RELIGION IN OHIO

RELIGION IN OHIO

Profiles of Faith Communities

EDITED BY

Tarunjit Singh Butalia
Dianne P. Small

Published by Ohio University Press
in association with
the Religious Experience Advisory Council
of the Ohio Bicentennial Commission and
the Interfaith Association of Central Ohio

ATHENS

Ohio University Press, Athens, Ohio 45701
© 2004 by Ohio University Press
Printed in the United States of America

1803 ❦ *2003*

12 11 10 09 08 07 06 05 04   5 4 3 2 1

Cover art courtesy of Farnoosh Lanjani

Library of Congress Cataloging-in-Publication Data
Religion in Ohio : profiles of faith communities / edited by Tarunjit Singh
     Butalia, Dianne P. Small.
        p. cm.
     Includes bibliographical references and index.
     ISBN 0-8214-1551-4 (alk. paper) — ISBN 0-8214-1552-2 (pbk. : alk. paper)
     1. Ohio—Religion. I. Butalia, Tarunjit S. (Tarunjit Singh), 1965– II. Small,
Dianne P.
     BL 2527.O3R45 2004
     200'.9771—dc22
                                                                    2003025434

CONTENTS

ILLUSTRATIONS

MESSAGE FROM
GOVERNOR TAFT

Ohio's Bicentennial celebration is a time for all Ohioans to look back on our rich history and celebrate the growth of our state from its frontier beginnings to its current place of prominence in our nation.

Faith has always been an important foundation for Ohioans, from the time of the first Native American footsteps into what would become Ohio in 1803, to the present day. The earliest planners laid out town squares that featured courthouses and churches in close proximity, to re-inforce the message that our state would be mindful of the role faith plays in our lives and that people would always be free to practice their faiths as they saw fit.

From those modest beginnings, religious observance has grown in numbers. Present-day churches, temples, mosques, and worship centers are visual testaments to the depth and diversity of Ohio's faith-based communities. These communities serve a greater purpose than religious observance—they provide a social network, community services, education, and much more to the people they serve—and the people of Ohio are all the better for these contributions.

As we celebrate our state's two hundredth birthday, I would encourage Ohioans to look back on the growth and role of faith in the development of our state and to be thankful that Ohio's many religious communities remain the foundation of our state's greatness and the continued advancement of our citizens.

I hope you enjoy this book, which honors the growth of Ohio's religious communities and gives us all something on which to reflect during our bicentennial celebration.

Governor Bob Taft
March, 2003

PREFACE AND
ACKNOWLEDGMENTS

Building upon the work of the Ohio Sesquicentennial Commission in 1953, the Ohio Bicentennial Commission's Religious Experience Advisory Council sought to expand and update the history and influence of faith groups in Ohio for the state's 2003 bicentennial celebration. This is largely an untold story, at least to the extent that our experiences here are gathered in one volume so they might be appreciated in their full breadth and diversity.

Ohio's religious and spiritual heritage goes back thousands of years to the state's original Native American population and then continues in the westward migration of settlers to this region, each group bringing with it cherished traditions. We have been blessed, too, with the arrival of many new immigrants in the last fifty years—immigrants whose faith has thrived in new soil. This book is our unique recollection as people of faith of two hundred years of statehood and the years leading up to it.

Information for this volume was gathered with great care and effort. Rather than write about the various faiths present in Ohio, the Advisory Council asked the groups themselves to tell us their stories in their own words.

The faiths represented in this book are a sampling of the religious diversity in Ohio at the beginning of the twenty-first century. Some religious organizations may be missing. A concerted effort was made to reach as many faith groups as possible. Some chose not to respond; others proved difficult to locate. We were persistent, however, in our effort to solicit as many acceptable submissions as possible.

Full accuracy has been the goal of this book. Historical facts are naturally dependent on the reliability of sources, and interpretation can be somewhat subjective. Be assured that, to the greatest extent possible, we have striven to see that all information included is correct. All opinions expressed in the chapters are those of the chapter authors. All addresses —street, internet, and email—and phone numbers were correct at the time of publication.

Special acknowledgment is given to Tarunjit Singh Butalia and Dianne Small, co-chairs of our book committee and editors of this volume. Without their tireless dedication and effort, this publication would not have been possible. The help and valuable advice provided by Steve George, Executive Director, Ohio Bicentennial Commission, and Molly Ryan, Program Coordinator, Ohio Bicentennial Commission, is greatly appreciated. We gratefully recognize the Interfaith Association of Central Ohio, which also served as a sponsoring organization. The assistance provided by Leslie Stansbery in the formation of the Religious Experience Advisory Council is appreciated. And our sincere appreciation goes to David Hedden for his legal advice. Finally, we want to thank the Ohio Bicentennial Commission and other cofunders for the contributions that made this work a reality.

Publication of this book is made possible by the gracious financial support of the Ohio Bicentennial Commission, Theodore R. Simson, and the following organizations and individuals:

Organizations:

Bahá'ís of Ohio (including the Bahá'í communities of Bexley, Carroll County, Columbus, Fairborn, New Albany, Stark County, and Upper Arlington)
Bharatiya Hindu Temple of Columbus
Buddhist community of Ohio (Buddhist Council of Ohio, Soka Gakkai International–USA/Southern Ohio Area, Karma Thegsum Choling Columbus, Buddhist Bodhi Association of Columbus)
Catholic Conference of Ohio (on behalf of the Archdiocese of Cincinnati, Diocese of Cleveland, Diocese of Columbus and its Department of Social Concerns, Diocese of Steubenville, Diocese of Toledo, Diocese of Youngstown, Parma Byzantine Eparchy, Romanian Catholic Diocese of Canton, and Ukrainian Catholic Diocese of St. Josaphat in Parma)
Central Ohioans for Peace
Church of Jesus Christ of Latter-day Saints–Ohio Stakes
Church of the Covenant of Cleveland
Columbus Metropolitan Area Church Council
Community Organizing Center
Faith Communities Uniting for Peace
Interfaith Alliance of Greater Cincinnati
Interfaith Center for Peace

Jain community (Jain Center of Central Ohio, Mahavir World Vision, Brahmi Jain Society)
Methodist Theological School in Ohio
Muslim community of Ohio (Council on American-Islamic Relations–Ohio Chapter, Islamic Council of Ohio, Islamic Society of Greater Columbus, Islamic Foundation of Central Ohio, Islamic Society of Central Ohio)
Ohio Baptist General Convention
Ohio Council of Churches Foundation
Ohio Empowerment Coalition
Ohio Jewish Communities, Inc.
Ohio Theological Library Association
Old First Presbyterian Church of Columbus
Pastors for Peace
Peacemaking and Justice Committee of the Presbytery of Scioto Valley
Pluralism Project at Harvard University
Port Columbus Interfaith Services
Sikh community (World Sikh Council–America Region, Sikh Society of Dayton, Guru Nanak Foundation of Greater Cleveland, Guru Nanak Society of Greater Cincinnati, Guru Nanak Religious Society of Central Ohio, Guru Gobind Singh Sikh Society of Bedford, Sikh Educational and Religious Foundation, Sikh Youth Federation)

St. Stephen's Episcopal Church of Columbus
St. Thomas More Newman Center at the
Ohio State University
Trinity Lutheran Seminary
Trinity United Methodist Church of Marble
Cliff
Unity Church of Christianity of Columbus
University Interfaith Association at the
Ohio State University
USA Ahmadiyya Anjuman Ishaat Islam
Walnut Hills Retirement Home of Walnut
Creek
West Ohio Conference of the United
Methodist Church

Individuals:
Tejinder Singh and Surjit Kaur Bal
William G. and Laura T. Barndt
Satinder Kaur and Kanverjit Singh Bedi
Satinder Singh and Tejinder Kaur Bhullar
N. Singh and Parminder Kaur Brar
Maryca N. Brooks
Karamjit Singh and Tripat Kaur Butalia
Inder S. and Suresh Chandra
Surinder Singh and Nariinder Kaur
Chauhan
Raj Kamaljit and Jaswant Cheema
Margaret Lewis Church
I. David and Rita K. Cohen
Erin L. Cordle
Jack Davis
John T. and Barbara B. Davis
Robert L. and Dot Erickson
Ahmed and Janet Fellague
Galip Feyzioglu
Clyde C. and Elsie B. Fry
Wallace C. and Sarah E. Giffen
George Glazier
James R. Hanson
Bruce O. and Catherine M. Hickin
Donald L. and Shirley A. Huber
Skip Jackson
Mazhar and Betty Jalil
Balpreet Singh and Baljeet Kaur Jammu

Donley Johnson
Howard J. and A. Elaine Dodd Johnson
Abdul H. Khan
Amir U. and Shaheda A. Khan
Habib U. Khan
Munawwar J. and Abdul H. Khan
Nasr U. and Brian Khan
Karamjit Singh and Gurjit Kaur Khanduja
Curt A. and Katharine S. Levis
Houshang Ma'ani
Louis Ma'ani
Farouki A. Majeed
Michael S. and Melody Layton McMahon
Leah and Dyed Minhaj Mohiuddin
Gurbilash Kaur Nagpaul
M. Razi and Shahida Rafeeq
Sepehr Rajaie
Harbir Kaur Rekhi
Raghbir Singh Sandhu
Darshan Singh, Simran Kaur, Sandeep
Singh, Darsheel Kaur, Santosh Singh,
and Baljit Singh Sehbi
David A. and Sheila Seifert
T. O. and Faizi Jihan Shanavas
Marilyn and N. Lance Shreffler
Avtar Singh, Sarabjeet Singh, Karanvir
Singh, Manpreet Singh, Harjeet Kaur,
and Ravjot K. Singh
Daljeet and Jagdish Kaur Singh
Inder Paul and Kawal Jit Kaur Singh
Kanwaljit and Gurpreet Kaur Singh
Surjit Singh, Jatinder Kaur, Ganeev Singh,
and Aneet Kaur Singh
Yadwinder and Harbir Kaur Singh
Sidney A. and Delores K. Small
Kevin L. and Vicki L. Smith
Leslie E. and Margaret D. Stansbery
Gwyn E. and Gary L. Stetler
L. Gordon Tait
Barbara A. Thompson
Rebecca J. Tollefson
Ajit Singh and Manjit Kaur Walia
Lane J. and Rhonda L. Wallace
Laura Cean Wilson

We hope this book will serve the interests of Ohioans who wish to be more knowledgeable about the state's religious past. May it also be a springboard into a future where we can learn to work together more closely for the greater good of all humanity.

The Religious Experience Advisory Council
of the Ohio Bicentennial Commission

Ronald W. Botts, United Church of Christ
Tarunjit Singh Butalia, World Sikh Council–America Region
Jack B. Davis, United Church of Christ
Steven R. Dimler, Interfaith Association of Central Ohio
Dilip Doshi, Jain Community of Central Ohio
Alvin R. Hadley, Columbus Metropolitan Area Church Council
J. S. Jindal, Spiritual Sadhna Society
Joyce Garver Keller, Ohio Jewish Communities, Inc.
Habib Khan, Islamic Council of Ohio
Meena Khan, Muslim
Houshang Ma'ani, Bahá'í Faith of Central Ohio
Patrick Mooney, Roman Catholic Diocese of Columbus
Michael Morello, The Church of Jesus Christ of Latter-day Saints
Bishun D. Pandey, Bharatiya Hindu Temple
Paul F. H. Reichert II, Evangelical Lutheran Church in America
Molly Ryan, Ohio Bicentennial Commission
Tansukh J. Salgia, Bramhi Jain Society
Ranbir Singh, Sikh Educational and Religious Foundation
Dianne Small, Bahá'í Faith of Central Ohio
Rebecca Tollefson, Ohio Council of Churches
Winifred C. Wirth, Buddhist Council of Ohio
Jayne M. Zborowsky, Presbyterian Church (U.S.A.)

RELIGION IN OHIO

INTRODUCTION

More Than Two Centuries of Religion in Ohio

Donald L. Huber

L AYERS OF SEDIMENTARY ROCK OFTEN GREET THE EYE AS ONE DRIVES through the hilly portions of Ohio. Sometimes horizontal, but more often tipped topsy-turvy, the rock layers give clear evidence both that the present terrain of Ohio has been built up over time and that it has occasionally been affected by cataclysmic events.

So it is with religion in Ohio. The religious topography of Ohio includes many layers, and also gives evidence of significant upheavals. Both the layering and the upheavals have had a number of consequences, some of which are explored in the essays that follow in this volume. In this essay, the goal will be to look at the general "lay of the land," so that the individual essays that follow can be understood in a larger context.

Humans have lived in Ohio for thousands of years. Although we know very little about the first inhabitants, they left a legacy that continues to awe and inspire us—the mounds and other earthworks that are still prominent on the landscape, in spite of centuries of neglect and destruction. Many Ohioans have at least a passing acquaintance with the names —Adena, Hopewell, Fort Ancient—associated with the mound builders and their immediate successors.

SERPENT MOUND

Effigy mounds, such as the famous Serpent Mound in Adams County, were probably constructed for ceremonial purposes that we today would describe as "religious." (Courtesy of the Ohio Historical Society)

Were these prehistoric peoples "religious"? No doubt they were. They certainly paid attention to those events—birth, death, the passing of the seasons, the vagaries of nature and human behavior—that give rise to religious reflection, as is evidenced in their artifacts. But we can know few of the details of their perspectives on life, or of their specific behaviors, because there is too little available evidence.

Much more is known of the religious views of the historic Native Americans, whose beliefs and customs European explorers and settlers recorded from the time of the first contact between the two peoples. In Ohio, the major Indian tribes in the eighteenth century, just prior to large-scale white settlement, were the Delaware, Miami, Mingo, Ottawa, Shawnee, and Wyandotte. Their religion was part and parcel of everyday life, with no distinction between "sacred" and "secular." Elders, shamans, and other religious leaders of these communities interpreted the significance of, and were involved in, all aspects of life. Sometimes looked down upon by European Americans as "pagans" or "animists"—because of their belief that all living creatures, and even some inanimate ones, contained spirits—most Native Americans combined this view with belief in a Great

A bird's-eye view of the reconstructed village at Schoenbrunn, Tuscarawas County. Schoenbrunn was established in 1772 by Moravian missionaries. (Courtesy of the Ohio Historical Society)

Spirit who ruled over the lesser spirits. Indeed, Native Americans in Ohio were indignant when early Christian missionaries intimated that they were hearing of the one true God for the first time.

Contact between Europeans and Native Americans had profound religious implications for the latter, as they became the objects of missionary efforts by various Christian groups. In Ohio, the best-known Christian missions were those of the Moravians among the Delawares on the Tuscarawas River just before and during the American Revolution, and of the Methodists among the Wyandottes at Upper Sandusky after the War of 1812. Both stories had unhappy endings, giving credence to the views of those Native Americans who argued that they had no business being involved with a "white man's religion."

Both sides in the Revolution suspected the peaceful Moravian Delaware Indians of giving aid and comfort to the enemy. On March 9, 1782, a day of infamy in Ohio history, American militia—acting on the flimsiest of pretences—massacred ninety-eight nonresisting Moravians at Gnadenhutten. Although American authorities decried this deed, it reflected the widespread belief among frontier whites that Native Americans—no matter what their formal religious affiliations—were never to be trusted. For their part, Native Americans avenged their kinsmen's deaths with the subsequent capture, torture, and execution of Col. William Crawford, who had led a military expedition against them in May of that same year. After the war, a few Moravian Delawares did return to the Tuscarawas River valley with the aid of the U.S. government. Regardless of such conciliatory gestures, the credibility of Christian America remained at low ebb among most Native Americans.

Later, the Wyandottes, confined to a reservation at Upper Sandusky after the War of 1812, fared better. But in the end they fell victim to the white greed and racism that had always troubled European–Native American relationships. The fact that a majority of the Wyandottes converted to Methodist Christianity during the 1820s and 1830s, under the empathetic tutelage of black and white missionaries, and that the tribe had considerable success in adapting to European American methods of agriculture and commerce, was not enough to prevent their white neighbors and the state and federal governments from forcing them to sell their reservation in 1843. As the last organized tribe in Ohio began its westward trek to Kansas, one of its preachers noted: "Here our dead are buried. Soon they shall be forgotten, for the onward march of the strong White Man will not turn aside for the Indian graves" (Thelma R. Marsh, *Moccasin Trails to the Cross: A History of the Mission to the Wyandott Indians on the Sandusky Plains* [Upper Sandusky, Ohio: John Stewart United Methodist Church, 1974], 121).

Indian graves, and the cataclysmic end to the ancient culture that they symbolized, were of little consequence to the European American settlers who had flooded into eastern and southern Ohio after the Treaty of Greenville in 1795. With Native Americans confined to the northwestern part of the territory after this date (although this arrangement was disturbed both by continuing Native American resistance and by white violations of the treaty line), white settlement proceeded rapidly. It would take only a short eight years to achieve statehood.

As white settlers streamed in from the East, they brought their religion, or lack thereof, with them. Nominally, most were Protestant Christians, whose "layer" of religion in Ohio has been particularly thick and durable. Naturally, churches that were prominent in the East followed their adherents to Ohio, providing various forms of assistance to the migrants, including missionary clergy. Several of the churches described later in this book—including the Congregationalists, Episcopalians, German Reformed, Lutherans, Mennonites, Presbyterians, Quakers, Universalists, and Unitarians—got their start in Ohio this way.

The established churches had to cope with one indisputable fact of frontier life, namely widespread irreligion among the new settlers. Some migrants to Ohio had never been a part of organized religion. Some were outspoken disbelievers. Some shed their nominal religious allegiances, as a snake sheds its skin, as they crossed the Appalachian ranges. Although it would not be until 1834 that the Reverend Lyman Beecher of Cincinnati would publish his *Plea for the West,* in which he identified the dangers of "barbarism" for this vast region, the worry that western Americans would not remain—or become—good Protestants was there from the beginning.

Protestants did more than worry. They took concerted action to win the West for their faiths. In addition to the missionary efforts of older groups, newer denominations entered the effort. These denominations either originated in, or were invigorated by, the phenomenon known as the Second Great Awakening, beginning around 1800. The western form of the Awakening was identified with colorful camp meetings and "protracted meetings" that gathered large crowds for emotional seasons of praying, preaching, singing, and sacramental celebration. New members were added to the churches, and backsliders were reclaimed. Baptists and Methodists were especially adept at this work, and their churches grew rapidly in the first decades of the nineteenth century. A new group, the Christian Churches (Disciples of Christ) also established itself during this period, winning numerous adherents in Ohio.

Outside the Protestant mainstream, Amish Christians entered Ohio from Pennsylvania early in the nineteenth century. Widely noted for a conservative lifestyle that set them apart both from their fellow Christians and from society at large, the Amish settled in northeastern Ohio, where they were and are particularly prominent in Holmes, Wayne, and Geauga counties. Although viewed by many outsiders in recent years as "quaint," or as "living ancestors," the Amish way of life is in fact founded upon a thoughtful Anabaptist theology that eschews worldliness in favor of what is believed to be a primitive Christian simplicity. Amish beliefs, and those of their Mennonite cousins, are explained at the Amish and Mennonite Heritage Center at Berlin, the centerpiece of which is the 265-foot-long *Behalt,* a cycloramic painting that depicts the history of Christianity from an Anabaptist perspective.

Not all of the new Buckeyes were migrants from the eastern United States. After the end of the napoleonic era in Europe and the opening of the Erie Canal (1825) in this country, a steady stream of immigrants came to Ohio directly from Europe. Irish, Germans, and—a bit later—Eastern and Southern Europeans came in ever larger numbers. They strengthened existing churches and added new Christian denominations as well. Roman Catholic churches, which had been relatively small in size and number, now grew rapidly. Eventually Catholics would become the largest religious body in the state. German Catholics in Columbus founded the Pontifical College Josephinum in 1888; this was, and still is, the only school for priests in North America that is under the direct control of the Vatican. Lutheran and German Reformed churches also grew dramatically as a result of immigration. Eastern Orthodox churches, organized along linguistic lines, were established a bit later, adding another layer to the religious landscape. With the exception of the Civil War years, this immigration continued at a high level until the early twentieth century.

Some of the newer groups did not fit preexisting patterns. Notable among these was the Church of Jesus Christ of Latter-day Saints (Mormons), which claimed both a restoration of an ancient revelation in *The Book of Mormon* and new revelations through its prophet, Joseph Smith Jr. From 1831 to 1838 Smith had his headquarters at Kirtland, where a venerable temple still stands as testimony to the ingenuity and persistence of the early Mormons. The Swedenborgians (Church of the New Jerusalem), a small theosophist group, were also active in the state in the early nineteenth century. Their most famous member was John Chapman, better known to generations of Ohio schoolchildren as "Johnny Appleseed."

Communal religious societies also found a congenial home in Ohio. The Shakers and "Zoarites" (Society of Separatists at Zoar) are discussed in an essay in this book. They are representative of a widespread phenomenon in the early nineteenth century, when many groups attempted to form utopian societies throughout the United States. These societies, usually grounded in a religious point of view, intended not only to provide an ideal society for their own members but to present an example to the larger world of how people should live together. Both migrants from the East (for example, the Shakers), and immigrants from Europe (for example, the Zoarites), founded utopian societies on the western frontier.

Utopianism was not the only way to address the ills of society in the nineteenth century. Many other religiously motivated people were also keenly aware that there were a multitude of societal wrongs that needed righting. By 1850 Ohio was a hotbed of reforming groups that were promoting particular causes—temperance, abolition of slavery, women's rights, prison reform, and many more. Theodore Dwight Weld, for a time one of the most prominent of the abolitionists, began his active antislavery career while a student at Lane Seminary (Presbyterian) in Cincinnati in the 1830s. When Lane proved less than hospitable to his abolitionist activity, he and seventy-five of his student colleagues left the seminary. Many of these "Lane Rebels" completed their theological educations at nascent Oberlin College, an evangelical Protestant school that became nationally famous for its policy of admitting women and African American students alongside white males. Harriet Beecher Stowe, author of the religiously motivated antislavery novel *Uncle Tom's Cabin* (1852), lived for many years in Cincinnati, where her father Lyman was president of Lane Seminary. Living just across the river from the slave state of Kentucky provided her with important information for her antislavery writings. She also learned much from Theodore Dwight Weld, having more appreciation for his intense abolitionism than did her father.

African Americans migrated to Ohio under the most difficult of circumstances, whether they were free or enslaved. In spite of the presence of active abolitionists and the state's reputation as a "main line" on the Underground Railroad, not all white Ohioans welcomed blacks, whether transient or newly resident. As early as 1804, "black laws" were passed to discourage migration to Ohio. There was a major riot in Cincinnati in 1829 that led to the forcible removal of eleven hundred blacks from that city. Nonetheless, both free blacks and fugitive slaves continued to come to Ohio. Soon they had founded congregations and began to support denominations. Macedonia Baptist Church at Burlington (1849), founded by emancipated slaves from Virginia, is one of the oldest African American church buildings in the United States. The African Methodist Episcopal

The arrival of thirty-two freed slaves from Virginia in 1849 enabled a congregation that had been in existence in Lawrence County near Burlington since 1820 to build the Macedonia Baptist Church, now one of the oldest surviving African American church buildings in the United States. (Courtesy of Dianne Small)

Church, the first organized black denomination in the United States, already had a significant presence in Ohio prior to the Civil War. In the 1860s it took over the operation of Wilberforce College (1856), the first college founded by African Americans in the United States. After the war, several black denominations prospered in Ohio as the African American population increased, adding an important layer to the religious topography of the state.

The Civil War was a cataclysmic event for religion as well as for all other aspects of American society. Some of the religious upheaval before and during the war was organizational, as in the splitting of denominations into northern and southern branches. Some of it was spiritual—the debates over slavery caused some to reexamine the teachings of the Bible, and the immense number of deaths during the war led many to question their traditional beliefs, or to seek out new spiritual experiences. Cultural upheaval was also significant during this period. Some of these changes, as for example those which took place during and after the war, affected the churches directly. Other changes, as for example those that were precipitated by increasing industrialization and urbanization, had a more indirect impact.

Growing cities had both good and bad consequences for the churches. On the positive side, large urban congregations often developed sophisticated programs housed in new facilities that met the religious needs of many people. On the negative side, industrialization was accompanied by widespread poverty and disruption of traditional family life among the working classes. Churches responded to these challenges in a variety of ways—most often by helping to ameliorate immediate needs (through settlement houses, soup kitchens, orphanages, hospitals, etc.), and sometimes by seeking to change the societal conditions that led to poverty, hunger, disease, crime, and premature death. Many Ohio Protestants became adherents of the "Social Gospel," which argued that Christians have a duty to make society as a whole more just and compassionate. Rev. Washington Gladden, Congregationalist pastor in Columbus from 1882 until his death in 1918, was a national leader of this movement.

By 1890, Ohio had many, mostly Christian, layers in its religious landscape. The ten largest religious groupings in the state at that time were the Roman Catholic, Methodist, Presbyterian, Lutheran, Baptist, Christians/Disciples of Christ, United Brethren (now United Methodist), German Reformed (now United Church of Christ), Congregationalist (now United Church of Christ), and German Evangelical Synod (now United Church of Christ). Judaism was the only significant non-Christian religion.

Jews came to Ohio early in its history; the first Jewish congregation was established in Cincinnati in 1824. By the 1860s there were organized Jewish communities in all of the larger cities and some of the smaller ones. Rabbi Isaac Mayer Wise of Cincinnati became a national leader of the Reform movement, which advocated the modernizing of Jewish worship and customs. Hebrew Union College was founded by this group in Cincinnati in 1875. It was the first rabbinical college in America and remains the center of Reform Judaism in North America. Other Jewish groups also flourished in the state in the nineteenth century, and on into the twentieth and twenty-first.

The Islamic Center of Greater Toledo, a striking mosque designed by Talat Itil and constructed in 1982–83, overlooks the junction of Interstates 75 and 475 at Perrysburg in Wood County. It is the first mosque in North America constructed in classical Islamic architectural style. (Courtesy of Dianne Small)

The twentieth century saw several new religious layers added to the Ohio religious landscape and some upheavals as well. A symbolic turning point in the ever-changing and expanding American religious landscape was the Parliament of the World's Religions, held at Chicago in 1893. Although hardly all-inclusive, this gathering did introduce many Americans for the first time, and in a positive context, to religious traditions other than Judaism and Christianity. Hinduism had a permanent presence in the United States from that time forward, in the form of the Vedanta Society, although organized Hinduism would not be present in Ohio until the 1960s. Buddhism was also much better known after the parliament, but it remained mostly a coastal phenomenon among Asian Americans until the 1960s. Jain representatives were also present at the 1893 parliament. The Bahá'í Faith entered American consciousness after the parliament and managed to found its first permanent organizations in Ohio as early as the 1930s. And the Muslim community in northwest

Ohio, which was an extension of a significant Muslim presence in the Detroit area, achieved its first formal organization in 1939. Today, the growing Muslim community in Ohio is perhaps best symbolized by the magnificent mosque at Perrysburg. It is the first mosque in North America to utilize classic Islamic architecture.

Still, Ohio was largely a Judeo-Christian society until after World War II. This was reflected in this volume's predecessor, the slim sesquicentennial volume *Churches in the Buckeye Country: A History of Ohio's Religious Groups Published in Commemoration of the State's Sesquicentennial, 1953,* which contains accounts of only Christian and Jewish groups.

At this point it is important to take note of one early-twentieth-century upheaval that affected many Ohio churches. This was the persecution of German Americans during World War I, a phenomenon which had religious as well as secular consequences. In 1917–18, after comments by Attorney General Thomas Gregory, former President Theodore Roosevelt, and others about "the Huns within our own gates," local vigilantes (called "Councils of Defense") set to work harassing the German American community, including its churches. In Ohio, a Lutheran minister was attacked by a mob and a German parochial school was dynamited. German religious books were burned in several cities. Clergy were regularly vilified on the street and in the press. Individual Mennonites and Amish suffered more than most—many were imprisoned—because of their conscientious objection to war. The churches of German background—Roman Catholic, Lutheran, Reformed, Mennonite, and others—defended themselves as best they could, calling attention to the patriotism of their members and to their many contributions to the state and nation. Their most effective defense, however, was to become "less German." Protestant worship in the German language and German-language instruction in both Protestant and Catholic parochial schools declined rapidly, except in the socially conservative Amish community. Many Protestant parochial schools closed, never to reopen. Churches of German heritage struggled with the implications of these changes for many years after the war. Coupled with the restrictive immigration policies enacted by the United States government in the 1920s and the economic hardships they shared with all Americans in the 1930s, they struggled to retain the allegiance of their traditional members as they sought to determine their place in the larger American scene. This struggle was evident in Ohio, where four of the ten largest Christian denominations in 1890 (Lutheran, United Brethren, German Reformed, and German Evangelical Synod) were largely of German background, and where two others (Roman Catholic, Methodist) had significant numbers of German American members. Many Ohio Jews, also, were immigrants, or descendants of immigrants, from Germany.

Significant religious change followed the Second World War, as well, and has continued to the present time, providing still more layers to the religious landscape. Many refugees and "displaced persons" came to Ohio soon after the war, including Jewish survivors of the Holocaust. While the religiously inclined among them usually joined existing groups, new perspectives and customs were introduced. Then came the Korean War and its aftermath, followed little more than a decade later by the Vietnam War. Both of these wars brought refugees to Ohio. For the first time, Ohio had a numerically significant Asian American population, which was reflected in the growth of traditionally Asian religions in the state. The liberalization of immigration laws in the 1960s also contributed to increasing religious diversity, as did the arrival of large numbers of international students, including those from Latin America, at the major universities. For example, many Sikhs from Punjab, India, came to study at the Ohio State University, bringing their faith with them. Jains from India, and Zoroastrians from India and Iran have had similar histories in Ohio. By the 1970s, the larger cities especially were becoming religiously cosmopolitan. Some of that diversity has been captured in the essays that follow in this book.

Ohio is more religiously diverse today than it has ever been. Still, the ten largest religious groupings in Ohio as late as 2000 continued to be Christian and Jewish. From largest to smallest, they were: Roman Catholics, Methodists, Baptists, Lutherans, Pentecostal/Holiness, Christians/Disciples of Christ, Presbyterians, United Church of Christ, Jewish, and Anabaptist/Pietist (primarily Mennonites, Amish, and Brethren).

Happily, what is largely missing from the above account is any tale of sustained interreligious conflict. While Ohioans certainly participated in the nativist movement of the nineteenth century, with its strong anti-Catholic and anti-Jewish sentiments, virulent nativism was of relatively short duration. Anti-Catholic rioting in Cincinnati in the 1850s, parallel-ing similar outbursts in other large American cities, did not provide a pattern for the future. Sadly, Ohio has had its share of anti-black, anti-Semitic, and anti-immigrant attitudes and activities. But these have sel-dom been framed in terms of religious ideas or practices. They have instead been expressed mostly in the language of ethnic prejudice, racism, and xenophobic nationalism. The American tradition of religious freedom seems well established in Ohio. With the growth of religious diversity across the state, interfaith and ecumenical tolerance and understanding have increased, further strengthening the foundations of religious freedom.

What about the future? Clearly, if present trends continue, Ohio will become more religiously diverse in the coming decades. Protestant dom-inance has decreased significantly over two centuries. In 1803, almost all religiously affiliated Buckeyes were Protestant Christians. By 1890, ap-proximately 67 percent were Protestants; a century later this number had fallen to 56 percent. The big gainers were Catholics (who increased from a minuscule percentage in 1803 to 28 percent in 1890 and more than 40 percent today), Jews (who rose to more than 2 percent of the total), and a potpourri of "others" (who represent approximately 2 percent). These figures include only those persons who are at least nominally affiliated with a religious organization. By most estimates, however, only half of all Ohioans had any kind of formal religious affiliation as the bicentennial approached. It should immediately be added that there are some groups that keep no statistics and others who deliberately function far from the public eye, so that it is very hard to estimate their numbers. Still, there is plenty of opportunity for religious groups in Ohio to grow if that is their desire.

While we cannot know with certainty what the future will bring, it is clear that the religious topography of Ohio has altered drastically over the centuries, and especially over the past two hundred years. As it continues to change, more layers will probably be added, and perhaps additional upheavals will occur. The Protestant pluralism of two hundred years ago is fast becoming a religious pluralism more extensive than our ancestors could have dreamed possible. It is unlikely that this process is complete. An especially promising harbinger of the future may be found in the fact that the almost universal dismissal of Native American religion in the past is slowly being replaced with a modicum of understanding and appreciation. Within our treasured, albeit imperfect, American tradition of religious freedom, we can hope that mutual understanding and appreciation between and among all religions will continue to grow, even as people of faith honestly and forthrightly express their deepest convictions about the meaning of life. The essays that follow are offered in that spirit and as a contribution to that end.

Our Common Future

Steven R. Dimler

As we celebrate Ohio's bicentennial, we would do well to remember all the things that have made this state such a great place to live—from our beautiful hills and lakes and streams, to our abundant material and intellectual resources, to the warm and friendly people who live here. Truly, Ohio is blessed with all these things and more. And one of our greatest blessings in Ohio is the diversity and strength of our religious faith. We who are Native Americans, Protestants, Catholics, Jews, Muslims, Sikhs, Hindus, Buddhists, Bahá'ís, Zoroastrians, and Jains . . . we are all people of faith who are trying to live and work together to build a better life for our children and grandchildren.

America's principle of religious freedom has brought people from all over the world to Ohio, people who have blessed us with the full diversity of the world's religious beliefs. The first essay in this book compared the various religious experiences in Ohio to the layers of rock and sediment deposited on our landscape over millions of years. Now, as we celebrate Ohio's bicentennial, our faith-based landscape is as diverse and beautiful as our natural landscape. Here are some fascinating examples to consider:

- Nearly a hundred mosques and Islamic community centers are present within the state's metropolitan areas, serving the needs of more than 150,000 Muslims who represent more than thirty different ethnic and national groups.

- Every year in late October and early November, Hindus can be seen putting up lights around their houses. Neighbors may ask, "Why are you putting up Christmas lights so early?" Hindus respond that they are preparing for Diwali, the festival of lights, a major celebration in which thousands attend the many Hindu temples across Ohio.

- Nearly a dozen Buddhist organizations are present in the city of Columbus alone. The *Columbus Dispatch* reported that Buddhism was the faith with the most rapid percentage increase in membership in the state during the last decade.

- In May 2001 Ohio's religious and community leaders were invited to a live satellite broadcast for the opening ceremonies of the Bahá'í terraces on Mt. Carmel, which lead up to the Bahá'í World Centre in Haifa, Israel.

- For the first time in Ohio's history, on September 18, 2001, representatives of the Ohio Jain community read the opening prayer in the Ohio Senate. The Jains were invited to do so in recognition of the twenty-six hundredth anniversary of the birth of the Jain prophet Lord Mahavira.

- Less than twenty-five years ago, federal laws prohibited American Indian ceremonial dancing. Now, a Pow Wow is held nearly every summer weekend in Ohio or one of the surrounding states.

- Nearly a thousand Sikh families have chosen Ohio as their home. Sikh men continue to proudly wear the symbols of their tradition, including turbans of nearly all colors, as a constitutionally guaranteed expression of their faith.

Many of us are familiar with the different Christian denominations in our cities and towns. They may range from Methodist, Baptist, and Pentecostal to Roman Catholic, Eastern Orthodox, Jehovah's Witness, Seventh-day Adventist, and Church of Jesus Christ of Latter-day Saints to the more recent nondenominational megachurches.

We also certainly know about the Jewish synagogues in our cities, and we may also have seen mosques and Islamic centers beginning to appear. In addition, there are nearly fifty distinct Buddhist and twenty Hindu groups in Ohio, and twenty-one Bahá'í Local Spiritual Assemblies, five Sikh *gurdwaras* (places of worship), and several Jain centers have been established throughout the state.

INTERACTING WITH EACH OTHER

Today America is one of the most faith-diverse nations on earth, and we see this diversity in Ohio. Part of the greatness of our country has been our principles of justice and fairness and our willingness to interact with others on the basis of equality and respect. A new challenge faces us now with so many different religions in our cities and neighborhoods. As Harvard University professor of comparative religion and director of the Pluralism Project Diana Eck writes, "[T]he most interesting and important phase of our nation's history lies ahead. The very principles on which America was founded will be tested for their strength and vision in the new religious America. And the opportunity to create a positive multireligious society out of the fabric of a democracy . . . is now ours."[1]

We are living with increasing religious diversity, or what is called "religious plurality." But are we merely viewing each other from a distance or are we interacting with each other in significant and meaningful ways? Professor Eck continues:

> First, I would want to insist that pluralism is not the sheer fact of this plurality alone, but is active engagement with plurality. Pluralism and plurality are sometimes used as if they were synonymous. But plurality is just diversity . . . Such diversity does not, however, have to affect me. I can observe diversity. I can even celebrate diversity . . . But I have to participate in pluralism . . . Pluralism requires the cultivation of public space where we all encounter one another . . . The encounter of a pluralistic society is not premised on achieving agreement, but on achieving relationship.[2]

Organized interfaith activities where we can practice interacting with each other are a relatively new phenomenon in Ohio. "Interfaith dialogues" used to mean discussions between Christians and Jews, but now the word "interfaith" has been expanded to include members of other religions such as Islam, Bahá'í, Buddhist, Hindu, Jain, and Sikh.

Is it possible to be true to our own faith and pray and worship with someone of another religion? Members of many faiths are asking these questions. S. Wesley Ariarajah (formerly of the World Council of Churches) wrote in 1999:

Is inter-religious worship or prayer a pointless pursuit that will in the end leave everyone dissatisfied? In spite of all the pressures of living, working and struggling together, should we decide that when it comes to praying we must maintain our separate identities and consider our ways and forms of worship as necessary and unchangeable? Will attempts at interfaith prayer eventually lead to the watering down of all our worship experiences ?[3]

These are genuine concerns. Interfaith interactions are not intended to blend different faiths into one eclectic faith. Each faith has a right to define itself and conduct its affairs according to its own beliefs. However, we are now living in a new reality that can no longer be ignored. Dr. Ariarajah further writes:

> As [religious] communities live in close proximity and face common issues and common problems, and share common visions for a just, reconciled and peaceful world, they come under enormous pressure also to pool their spiritual resources in dealing with them ... in an increasingly multifaith world we constantly face situations that demand new initiatives and new ways of holding our faith in relationship to others.[4]

HISTORICAL DEVELOPMENTS

What international and national events have led to this amazingly rich diversity of faiths in Ohio? The following are a few of the most significant factors:

- In 1893 the first Parliament of the World's Religions was held in Chicago. At this meeting representatives of eastern and western traditions came together for the first time to consult with each other on a common platform. That meeting in 1893 is today recognized as the birth of formal interreligious dialogue worldwide. Following that meeting, representatives of several eastern faiths toured America and gave lectures on their religions, bringing eastern spiritual traditions to the attention of the general American public for the first time.

- On December 10, 1948, the United Nations General Assembly, under the leadership of Eleanor Roosevelt as the chairperson of the Commission on Human Rights, adopted the Universal Declaration of Human

Rights, which recognizes the "inherent dignity and the equal and inalienable rights of all members of the human family" as "the foundation of freedom, justice, and peace in the world." Article 18 of the declaration formally recognized that "everyone has the right to freedom of thought, conscience, and religion; this right includes freedom to change his religion or belief, and freedom, either alone or in community with others and in public or private, to manifest his religion or belief in teaching, practice, worship, and observance."

- In the mid-1960s, the Second Vatican Council of the Roman Catholic Church issued a Decree on Ecumenism (1964), and a Declaration on the Relation of the Church to Non-Christian Religions (1965). The Decree on Ecumenism made "the restoration of unity among all Christians one of the principal concerns of the Second Vatican Council." The term ecumenism was defined to include "initiatives and activities planned and undertaken, according to the various Christian needs of the Church and as opportunities offer, to promote Christian unity." The Declaration of the Relation of the Church to Non-Christian Religions examined the relationship of the Catholic Church to "non-Christian religions" and declared that "the Catholic church rejects nothing that is true and holy in these religions." In particular the declaration addressed the Buddhist, Hindu, Islamic, and Jewish faiths. As a result of the Second Vatican Council, on Pentecost Sunday, 1964, Pope Paul VI instituted a special department of the Roman Curia for relations with people of other religions. First known as the Secretariat for Non Christians, it was renamed the Pontifical Council for Interreligious Dialogue in 1988.

- The U.S. Immigration Act of 1965 opened the country's doors to the world. The old quota system that linked immigration to national origin and favored Europeans was abolished. As a result of the act, millions of Buddhists, Muslims, Sikhs, Bahá'ís, Jains, Hindus, Jews, and Christians immigrated to the United States for better educational and economic opportunities and more religious freedom. The Immigration Act coincided with the Civil Rights Act of 1964, which prohibited discrimination based on religion. These two acts began a new reality for many faithful immigrants.

- Since the 1960s, continuing human rights violations across the world brought new groups of refugees to the United States. Many of these refugees were given asylum in the United States and settled in Ohio. A recent example was the influx of Somalis, who are predominantly Muslim, to central Ohio in the late 1990s.

- Within the United States, Native Americans have endured horrendous spiritual and physical hardships for centuries. Now there is a growing appreciation for the spiritual traditions of the American Indians and for their presence in American society.

These developments have influenced the diversity of faith traditions in Ohio. Many immigrants admit they have greater religious freedom in the United States than they did in their countries of origin. They appreciate their new freedom and often remark how grateful they are to live in a country where they can freely practice their religion. The United States has become a religiously diverse nation, and the number of interactions between people of different faiths at work, at home, and in the public arena is increasing rapidly.

CHRISTIAN ECUMENISM

The Christian ecumenical movement is concerned with the unity and renewal of the church. Many Christian denominations with similar names remain separated because of particular beliefs or ways of organization. In various countries around the world, including the United States, Christians are grouped into denominations, such as Baptist, Episcopalian, Lutheran, Presbyterian, and United Methodist. These denominations then come together in councils. Around the world there are numerous national councils of churches. They are usually organized around a common commitment to one another and to the witness of the Gospel of Jesus Christ, which is demonstrated in various ways—through public policy, education, dialogue, mission and evangelism, and justice and peace.

There have been numerous conversations and agreements among Christian groups worldwide. There are also joint working groups, such as the Roman Catholics and the World Council of Churches, and the Lutherans and Orthodox. In the past fifty years there have been significant events marking the willingness of denominations to move beyond differences and work from common ground. For example:

- In 1960, consultation among nine denominations began from a sermon preached at an Episcopal church in California. Called the Consultation on Christian Union, it gradually changed and in January 2001 became

The Ohio Pastors Convocation was begun in 1920 and continued through 1993. In 1996 it was revived as the Ohio Ministries Convocation and continues to be a hallmark of ecumenical spirit for Christian clergy and laity across the state. This photo of Dr. Billy Graham, Rev. Weir Hartman, Rev. Smyth, and Dr. B. F. Lamb was taken at the 1963 convocation. (Courtesy of the Ohio Historical Society)

Churches Uniting in Christ. Its mission is to live together intentionally and differently, with a commitment to combat racism.

- Four denominations (the Evangelical Lutheran Church in America, the Presbyterian Church U.S.A., the Reformed Church in America, and the United Church of Christ) agreed on "A Formula Of Agreement" in 1998 to recognize each other as churches in which the Gospel is rightly preached and the sacraments rightly administered. They agreed to withdraw historic condemnations and are now working toward sharing pastors.

- The Joint Declaration on the Doctrine of Justification, signed in 1999 between the Roman Catholic Church and the Lutheran World Federation, was an important milestone in putting to rest centuries of conflict over a key element of the Christian faith—the issue of justification. The two bodies agreed they could live with remaining differences and have committed to pray for each other, to continue to discuss matters of faith, and to work toward common understanding.

- Called to Common Mission is an agreement of full communion between the Episcopal Church and the Evangelical Lutheran Church in America, formally approved in 2000. Each church will retain its own liturgical, theological, and organizational uniqueness and integrity, but the two will be able to exchange clergy and cooperatively plan pastoral and outreach ministries.

- The United Methodist Church and the three historically African American Methodist churches—African Methodist Episcopal, African Methodist Episcopal Zion, and Christian Methodist Episcopal—are in a dialogue known as "Pan-Methodism" to explore the possibility of coming together; and the African Methodist Episcopal Zion and the Christian Methodist Episcopal churches may join in the near future to form a new denomination.

With more than one hundred dialogues and conversations going on around the world among Christian denominations and churches, shared theological convictions will continue to emerge.

Only in the United States are there state councils/conferences of churches. Today, there are forty-six such statewide organizations. The Ohio Council of Churches (OCC), established in 1919, is a statewide ecumenical organization currently made up of representatives of seventeen Christian denominations. The OCC has a long history of drawing Christians from various denominations together around public policy concerns, theological discussions, educational events, and social justice. In addition, many local church councils and other ecumenical organizations unite different denominations in areas of joint concern. Examples include Metro-Toledo Churches United, Alliance of Churches in Alliance, Jackson Area Ministry, Tuscarawas County Council for Church and Community, and Columbus Metropolitan Area Church Council. Not all Christian churches choose to participate in these ecumenical councils and gatherings, but many do. Many Christians have also recognized the value of learning and working with people of other faiths.

THE INTERFAITH MOVEMENT

Interfaith gatherings and dialogues have grown increasingly common. "Interfaith" means the interactions of people of different religions who come together in a common arena of dialogue, study, and action. What are some of the factors propelling the interfaith movement forward?

Globally

In 1979 the World Council of Churches (an international organization of about 330 Christian denominations) developed guidelines for interfaith dialogue and understanding. These guidelines encouraged members of affiliated churches to enter into dialogue with their neighbors of different faiths and ideologies, to share their lives, to pursue common activities within their communities, and to open their minds and hearts to people of different faiths.

In 1986, Pope John Paul II created a model for interfaith prayer during his historic Day of Prayer for Peace at Assisi, where leaders representing several world faiths recited prayers from various traditions. This model has been recreated in many interfaith prayer services throughout the world, including Ohio. In addition, in October 1999 Pope John Paul II hosted 230 representatives from twenty of the world's religions at the Vatican to set goals for interfaith cooperation in the next millennium.

The Parliament of the World's Religions has continued to bring faith leaders together from across the world, in Chicago in 1993, and again in Cape Town, South Africa, in 1999.

Nationally

Within the United States several interfaith activities and organizations have taken root. Many Christian groups have developed guidelines for interfaith dialogue and have joined newly formed organizations in working together. The African American Muslim leadership is encouraging its members to interact with people of all races and religions. Interfaith organizations and programs, such as North American Interfaith Network, National Conference for Community and Justice, Interfaith Alliance, the

Bahá'ís, Buddhists, Christians, Hindus, Jews, Muslims, and Sikhs join hands at an interfaith prayer service for peace in Kosovo and the Balkans held in June 1999 at the Ohio Statehouse Atrium in Columbus. (Reprinted, with permission, from the *Columbus Dispatch*)

Parliament of the World's Religions, the United States Conference of Religions for Peace, and Harvard University's Pluralism Project, have all encouraged interfaith dialogue in the United States.

Statewide

In the last ten years, interfaith activities in Ohio have intensified quite significantly. A few examples include:

- The Christian-Jewish dialogue in Dayton is one of the oldest surviving formally organized interfaith interactions in the nation.

- The Brueggeman Center for Interreligious Dialogue at Xavier University in Cincinnati is actively involved in promoting interfaith understanding. In September 2000 the Brueggeman Center hosted a Millennium Peace Celebration in which members of the International Interreligious Peace Council presided over the ceremonies, and local representatives of the world's faiths made presentations. Thousands of Ohioans attended.

- In 2000 the Ohio Bicentennial Commission appointed the multifaith Religious Experience Advisory Council, which planned and coordinated faith-based activities in celebration of Ohio's two-hundredth birthday. (This book is a collaborative interfaith effort by the members of that council.)
- Many Ohio hospitals are expanding their chapel rooms to include symbols and information from various faiths, and libraries are producing brochures listing books about the major religions of the world.
- In 2002 Port Columbus International Airport dedicated a meditation room for use by employees and travelers. Symbols of eight world religions adorn the walls, and literature and prayer books from a wide variety of faiths are available.
- Ohio educators are increasingly being challenged to include religion in their study of world history and cultures. In response to this need, Harvard University's Pluralism Project has produced a multimedia CD-ROM video entitled "On Common Ground," which explains the history, beliefs, and practices of more than fifteen different faiths in the United States. Additional instructional materials have been developed by other organizations to help high school teachers present information about the world's religions to their students and to teach about how these faiths are linked to ethics, values, literature, and the cultures of the world.
- After September 11, 2001, a few mosques and other Islamic religious centers were vandalized in Ohio. In response, local people from various faiths, including those from neighboring churches and synagogues, supported these faith communities emotionally, financially, and socially.
- People across Ohio are increasingly seeing the need for interfaith discussion and collaboration. Some mayors in metropolitan areas have formed interfaith and ecumenical advisory groups. For example, Columbus Mayor Michael Coleman formed a Religious Advisory Council composed of members from the major faith groups, and his office developed a citywide pledge "to come together from various life experiences and faith beliefs to uplift our common humanity and to come together in a series of educational and peaceful activities focusing on understanding, acceptance, and unity among all of us."

Locally

Both formal and loose-knit interfaith groups exist in Cleveland, Youngstown, Akron-Canton, Dayton, Cincinnati, Toledo, and Columbus. One of the best known interfaith organizations in Ohio is the Columbus-based Interfaith Association of Central Ohio (IACO), which has been recognized by the *Columbus Dispatch* and by Harvard University's Pluralism Project as a model for grassroots interfaith organizations.[5] The IACO was formed in 1986, following an interfaith prayer service in November 1985 to focus attention on the summit meeting between President Ronald Reagan of the United States and President Mikhail Gorbachev of the USSR.

In the early 1990s the IACO worked with the World of Difference campaign, an Anti-Defamation League of B'nai B'rith effort, to reduce faith-based prejudice in the central Ohio region. In the last ten years, the association has laid a foundation of friendship and trust with members of different faiths. This was evident after the terrorist attack on the World Trade Center on September 11, 2001—only a few documented hate crimes were carried out in central Ohio in the wake of the attack. In fact, the events of September 11 seemed to bring the Columbus community together instead of dividing it. An excellent example of this was the first statewide interfaith prayer service held in Columbus at the Ohio Statehouse on September 30, 2001, where adherents of nine different faiths shared prayers of hope, peace, and justice.[6] More than 350 people attended. In August 2003 IACO hosted the North American Interfaith Network Annual Conference titled "Journeys of Faith, Freedom, and Justice." The conference was attended by more than 100 persons from across North America.

The IACO has also helped to start interfaith dialogue at the Ohio State University. In spring 2002 students from different campus religious groups formed the Campus Interfaith Council. Members of the Bahá'í, Buddhist, Christian, Hindu, Islamic, Jewish, Native American, and Sikh faiths participate.

People of diverse faiths and denominations in Ohio have blessed our state, and learning to live and work together with understanding, appreciation, and respect for each other is the challenge now before us.

OUR COMMON FUTURE

Ohio is more diverse in religion and faith traditions today than it has ever been. Hindus, Buddhists, Muslims, Christians, Jews, Sikhs, Native Americans, Bahá'ís, Jains, Zoroastrians . . . all are now citizens of the

Buckeye state. But what about our future? What will Ohioans fifty years from now write about us and how we faced the challenges ahead of us?

Knowledge of another faith does not need to threaten our own. On the contrary, many people involved in interfaith dialogue report that interfaith experiences have led to a better understanding of their own religious beliefs. Rita M. Gross observes: "[O]nce one really begins to understand other religions accurately, one is in a position also to appreciate one's own religion much more fully. This appreciation results from having the basis to understand the uniqueness and specificity of one's own tradition."[7] A common conclusion of those engaged in interfaith discussion groups is that exposure to other religious traditions enriches and enhances their own knowledge and beliefs.

And on a communal or societal level one may ask, "Is there value in diverse faiths working together, pooling their strengths and perspectives to make a better society?" Ultimately, the answer must be yes. The alternative is dissension and strife, and possibly the loss of life and bloodshed as has been seen in so many other parts of the world. To live and work together in peace for the common good of all must be the goal of a civilized society.

One goal we can certainly all agree on is that we want to be treated with respect. Our neighbors, friends, and family of different faiths would also like to be treated with respect. Each of the faiths has a "Golden Rule" that encourages its followers to "do unto others as they would have done unto them." What better way to start the next hundred years of Ohio's history than by renewing and reaffirming the centuries-old values and beliefs of those gone before us?

> One should treat all creatures in the world as one would like to be treated.
>> *Jainism, Mahavira, Sutrakritanga*

> No one is an enemy, none a stranger; I get along with all.
>> *Sikh Faith, Siri Guru Granth Sahib*

> In everything, do to others as you would have them do to you; for this is the law and the prophets.
>> *Christianity, Jesus, Matthew 7:12*

> Treat not others in ways that you yourself would find hurtful.
>> *Buddhism, The Buddha, Udana-Varga 5.18*

This is the sum of duty: do not do to others what would cause pain if done to you.

Hinduism, Mahabharata 5:1517

Not one of you truly believes until you wish for others what you wish for yourself.

Islam, The Prophet Muhammad, thirteenth of the forty Hadiths of Nawawi

Lay not on any soul a load that you would not wish to be laid upon you, and desire not for anyone the things you would not desire for yourself.

The Bahá'í Faith, Bahá'u'lláh, Gleanings

We are all related.

Lakota prayer

Do not do unto others whatever is injurious to yourself.

Zoroastrianism, Zoroaster, Shayast-na-Shayast 13.29

What is hateful to you, do not do to your neighbor. This is the whole Torah; all the rest is commentary.

Judaism, Hillel, Talmud, Shabbath 31a

NOTES

1. Diana L. Eck, *A New Religious America* (San Francisco: Harper, 2001), 383.

2. Diana L. Eck, "The Challenge of Pluralism," *Nieman Reports* 47, no. 2 (summer 1993).

3. S. Wesley Ariarajah, *Not without My Neighbour: Issues in Interfaith Relations* (Geneva: World Council of Churches, 1999), 35.

4. Ibid., 37.

5. "Group Unites Eight Faiths for Mutual Enlightenment," *Columbus Dispatch,* May 10, 2002.

6. "Faithful from Ohio Gather to Pray for End to Terrorism," *Columbus Dispatch,* October 1, 2001.

7. Rita M. Gross, "Religious Diversity: Some Implications for Monotheism," *Wisconsin Dialogue: A Faculty Journal for the University of Wisconsin-Eau Claire* 11 (1991): 11.

NATIVE AMERICAN INDIAN SPIRITUAL TRADITIONS

Barry Landeros-Thomas

NATIVE AMERICAN INDIANS HAVE LIVED IN OHIO FOR THOUSANDS of years. When European settlers came to Ohio, they brought different religions and different ways of doing things. The European settlers did not understand Native American Indians, and they thought that European ways were better. Because they thought that Christianity was superior to native beliefs, they tried to convince Indians to change their ways. The settlers used many different methods to try and make Indians change. Many missionaries tried to "educate" Indians about why these new ways were better and why Indian ways were bad. The settlers made laws against Indian religions and punished anyone they caught breaking those laws. Sometimes Indian people were killed if they did not change to these new ways. The settlers believed in a doctrine that held that European Americans had a divine right to the continent and a religious mission to bring Christian "civilization" to the "heathens." These beliefs later came to be known as Manifest Destiny. Many Native American Indians were hurt because of these ideas.

The American Indian Religious Freedom Act was passed in 1978. Even though this law was enacted, some problems still persist. Some native people are still not allowed to fully practice their religions. Many native prisoners are harassed when they try to pray in a Native American way. In early 2003, a woman was arrested for praying at the Circle and Octagon Mounds in Newark, Ohio.

More than one hundred thousand people in the state of Ohio have at least some native heritage. In Ohio today, there are people from more than a hundred tribes and nations. Each tribe has its own set of beliefs and traditions. Even though each tribe is different, there are still some basic ideas that connect Indian beliefs. These core beliefs connect Native American Indians to each other in unique ways.

HISTORY

Many different tribes and nations have lived in Ohio for thousands of years. Dozens of tribes lived in Ohio before the settlers arrived. Most tribes had these beliefs in common:

1. Native American Indian belief systems were complex. Creation myths and other stories explained how tribes came to be.

2. Most Native American Indian people worshiped a creator. They saw themselves as part of God's creation. They did not see themselves as above the rest of creation. They saw themselves as connected to the rest of the world.

3. Most tribes believed in the immortality of the human soul. The afterlife was a place of abundance and security.

Like other cultures, the Native American Indian societies of North America hoped to enlist the aid of supernatural forces in controlling the natural and social worlds. Each tribe had its own set of religious ceremonies and observances devoted to that aim. Individuals spoke to the Creator with private prayers or ceremonies. Tobacco, sweetgrass, sage, and cedar were used in these prayers. Spiritual leaders were believed to have special knowledge and had sacred visions. They helped communities in times of need. Beliefs and practices of native and European cultures were similar in many ways, including:

1. Europeans and Native American Indians each had creation myths.

2. European and Native American cultures both worshiped a Creator God.

3. Both cultures feared a wicked being.

4. Both cultures believed in an afterlife and an immortal soul.

5. Both cultures communicated with their deity through prayers and offerings.

6. Both cultures had spiritual leaders who helped sustain their societies.

There were also major differences between these cultures. Native American Indians did not see the supernatural as separate. They perceived both the "material" and the "spiritual" as part of creation. In this view, plants, animals, and humans are closely connected with each other as part of creation. Human beings are viewed as part of this interconnected universe. They are not above or superior to any other part of creation. Europeans saw this worldview as "pagan." They portrayed Native American Indians as "worshiping" animals, plants, and trees. By contrast, Europeans focused on the separation between the mundane and the divine. The spiritual beings in heaven were separated from sinful men and women in a world filled with temptation and evil.

Precontact Era

One culture that existed in the Ohio region was the Adena. This is the name given by western scientists. These Native people inhabited parts of Ohio more than two thousand years ago. They lived in villages and survived by hunting, fishing, and gathering wild plants. Much of what we know of them today is drawn from their sacred mounds. Many artifacts have been found throughout Ohio. The Adena's culture is also distinguished by their siltstone smoking pipes. These pipes are fine examples of prehistoric Indian art.

It is believed that the building of the mounds began around 500 B.C.E. Mounds were used for many purposes. Conical mounds were used for burials. Other mounds were used for various ritual purposes. Chillicothe holds one of the earliest and most important Adena sites. Western scientists are not sure whether or not the mounds were used for religious purposes. However, Vine Deloria Jr. and other Native scholars state that it is clear that the sites are sacred. This confirms the position of many Native elders and spiritual leaders such as Asa Primeaux Sr. One of the most famous of these mounds is the Great Serpent Mound. Western scientists remain unsure of its significance. Native experts believe that it was used as a ceremonial site. It was made in the shape of a serpent swallowing an oval object. Native experts believe that the oval was the center of ceremonies. There are also burial mounds adjacent to the serpent mound. It is thought that these belonged to families that took care of the site.

The Hopewell culture grew out of the Adena culture. As with the Adena, these Native people did not call themselves "Hopewell." It is the name that western archaeologists and anthropologists have given to them. They were named for Captain Mordecai Hopewell, on whose land some of the first artifacts were found. The Hopewell continued the mound-building tradition of the Adena, building mounds and enclosures that were larger and more varied in design. Their villages were small and scattered around large ceremonial centers. They built earthen enclosures in the shapes of circles, squares, octagons, parallel lines, and other forms. They used these earthworks for many different purposes—as ceremonial centers, social gathering places, trading posts, and places of worship. The Circle and Octagon Mounds are part of what remains of the Newark Earthworks. The mounds in Newark are the largest geometric earthworks ever built. Many people from different villages worked together to build these giant mounds and enclosures. They were considered sacred by the Native people of the time. They continue to be of importance to Native people today. They are a place to which Native people come today to pray.

Another group of Natives in Ohio are known as the Fort Ancient people. Western observers have misnamed them. Natives of the late Woodland period did not continue building earthworks. These people lived in an area that was developed earlier. Groups of "Fort Ancient" Indians lived in the "South Fort" and in the valley of the Little Miami River. For years, archeologists believed that these Natives built Fort Ancient. Therefore, they were incorrectly named the Fort Ancient Indians. One of their villages, Anderson Village, is located on the east side of the Little Miami in the shadow of Fort Ancient. Two distinct Indian tribes lived within what is now Fort Ancient State Memorial. They lived in this area at different times. These were the Hopewell people and the Fort Ancient people. Of these two groups, the Hopewell people were the first to settle in the area. They were also the builders of the great Fort Ancient Earthworks. Later, people of the Fort Ancient culture came into the area and established their stockade villages. One interesting difference was the Fort Ancient people worked with stone, bone, and shell. They never developed the high degree of craftsmanship shown by the tools and ornaments of the Hopewell.

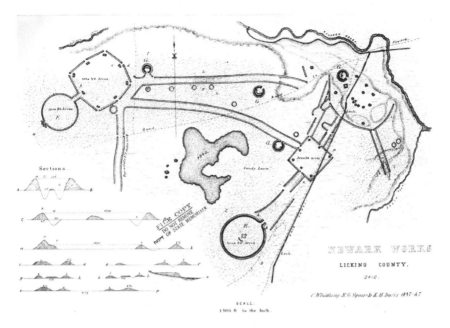

The geometric earthworks in Newark were constructed by prehistoric indigenous people more than two thousand years ago. The earthworks are believed to have been used as a ceremonial, spiritual, and social center by their builders. They are a majestic remnant of prehistoric Ohio. A part of this site is currently being used as an eighteen-hole golf course and private country club, which has caused some disagreement between club members and Native people who come to pray. (Courtesy of the Ohio Historical Society)

Early Colonial Era

From the beginning of contact with Native American Indians, Europeans thought that their society was better. They thought that Native American Indians were not civilized. They believed that the world could be separated into two parts, good and evil, body and spirit, man and nature, head and heart, European and primitive. Native American Indians did not separate things in this way. Native languages express the oneness of all things. They believed that all of God's creation is related. God is not the transcendent Father but the Mother Earth, the Corn Mother, the Great Spirit who nourishes all. The Europeans did not understand these views. They thought that Native peoples believed in many gods and worshiped plants and animals. They saw Native beliefs as inferior to European beliefs. The founding idea of most Native belief systems is that all of creation is connected. The Creator was viewed as an invisible force, a powerful spirit. This spirit created the entire universe and ordered the cycles of birth and death for all living things. This core belief included literally all of creation. Plants, animals, stars, mountains, people, and so forth are all connected. Such phrases as "my relatives" or "all my relations" reflect this idea. Phrases such as these can be found in most Native languages. Such ideas show that Native people did not set themselves apart from or above the rest of God's creation. Their world was infused with the divine—often described as "The Sacred Hoop" or a similar phrase. This was not at all a personal divine being who presided over an individual and his or her salvation. In contrast, Europeans believed that God judged each individual's conduct and either let the person enter Heaven or damned the person to Hell.

Europeans viewed the Native beliefs as "pagan." Thus, the conquest was seen as a necessary evil. They sought to bestow upon the "heathen Indians" a moral consciousness that would redeem their souls. Using these views, the Europeans portrayed themselves as noble. The true basis for conquest was economics—the desire to accumulate treasure and land and exploit cheap labor. The Christian religion was used by the European conquerors. They demanded fealty from all cultures in the name of Christianity. In this way, the invaders rationalized their actions.

Early American Era

Two treaties were signed at Fort Stanwix. The first was signed in 1768, and the second in 1784. This second treaty forced the Iroquois to cede lands in western New York and Pennsylvania, losing their ancestral homes. The conditions for Iroquois in the United States quickly worsened after this. They lost most of their remaining lands and much of their ability to cope. Many of the tribes in Ohio watched what happened to the Iroquois. These tribes included the Shawnee, Miami, Delaware, Ottawa, Wyandotte, and Potawatomi. These tribes formed their own confederacy. They informed the United States that there would be a boundary between them and the settlers. The Ohio River was the boundary between their lands and those of the settlers, with the Natives occupying much-desired lands in Ohio. It was just a matter of time before further hostilities ensued.

Tecumseh was a renowned Shawnee leader in the early nineteenth century. He had much experience with the invading whites. He determined that the best way to stop the settlers was to form a confederacy. He approached most of the leaders of other Indian tribes west of the Appalachian Mountains in 1808. Tecumseh's younger brother was Tenskwatawa, also known as the Prophet. The Prophet helped to unite the tribes. The Prophet, a spiritual leader, had a vision in which the Creator told him to have the Indians give up all white customs and products. The influence of the Europeans was seen as poisoning Native culture. By turning their backs on their traditional ways the Indians had offended the Creator. If they returned to Native customs, the Creator would reward them by driving the whites from their land. Many Natives embraced the Prophet's message and joined the two brothers at Prophetstown. This was a village the two had established in 1808 in the Indiana Territory.

William Henry Harrison was the governor of the territory. He led an army toward the village in 1811. Tecumseh was not there at the time. He was recruiting allies in the southern United States. He left his brother with orders not to attack the Americans. The Prophet claimed to have received another vision from the Creator. In this vision, the Creator told him to send his warriors against the Americans. The Creator also told him that the soldiers' bullets would not harm them. The resulting battle was known as the Battle of Tippecanoe. The Americans defeated the Prophet and his followers and destroyed Prophetstown.

The confederacy was weakened by this defeat. Many of the allies returned to their own villages and towns. The War of 1812 seemed to be another chance for his confederacy. Tecumseh and his remaining followers allied themselves with the British. They hoped that the British would return their homeland to them. The war ended in a stalemate. Tecumseh died at one of the most important battles of the conflict, the Battle of the Thames. In this battle, combined English-Indian forces met the American army. William Henry Harrison led the Americans. The British soldiers fled and left Tecumseh's followers to continue on their own. The Americans eventually drove the Natives from the field. As they did, an American bullet felled Tecumseh. His death signaled the end of united Indian resistance against the Americans, and Tecumseh's dream of a united Indian front died with him.

Not all relationships between Europeans and Natives were bad. There were many times in which Native people and settlers lived in peace with one another. The Christian missionary work of the Moravians in Gnadenhutten is one of these stories. However, there was a very sad end to this tale. On March 9, 1782, American soldiers killed ninety-six Indians—men, women, and children. All of them were Native American Christians. Witnesses reported that they did not resist and sang hymns and prayers as they were killed. Those killed at Gnadenhutten were true Native American Indian Christian martyrs. Government officials condemned the action. However, it reflected the widespread attitudes of the settlers towards Native peoples.

Other tactics were much more insidious. One such method focused on "cleansing" Native children of their culture. These were strategies of assimilation. All too often, they began with violence. Jesuits in the Great Lakes region built forts in which Native youths were incarcerated. The priests indoctrinated them with Christian values and forced them to do manual labor. This type of education was a crucial tool. It changed not only the language but also the culture of impressionable children. In boarding schools, students were immersed in an environment of assimilation twenty-four hours a day. The founder of the Carlisle School in Pennsylvania was Captain Richard H. Pratt. Pratt stated that "Carlisle has always planted treason to the tribe and loyalty to the nation at large." More crudely put, the Carlisle philosophy was "Kill the Indian to save the man." Soldiers took the children from their families. The children were forced to stay at the boarding schools for years with no contact with their families. Their hair was cut and they were made to wear military uniforms. After years of "education" and harsh treatment at the schools, the children lost their native language and much of their culture. They were strangers in their own world; there was a loss, a void of not belonging in either the Native world or the white world. As illustrated in the movie *Lakota Women,* these children are often referred to as "Apple Children" (red on the outside, white on the inside); they did not know where they fit; they were unable to assimilate into either culture. This confusion and loss of cultural identity led to many problems. Suicide, drinking, drugs, violence, and other symptoms of multigenerational trauma are just some of the results. One of the more dire aspects of multigenerational trauma is the fact that the adverse effects are passed on to successive generations. Boarding-school students were not prepared for parenthood. They had been deprived of the necessary learning of skills needed in this area. This type of learning takes place within a loving family and community, not an institution. Put simply, in addition to being stripped of their cultural identity, they never learned how to be parents.

The Indian Removal Act was passed in 1830. The Indian Removal policy was designed to clear land for white settlers. Removal was more than simply another assault on Indian land. It was more than just greed for land, although that was still a primary reason. Many white Americans thought that it was a way to save Indians. There was still overt violence and other problems wherever Indians lived close to white settlements. Removal was often accomplished by forced marches, which usually saw high mortality rates.

The Wyandotte in Ohio were removed by such a policy. They were confined to a reservation after the War of 1812. Greed and racism were driving forces behind the push to rid Ohio of the "Indian problem." By the 1830s, many Wyandotte were Christian converts. The tribe was also successful in adapting to western methods of agriculture and commerce. Despite this, their white neighbors and the state and federal governments forced them from their land in 1843. As the last organized tribe in Ohio began its westward trek to Kansas, Squire Grey Eyes, a Wyandotte spiritual leader and ordained minister, noted: "Here our dead are buried. . . . Soon they shall be forgotten, for the onward march of the strong White Man will not turn aside for the Indian graves" (from "Farewell to a Beloved Land," July 9, 1843; text at www.sfo.com/~denglish/wynaks/farewell.htm).

Indian graves were a symbol of the cataclysmic end. Many settlers came into eastern and southern Ohio after the Treaty of Greenville was signed in 1795. They did not worry about what this meant to Native culture. Indians were confined to the northwestern part of the territory. It would take European American settlers only a short eight years to achieve statehood.

Contemporary American Era

European contact radically changed and/or eliminated a whole way of Indian life. This was often done by ruthless exploitation. Natural resources were often the target. The destruction of sacred sites or ancient homelands is evident in many places. This was due to economic development in most cases. The following are a few examples:

- The purposeful destruction of an ancient petroglyph at Blackhand Gorge in Licking County by builders of the Ohio and Erie Canal in 1828;
- The ancient sacred site of the Circle and Octagon Mounds in Newark, Ohio, now occupied by a private country club, although it is public property, and whose membership continues to deface and desecrate the mounds as well as harass Native Americans who come to pray at the site;
- The strip mining of coal in the Ohio Valley that destroyed numerous sacred sites.

To this day, Native American people in Ohio encounter problems. There are many sacred mounds located throughout the state. These mounds are both burial and ceremonial sites. However, protection of these sites is minimal at best. It is a seemingly constant battle. Developers and relic hunters alike continue to threaten the mounds. They dig into, plunder, excavate, or simply bulldoze over the mounds. They have little to no regard for Indian spiritual beliefs. They often treat physical remains like baseball cards. Hundreds of thousands of skeletal remains and burial artifacts have been taken. There are many private collectors. Many public groups also have large collections. Such organizations may hold as many as hundreds of thousands of burial artifacts. Some do approach the Native community and return remains so they can be reburied. Muskingum College returned more than eighty skeletal remains. These ancestors were reburied in 2001. Some organizations and collectors hold onto bones and artifacts taken from graves and try to rationalize their actions.

Another current policy that reflects these problems deals with freedom of religion. Natives in jails and prisons are deprived of their rights. They are not allowed to take part in traditional ceremonies, while other prisoners are free to hold worship services with no interference.

BELIEFS

It is difficult to give a short description of the spiritual beliefs of the many Native cultures of Ohio. In Ohio today there are people from more than one hundred tribes and nations. Each tribe has its own history, practices, and belief systems. However, a common thread that can be found in many Native traditions is the idea of "connectedness." Basically, Native

The sweat lodge, or *inipi,* is an integral part of many historical Native faith traditions. It serves as a way to purify and renew one's spirit through prayer. The design of the lodge and the rituals performed or songs sung may differ from place to place. Photograph by Barry Landeros-Thomas. (Courtesy of the photographer)

people believe that all of creation is connected. Everything has a spirit, whether human being, bird, fish, tree, or stone. All are seen as part of creation and one is not set above the other. Human beings are to remain mindful of their actions and how those actions affect the rest of creation.

The Medicine Wheel, which is used by many Native traditions, illustrates this belief. The wheel depicts the Four Directions. These directions are similar to the cardinal points on the compass. The directions are represented by four colors, often red, white, yellow, and black. The directions/colors are set in a sacred circle. They symbolize the cyclic nature of creation and the interconnectedness of all things. The Medicine Wheel also represents other cycles and relationships. It represents the cycle of life (child, youth, adult, elder). It corresponds to the aspects of individual well-being (physical, mental, emotional, spiritual). It illustrates relations with the people of the world (red, white, black, yellow). The Medicine Wheel teaches the importance of balance, which is important in our lives and everyday activities.

Core beliefs and cultural practices form the foundation of Native spirituality. Modern Natives use this foundation to build a sense of identity. The Native view joins together the realms of religion, art, and utility. These areas are separate in the Western way of thinking. They are seen as special individual skills. The Native holistic way of thinking is shown in many ways. It can be seen in the artifacts—pots, blankets, moccasins, saddles, cradleboards—of various nations. Iconographic decoration and symbols often reveal this similarity. Woven into a Cherokee sash or beaded into a Lakota pipe bag, the same message is shown. They can both honor the power of natural and supernatural forces. Many of these traditional skills have been preserved, and programs of cultural restoration help in this.

There are common purposes in many Native cultural items. Differences in history and styles are also shown. These differences often have a regional base. The arts of the early Woodland period are an example of this. They have been discovered in burial mounds and religious sites. Archaeologists identify these Ohio sites with Adena and Hopewell cultures. Some items include figures, pipes, and other carvings. The famous Hopewellian serpent effigy is one of these items. It was found in a mound in southern Ohio. The serpent is made out of mica. Its production involved many types of technology. Whetstones, grindstones, hand hammers, chisels, and flint knives were used to make it. The Hopewell artists also made ornaments. These items, made from stone, flint, and pearl, often included bird images. They are also credited with the first human-shaped form in Indian art. These were miniature clay figures, often with infants on their backs. This Woodland culture was among the first to be displaced and nearly destroyed by the colonists. By this time, the Woodland cultures had developed to include symbolic animal forms. Medicine bags were made from the pelts of sacred animals. The otter, the muskrat, and the water panther were some of these animals. One example of an important cultural artifact that survives from this Woodland culture is the mantle of Powhatan, who was the leader of the Algonquin people. He led at the time of the coming of the Puritan colonists in the early seventeenth century.

Many native religions have a therapeutic role. Tribal, rather than individual, concepts of rights are emphasized. All these elements indicate that Native culture is a viable way of life. This has just not been understood or acknowledged by the mainstream. Many white Americans still want to cancel the special status of Natives. Many still argue for assimilation.

There are a great number of traditions in the Native community. This results from the experiences of Native peoples. Christian missionaries and schools tried to get rid of Native religions. They tried to replace them with various Christian traditions. Many Native traditions have survived despite European American efforts to eradicate them. One way Native religions survive is to attach themselves to Christian forms in a process known as syncretism. Using sage or sweetgrass as part of prayer or other liturgical activities is one way this is done. One example is the Native American Church, which originated among the Yacqui and other Mexican Indians in the late nineteenth century. It has spread to other Native peoples in Oklahoma and the Midwest, attracting followers from many nations. This religion combines Christian and native traditions. Peyote is used in some ceremonies. However, it is still deemed illegal in the state of Ohio. Despite this, the Native American Church holds regular meetings and has a great number of followers in the Buckeye state.

Our Lady of the Sioux Catholic Church provides another example. This church was first established at Pine Ridge, South Dakota, and now has followers all across the country, including Ohio. Native images like the buffalo, peace pipe, and thunderbird are central. They have been added to and substituted for Christian images. Smoking of the sacred pipe replaces the wine and wafer of the Eucharist. In the Southwest, many Native beliefs have continued without drastic change or adaptation, and the Navajo, Hopi, and Pueblo people still have strong ties to their traditions. Many of those living in Ohio still maintain their traditional practices.

It should be mentioned that there is a large number of Native Christians today in Ohio. This is to be expected. There have been hundreds of years of cultural contact. Native people have been exposed to Christian beliefs and traditions for a long time. These many years of contact have obvious results. Many Natives now feel more comfortable in a mainstream church. Many have little experience with Native traditions. It is safe to say that the majority of Natives in Ohio practice some form of Christian tradition. A number of Native Christians have chosen the path of pastoral leadership or lay ministry. They serve the Native community and act as bridges between cultures. They address issues affecting Native people within their own denominations, as well as doing interdenominational work.

CURRENT DEMOGRAPHICS

There are about twenty-seven thousand Natives living in Ohio. This number is based on the 2000 census. That number increases to over one hundred thousand when people of mixed ancestry are included. For example, many Latinos can trace their roots to the Yacqui, Otomi, Mixteca, or other tribes. Considering this, it is safe to say that well over one hundred thousand people in the state of Ohio have at least some Native heritage. This heritage comes from dozens of tribal nations.

CONTACT INFORMATION

The contact information for Indian centers throughout Ohio is as follows:

The Ohio Center for Native American Affairs, 7916 Braun Road, Groveport, Ohio 43125, 614-830-0562, *info@ocnaa.org*

Native American Indian Center of Central Ohio, 67 East Innis Avenue, Columbus, Ohio 43207, 614-443-6120, *naicco@aol.com*

North American Indian Cultural Centers, Inc., 1062 Triplett Boulevard, Akron, Ohio 44306, 330-724-1280, *NAICC2@aol.com*

The Miami Valley Council for Native Americans, P.O. Box 637, Dayton, Ohio 45401, 937-275-8599, *TMVCNA89@aol.com*

Land of the Singing Coyote Indian Center, 17992 Main Street, Seaman, Ohio 45679, 937-386-0222 / 866-500-1112.

Lake Erie Native American Council, P.O. Box 620054, Cleveland, Ohio 44102, 216-634-8408.

RESOURCES

Champagne, Duane. "The Delaware Revitalization Movement of the Early 1760s: A Suggested Reinterpretation." *American Indian Quarterly* 12 (spring 1988): 107–25.

Deloria, Vine. *God Is Red.* New York: Grosset & Dunlap, 1973.

Erdoes, Richard, and Alfonso Ortiz, eds. *American Indian Myths and Legends.* New York: Pantheon Books, 1984.

Hultkrantz, Ake. *Belief and Worship in Native North America.* Syracuse, N.Y.: Syracuse University Press, 1981.

Neihardt, John. *The Sixth Grandfather: Black Elk's Teachings Given to John Niehardt.* Edited by Raymond DeMallie. Lincoln: University of Nebraska Press, 1984.

Paper, Jordan. *Offering Smoke: The Sacred Pipe and Native American Religion.* Moscow: University of Idaho Press, 1988.

Slotkin, James. *The Peyote Religion: A Study in Indian-White Relations.* Glencoe, Ill.: Free Press, 1956.

CHRISTIANITY

Amish and Mennonite

AMISH

David Kline

HISTORY

THE AMISH CAME TO OHIO IN 1803, NOT TO SETTLE, BUT TO EXPLORE the region around what is now eastern Holmes and western Tuscarawas counties for its potential as a site for an agrarian community. Attracted by the excellent springs and vast white oak forests, which indicated fine limestone soils, they selected tracts of lands for a settlement and then returned to their homes in Somerset County, Pennsylvania.

Deeds for their new land, signed by Thomas Jefferson, were secured in 1807. The following spring Jacob Miller and his two sons, Henry and Jacob, came to their section of land, about a mile northeast of Sugarcreek. They cleared a parcel of land and planted some crops. After two cabins were built, Jacob Sr. returned to Pennsylvania. In the spring of 1809 Jacob Sr. moved the rest of his family to Ohio and brought with him his wife's twenty-year-old nephew, Jonas Stutzman, who then traveled five miles farther west and settled on 160 acres just south of Walnut Creek. Jacob Miller Sr. was a minister; he preached the first Amish sermon in Ohio.

More settlers soon arrived in the fertile valley, and by 1815 a cabin schoolhouse was built. Even though the War of 1812 slowed the influx of settlers to the area, by the 1820s the settlement was flourishing and there were four churches.

By 1840 there were ten Amish communities spread across the state. Between 1865 and 1880 most of these merged with the more progressive but similar Mennonite Church. At that time the Amish came to be called (by historians) Old Order, to differentiate them from the more progressive Amish/Mennonites.

The Amish are Christians. The group came out of the Protestant Reformation in Switzerland in the early 1500s, when Conrad Grebel and several other young associates of Swiss reformer Ulrich Zwingli believed he had stopped short of a total scriptural reformation of the Church. Grebel especially hoped for far-reaching change. In 1525 the zealous young university-trained men who believed in nonresistance, believer's (adult) baptism, and complete separation of church and state, broke away from Zwingli and started their own movement by baptizing each other. The foundation of their faith was the word of God, with an emphasis on the Gospels. They believed that there should be complete freedom of conscience and no use of force or compulsion by state or church; faith must be free. They were called Anabaptists (meaning "to be baptized again") and soon began suffering persecution from the state church, which considered them heretics. The small group was arrested, imprisoned, and banished from Zurich.

Religious persecution in Europe during the 1600s drove the Anabaptists into mountainous rural regions, where they became agriculturists. In time they came to be known as "the quiet in the land." Following the Thirty Years War (1618–48) and the Treaty of Westphalia, many of the Swiss Anabaptists, or Swiss Brethren, moved north into the Alsace-Lorraine and Palatinate areas to escape compulsory military service in Switzerland. The German dialect the Amish speak, Pennsylvania Dutch or Deutsch, originates from the Alsatian region. The conservative branch of Anabaptists that came to be called Amish separated from the main group of Swiss Brethren during the decade of the 1690s. One of their early leaders was a minister named Jacob Amman, hence the name Amish.

It was in the farmlands of Alsace-Lorraine (the little spit of fertile land west of the Rhine River that was a prize in the many wars fought between France and Germany from the 700s until 1945 and now belongs to France)

An Amish farmer plowing his field in Holmes County. The Amish have always considered the agrarian life their ultimate goal. Photo by Ian Adams. (Courtesy of David Kline)

that the Amish developed the agricultural practices they still use in Ohio today. They plant a diversity of crops and follow an annual rotation of plants to naturally control insects and weeds. The Amish are primarily livestock farmers—hogs, chickens, sheep, and dairy cows. Dairy farming is the primary source of income, particularly in the Holmes County area. The average herd size is between thirty and forty cows. While much of the milk is made into cheese by local cheese makers, more and more of it is Grade A and is sold to bottling plants in northeastern Ohio.

As recently as thirty years ago, three-fourths of the Amish were farmers or retired farmers. That percentage has now dropped to 25 percent, as their population doubles about every twenty years and the scarcity and cost of farmland prohibit many young people from farming. The Amish have always considered an agrarian life their ultimate goal. They never accepted the American notion that farming is dull or tedious. They believe that there is drama in every day and in every blade of grass and stalk of corn. Their desire is to stay close to the softening influence of nature and its Creator. They hold to the Psalm that says, "The Earth is the Lord's and the fullness thereof" (Ps. 24:1).

A considerable number of the nonfarming Amish are involved in agriculture-related enterprises. They work as wheelwrights; harness makers; horse-collar, equipment, and home manufacturers; and farm equipment repairers. Many others are woodworkers; they make quality hardwood furniture. Some work in local factories.

BELIEFS

The Amish in Ohio hold worship services in their homes every other Sunday. On "between" Sundays they often attend services at friends', relatives', or neighbors' homes. During the warm months services are held in barns or woodworking shops, and in the winter they are held in the house or some other heated building. Services are from nine in the morning to about noon. Services include hymn singing and two sermons—a fairly brief opening sermon and then the main sermon. While only New Testament scriptures are read during the service, the entire Bible is used in the sermons. They use Martin Luther's German translation of the Bible. The minister speaks a blend of German, Pennsylvania Dutch, and English. All Amish are bilingual. Communion services are held semiannually; at Easter and in the fall at the end of harvest. The Amish also practice the ordinance of foot-washing. The Amish keep Christmas, Good Friday, Easter, Ascension Day, and Thanksgiving Day as holy days.

Early in the twentieth century, after living in Ohio for more than a hundred years, the Amish made the decision *not* to use the tractor for field traction. They chose to stay with animal power, both for the farm and for road travel. That wise decision to restrict technology prevented the Amish from following the agribusiness tendency to "get big or get out." It also saved all the small towns and villages in their communities, which have now become tourist destinations for hundreds of thousands of visitors annually. Amish examine new technology thoroughly before accepting it. Much is rejected because of its long-term negative effects on the family, the church, and the community. Television is rejected because they believe that allowing a pipe into the sanctity of the home spewing forth 5 percent springwater and 95 percent raw sewage is contrary to the teachings of Jesus Christ.

The Amish strongly believe that technology and material things can never liberate you but tend to squeeze you into their own image. The Amish philosophy of "small farms are beautiful" and other conservative values are held by choice. They are very aware of what mainstream society has to offer and choose to reject much of it. They struggle to be "in the world, but not of the world." Around 70 percent of Amish children attend parochial schools, while the others go to public schools. Their formal education ends with the eighth grade.

CURRENT DEMOGRAPHICS

The Amish community in Holmes County and the surrounding counties of Wayne, Tuscarawas, Coshocton, Ashland, and Stark thrived in the fertile soils and today there are nearly two hundred congregations (more than forty thousand Amish) in the six-county area. It is the largest community of Amish in the world.

CONTACT INFORMATION

Each Amish church is autonomous and under the oversight of its elders. The Amish do not have local, state, or national administrative offices.

RESOURCES

Amish and Mennonite Information Center, 5798 County Road 77, Berlin, Ohio 44610, 330-893-3192.

The Budget, 134 Factory St., P.O. Box 249, Sugarcreek, Ohio 44681. (*The Budget* is published weekly [Wednesday] and has letters from Amish writers in communities across North America.)

Hostetler, John. *Amish Society*. Baltimore: Johns Hopkins University Press, 1993.

Miller, Levi. *Our People: The Amish and Mennonites of Ohio*. Scottdale, Penn.: Herald Press, 1992.

Ohio Amish Library, 4292 State Route 39, Millersburg, Ohio 44654.

MENNONITE

Bruce Stambaugh

HISTORY

MENNONITES FIRST CAME TO OHIO DURING THE LATE EIGHTEENTH and early nineteenth centuries. They arrived using the same modes of transportation as other pioneers. They drove wagons, rode on horseback, walked, and a few even traveled by flatboat on rivers.

The Mennonites journeyed to the young state for many of the same reasons as other settlers. They wanted economic betterment, hoping to own and develop their own land. They wanted the freedom to worship in their own way, as well as a place to raise and nurture their families without fear of being arrested and persecuted for their beliefs as they had been in Europe.

Mennonites had good reason to seek new land in the new world. From the beginning of the Anabaptist movement in 1525, Mennonites were persecuted and sometimes martyred by being drowned or burned at the stake in Germany, Switzerland, and eventually Holland for practicing their faith. This caused them to seek safer, more hospitable environs.

Because they baptized adult "believers" instead of infants, followers of the faith were called Anabaptists or "re-baptizers" by their persecutors in Europe. Mennonites were imprisoned, tortured, and martyred for their adult baptisms and for refusing to swear allegiance to the state. They were forced to live and farm on the poorest, steepest land and to meet secretly for worship in caves and forests.

In 1693, a split occurred in the church, dividing the Anabaptists. One group eventually became known as the Mennonites. The name Mennonite came from one of their early leaders in Holland, Menno Simons. He had been a Catholic priest before deciding to join the Anabaptists. The other group was the Amish, named for Jacob Amman, another Anabaptist leader.

Mennonites settled in Philadelphia, Pennsylvania, in 1683 before migrating west. The first Mennonites explored Ohio as early as 1785. The early Mennonite settlers liked the rich, well-drained soil and abundant water supply. In letters to relatives and friends back home in eastern Pennsylvania and in the Shenandoah Valley in Virginia, they raved about the availability of cheap, fertile land.

In addition to those from Pennsylvania and Virginia, many early Ohio Mennonites also came directly from Holland, Germany, and Switzerland. In the aftermath of World War I, Mennonites from Russia also came to Ohio.

The first Mennonite congregation in Ohio was Turkey Run, established near Bremen in Perry County in 1803. It is now part of the Conservative Mennonite Conference in Ohio. Midway Mennonite Church, founded in 1807 and built in 1825 near Columbiana, has more continuous years of service than any other Mennonite church in Ohio.

Industrious and unassuming, these early Mennonite settlers were almost exclusively farmers. They built their homes and barns with the lumber from the trees that they felled on their land as they cleared it for the planting of crops. Their attention and energies were focused on providing for their families and gathering for worship. The crops they grew—flax, wheat, timothy, corn, and oats—and the animals they raised—cows, sheep, goats, and chickens—allowed them to be self-sustaining. The families were often large, and the children helped on the farm.

Their division of labor was well defined. For example, the father and sons planted, raised, and harvested flax and broke it into fibers. The mother and daughters spun the fibers into thread, wove the thread into cloth, and used the cloth to sew clothes. After harvesting, the wheat was milled into flour, which was used for baking.

In the winter months, the men became proficient craftsmen, such as cheese makers, cabinetmakers, shoemakers, and weavers, to name a few. In the spirit of mutual aid, Mennonites helped each other by using these gifts in providing for all of the families.

The original building that first served as Turkey Run Mennonite Church near Bremen. Turkey Run (1803) was the first Mennonite congregation established in Ohio. (Courtesy of Leota Wesselhoeft)

Although their methods of travel and reasons for moving to Ohio were similar to those of other groups that settled the state, the Mennonite way of life was not. Mennonites intentionally chose to live differently. They wanted to be "in this world, but not of it," as their teachings professed. To do that, they chose a simple life, mostly rooted in farming. Initially, they avoided living in urban areas or even small towns. They did not participate in any form of government.

Their values were centered on hard work, family, church, and community. They read the Bible faithfully and believed it literally. They applied what they believed to their everyday lives, following Jesus' example in their behavior.

BELIEFS

Though not communal, Mennonites lived in close proximity for practical and theological reasons. Living close together permitted them to help each other with farming and household chores. It also allowed them to worship together easily, first in homes and barns, then in churches, as these were built. This was critical for their survival, since transportation was so difficult and dangerous.

However, Mennonite communities were not exclusive. In addition to living close to other Mennonites, they lived side by side with people of other faiths. The Mennonites also believed in a good education, either building their own schools or pushing for public ones to be opened close by. Again, this kept travel to a minimum so that their children could return to the farm to help with chores once school was over.

Another reason for settling together was their strong belief in the separation of church and state. They did not want to be a part of mainstream society, and chose to follow the biblical teachings of Jesus by living their faith. They were pacifists, which meant that they would not participate in the military. Believing their loyalty was to Christ and not country, Mennonites did not swear oaths. Instead, they expected each person to simply tell the truth at all times.

In the two hundred years since the first Mennonites moved to Ohio, much has changed in terms of how Mennonites look, what they do for a living, and even where they live. But their basic beliefs have remained constant.

Mennonites are mission oriented through service to others, locally, nationally, and internationally. Education, camps, and helping the less fortunate are priorities in their church organizations. Individuals may assist their communities by serving on civic boards, such as schools and hospitals, and in services like volunteer fire departments and thrift shops. Sharing their faith and their story, Mennonites have brought converts from a variety of cultural and ethnic backgrounds, not just Dutch, German, Swiss, or Russian, to the faith.

Mennonites have changed their lifestyle since their arrival in Ohio. However, the original Mennonite values of church, family, community, service, a strong work ethic, and sharing Christ's love remain important elements of their theology. Most Mennonites today have adopted the current styles of dress, while Conservative Mennonites tend to dress more plainly, with the women still wearing head coverings.

CURRENT DEMOGRAPHICS

As the early settlements expanded, Mennonites began streaming into other parts of Ohio. Stark, Wayne, and Holmes counties were initial destinations, and later Allen, Fulton, and Logan counties in western Ohio became popular locations for settling. Those counties continue to be home to the largest populations of Mennonites in Ohio. Altogether, Mennonites, including Conservative Mennonites, totaled about seventeen thousand in thirty-five Ohio counties in 2002. Congregations average about one hundred members. Many Ohio Mennonites have Amish ancestors. Members of the two groups even live in the same communities, especially in Holmes and Wayne counties.

CONTACT INFORMATION

Mennonites have organized their congregations into conferences, although some churches remain independent. Representatives from the congregations make decisions at annual meetings held at different locations around Ohio. In general, the congregations follow the organizational guidelines set by the conference to maintain a commonality in carrying out Mennonite beliefs as outlined in the Mennonite Confession of Faith.

Mennonites in Ohio are divided into three different conferences: the Ohio Conference and the Central District Conference, both of the Mennonite Church USA, and the Conservative Mennonites. Some churches belong to both the Central District Conference and the Ohio Conference.

Mennonite Church USA, Great Lakes Office, 500 South Main Street, P.O. Box 1245, Elkhart, Indiana, 46515-1245, 888-866-2872, *www.Mennonite-ChurchUSA.org*

Mennolink: *www.mennolink.org*

Ohio Conference of the Mennonite Church, 13363 Jericho Road, P.O. Box 210, Kidron, Ohio 44636, 330-857-5421, *ohmc@zoominternet.net, www.ohio.mennonite.net*

Central District Conference, 1015 Division St., Goshen, Indiana 46528, 800-662-2264, *cdoffice@hoosierlink.net, www.centraldistrict.mennonite.net*

Conservative Mennonite Conference, 9910 Rosedale Milford Center Road, Irwin, Ohio 43029, 740-857-1234, *steve@cmcrosedale.org, www.cmcrosedale.org*

Amish and Mennonite Heritage Center, 5798 County Road 77, P. O. Box 324, Berlin, Ohio 44610, 330-893-3192.

Third Way Café: *www.thirdway.com*

RESOURCES

Snyder, C. Arnold. *Anabaptist History and Theology*. Kitchener, Ont.: Pandora Press, 1997.

Baptist

AMERICAN BAPTIST

Alvin R. Hadley

HISTORY

BAPTIST HISTORY IN OHIO HAD ITS BEGINNING WHEN A FLATBOAT with twenty-eight persons aboard (two of them children) drifted down the Ohio River and landed near the point where the Little Miami River flows into the Ohio. This was about five miles above what is now the city of Cincinnati. The pioneers named their new settlement Columbia. The date of their arrival was the evening of November 18, 1788.

On January 20, 1790, nine people joined together at the Columbia home of Benjamin Davis to organize a church. Led by Rev. Stephen Gano, pastor of the First Baptist Church of New York City, who was visiting his brother, Major John Stites Gano of Columbia, the small group was "duly constituted" a Baptist church and "messengers" were appointed to attend the Elkhorn Baptist Association of Kentucky in order to be received into the wider Baptist fellowship. Stephen and John Gano's father, Rev. John Gano, a great name among Baptist leaders in the Philadelphia Baptist Association, had come west in his elderly years and was serving as moderator of the Elkhorn Association at about that time.

The newly organized church was called the Columbia Baptist Church. It may indeed be regarded as the mother church of the many Baptist

The Columbia Baptist Meeting House, near Cincinnati, as it looked in 1830. Columbia Baptist was established in 1790 and is considered by many to be Ohio's Baptist mother church. (Courtesy of Columbia Baptist Meeting House)

churches which were organized by the pioneers of the Miami Valley in the two decades which followed. Rev. John Smith, the most celebrated Baptist in the region and the first pastor of the Columbia church, was later chosen as the first United States Senator from Ohio (1803).

The first meetinghouse of this church was completed in 1793. A sketch published in 1842 in the *American Pioneer* shows the edifice as it stood in 1830. It was destroyed by fire in 1835.

In 1797, delegates from four pioneer Baptist churches—Columbia, Miami Island, Carpenters Run, and Clear Creek—met at Columbia for the purpose of organizing the group into a Baptist association and drafting general principles of faith, practice, and decorum. Rev. John Smith was the moderator of this meeting. The new association was called the Miami Baptist Association.

By the time Ohio, our seventeenth state, was admitted to the Union (1803), twenty-two churches had been organized and received into the Miami Baptist Association. Between 1819 and 1830 no fewer than fourteen associations were organized in Ohio.

No theme in the early nineteenth century among Ohio Baptists was as profoundly emphasized as that of missions—all kinds of missions, but foreign missions first and foremost. Baptists in Ohio supported the call of Luther Rice, an official of the National Triennial Convention (later named the Baptist Board of Foreign Missions), to support the foreign mission work of Adoniram Judson and through this support became a vital part of the National Triennial Convention. Judson served as a missionary in Burma with his wife, Ann, and was instrumental in the formation of the American Board of Commissioners for Foreign Missions. There were also home missions, which involved, among other projects, building new churches in western lands. And there were other missionary organizations: the American Tract Society, the American Bible Society, and the American Sunday School Union, to name the most important.

Baptists' concern for education made an early appearance. A committee of ministers described as "The Baptist theological Society for the education of young men for the ministry" was gathered in 1816. Out of this beginning, the Ohio Baptist Education Society was formed at Youngstown in the same year. The society was not active until 1830, when members met at Lebanon to reorganize and rewrite a constitution. Out of this and subsequent meetings came the proposal to establish a literary and theological seminary to train ministers in Ohio. A decision was made to locate in Granville, which was in the center of the state. The school originally opened in 1831 as the Granville Literary and Theological Institute and eventually became known as Dennison University.

On May 22, 1826, the Ohio Baptist Convention was born, gathering delegates from virtually every section of Ohio. Held in Zanesville, the convention brought together thirty-nine messengers representing seven thousand Baptist communicants in Ohio.

One of the leadership offices created by the new organization was that of corresponding secretary, an office first held by Rev. George C. Sedwick of the Zanesville church. This position, important in the function of communication from the beginning, was eventually to evolve into that of the convention's executive minister, the chief executive office of the convention.

Famous executive ministers include Rev. George C. Sedwick, 1826; Rev. J. B. Sackett, 1865; Rev. Dr. T. F. Chambers, 1915–39; Rev. Paul J. Morris, 1939–57; Rev. Clifford G. Hansen, 1958–60; Rev. Dr. Joseph Chapman, 1968–75; Rev. John Sandquist, 1977–85; Rev. Robert A. Fisher, 1986–95; and Rev. Dr. C. Jeff Woods, 1996–2003.

Ohio Baptist Convention delegates approved a reorganization plan at the convention's annual meeting in October 1990. The plan was developed by the PRAY Committee, under the theme "Decade of Adventure: Planning, Restructuring, Action Years." The action by the delegates resulted in a new name, American Baptist Churches of Ohio; a new constitution; and a new mission statement and goals.

BELIEFS

The 1.5 million members and fifty-eight hundred congregations of the American Baptist Churches in the USA share with more than 43 million Baptists around the world a common tradition begun in the early seventeenth century. That tradition has emphasized the Lordship and atoning sacrifice of Jesus Christ, believers' baptism, the competency of all believers to be in direct relationship with God and to interpret scripture, the importance of the local church, the assurance of worship and opinion, and the need to be Christ's witnesses within society.

The following areas are representative of the beliefs and practice of American Baptists:

- American Baptists believe that Jesus Christ is Lord and Savior, and that the Bible is the divinely inspired word of God that serves as the final written authority for living out the Christian faith.
- For American Baptists the local church is the fundamental unit of mission in denominational life.
- American Baptists partake of two ordinances: believers' baptism and the Lord's Supper.
- American Baptists believe that the committed individual Christian can and should approach God directly, and that individual gifts of ministry should be shared.
- American Baptists take seriously the call to evangelism and missionary word.
- American Baptists support religious freedom and respect the expressions of faith of others.
- American Baptists acknowledge that God's family extends beyond our local churches, and that God calls us to cooperative ministries.
- American Baptists have been called to be Christ's witnesses for justice and wholeness within a broken society.

CURRENT DEMOGRAPHICS

The American Baptist Churches in the USA is one of the most ethnically diverse denominations in America, and the Ohio membership reflects that diversity. The churches include European American, African American, Hispanic, Japanese, Vietnamese, Rwandan, as well as several multicultural congregations.

The American Baptist Churches of Ohio is a regional denominational agency composed of more than 290 congregations and a total of eighty thousand members. Ohio is the fifth largest of thirty-four American Baptist regions in the United States. Our region includes nineteen associations, with urban areas having larger numbers of churches, for example, Columbus, thirty-seven; Miami (Cincinnati), thirty-one; Akron, twenty-three; Dayton, twenty-one; Trumbull, seventeen; North Central, sixteen; Western, sixteen; Marietta, fifteen; Marion, fifteen. The remaining ten associations have less than fifteen churches each.

CONTACT INFORMATION

American Baptists Churches in the USA, 9 Mission Center, P.O. Box 851, Valley Forge, Pennsylvania 19482–0851, 610-768-2000 or 800-ABC-3USA, *www.abc-usa.org*

American Baptist Churches of Ohio Central Administrative Office, 136 Galway Drive North, P.O. Box 376, Granville, Ohio 43023–0376, 740-587-0804, *www.abc-ohio.org*

RESOURCES

10 Facts You Should Know about American Baptists. Valley Forge, Penn.: Office of Communications, General Ministries, American Baptist Churches Mission Center, 2000.

Clossman, Richard H. *A History of the Ohio Baptist Convention.* Ohio Baptist Convention, 1975.

A Sketch of Early Primitive Baptist History in the State of Ohio. Carthage, Ill.: The Primitive Baptist Library, 2001; also at *www.carthage.lib.il.us/community/churches/primbap/FamHist-Ohio.html*

OHIO BAPTIST GENERAL CONVENTION

Joel L. King Jr.

HISTORY

THE OHIO BAPTIST GENERAL CONVENTION (OBGC), INCORPORATED as it is known today, began as the Ohio Baptist State Convention (colored) (OBSC) in 1896. There were three associations that formed earlier, namely, Providence in 1834, Eastern in 1872, and Western, also in 1872. Each association formed as an anti-slavery missionary Baptist association after the "Negro" ministers were expelled from the Teays Valley Association. In 1893 the Eastern Union Association voted that a committee of five be appointed to meet with a committee of five from the Western Union Association to devise plans for a state convention. In keeping with the resolution to organize a state convention, on May 28–29, 1896, a meeting was held at the Curry School in Mechanicsburg and the OBSC was born. Twenty-six churches were represented at this organizational meeting. Also at the Mechanicsburg meeting, the Women's Baptist Educational Society was organized with G. E. Curry of Delaware as president. By 1899 this organization had resolved itself into the Women's Convention Auxiliary to the OBSC.

Determined to survive without the financial help of sympathetic whites, the OBSC kept holding its course until the fog began to clear and the true goals for which the convention was formed became clearer. In

1905 the Northern Ohio Baptist Association was organized. It sought to embrace all that the other associations had, to capture all the good that had been discovered, and to capitalize on the experience of the other three. In 1915 the Northwestern Baptist Association of Ohio was organized and quickly joined the other four associations in providing missionary work and education throughout Ohio.

From 1919 to 1930 several endeavors were begun: a printing press, the State Sunday School Convention, the Baptist Young People's Union, and the Laymen's League. OBGC's first headquarters was located at 106 Lexington Avenue in Columbus. In 1954 a second headquarters building was purchased. It was located at 48 Parkwood Avenue in Columbus. The State Sunday School Convention and Baptist Training Union became the Congress of Christian Education in 1972. A Youth Mission Task Force began, and the Committee on Evangelism was expanded. Six new departments were established between 1983 and 1987: Economics, Education, Evangelism, Programs, Public Relations, and Social Concerns. In the early 1980s two properties adjacent to the headquarters were acquired, and three apartment units were purchased around the state. In 1994 the convention adopted the following proposal concerning women preachers: "We will not recognize, nor endorse, nor register, nor have participation with, in the life of the Convention, women preachers." The Ohio Baptist General Convention has countless individuals who have contributed to its vast history. Neither time nor space can accommodate the roll call. There have been fifteen presidents and nine executive secretaries to date.

BELIEFS

The preamble of the Ohio Baptist General Convention constitution states: "We, the consenting Baptist Churches of Ohio, united by our faith in the Lord Jesus Christ; organized for the promulgation of His gospel in Ohio and the extension thereof throughout the entire world; seeking to fulfill the Great Commission as recorded in Matthew 28:19, and to perpetuate the ministries of the New Testament Church (evangelism, mission, Christian education and charity) do hereby adopted this constitution for the Ohio Baptist General Convention, Inc."

The Ohio Baptist General Convention affirms the twenty-four Articles

Ohio Baptist General Convention, Inc., headquarters on Parkwood Avenue in Columbus, purchased by the church in 1954. (Courtesy of Ohio Baptist General Convention)

of Faith, which are: "We believe that the Holy Bible was written by men divinely inspired; that there is one and only one living and true God; that man was created by the special act of God; that he was created in a state of holiness under the law of his Maker, but through the temptation of Satan, he transgressed the command of God and fell; that salvation is wholly of grace through the mediatorial office of the Son of God; justification is God's gracious and full acquittal upon principles of righteousness of all sinners who believe in Christ; the freeness of salvation; grace in regeneration; repentance and faith; God's purpose of grace; sanctification; the perseverance of saints; the harmony of the law and the Gospel; a Gospel Church; baptism and the Lord's Supper; the Christian Sabbath; civil government; the righteousness and the wicked; Christian education; social service; stewardship; evangelism and missions; the resurrection; the return of the Lord and the world to come."

The Great Commission stands at the heart of the Christian enterprise. It is the center of what the Church is called to do. The Church of Jesus Christ has but one primary mandate, to "make disciples" of men and women and lead them into a vital relationship with Jesus Christ. If it seeks to do ministry without mission, it is only half fulfilling its purpose.

This is very important for African American churches to grasp. Mission is presenting the gospel. Ministry is the church rendering service to the least of the earth.

CURRENT DEMOGRAPHICS

Currently there are about 250 congregations, five associations, and 135,000 members in Ohio.

CONTACT INFORMATION

Ohio Baptist General Convention, 1780 E. Broad Street, Columbus, Ohio 43203, 614-253-5563 or 888-877-6446, *obgc1896@ameritech.net, www.ohiobaptist.org*

The Ohio Baptist General Convention is affiliated with and part of the following:

American Baptist Convention: *www.americanbaptist.com*

Lott Carey Foreign Mission Convention: *www.lottcarey.org*

National Baptist Convention of America: *www.nbc.org*

National Baptist Convention U.S.A.: *www.nationalbaptist.com*

Progressive National Baptist Convention, Inc: *www.pnbc.org*

SOUTHERN BAPTIST CONVENTION

Willis C. Pollard

HISTORY

A MAN WHO NEVER LIVED IN OHIO STARTED SOUTHERN BAPTIST church work in our state. He was a Baptist farmer-preacher named William A. Helton. In 1928 he moved from Owsley County, Kentucky, to Franklin County, Indiana, to the area just south of Richmond. When he could not find a Baptist church in the area, he began church services in his home. On Saturdays, after he had finished work on the farm, he traveled to surrounding communities to conduct church services. Because of his efforts, three churches began in Indiana.

Some relatives of the members of the Indiana churches started by Helton moved to the Cincinnati-Hamilton area. Relatives living in New Miami, Ohio, six miles north of Hamilton, traveled to Indiana and asked William Helton to come to New Miami to preach and help them start a church. He came to preach in August 1931, and the New Zion Baptist Church of New Miami came into existence on August 30, 1931. This was the first Southern Baptist church in Ohio. The New Zion church found property on Western Avenue in Hamilton and became the Western Avenue Baptist Church. Today this congregation has moved to another location and changed its name to Hamilton West Baptist Church.

V. B. Castleberry, a former missionary to Brazil, influenced the first decade of Southern Baptist life in Ohio greatly. He served as the pastor at Hamilton West Baptist Church and later became the first director of

Western Avenue Baptist Church in Hamilton. This congregation, established in 1931, was the first Southern Baptist church in Ohio. It was originally called the New Zion Baptist Church, but changed its name when it moved to its new building on Western Avenue. Today it is the Hamilton West Baptist Church on Washington Boulevard. (Courtesy of Will Pollard)

missions for Ohio Southern Baptists. Prior to 1954, Ohio Baptists were part of the Kentucky Baptist Convention known as the Whitewater Baptist Association, which consisted primarily of congregations from Ohio and Indiana.

In 1952 Ray Roberts, the pastor of the First Baptist Church of Danville, Kentucky, accepted the invitation to become director of missions of the Whitewater Baptist Association. He led the work of Ohio Southern Baptists through significant growth and progress. In 1954, 160 messengers from thirty-eight churches met at the Hamilton West Baptist Church to organize the State Convention of Baptists in Ohio. They elected Roberts as the convention's first executive director.

Excerpts of Roberts's first speech to Ohio Baptists were quoted in the November 1952 issue of the *Ohio Baptist Messenger*. Speaking on the topic "Why I came to Ohio," Roberts said, "It is my deep conviction that the ripest field for Southern Baptist work in the USA lies within the boundaries of the state of Ohio. . . . There are no geographical boundaries on the Great Commission, and it would certainly be a gross sin, if we fail God in this ripe field of opportunity."

Like they had with Helton and Castleberry before him, people who desired a Baptist church contacted Ray Roberts to come and help them start a church in their community. In 1952 the first such call came from Kathy Cochran, who now lives in Reynoldsburg. Her husband was a military officer stationed at Wright-Patterson Air Force Base in Dayton. Out of Cochran's desire for a church in Fairborn and the efforts of Ray Roberts came the First Baptist Church of Fairborn.

Southern Baptists' work in Northeast Ohio began in 1949, when a group of people from Rittman began the Main Street Baptist Church (now Ridgewood Baptist Church) in Wadsworth. Southern Baptist work in Northwest Ohio began with the start of the Sylvania Baptist Church in Toledo in 1951. Southern Baptist work in southeastern Ohio began with the establishment of the First Baptist Church in Athens in 1952. Work in central Ohio started when the Whitehall Baptist Church began in Columbus in 1953. These are the churches from which the expansion of Ohio Southern Baptists began.

Roberts continued to hear the request "Will you come and help us start a church?" until he retired in 1979. Such requests took him to cities in New York, Pennsylvania, and West Virginia to begin churches under the auspices of the State Convention of Baptists in Ohio. Congregations (including those in New York, Pennsylvania, and West Virginia) grew to five hundred. Each time the total number of churches in a state surpassed five hundred, that state became strong enough to form its own state convention.

Near the end of Roberts's leadership in Ohio he received a call from some families in Dublin, Ohio. They wanted a Baptist church in their community. Roberts was instrumental in leading the Bible studies and worship services which led to the formation of Dublin Baptist Church.

Three other men have served as Ohio executive directors since Roberts's retirement. They are Tal D. Bonham, Orville Griffin, and the present executive director, Jack Kwok. Kwok has led Ohio Baptists to accept the challenge of "Mission Ohio"—a million Southern Baptists in 2020 churches by the end of the year 2020.

Ohio Southern Baptists are involved in disaster relief efforts. The development of the feeding unit was the beginning of Ohio involvement. Sam Kelley, a member of First Baptist Church, Groveport, is the volunteer coordinator of this ministry. Working with the American Red Cross and the Salvation Army, the Ohio team has provided more than 550,000 meals in response to twenty-five national disasters. In addition to those responses, Ohio volunteers participated in the national efforts in New York after September 11, 2001. They helped prepare more than 700,000 meals for the rescue and demolition workers.

Shortly after the terrorist attacks, the governor of New Jersey, Donald T. DiFrancesco, through the American Red Cross, called up the Ohio

Southern Baptist Temporary Emergency Child Care Unit. They cared for the children touched by September 11, 2001. Betty Sampley, a member of Huber Heights First Baptist Church, is the volunteer coordinator of this ministry. The childcare they provided allowed parents to work through the twenty-nine agencies set up to help them. From October 7 until December 21, 2001, our workers provided care for 650 children in crisis in New Jersey.

BELIEFS

Missions and evangelism are the heartbeat of Ohio Southern Baptists. They believe that the Bible was written by men divinely inspired and is God's revelation of Himself to man. It is a perfect treasure of divine instruction. The Bible teaches that God created heaven and earth and set the universe in motion. The message is that God created man in His own image, which means that man has the capacity to choose to respond to God and have fellowship with his Creator. Baptists believe the account of Genesis 3, that man in Adam and Eve chose to sin and that all men and women since that time have also chosen to disobey God.

Ohio Baptists believe Romans 3:23, which states, "[F]or all have sinned and fall short of the glory of God." The Bible follows up this statement with a message of hope for all people in Romans 6:23: "For the wages of sin is death, but the gift of God is eternal life in Christ Jesus our Lord." The path to accomplish a new relationship with God is stated in Romans 10:9: "That if you confess with your mouth, 'Jesus is Lord,' and believe in your heart that God raised him from the dead, you will be saved." Ohio Baptists believe that the greatest statement of love expressed in the Bible is John 3:16: "For God so loved the world, that He gave His only begotten Son, that whosoever believes in Him shall not perish, but have eternal life."

CURRENT DEMOGRAPHICS

More than 140,000 Southern Baptists live in Ohio. The number of congregations has grown from 39 in 1954 to 642 in 2002.

CONTACT INFORMATION

Southern Baptist Convention: *www.sbc.net*

State Convention of Baptists in Ohio, 1680 East Broad Street, Columbus, Ohio 43203, 614-258-8491, *www.scbo.org*

RESOURCES

Moore, L. H. *The History of Southern Baptists in Ohio.* Columbus: State Convention of Baptists in Ohio, 1979.

Ohio Baptist Messenger. 1680 Broad Street, Columbus, Ohio 43203, 614-827-1766, *http://messenger.ohbaptist.org*

Brethren Churches

THE CHURCH OF THE BRETHREN

Clyde C. Fry

HISTORY

EIGHT SOULS COMPOSED THE FIRST ORGANIZATION OF THE CHURCH of the Brethren in 1708 at Schwarzenau, Germany. Moved by their perception that the state churches were spiritually compromised, the growing fellowship rejected the established church creeds and looked to the New Testament as its only rule of faith and practice. The Brethren rejected the baptism of infants and accepted adult, or "believers," baptism in its place. They rejected violence in personal and national affairs and refused to serve in the military. These deviations from established orthodoxy led to persecution and the eventual migration of the Brethren to America in 1719. The first arrivals to America settled in the vicinity of Philadelphia, Pennsylvania, near Germantown, where in 1723 they organized a congregation. Germantown became the "mother church" from which the church spread both south and west.

The Brethren were often known in America by the nickname "Dunkers," given because of their mode of baptism, "trine immersion" (three "dips" forward). In 1871 the official name for the purpose of granting letters of membership was "German Baptist Brethren." In 1908 the name changed to "Church of the Brethren."

Stonelick Church in Clermont County, organized about 1795. This building was erected in 1854. (From *Churches in the Buckeye Country*, 1953)

The Brethren began to move to Ohio about 1795. Groups of Brethren families and their non-Brethren neighbors organized congregations that met in homes or barns. Since the real "Church" is not a building but the "people who belong to the Lord," when buildings were built they were known as "meetinghouses." These were simple structures where the men and boys sat on one side and the women and girls sat on the other. There was no raised platform, since all were "ministers in Christ." Those called by the congregation as preachers sat at the "ministers' table" (a long table with as many spaces as there were preachers). It was from this table that sermons were delivered. There were no musical instruments, and the hymns were sometimes "lined" by the song leader so that the congregation could follow along. Congregations often had more than one "meetinghouse" to accommodate the clusters of families in outlying areas. In 1856 adjoining congregations were formed into groups of five or more churches called "Districts," which met annually for fellowship and to conduct the business of the church.

The first settlers came to Ohio through Pittsburgh down the Ohio River and from Virginia through Kentucky. The earliest settlements in Southern Ohio were in the Virginia Military Tract east of Cincinnati where, by 1805, at least two congregations were organized: O'Bannon

Creek (now Stonelick Church, on State Route 727 near Pleasant Plain) and Brush Creek in Adams and Highland counties. The Brethren continued to grow, establishing congregations in the Scioto River Valley, where preachers like Sara Major and her husband Thomas served. A female preacher at a time when women were not well accepted in pulpits, Sara (1808–84) was accepted in many area congregations, even in the face of pressures from the larger church. With the help of other Brethren, Samuel Weir (1812–84), born a slave in Bath County, Virginia, escaped to Ohio, where in 1849 he joined the Paint Creek congregation (Bush meetinghouse), was licensed to preach, and began a ministry among the blacks in the area. His first convert, Harvey Carter, was also elected to the preaching ministry. Through the labors of men like Jacob Miller (1735–1815), a prolific church planter (began five congregations in Virginia), the Miami congregation was established in the Miami Valley southwest of Dayton in 1805. Brethren from the east settled in the surrounding four counties. By 1840 fifteen congregations were organized and became the Miami District. The Miami District is the historical base upon which the present "District of Southern Ohio" was formed.

By 1805 Brethren were also moving into Northeastern Ohio, where John Gans, a minister from Pennsylvania, moved to Stark County near Canton and established the Nimishillen congregation. The first denomination-wide annual meeting west of the Allegheny Mountains was held in Nimishillen church territory, eight miles northeast of Canton. As the congregation grew it was divided into a number of congregations, four of which still exist today. The oldest building still standing was built in 1899 using brick from the 1856 structure for the interior walls (East Nimishillen, two miles south of Hartville on Route 43, one mile east on Nimishillen Church Street). East Nimishillen was also the home church of Andrew W. Cordier, who for fifteen years was executive assistant to the secretary general of the United Nations and dean of the Department of International Relations at Columbia University.

One of the most influential men for the whole church was Henry Kurtz (1796–1874), a Lutheran pastor from Germany who moved his family to Stark County, where he joined the Brethren and was rebaptized on April 6, 1828. He became pastor of the Mill Creek congregation in nearby Mahoning County, where he moved in 1842. In the early 1830s he purchased a printing press and eventually published the first denomination-wide magazine, the *Gospel Visitor* (forerunner of the current denominational magazine the *Messenger*). James Quinter (1816–88) joined Kurtz in 1866 as an editor. The printing operation was moved to Covington in 1866 and then to Dayton in 1869 under Quinter's management. The Kurtz gravesite is in the Zion Hill churchyard (14550 New Buffalo Road, Columbiana).

By the 1840s there were at least ten congregations spread over Columbiana, Mahoning, Stark, Tuscarawas, Richland, and Knox Counties. They formed the Northeastern District. The last area settled by the Brethren was the Great Black Swamp area in northwestern Ohio, where in 1836 the Sugar Creek congregation in Allen County and the Lick Creek congregation in Williams County were organized. In 1963 the Northeastern and Northwestern Districts merged to form the Northern Ohio District.

For good or ill, the "Dunkers" have in significant ways become "mainline Protestants." Today many of our once-rural congregations find themselves in the midst of or on the very edge of urban sprawl. The Brethren emphasis on peace, justice, and service remains intact, but there is a new emphasis on worship and evangelism. "Service" is their specialty, and Brethren remain involved in refugee relief and resettlement, disaster child care, disaster cleanup and rebuilding, and nonviolent training and conflict intervention.

BELIEFS

The Brethren were influenced by the Pietist and Anabaptist movements of the sixteenth and seventeenth centuries. A "heartfelt" faith that expressed itself in a life of "practical goodness" was at the center of the Brethren belief system. In 1964 the annual conference (denominational business meeting composed of lay and clergy delegates from all the congregations in the United States) passed this brief statement of belief:

The Church of the Brethren:

    1. Is founded upon the faith that there is but one God who is a personal God who in holy love creates, sustains, and orders all.

    2. Confesses Jesus Christ as the Lord of the church and of all life.

3. Believes that the Holy Spirit is at work in the hearts and minds of believers, creating and sustaining the church through the Gospel, giving guidance and comfort, and uniting believers with their Lord and with one another.

4. Maintains the New Testament as its only creed and rule of faith. In the Holy Scriptures is recorded God's search for all persons, which is climaxed in God's redemptive act in and through Christ. Through the Bible God continues to speak and to accomplish God's redemptive purpose.

5. Believes that the gospel is the good news that God was in Christ reconciling the world unto himself. Through the gospel God's sovereign will and Christ's redeeming grace are revealed.

6. Holds that the church is the body of Christ and is under the Lord's mandate to be faithful in accepting and transmitting the gospel by word and deed.

7. Considers that all members of the congregation, of the body of believers, are responsible for the total ministry of the church (priesthood of all believers).

8. Accepts the ministry of the church to be the proclamation and fulfillment of the gospel for all people both near and far, and the nurture of individual believers in the Christian faith and life.

CURRENT DEMOGRAPHICS

The Northern Ohio District (2001) has fifty-three congregations in twenty-six counties—twenty-seven of these churches are west and twenty-six east of I-71—and 5,989 members, 3,697 of whom are in active attendance. The Southern Ohio District (2001) covers fifteen counties and includes fifty-four congregations, twenty-one of which are located in four counties around Dayton, and 8,921 members, 4,583 of whom are in active attendance.

CONTACT INFORMATION

Church of the Brethren: *www.brethren.org*
Northern Ohio District Office: 1107 E. Main St., Ashland, Ohio 44805–2806, 419-281-3058, *www.cob-net.org/church/ohio_northern.htm*

Southern Ohio District Office: 1001 Mill Ridge Circle, Union, Ohio 45322–8782, 937-832-6399, *www.cob-net.org/church/ohio_southern.htm*

RESOURCES

The Brethren Encyclopedia. 3 vols. Willard, Ohio: The Lakeside Press, R. R. Donnelley & Sons Company, 1983.

Brown, Dale W. *Understanding Pietism.* Grand Rapids, Mich.: William B. Eerdmans Publishing Company, 1978.

Durnbaugh, Donald F. *The Believers' Church: The History and Character of Radical Protestantism.* New York: Collier-Macmillan Company, 1968.

Weaver, J. Denny. *Becoming Anabaptist: The Origin and Significance of Sixteenth-Century Anabaptism.* Scottdale, Penn.: Herald Press, 1987.

THE BRETHREN CHURCH
(ASHLAND BRETHREN)

Dale R. Stoffer

HISTORY

THE ORIGIN OF THE BRETHREN CHURCH IS SET AGAINST THE backdrop of a three-way division that occurred in the German Baptist Brethren Church between 1881 and 1883. The German Baptist Brethren had begun in Germany in 1708, but most of the Brethren had come to America by the early 1730s due to persecution and harsh economic conditions in Europe. Until the 1830s and '40s the Brethren were a subculture in America due to their German language and their tendency to form agrarian settlements on the frontier in their search for good land.

By 1850, however, the Brethren were interacting increasingly with the surrounding American culture as they adopted English as their primary language, and as their rural settlements became home to a more diverse population. Over the next thirty years three distinct groups developed among the German Baptist Brethren in response to the challenges posed by the impact of culture. One group, the Old Order Brethren, wanted strict observance of the traditional ways ("old order") of the church and opposed all new religious practices (Sunday schools, revivals, higher education, a paid ministry). On the opposite side were the Progressive Brethren, who felt that these and other modern advances should be accepted if the church was to have any significant outreach into the wider

American society. In the middle were the Conservatives, who were willing to accept change, but insisted that it must be slow so as not to disrupt the unity of the church.

The tension among these three positions led to a division among the German Baptist Brethren between 1881 and 1883. The Old Order Brethren withdrew from the church, forming the Old German Baptist Brethren. The Progressive Brethren, guided especially by Henry R. Holsinger, were disfellowshipped from the main body of the church and in 1883 formed The Brethren Church. The Conservatives—the vast majority of the German Baptist Brethren—would adopt the name the Church of the Brethren in 1908.

The controversy of the 1870s and '80s had both positive and negative effects on the Brethren Church. On the positive side, many practices supported by the Progressives have continued to be important for the Brethren Church. These include Christian education through Sunday schools; higher education through Ashland College in Ashland, Ohio, which was founded in 1878 and came under the control of the Progressives at the time of the division; an educated and salaried ministry; evangelism in the wider American culture, especially urban centers; and foreign missions.

The division of the 1880s also negatively affected the Brethren Church. Financial hardships made the future of Ashland College questionable during the 1880s and '90s, and an unreasonable fear of centralized government prevented the denomination from addressing some of its most pressing issues in a united way. In spite of these hardships the Brethren Church did manage to make considerable headway through the early 1900s, founding many new congregations, beginning foreign mission work, and maintaining consistent numerical growth. Ashland College finally achieved a firmer financial footing through the very capable leadership of J. Allen Miller. He served as president of the college from 1898 until 1906, when he resigned to become the dean of the newly organized seminary. Due to the location of the college and the Brethren Publishing Company in Ashland, the denominational offices would eventually be headquartered there as well.

Its progressive and open attitude enabled the Brethren Church to move more fully into the mainstream of American culture in the twentieth century. But it also opened the church to the influence of liberalism and fundamentalism. Between 1913 and 1921 the Brethren experienced occasional controversy due to the association of a few well-educated Brethren with liberalism and the social gospel. This controversy was brought to an end in 1921, when the Ministerial Association, the auxiliary organization composed of ordained Brethren ministers, adopted a conservative statement of faith and those with liberal persuasions left the church for more compatible denominations.

Though the church was conservative theologically, there were those in the denomination who wanted to steer the church into fundamentalism. By the 1930s, American fundamentalism had adopted a very aggressive stance toward anything deemed liberal and frowned on any association with those having liberal sentiments. Some Brethren with fundamentalist persuasions feared that liberalism was gaining a foothold at Ashland College and sought to turn Ashland College into a fundamentalist Bible institute. They were opposed by the Ashland College trustees and many Brethren who preferred to maintain a Christian liberal arts education at the institution.

This controversy spilled over into the Brethren Church during the latter 1930s. The clash of strong personalities on both sides of the conflict, as well as some theological differences, served to intensify the controversy. In 1939 the nearly thirty thousand members divided almost equally between the Grace Brethren, so named because they supported the newly founded Grace Theological Seminary, and the Ashland Brethren, who continued their connection to Ashland College.

It would be nearly twenty years before the Brethren Church (Ashland) would be able to shake off the disillusionment that plagued the denomination in the wake of the 1939 division. By the 1960s, however, a new generation of leaders began to move the church forward. Significant signs of progress have been new home and foreign mission works, a vibrant youth ministry, reawakening interest in the history and thought of the church, and the exciting growth of Ashland Theological Seminary (now the twelfth largest seminary in North America).

Because the Brethren Church was formed as a part of a division from the German Baptist Brethren Church in the 1880s, there is no "oldest church" in the denomination. Numerous churches in Ohio and other states in the Midwest and East formed in the aftermath of the division. Ohio has remained one of the key states of Brethren Church activity. Not only does it have the second largest number of members in the denomination (behind Indiana), but it is also home to the denominational headquarters, Ashland University, and Ashland Theological Seminary.

BELIEFS

The Brethren Church identifies with the evangelical movement in America. It shares many of the historic views of the Christian faith in general. Brethren have generally accepted scripture "as it reads," in a straightforward, obedient manner. Scripture bears authority for Brethren because it is the final revelation of God to humanity in and through Jesus Christ. Brethren believe that scripture tells the story of God's desire to form a people for Himself, that is, the church. Because of sin, however, humanity has been in rebellion against God and His purposes. Nevertheless, God, out of His mercy and love, has provided a means for humanity to be restored to fellowship with Himself though the life, death, and resurrection of Jesus Christ. Through the preaching of scripture and the work of the Holy Spirit, people are confronted with the need to repent of their sins, turn toward God, and respond in faith and faithfulness to Jesus Christ as their savior and lord. The initial confession of Jesus Christ as saving lord is merely the first step, however, in a lifelong call to serve God and one's neighbor, to testify to one's faith by word and deed, and, ultimately, to continue to grow in Christlikeness. This call cannot be lived out in isolation, however. Every believer must be a part of a local body of Christians in order to continue the growth process toward Christian maturity. God's eternal purpose to have a people for Himself will be realized only in the future when His people, drawn from every nation, language, and culture, are once again united with God in His very presence in a new creation.

CURRENT DEMOGRAPHICS

Today there are 119 congregations in the denomination, 23 of which are in Ohio. Ohio churches account for 2,237 members out of a total of 10,381 for the denomination. The main concentrations of Brethren Church congregations are in the Miami Valley (southwest Ohio) and north central Ohio.

CONTACT INFORMATION

The Brethren Church (Ashland Brethren), 524 College Avenue, Ashland, Ohio 44805, 419-289-1708, *brethren@brethrenchurch.org, www.brethrenchurch.org*

RESOURCES

Committee on Doctrine, Research, and Publication. *Pilgrimage of Faith: The Witness of The Brethren Church.* Thirteen-part video series produced by David Sollenberger. Ashland, Ohio: The Brethren Church, Inc., 2000.

Durnbaugh, Donald F., ed. *The Brethren Encyclopedia.* Philadelphia: The Brethren Encyclopedia, Inc., 1983.

———. *Meet the Brethren.* Elgin, Ill.: Brethren Press, 1984.

Christian Churches

CHURCHES OF CHRIST

Rachel Reinhard

HISTORY

To understand the Churches of Christ in Ohio, it is necessary to consider the goal of the Reformation in Europe. Martin Luther, John Calvin, and other great men sought to reform the Catholic Church and to correct errors they found in its practices. By the time Europeans moved into Ohio, more than two hundred years had passed since this movement began, and the new churches formed by these men and their followers had governing bodies. The Protestant church organizations were less formal than the Catholic Church, but nevertheless, councils told the churches what to do.

When Ohio was opened for settlement after the American Revolution, some communities were formed, but there were few roads, and most people were separated by expanses of land and streams that were difficult to cross. Therefore, individual landowners and settlements were isolated. Not many ministers who trained at Harvard Divinity School or other schools in the original colonies wanted to move to such an outpost. A few hardy ministers chose to work in these areas, but for the most part, religious groups were few and loosely organized. Members of these congregations were by necessity self-reliant and disliked being told what to do by governing bodies far removed from them.

Ohio was ripe for the Restoration Movement. This movement proposed not to reform the church but to restore the church to its New Testament simplicity. This movement seemed to spring up spontaneously in various parts of the country and among many of the mainline Protestant groups. Many men could be named as leaders of this movement, but perhaps the most influential leaders were two men who lived in what is now West Virginia: Thomas Campbell and his gifted son Alexander. They left the Springfield Presbytery, contending that nothing should be bound on Christians that was not as old as the church described in the New Testament.

Thomas and Alexander Campbell preached often in Ohio. Alexander settled on property in Bethany, Virginia (now West Virginia), given to him by his father-in-law and from there preached widely in the Western Reserve. Walter Scott, an eloquent speaker who had been educated at Edinburgh University, also did much to popularize Campbell's message. He would enter an Ohio community, start a class for children during the day, teach them the "five-finger exercise" (faith, repentance, confession, baptism, and the gift of the Holy Spirit), and send them home to tell their parents what they had learned. The parents then attended the evening meeting. Scott stayed as long as he felt he should and then went on to another area.

The preaching of the Restoration Movement stressed reason rather than emotion. Many people who attended revivals were told that they could not become members of a church because they had not had an emotional religious experience. Scott said that those experiences were unnecessary and that he would baptize anyone for the remission of sins who had repented of them. In the debates that were popular at the time, civility reigned. Alexander Campbell debated and became friends with Robert Owen, an influential man who believed and taught a form of enlightened atheism. The teachings of the men of the Restoration produced congregations in Ohio that extended along the Ohio River and many of its tributaries from Cincinnati to the northern boundaries of the state.

G. Tidwell, a historian and minister of the Church of Christ, states, "Early in the 1830's the churches from the Stone and Campbell groups commenced merging in Kentucky. The union encompassed congregations in Pennsylvania, Ohio, Virginia, Tennessee, Indiana, Illinois, and Missouri. These churches usually identified by the name Christian Churches multiplied rapidly, becoming the fastest growing American religion, reaching

The Bush Church of Christ in Monroe County is one of the oldest congregations in Ohio. It celebrated its 150th anniversary in July 1998. (Courtesy of Paul E. Young Jr.)

a million members before 1900" (personal communication, September 4, 2002).

After the Civil War, differences among members of the Restoration began to create serious problems. One difference lay in the direction of state and national missionary societies. The conservatives opposed such mission societies but eventually lost the fight. Another major difference originated when musical instruments became available in Ohio. Some believed that they should be a part of the worship service; others thought that they should not be used because no record exists in the New Testament of their use in worship. In 1906 the churches divided into three groups: the Disciples of Christ, the Independent Christian Churches, and the most conservative, the Churches of Christ. Some groups were left without a place to meet, so they met in homes, schools, or rented buildings until they could purchase or build a place to worship.

Even after buying or building meetinghouses, few congregations hired ministers to serve their needs. Instead, following in the steps of the churches of the first half of the nineteenth century, they used the resources of the gifted men in their church, or they hired someone to preach on Sundays. Revivals or protracted meetings provided inspiration and often new members. After World War II, many churches added educational wings to their buildings to provide more space for Bible classes. Fellowship halls were also added during this period to encourage members to relax and enjoy meals together. During this time, many churches elected to hire ministers. In the ensuing years the Churches of Christ grew faster than most churches nationwide.

BELIEFS

The Churches of Christ model their beliefs and practices on those of the early church. For instance, anyone who believes and confesses Jesus to be the Son of God, repents of sin, and is baptized becomes a member of the church. Acts 2:38 is often cited to show how the believers reacted to the first gospel sermon of the apostles, and Romans 6:8 to show the beauty of baptism as a symbol of the death, burial, and resurrection of Jesus. The Churches of Christ are sacramental churches that observe communion every Sunday as a solemn memorial to his victory over death and the certainty of a life that is everlasting.

Bible study is stressed, and classes are held for all ages in most churches on Sunday mornings and on Wednesday nights. It is believed that Christ's death completed the laws found in the Old Testament; however, the Old Testament is important because, as the Apostle Paul said, "The law was a schoolmaster to bring us to Christ" (Gal. 3:24). Therefore, the lessons about God and His interaction with humanity at that time are helpful lessons for people today. Knowledge of scripture enables Christians to live a God-filled life and to become more like Him each day. The Bible further teaches that those who do not remain faithful to the teachings of Christ will be unable to live with him in heaven.

Worship services vary somewhat among congregations, but all include singing with no instrumental accompaniment, communion, prayers, reading of scripture, and either comments by men of the congregation or a sermon. Each member of the church is asked to give to the church treasury so that the ongoing programs of the church and other needs the elders deem important can be supported.

Women serve the congregation in many ways, but almost all churches exclude them from public speaking when the congregation is assembled. Women are encouraged to serve as teachers of the young and may, in some congregations, serve as coteachers with men in adult classes. They are encouraged to participate fully in Bible classes, to visit the sick, and to serve on committees.

CURRENT DEMOGRAPHICS

In a census taken in 2000, Ohio had 428 congregations and 47,472 adherents, a term that refers to baptized believers and their minor children. Nationwide the number is 1.6 million. A majority of the churches are located in small towns and rural areas; however, some southern states have strong concentrations in big cities. Monroe County in Ohio has the distinction of being the only county north of the Mason-Dixon line more than 10 percent of whose population are members of the Churches of Christ.

CONTACT INFORMATION

The Churches of Christ have no state or national administrative offices. Each church is autonomous and under the oversight of its elders. Cooperation among the churches does occur on an informal basis in regard to educational projects, missionary efforts, and the care of the poor and hungry.

RESOURCES

Ferguson, Everett. *The Church of Christ: A Biblical Ecclesiology for Today.* Grand Rapids, Mich.: Wm. B. Eerdmans Publishing Co., 1996.

Hayden, A. S. *Early History of the Disciples in the Western Reserve, Ohio.* Cincinnati: Chase and Hall, 1876.

Hooper, Robert E. *A Distinct People: A History of the Churches of Christ in the 20th Century.* West Monroe, La. : Howard Publishing Co., 1993.

Hughes, Richard T. *Reviving the Ancient Faith: The Story of Churches of Christ in America.* Grand Rapids, Mich., and Cambridge, UK: William B. Eerdmans Publishing Co., 1996.

Shaw, Henry K. *Buckeye Disciples: A History of the Disciples of Christ in Ohio.* St. Louis: Christian Board of Publication, 1952.

CHRISTIAN CHURCH (DISCIPLES OF CHRIST)

Jeff Gill and Dennis Sparks

HISTORY

IN ORDER TO REACH AMERICA'S FRONTIER PEOPLE, MANY CHURCH leaders discovered at the beginning of the nineteenth century the need for change within denominational structures. Communities in the Ohio River Valley, used to doing everything from barn raisings to militia drilling together, wanted to hold revival services together as well. Pastors started to wonder, "Why not?"

The largest of these revivals, hosted by Barton W. Stone, a Presbyterian pastor, occurred in 1801 at Cane Ridge, Kentucky, where Daniel Boone had directed settlers. Methodists, Baptists, Shakers, and scattered other Christian groups were represented in both the preaching and hearing at this celebrated event, which drew an estimated twenty to thirty thousand people from both sides of the Ohio River. By 1804, those who joined Stone were calling themselves simply *Christians,* acknowledged no church organization above that of a congregation and pointed to the Bible as their single authoritative guide.

Not long after, and also near the waters of the Ohio, a Scotch-Irish preacher migrated to western Pennsylvania. Thomas Campbell was weary of the divisions in the Presbyterian Church of Ireland, but hoped as he left family behind in 1807 that a new start for Christ's church could be found in this new world. Instead, he was quickly embroiled in similar controversies. Like Stone, Campbell withdrew from denominational structures and organized on the local, congregational level. He defended his actions in a publication called "Declaration and Address," which promoted the "restoration" of the New Testament church, Christian unity, and concluded with a reformer's motto that predates both Stone and Campbell: "In essentials, unity; in non-essentials, liberty; in all things, charity."

Having been delayed by a shipwreck near Scotland, the rest of Campbell's family arrived in Pennsylvania in 1809. While awaiting passage, son Alexander, age twenty-one, had studied theology at the University of Glasgow. There he was exposed to Scottish reformers, whose ideas about congregational independence, weekly communion, and believer's baptism by immersion at the "age of accountability" instead of infant baptism were to have a lasting impact. Both father and son had broken with the Church of Scotland, primarily over the practice of "testing" church members to determine their fitness to receive communion at the Lord's Table.

Alexander Campbell traveled frequently in Ohio to such places as the area that had been the Western Reserve, Cincinnati, and Zanesville, where his father had settled. While traveling he preached on the Restoration Movement (as the Christian unity effort was called), debated, and promoted his publications. A compelling preacher from Pittsburgh named Walter Scott joined the growing movement and began to preach in existing churches and begin new congregations in Ohio. Many church historians agree the first of these was the Mantua Center Christian Church in Mantua (Portage County), which was established in 1827 by both Campbell and Scott. At the founding meeting at the old South School on January 27 were many prominent "circuit-riding preachers," including future U.S. president James A. Garfield. He was also president of Hiram College, an Ohio Disciple College that was modeled after Campbell's Bethany College in present-day West Virginia. Also present was Sidney Rigdon, who later joined Joseph Smith and became one of the "Twelve Apostles" of the Church of Jesus Christ of Latter-day Saints (Mormons). The Mantua congregation is still located on the original site, in a church built in 1840.

When Scott moved the center of his ministry from Pittsburgh to the Cincinnati area, more connections developed between the "Christians" of

Barton Stone and the "Disciples," who had been influenced by the Campbells. New Year's Day 1832 brought these two streams together in a formal greeting at a worship service in Lexington, Kentucky. The church has been known by both names since that time.

As the 1800s drew to a close, the issue of slavery, the Civil War, modernism, innovations such as musical instruments in worship, and resistance to cooperative mission work as "unscriptural" brought division within a movement that had been based on the dream of Christian unity. The Churches of Christ withdrew to take a separate path. Independent Christian Churches loosely organized around the North American Christian Convention as they parted from the congregations and state societies that came together as the Christian Church (Disciples of Christ), the formal name and structure adopted in the late 1960s.

Ohio Disciples spread their teachings through the state missionary and Sunday school societies, whose cooperative work had grown out of the initial association started in Cincinnati in 1849, with Alexander Campbell as first president. Today Ohio Disciples are organized into the Christian Church in Ohio, made up of two hundred congregations across the state. Ohio Disciples cherish their vital camp and conference ministry, which found its focal point at Camp Christian near Magnetic Springs (Union County), purchased in 1949. What had been a century before a place for water therapy had become for Disciples a place for thousands of young people to experience spiritual growth. With that same enthusiasm, Disciples of Christ in Ohio, like Disciples throughout the world, continue to promote Christian unity as the church works in ecumenical partnerships with its sister church (the United Church of Christ), the Ohio Council of Churches, and Churches Uniting in Christ, which evolved in 2001. With Barton Stone, the church still affirms, "Christian unity is our polar star."

BELIEFS

The mission—to be and to share the Good News of Jesus Christ, loving, witnessing, and serving from one's doorstep to the ends of the earth—comes straight from the New Testament portion of the Bible.

Disciples believe that God is calling us to be a faithful, growing church that demonstrates true community, deep Christian spirituality, and a passion for justice.

In 1832, two American frontier religious movements came together. One, led by Barton Stone, called itself simply "Christians." Thomas and Alexander Campbell's group was called "Disciples of Christ." One important belief then and now is that people should not be forced to put faith in creeds, but only in Jesus Christ. On the other hand, in an effort to be in unity with other churches (a strong Disciple belief), the Disciple hymnal, *Chalice Hymnal* (St. Louis: Chalice Press, 1995) includes several common creeds called "affirmations of faith." It also includes the Disciples' "Affirmation of Faith" (number 355).

Most Disciples of Christ congregations partake of the Lord's Supper or Holy Communion in remembrance of Christ each Sunday. For most congregations, communion is "open," meaning that all believers from any Christian background are invited to share in the celebration. Many congregations regularly extend an "invitation" during Sunday worship, asking people to "accept Jesus Christ as their Lord and Savior of their Life." Those who have newly "confessed" their faith in Christ are invited to prepare for baptism at a later date. While most Disciple congregations practice "believers'" baptism by immersion at an age of accountability (around eleven), most also accept people from other Christian faiths who have been baptized by other forms, including infant baptism.

CURRENT DEMOGRAPHICS

According to 2001 statistics, the Christian Church (Disciples of Christ) is a body of approximately eight hundred thousand Christian believers in some thirty-seven hundred congregations in the United States and Canada.

There are 55,053 members in the 200 congregations that make up the Christian Church in Ohio. Of these, 36,416 are active. The average weekly worship attendance is 17,074, and 6,445 children and adults attend Sunday school weekly. The Christian Women's Fellowship has 4,949 participating members.

CONTACT INFORMATION

Christian Church in Ohio, P.O. Box 299, Elyria, Ohio 44036–0299. Street address: 38007 Butternut Ridge Road, Elyria, Ohio 44035, 440-458-5112, *www.christianchurchinohio.org*

Christian Church (Disciples of Christ), 130 East Washington Street, Indianapolis, Indiana 46204–3645, 317-635-3100, *www.disciples.org*

Disciples of Christ Historical Society, Nashville, Tennessee: *www.members.aol.com/dishistsoc/*

Hiram College: *www.hiram.edu*

RESOURCES

Shaw, Henry K. *Buckeye Disciples: A History of the Disciples of Christ in Ohio.* St. Louis: Christian Board of Publication, 1952.

The Church of the New Jerusalem (Swedenborgian)

Ken Turley

HISTORY

T HE EARLY GROWTH OF THE NEW CHURCH IN WHAT WAS THEN THE Ohio Territory and is now the state of Ohio is closely linked to the life of John Chapman (1774–1845). Today he is better known as "Johnny Appleseed," the wilderness wanderer and peaceful planter of apple trees. Yet Chapman's true purpose was to plant, in the hearts and minds of the frontier people, spiritual seeds from the Bible and the writings of Emanuel Swedenborg, seeds he called "good news right fresh from heaven."

All over the world, in all realms of life, the early eighteenth century was a time of innovation, turmoil, rebellion, independence, and discovery. The Revolutionary War had given birth to a new nation in the "new world," a nation entirely independent of the "old world." And it was to the Ohio Territories at the growing edge of this new nation that John Chapman would bring the writings of Swedenborg and the doctrines of the New Church. Somewhere around 1789, the year George Washington was elected president, between leaving home and establishing himself as a provider of apple seedlings, Chapman discovered Swedenborg's writings. He devoted the rest of his life to sharing his discovery with others.

Chapman was not the only New Church missionary of those times. For several years, a Philadelphia merchant by the name of William Shlatter had been slipping Swedenborg's writings and New Church teachings—in the form of books and pamphlets printed by Francis Bailey, a friend of Benjamin Franklin—into the bales of merchandise that he shipped to the frontier. And there were other preachers of New Church persuasion speaking and leading worship on a regular basis in the Ohio Territories. Reading groups and then societies began to form as people gathered together and found community around New Church worship and the life of charity. In the late 1790s a reading circle led by David Powell formed in Steubenville. By 1809 the group had formed into what was then the second "Swedenborgian Church" in the United States. In 1808 Adam Hurdus arrived in Cincinnati and began to preach New Church teachings and play a pump organ he built himself. He attracted many listeners, including members of some of the local native tribes. In 1812 a group at Turtle Creek near Lebanon gathered around the leadership of Thomas Newport.

Records from 1817 show eighteen different Ohio groups gathering to worship and study the Bible and the teachings of Swedenborg. There were enough *bona fide* Swedenborgians or "New Church folk," as they preferred to be called, to send nearly one hundred representatives to the first General Convention of the New Jerusalem, held in Philadelphia. In 1818 forty-five members in Cincinnati incorporated into a "society," and in 1819 they built the first New Jerusalem church building west of the Alleghenies. By 1822 Hannah Holland Smith had moved from New England to Cincinnati. She and her ten sons, all over six feet tall and called by locals "the sixty-foot Smiths," were leading citizens and New Church folk.

In the early 1800s quite a number of Ohio New Church folk, out of necessity, frustration, and even religious persecution, were seeking opportunities to combine instruction in spiritual matters with the elements of a good higher education. After establishing the first New Church Sunday school in America, Milo G. Williams, a pioneer educator, began to look further. His friend Col. John H. James, who had married a daughter of Francis Bailey (the printer of Swedenborg's writings mentioned earlier), had settled in Urbana, Ohio. Other proponents of Swedenborg, such as Frederick Eckstein, who had married another daughter of Francis Bailey and was becoming an influential artist, settled in nearby Cincinnati, the cultural center of the West.

In 1849, when approached by New Church minister Rev. James Stuart, Col. James agreed to donate ten acres of land and, along with Milo

The Urbana Swedenborgian Church (Church of the New Jerusalem). This is the second church building on this site. The first building was a two-room log structure built circa 1846. This stone building was begun in 1880 and dedicated in 1882. (Courtesy of Richard Sommer)

Williams, helped organize the effort to build and establish an innovative new college based on New Church teachings and values. In 1853 Urbana College opened its doors. At that time, it and Oberlin College were the only coeducational institutions of higher learning in the United States. Since the freedom to pursue truth was and is a basic tenet of the Swedenborgian perspective, the founders mandated that "any subject, secular or religious, should be open to inquiry."

By this time, the number of Swedenborgians in Ohio had grown considerably, and they were now present in sixty-two cities. Yet political turmoil had already embroiled a growing and all-too-human church bureaucracy, even one carved out of the Ohio wilderness by the frontier spirit and built in the sincere attempt to know and worship God in freedom. During the Civil War, the question of slavery divided many of the independent-thinking New Church societies. The authority of clergy also became a point of contention. And it was not many years later that money from successful businessmen in the glass industry entered the picture. By the early 1900s, as a result of a controversial theological split, there came to be two Swedenborgian denominations: one centered in Philadelphia called the General Church, and the other centered in Boston called the General Convention. Yet even in the midst of these internal disagreements, it was a Swedenborgian, Charles Carroll Bouney, who, demonstrating the church's acknowledgement of and respect for the diversity of human responses to the divine, proposed and oversaw the first Parliament of the World's Religions, held as part of the Chicago exposition in 1893. Beginning in the 1980s, after years of rancor, an era of peaceful coexistence and growing affection has settled between the two denominations.

Small in number yet large in influence, readers of Swedenborg include George Washington, Benjamin Franklin, Thomas Jefferson, Abraham Lincoln, Ralph Waldo Emerson, Henry David Thoreau, Robert Frost, and Helen Keller. Independent, free-thinking, biblically based, Christ-centered, ecumenical and interfaith, conservative and liberal, faithful and charitable, politically and economically aware, artistic, practical and spiritual: all these describe Swedenborgians or New Church folk. Throughout the years, the practical spirituality of Swedenborgians has played an important part in the history of Ohio. And even today they continue to live quietly useful lives, blending faith and charity, loving God and neighbor, and expressing spirituality in the natural world.

BELIEFS

The Church of New Jerusalem is a Bible-based Christian church strongly influenced by the writings of Emanuel Swedenborg. Born the son of a Lutheran minister in Sweden in 1688, he was a renowned scientist and published prolifically on all manner of subjects. In his early fifties he had a series of spiritual awakenings, after which he devoted himself to theological studies until his death in 1772. During this time he lived in England and published more than thirty volumes of theology.

In Swedenborg's writings John Chapman discovered, as have so many people before and since, a way of understanding scripture, Christianity, and life that did not require that he choose between faith and knowledge.

He found a perspective that brought the intellect and the emotions into balance and harmony in the spirit, the way light and heat are in balance and harmony in the flame. In his readings of Swedenborg and contemplations of God and nature, he found a vocabulary expressing a divinely inspired and "God-given" correspondence between things of spirit and things of nature. He found a level of meaning in the Bible that portrays the unfolding of the inner spiritual life of a person coming into being in a growing relationship with God. In a harmony of science and spirit, Chapman found a scriptural vision of life and salvation as a growth process extending from creation to the ultimate revelation we call dying. He saw life taking place in the natural world but having its highest meaning in the spiritual world.

It was this new way of seeing, this new perspective, that he loved sharing with the wide variety of people he encountered in his travels through the Ohio Territory. For more than fifty years, through times of war and times of peace, Chapman simply and quietly kept on with his work and travels. He was known by all as a kindly, if eccentric, man of God. All of the teachings of Jesus and the ideas of Swedenborg regarding the useful life of faith and charity found form and statement in John Chapman. His worldly life was the hard but rewarding work of bringing fruit trees to life in order to provide sustenance and joy to people. At the same time, his gentle and kindly spiritual work brought awareness of the divine presence in all of life, of the wonders of scripture and nature, and of the joys of a life that leads to Heaven. Johnny Appleseed is perhaps the best example of Swedenborgian beliefs in action, for he truly lived what he taught, both personally and professionally, and in a manner that was offensive to none.

CURRENT DEMOGRAPHICS

The General Convention of the New Jerusalem, with thirty-five churches and approximately two thousand members in North America (most along the East and West Coasts), is the smallest denomination in the National Council of Christian Churches. There are currently, along with the still active Urbana University, three active congregations in Ohio: Cincinnati, Cleveland, and Urbana.

CONTACT INFORMATION

The Swedenborgian Church (aka The General Convention of the New Jerusalem), 11 Highland Avenue, Newtonville, Massachusetts 02460, 617-969-4240, *www.swedenborg.org*

Urbana University, Box 840, College Way, Urbana, Ohio 43078, 937-484-1301.

J. Appleseed & Co: *www.jappleseed.org*

RESOURCES

Higgins, Francis J. *The Will to Survive: Urbana College, 1850–1975.* Urbana, Ohio: Urbana College, 1977.

Price, Robert. *Johnny Appleseed: Man and Myth.* Bloomington: Indiana University Press, 1954.

Smith, Ophia D. "The New Jerusalem Church in Ohio from 1840 to 1870." *Ohio State Archeological and Historical Quarterly* 62, no. 1 (January 1953): 25–32.

ACKNOWLEDGMENTS

Contributions to this chapter were made by Alice Skinner, Pete Toot, Betsy Coffman, and Dick Summers of The General Convention of the Church of the New Jerusalem.

Churches of Christ, Scientist

Donley Johnson

HISTORY

Mary Baker Eddy (1821–1910), a New England woman, discovered Christian Science in 1866. It was during the 1880s that Christian Science began spreading across the United States. Churches had been established in Toledo and Cleveland by 1889. At present there are more than fifty congregations in the state. The *Church Manual* by Eddy outlines the relationship between The Mother Church, located in Boston, Massachusetts, and the democratically governed branch churches. Readers elected from within each congregation conduct weekly Sunday services for the public. The sermon is read from the Bible and Eddy's book *Science and Health with Key to the Scriptures.* These books were ordained as pastors of the church by Eddy in 1895.

At the Wednesday evening service held each week for the public at Churches of Christ, Scientist, after a sermon from these books, anyone can share the spiritual insights and healings they have experienced. Robin Snider-Flor of Bloomington, Ohio, shared the following healing experiences at her church in Steubenville on November 3, 1999: "I am required by my place of employment to undergo an annual physical examination ... [The] physician ... stated that I was not [well] and proceeded to list all the symptoms I should be having and to indicate that surgery was certainly required. ... The next day I experienced every symptom the physician had listed. Soon I could no longer see clearly enough to drive and the

First Church of Christ, Scientist, Lancaster. Photo by Robert Echerd. (Courtesy of Donley Johnson)

pain in my face was unrelenting. I called a Christian Science Practitioner to pray for me, and immediately my thinking became clearer. Within a week, all symptoms were gone, and they have not returned. I have had many healings during my years as a Christian Scientist, including flu, smoking, drinking and sciatica."

An example of healing in the church's early history comes from nationally known Ohio artist Howard Chandler Christy: "Last March [1908] I was almost blind. For a year and a half my sight had been failing, and I had done no work. . . . I had always laughed at Christian Science, but my plight was now so serious that I grasped at any straw. . . . Twenty minutes after my first treatment I realized that I could see better, and my nerves were entirely calmed—the fear of blindness had left me. Three weeks later . . . I was cured" (quoted in *A Century of Christian Science Healing* [Boston: Christian Science Publishing Society, 1966], 50). Two murals by Christy hang in the east grand stairway of the Ohio Statehouse in Columbus. They are "The Signing," portraying the treaty of Greenville, and "Dawn of a New Light," depicting Thomas Edison.

Ohioans from all areas of the state have made significant contributions to the Church's history. At different times, Edward Merritt of Cleveland and Clayton Craig of Cincinnati served on the Christian Science Board of Directors, the five-member body responsible for administering the worldwide activities of The Mother Church.

The *Christian Science Monitor,* an award-winning daily newspaper founded by Mrs. Eddy in her eighty-eighth year, champions human rights for all. "The object of the *Monitor,*" in Eddy's words, "is to injure no man but to bless all mankind." Joseph Harsch, a Christian Scientist from Toledo, had a sixty-year relationship with the *Monitor* beginning in 1929. He received two Overseas Press Club awards.

An article profiling Mrs. Tommie Pattie of Cleveland appeared in the *Monitor* on April 2, 1973. Pattie, executive director of the Phyllis Wheatley Association in Cleveland from 1961 to 1983, was characterized by former U.S. Representative Louis Stokes as one of the great African American women in Cleveland's history. She was a member of the First Church of Christ, Scientist, Cleveland.

Philanthropic activities of Christian Scientists in Ohio include the gift of Thyrza Kiser in the 1930s of Kiser Lake State Park in Champaign County. Music lovers in Ohio have benefited from the generosity of Fynette and Elroy Kulas, who were church members in Cleveland. The Kulases established the Kulas Foundation, a major supporter of the musical arts. Many religious denominations in the northern part of the state have received grants from the foundation. Paul Smucker was a member of the First Church of Christ, Scientist in Wooster. He was instrumental, along with other members of the community, in establishing Wayne College in Orrville, a branch of the University of Akron. In 2001 the Learning Center at Wayne College was dedicated to Smucker and his wife Lorraine.

BELIEFS

Christian Science is dedicated to "commemorate the word and works of our Master [Christ Jesus], which should reinstate primitive Christianity, including its lost element of healing" (Eddy, *Church Manual,* 16–17).

The tenets or important points of Christian Science are given in *Science and Health* (497):

1. As adherents of Truth, we take the inspired Word of the Bible as our sufficient guide to eternal Life.

2. We acknowledge and adore one supreme and infinite God. We acknowledge His Son, one Christ; the Holy Ghost or Divine Comforter; and man in God's image and likeness.

3. We acknowledge God's forgiveness of sin in the destruction of sin and the spiritual understanding that casts out evil as unreal. But the belief in sin is punished so long as the belief lasts.

4. We acknowledge Jesus' atonement as the evidence of divine, efficacious love, unfolding man's unity with God through Christ Jesus the Way-shower; and we acknowledge that man is saved through Christ, through Truth, Life, and Love as demonstrated by the Galilean Prophet in healing the sick and overcoming sin and death.

5. We acknowledge that the crucifixion of Jesus and his resurrection served to uplift faith to understand eternal Life, even the illness of Soul, Spirit, and the nothingness of matter.

6. And we solemnly promise to watch, and pray for that Mind to be in us which was also in Christ Jesus; to do unto others as we would have them do unto us; and to be merciful, just, and pure.

Science and Health presents the rules for spiritual healing Eddy discerned from her study of the Bible. The relationship between health and thought is thoroughly explored in her text.

CURRENT DEMOGRAPHICS

By rule, since 1906, the church does not publish the number of members. However, the *Christian Science Journal* includes a directory of Christian Science practitioners and churches in Ohio. The journal is available at any of the Christian Science Reading Rooms, which are resource centers provided by the churches for the general public. There is no proselytizing toward any visitor. Practitioners devote themselves full time to the profession of spiritual healing. These practitioners are members who use prayer to heal anyone who calls seeking healing from physical, social, or emotional problems. There are more than forty-five Christian Science practitioners in Ohio.

CONTACT INFORMATION

The Church of Christ, Scientist: *www.tfccs.com*

Christian Science Committee on Publication, 85 E. Gay St. #400, Columbus, Ohio 43215–3118, 888-339-1466, 614-222-8937.

The First Church of Christ, Scientist, 175 Huntington Avenue, Boston, Massachusetts 02115, 617-450-3301.

RESOURCES

Christian Science Monitor: www.csmonitor.com

Eddy, Mary Baker. *Church Manual of the First Church of Christ, Scientist.* Boston: Christian Science Board of Directors, 1895.

————. *Science and Health with Key to the Scriptures.* Boston: Christian Science Board of Directors, 1994.

Nenneman, Richard A. *Persistent Pilgrim: The Life of Mary Baker Eddy.* Etna, N.H.: Nebbadoon Press, 1997.

Peel, Robert. *Spiritual Healing in a Scientific Age.* San Francisco: Harper & Row, 1987.

Erratum:
p. 98 no.5 line 2, read: allness of Soul

Communitarian Societies

Patrick Mooney

G ROUPS OF MEN AND WOMEN WHO IMAGINED SOCIAL CHANGE AND their role in it found opportunity in North America from the seventeenth century onward. In the century before the American Revolution there were twenty or more mostly religion-based attempts to build communitarian societies, that is, social organizations with equality of rank among members and common ownership of the means of production and subsistence. Some of these groups were utopian (attempts to create the perfect society on earth); others were communally based, but not utopian. Most of these early communities were composed of German immigrants and were short-lived. Of these the relatively long-lasting Seventh-Day German Baptist brother- and sisterhoods founded about 1730 by Conrad Beissel at Ephrata Cloister in Lancaster County, Pennsylvania, left an enduring mark.

In the nineteenth century the United States experienced a series of communitarian movements. Some were entirely secular, others religious in nature. The longest lasting tended to be based on some form of religious faith.

Two of these religious societies are important parts of the story of religious experience in Ohio's first century. The Shakers (1774) had their roots in English Quakerism, but became a peculiarly American and very successful communitarian experiment. They drew much of their early impetus from American revivalistic religion and later were influenced by the American millenarian and spiritualist movements of the 1840s. The Society of Separatists at Zoar (1817) was an organized attempt to break free of the restrictions of the state church system of the German states.

SHAKERS

HISTORY

THE GROUP COMMONLY KNOWN AS SHAKERS AND OFFICIALLY KNOWN as the United Society of Believers in Christ's Second Appearing owes its development in Ohio to the religious revival movement which began south of the Ohio River in 1801 and is often called the Great Kentucky Revival. After word of the attendance of thousands at outdoor gatherings for preaching and conversion reached Shaker communities in the East, they decided to investigate this "movement of the Spirit" in the West.

The Shakers had first been established in America in New York State, northwest of Albany, in the years during and immediately following the American Revolution by a small group of men and women. The group was led by thirty-eight-year-old Ann Lee (1736–84), who had brought the group to the English Colonies in 1774, after they had struggled for more than ten years to survive in industrial England. There they had been called Shaking Quakers or Shakers for their uninhibited style of worship and had been persecuted for their unconventional behavior and beliefs.

Eastern New York and western Massachusetts were experiencing an upsurge of revivalistic Christian preaching in the last decades of the eighteenth century. The place and time were ripe for Ann Lee's message that she embodied the Second Coming of Christ, revealing the female aspect of God and bringing a call to a millenarian lifestyle. (*Millenarian* and *millennial* refer to the tradition of the millennium, the thousand-year reign of Christ after his Second Coming.) By the time of Lee's death in 1784, Shaker groups had been formed in nearby Connecticut and western Massachusetts. "Mother Ann's" successors in leadership developed a communal lifestyle and attracted many followers. While they never reached their goal, "to convert the world," over time thousands of their converts lived in twenty-four communities in ten states.

On New Year's morning, 1805, John Meacham, Issachar Bates, and Benjamin Seth Youngs set out on foot from Shaker headquarters in New Lebanon, New York, for the new state of Ohio. Mother Lucy Wright of the New Lebanon Shaker ministry had read newspaper reports of the great revival going on in Kentucky and Ohio and had decided to send missionaries to the West. They found many receptive listeners to their message of repentance and the millennial lifestyle, and within the year the first Shaker settlement in the West had been established at Union Village in Warren County, Ohio. It was to be followed by more than a dozen Shaker sites in Ohio, Kentucky, Indiana, and Illinois.

The first Shaker convert in the West was Malcolm Worley, a prominent landowner. He was followed by neighbors William Beedle and Richard McNemar, a Presbyterian minister who had been much involved in the Great Kentucky Revival. McNemar's entire Turtle Creek congregation followed these three into the Shaker faith. These Ohioans were the nucleus of Union Village.

Conversion to the Shaker faith involved confession of one's past transgressions and a commitment to a celibate, communitarian life. All resources in land or personal property passed into communal ownership. Shakers did not rely heavily on written doctrines but preferred first-person religious experiences. Their lifestyle was comfortable but plain in every respect, from food and clothing to architecture and furniture. Men and women lived in separate but equal fashion, including leadership in ministry.

Children were cared for in separate dwellings. All members contributed to community work, from subsistence tasks to manufacturing, in ways appropriate to their age, sex, and skills. Mother Ann's motto, "Hearts to God and hands to work," became the touchstone of every task in Shaker communities. The simplest, most efficient method was sought in every endeavor.

Union Village grew rapidly in membership, acreage, industries, and buildings. By 1818 membership at Union Village was 634 Shakers living in eleven "family" groupings. The Shaker Central Ministry in New Lebanon, New York, had sent a small group of men and women to assist in leadership in the West, and in the first decades after 1805 Shaker communities in New York and New England contributed more than twenty-six thousand dollars to cover the expenses of their missionaries and for land purchases. As Ohio Shakerism grew in numbers and resources, the entire sum was eventually returned to the Eastern Shakers. Union Village became the overseeing organization for Shakers in the West, continually seeking to carry the word into other parts of Ohio and into Kentucky, Indiana, and even Georgia. Union Village's influence is reflected in the names of some of these new communities: North Union (1822) in Cuyahoga County, West Union (1808) in Indiana, and South Union (1807) in Kentucky. Other Shaker Villages in Ohio were Watervliet (1806) in Montgomery and Greene counties and White Water (1822) in Butler and Hamilton counties.

About 1840 a Midwestern group called the Millerites claimed to have determined the exact date of Christ's Second Coming. After several reschedulings, the expected event did not occur. A large number of Christians who had been stirred up and then disappointed by the Millerites became Shaker converts when they saw that the Shaker faith could claim to be already living in the millennial reign. During much of the nineteenth century the Shaker practice of raising orphans increased their numbers, although many of these children upon reaching maturity chose not to remain and become covenanted members of the Shaker faith. In their peak years of the mid-1800s, Ohio Shaker membership approached two thousand, and the Shakers owned thousands of acres of land. They became well known for their agricultural products, as well as for several of their own inventions, which they successfully marketed, and for their manufactured products, which included herbal remedies, garden seeds, brooms, baskets, wooden storage boxes, and furniture, especially chairs.

After the Civil War the increasing industrialization of America, new waves of immigration, and increasing urbanization ended much of the American fascination with communitarian and utopian social experiments. The severe simplicity of lifestyle, the requirement of celibacy, and the decreasing market for Shaker products all had a serious impact on the viability of Shaker communities. Shaker membership began a slow decline. Their presence in Ohio ended with the sale of their last land holdings in 1916 and the move in 1920 of the last few resident Ohio Shakers to Shaker villages in New England.

Shakers dancing by John W. Barber, 1847. (From *Historical Collections of Ohio* by Henry Howe, vol. 1, 1888)

During the twentieth century the New England Shakers continued to accept small numbers of new converts but basically closed their communities to the outside world. In the United States before the Civil War, Shakers numbered six thousand in nineteen communities. Today a few Shakers remain in Maine and New Hampshire in former Shaker villages, which have become historic sites and museums operated by trusts.

The late twentieth century saw great interest in Shaker material culture and life. Significant collections of artifacts and publications have been assembled in former Shaker villages and elsewhere. Much has been published about their music, song, dance, furniture, and other contributions to American religious life and general culture. Shaker music has been a source of themes for popular and orchestral compositions. The simple lines and superior workmanship of Shaker furniture, in particular, have created a style of continuing popularity.

The Shaker mark on Ohio remains. The site of North Union in Cuyahoga County is now the location of the Cleveland suburb of Shaker Heights. Twenty-three buildings of the former White Water Shaker Village are now owned and maintained by the Hamilton County Park Board. The largest collection of Shaker buildings in Ohio, it includes a Shaker burial ground. Three Shaker buildings survive at Otterbein-Lebanon, a United Methodist retirement community near Lebanon. Otterbein-Lebanon owns fifteen hundred acres of the former Union Village, which includes the original land of Malcolm Worley, the first Shaker convert in Ohio. The Western Shaker Study Group maintains its address at Otterbein-Lebanon. Important resources for the study of Ohio Shakers can be found in the Dayton and Montgomery County Public Library and at the Western Reserve Historical Society in Cleveland.

BELIEFS

The United Society of Believers in Christ's Second Appearing, commonly known as Shakers, was a millenarian, communitarian Christian sect with a unique belief in gender duality/equality. They conceived of God as a duality, male and female. Their eighteenth-century founder, Mother Ann Lee, was believed to embody the Second Coming of Christ, "appearing as Female, embodying Her loving spirit." The third leader of the group, Joseph Meacham, whose influence was strong in the rise of nineteenth-century Shakerism, developed four dispensations for salvation based on obedience, which were called "the lights of salvation":

1. God's promises to the patriarchs;
2. The Law of Moses;
3. Christ's First Appearance as Man;
4. The Coming of God to earth to build the new Kingdom.

Shaker lifestyle was based on celibacy and simplicity in daily life, which were seen as the two keys vital to building a truly selfless and spiritual community. Men and women held equal status in every respect. Simplicity was the keynote in dress, food, buildings, furniture, and all other aspects of daily life. Shaker worship was initially spontaneous and later became highly ritualized, incorporating ecstatic experience and dancing.

CURRENT DEMOGRAPHICS

There are no remaining Shakers in Ohio.

CONTACT INFORMATION

There is no administrative office for Shakers.

RESOURCES

During most of the twentieth century, Shakers archives were closed to "The World's People," as they called outsiders. Until very recently their publications, including hymns, doctrinal statements, personal revelations and testimonies, and accounts of their own history have been available only in museum and library archives and on microfilm. A selection of early Shaker material is now available at no charge through Pass the Word Services at *www.passtheword.org/SHAKER-MANUSCRIPTS/*

Boice, Martha, et al. *Maps of the Shaker West: A Journey of Discovery.* Dayton, Ohio: Knot Garden Press, 1997.

Rokicky, Catherine M. *Creating a Perfect World: Religious and Secular Utopias in Nineteenth-Century Ohio.* Athens: Ohio University Press, 2002.

The Shaker Manuscript Collection. Microfilm. 123 reels. Western Reserve Historical Society Library, 10825 East Boulevard, Cleveland, Ohio 44106, *www.wrhs.org*

The Shakers Collection: A special collection of three thousand items covering the period 1808–1983. Dayton and Montgomery County Public Library, 215 East Third Street, Dayton, Ohio 45402, *www.daytonmetrolibrary.org*

Western Shaker Study Group, c/o Otterbein Homes, 585 North State Route 741, Lebanon, Ohio 45036, *www.shakerwssg.org*

SOCIETY OF SEPARATISTS
AT ZOAR

HISTORY

IN 1817 A GROUP OF THREE HUNDRED GERMAN SEPARATISTS ARRIVED in the port of Philadelphia. Called Separatists because of their formal break with the established Lutheran state church in southeastern Germany, these people believed in a direct relationship with God, without any ceremony or ritual. Their statement of principles, written before their emigration from Wuerttemberg, clearly reflects their desire for freedom of religious practice, including their pacifist position in regard to military service.

Hosted at first by Philadelphia Quakers, the Separatists moved quickly toward the goal of establishing their own community in America. Under the leadership of Joseph Bimeler, they contracted for the purchase on credit of a tract of fifty-five hundred acres along the east side of the Tuscarawas River in Tuscarawas County, Ohio. The first cabin on the site was completed by December 1817.

They named the new settlement Zoar ("a sanctuary from evil"), which was the name of the biblical town where Lot sought refuge after the destruction of Sodom. By 1818 most of the Separatists had reached the new land in Ohio, where each family began cultivating its own acreage. It was immediately clear that this system would be insufficient to feed themselves and pay the land debt. Thus was born the communal Society of Separatists at Zoar. Both men and women signed articles of association on April 19, 1819.

Historic view of the village of Zoar by Henry Howe, 1846. (From *Historical Collections of Ohio* by Henry Howe, vol. 1, 1888)

Joseph Bimeler remained their leader. Organization of the society was democratic. Men and women held equal rights. All wealth and property was held in common. Each member agreed to follow the assignments of an annually elected board of trustees, and in return received food, clothing, and shelter.

The new system and Bimeler's astute business sense brought immediate success. Soon the Zoarites were producing an agricultural surplus. The village grew, mills for processing grain and lumber were built on the Tuscarawas, and brick- and rope making were developed as industries. The society contracted to build that portion of the Ohio and Erie Canal which passed through its land, bringing further prosperity. By 1834 the Zoarites had paid their debts and built a surplus. They had become virtually self-sustaining. Agricultural products and manufactured goods were being exported to surrounding towns. By 1852 the society numbered about six hundred persons and had assets of more than $1 million.

Religious, educational, and labor practices of the Zoarites remained simple. Two worship services were held each Sunday, with hymn singing, scripture reading, and explanation by a member of the society. Evening prayers were sometimes held during the week. School was held during the winter, in English and German. Childcare, baking, laundry, and other needs were carried out communally. Men and women shared equally in farming tasks.

In 1853, a traveler wrote in a letter:

> Sabbath was at Zoar, a small village of about three hundred inhabitants. The people are all German and somewhat Apostolical in their govern-mental arrangements as they hold all things in common. . . . I was highly pleased at their [church] meeting to see such excellent order. They were mostly dressed in uniform and gave the closest attention to what was said. Little girls and old women dressed just alike, wearing a small white cap on the head, a white scarf crossing the bosom, in front a long white linen apron. . . . The men were coatless, wore short vests, short pants, low short and mixed grey stockings. The music and singing was good and the preach-ing was just as interesting as any Dutch (German) book you ever read. (Griffing Papers, 1822–1883, reel 11723, Kansas State Historical Society; also at *http://www.griffingweb.com/sabbath_was_at_zoar.htm*)

The death of Joseph Bimeler in 1853 began Zoar's slow decline. A former schoolteacher, Bimeler had been the community's guide in spiritual and business matters even before their arrival in America, and much of the suc-cess of the Society of Separatists had been due to his leadership. The soci-ety continued its communal nature, but the Ohio around it was changing. The rise of mass production made its smaller hand-manufacturing opera-tions obsolete, and the coming of the railroad in the 1850s brought the outside world closer. Younger members began to drift away, and religious orthodoxy decreased.

In 1898 the Society of Separatists of Zoar was dissolved by a vote of the remaining members. Common property was divided, with each member receiving two hundred dollars and fifty acres.

In 1942 the Ohio Historical Society assumed management of the mu-seum and garden maintained by Zoar villagers and began to acquire more buildings. Since 1965 the state of Ohio and the Ohio Historical So-ciety have been involved in an extensive restoration program. Thanks to these programs and a great deal of local effort and cooperation, the story of the Society of Separatists of Zoar lives on as an example of a notable ex-periment in religious communalism in the history of Ohio and the nation.

The Separatist Principles

1. We believe and confess the Trinity of God, in the Father, Son, and the Holy Ghost;

2. the fall of Adam and of all mankind, and with the loss thereby of the likeness of God in them;

3. the return through Christ to God, our proper and lawful Father;

4. the Holy Scriptures as the rule of our lives. . . .

5. All ceremonies are banished from among us. . . .

6. We render to no mortal honors due only to God, such as to uncover the head or bend the knee. . . .

7. We separate ourselves from all ecclesiastical constitutions and ties. . . .

8. Our marriages are contracted by mutual consent before witnesses. . . .

9. All intercourse of the sexes, except what is necessary to continue the species, we hold to be sinful and contrary to the command of God. . . .

10. We cannot send our children into the schools of Babylon because they oppose our principles. . . .

11. We cannot serve the state as soldiers because a Christian cannot murder his enemy, much less his friend.

12. We recognize the temporal authority as necessary to maintain order. . . .

These therefore are the principles which for ten years have brought upon us many and varied persecutions. . . . We can testify before God and conscience that our purposes were never other than these: to forsake the godless life of the world, to fulfill faithfully our duties toward God and man, to live in an inner circle of love and friendship. (Abridged from the website of Zoar Community Association, *www.zca.org*)

CURRENT DEMOGRAPHICS

Descendants of the Zoarites can still be found in Ohio, but the Society of Separatists at Zoar was officially ended by a vote of the membership in 1898.

CONTACT INFORMATION

There is no administrative office for Society of Separatists at Zoar.

Zoar Community Association, P.O. Box 601, Zoar, Ohio 44697, *www.zca.org*

Zoar Village State Memorial (Ohio Historical Society), P.O. Box 404, Zoar, Ohio 44697, *www.ohiohistory.org/places/zoar/*

RESOURCES

Rokicky, Catherine M. *Creating a Perfect World: Religious and Secular Utopias in Nineteenth-Century Ohio.* Athens: Ohio University Press, 2002.

Community Churches

Jacqueline D. Cherry

HISTORY

COMMUNITY CHURCHES EXISTED IN OHIO THROUGHOUT THE nineteenth century. Some churches were established by a particular denomination, but later severed their denominational ties. Other nonsectarian community churches were organized to meet the religious needs of all Protestants in settlements that were too small to support more than one congregation.

Churches in the Buckeye Country: A History of Ohio's Religious Groups, published by the Sesquicentennial Commission in 1953, noted that Central Community Church of Columbus was organized in the Old Canal Hotel in February 1843. Its constitution reflected the independent nature and spirit of those who sought freedom from sectarianism. "A liberal, progressive, and tolerant Christianity has ever been, and shall always remain the cornerstone of our faith. . . . This Church shall never affiliate with any synod or other denominational organization which requires it to subscribe to a definite creed and to surrender its liberal principles." A church building had been erected by December 1843 and was still occupied in 1953.

The Community Church movement emerged about 1915 and was defined in the earliest book on the subject, *A Community Church,* published by Houghton Mifflin in 1919. A national organization known as the Community Church Workers of the United States of America was founded in 1923 as an association of pastors and lay workers in community churches across the nation. A second organization, the National Council of the People's Community Churches, was begun the same year among predominately black congregations and incorporated in 1933 as the Biennial Council of the People's Church of Christ and Community Centers of the United States and Elsewhere.

What these leaders envisioned can be illustrated through a brief sketch of First Community Church in Columbus. Residents of the suburban Tri-Village area decided in 1909 that they wanted a church, then through a democratic process chose the denomination preferred by the majority, and established Grandview Heights Congregational Church. The trustees announced that "this church was organized for every person in the community." In addition to fulfilling the traditional role of ministry, the church sought to meet social and cultural needs by establishing a library and community newspaper, showing movies, organizing vocal and instrumental music groups open to all, instituting religious education in the public schools, and hiring a kindergarten teacher for immigrant children.

The church flourished under the leadership of Rev. Oliver Weist, who arrived in 1915. He believed not only that what Christians have in common is far greater than what divides them, but also that a community could best be served by one large well-staffed church. His enthusiasm led the members to drop their Congregational ties and reorganize as an "undenominational" church in 1919. Weist eventually became associate secretary and field worker for the Community Church Workers. The work of this church paralleled what was happening across the country under the guidance of the Community Church movement. Several hundred people attended the first biennial conference at First Community Church in May 1926. The weekly bulletin announced, "The kind of churches represented will be Denominational Community Church, where one denomination goes into a field and all other denominations agree not to intrude; the Federated Church, where two or three denominational churches go together and form one church with each denominational group retaining its denominational connection; and the independent group represented by our church."

More than seven hundred community churches had been identified

Lincoln Road Chapel is part of the First Community Church complex in Columbus. This is the original church building, constructed in 1911. After a second, larger building was erected in 1926, the Lincoln Road Chapel continued to be used for Sunday school, youth programs, and other community activities. (Courtesy of First Community Church)

by 1928. A handbook listing all these churches was issued, and publication of a magazine to keep them informed was begun. Before long the list had grown to thirteen hundred.

Between 1935 and 1945 Community Churches sought to achieve recognition and membership in federal and international councils. When these attempts failed, Dr. Roy A. Burkhart, senior minister of First Community Church, spearheaded a statewide movement to found the Ohio Association for Community Centered Churches in 1945. This organization was to enable these churches to have a sense of fellowship until denominations could discover a way to give them leadership without absorbing them or destroying their community-centered quality.

Representatives from seventy-two churches in nineteen states and the District of Columbia again met at First Community in 1946 and formed the National Council of Community Churches, absorbing the Ohio Association founded the previous year. Almost immediately the black churches of the Biennial Council and the white congregations of the National Council began working toward a merger. In 1950 the two fellowships made history when they joined in the largest interracial merger up to that time and became the International Council of Community Churches. Initially offices were located in Columbus until the headquarters moved permanently to Illinois.

In recent years, more and more Community Churches have established denominational affiliations while still retaining their autonomy. A prime example is historic Howland Community Church, which in 1830 was chartered as Howland Christian Church by members who left the Christian Church in Warren, originally established by the Disciples of Christ. In 1948 this congregation became a charter member of the International Council of Community Churches. Since 1979 it has also shared a wider relationship with the United Church of Christ, and re-established ties to the Disciples of Christ. Presently the congregation is representative of the age and ethnic diversity within the community. The church continues to pursue ministries of reconciliation by strengthening cooperation with a predominantly black congregation in Warren, by reaching out to the Arab American community after the September 11, 2001, attacks, and by moving toward an official open and affirming stance to all.

BELIEFS

The Community Church has been defined as an attitude, a broad approach to Christianity. *Unity without Uniformity,* written by J. Ralph Shotwell, former executive director of the International Council of Community Churches, states that community means more than ministering to all the people in a given neighborhood. "It is an openness which does not set boundaries for investigation or expression. It neither solicits some majority opinion nor rejects any minority conviction. It works to achieve a unity of spirit while striving to express the spirit of unity." A Community Church believes its statements of faith will be as personal and as varied as its individual experiences of God. Members believe in the living Christ at work in the heart of the individual believer. They believe also in tolerance of another's point of view and in respect for the sincere conviction of every human being. Toleration of religious opinion is coupled with earnest faith in Jesus Christ. The Community Church movement can be defined as inclusiveness, not exclusiveness, by unity in diversity and diversity without divisiveness.

Community Churches can be found across the landscape of Ohio, and they mirror the diversity of the state's population. They range in size from a six-member congregation that meets in the Springfield home of its pastor to large churches such as First Community in Columbus with 3,376 active members who worship in two locations. Children, young people, and adults from these churches take an active role in responding to the needs of those around them. Sincerely believing that the basic tenets Christians hold in common are far more positive, unifying, and effective than those that would tend to divide them, members of a Community Church agree to differ, resolve to love, and unite to serve.

CURRENT DEMOGRAPHICS

The twenty-four congregations in the state that currently hold membership in the International Council of Community Churches are loosely associated as the Ohio Fellowship of Community Churches. However, the International Council is the movement's only administrative body. The council describes itself as committed to Christian unity and working toward a fellowship as comprehensive as the spirit and teachings of Christ and as inclusive as the love of God. There are numerous congregations that consider themselves to be "community" in nature because of their autonomy. Most are dependent solely upon their members for financial support since they receive no denominational funding.

CONTACT INFORMATION

Each Community Church is autonomous. There are no local, state, or national administrative offices for the Ohio Fellowship of Community Churches. For more information, please contact the International Council of Community Churches, 21116 Washington Parkway, Frankfort, Illinois 60423–3112, 815-464-5690, *www.akcache.com/community/iccc-nat.html*

RESOURCES

Melton, J. Gordon. "International Council of Community Churches." In *Encyclopedia of American Religions,* 6th ed., 331–32. Detroit: Gale Research, 1999.

Shotwell, J. Ralph. *Unity Without Uniformity: A History of the Postdenominational Community Church Movement.* Homewood, Illinois: Community Church Press, 1984.

Eastern Churches

GREEK ORTHODOX

Jim Golding

HISTORY

AMONG THE TIRED, POOR, AND HUDDLED MASSES SEEKING A BETTER life in the United States in the late nineteenth and early twentieth centuries were more than five hundred thousand Greeks from southeastern Europe and Asia Minor (present-day Turkey).

Fleeing an economically depressed agrarian economy and, in the case of those from the Ottoman Empire, political repression, most brought little with them in terms of material goods or education, but carried the richness of Orthodox Christianity and their ancient culture.

Hearing stories of America's wealth and the relative ease of earning a living here, most of these first arrivals came between 1890 and 1920 and were single young men. Many intended to stay only a few years until they could provide for their sisters' dowries in Greece or help their families financially. But their brief stays became permanent as they earned enough money to marry and establish roots in their adopted country.

Orthodox Christianity traces its history to Jesus Christ and his apostles. The church developed and spread over the subsequent centuries under the Roman and Byzantine Empires. During the Byzantine era, missionaries spread the faith north through Eastern Europe and Russia. Orthodox

Christianity today is the predominant faith in Russia, Bulgaria, Serbia, Romania, Ukraine, Belarus, Greece, and Cyprus, and Orthodox Christians make up a large percentage of the populations of Albania, Poland, Slovakia, and other lands. Immigrants from many of these countries settled in the United States, and their churches can be found in many cities. There are Orthodox Christians throughout the world on every continent.

About forty thousand Greeks settled in Ohio in those early years, eagerly seeking work in urban factories or with the railroads, or establishing their own small businesses, most notably restaurants.

With a strong desire to maintain their faith, culture, and heritage, they established Greek Orthodox church communities, known as parishes, in every major city and several mid-size cities of the Buckeye state. Beginning in the early 1920s, two fraternal organizations helped the immigrants adapt to their new country and maintain their culture. AHEPA (American Hellenic Educational Progressive Association) and GAPA (Greek American Progressive Association) were composed of Greek men in each parish. Over the years they offered strong support—financial and material—to their local communities. AHEPA, along with its women's and young people's auxiliaries, the Daughters of Penelope, Sons of Pericles, and Maids of Athena, continues to function as a strong supporter of the church to the present day. It has sponsored senior citizens centers in various parts of the country and taken on other humanitarian projects.

In the early 1950s the Greek Orthodox Archdiocese saw the need for a national organization to give Greek Orthodox youth a strong sense of identity. The result was the establishment of GOYA (Greek Orthodox Youth of America), which brings young people together for religious, cultural, and social activities. Most parishes have a GOYA chapter. The organization also promotes philanthropic activities, such as collecting food for the needy and toys for disadvantaged children. Each parish also has a Church school (Sunday school).

Most parishes also operate afternoon Greek-language schools for children in grades one through six or eight. The schools help children maintain Hellenic culture and expose them to the original language of the New Testament. In addition, between the spring and early fall, these communities offer the experience of their culture to the general public through their Greek festivals, which include church tours, food, and music. The festivals provide the parishes with supplemental income. Most of the parishes' revenue, however, comes from annual dues, fair-share steward-ship, or a combination of both.

After the 1920s, immigration from Greece and other Orthodox coun-tries decreased, though Greeks continued to arrive in smaller numbers in the ensuing decades. Today, parishes in Ohio consist of second-, third-, and fourth-generation Americans of Greek descent and many non-Greeks who came to the faith through intermarriage with Greek Americans or by voluntary conversion to Orthodox Christianity.

BELIEFS

The term "Greek Orthodox" does not derive from the fact these immi-grants were ethnic Greeks; rather, it signifies the ancient Christian Church's and the New Testament's original language and that the writings and teachings of the church fathers were in Greek.

The Orthodox Christian Church has two sources of authority: Holy Scripture and Holy Tradition. Holy Scripture consists of the writings in both the New and Old Testaments. Holy Tradition, of which Holy Scrip-ture is a part, also includes the writings and teachings of the apostles, saints, martyrs, and fathers of the Church, her liturgical and sacramental traditions through the ages, and the decisions of the seven Ecumenical Councils.

CURRENT DEMOGRAPHICS

Ohio's parishes are home to an estimated twenty thousand Greek Ortho-dox Christians. The Metropolis of Pittsburgh and the Metropolis of De-troit, to which the eastern and western halves of Ohio belong, along with seven other metropolises with a combined total of 450 parishes, compose the Greek Orthodox Archdiocese of America. The archdiocese, in turn, is a major province of the Ecumenical Patriarchate of Constantinople.

There are currently twenty-two Greek Orthodox parishes in Ohio. The following is a list of the state's parishes, with the year in which each was founded in parentheses: Akron, Annunciation Church (1918); Camp-bell, Archangel Michael (1955); Canton (two parishes), Holy Trinity (1917)

The Greek Orthodox Annunciation Cathedral in Columbus (1912) is one of the oldest Greek Orthodox churches in the state. (Courtesy of Dianne Small)

and St. Haralambos (1913); Cincinnati, Holy Trinity–St. Nicholas Church (1907), the oldest parish in Ohio; Greater Cleveland (four parishes), Annunciation (1913), Sts. Constantine and Helen (1956), St. Demetrios (Rocky River, 1960), and St. Paul (North Royalton, 1966); Columbus, Annunciation (1912); Dayton, Annunciation (1921); Lorain, St. Nicholas (1923); Mansfield, Sts. Constantine and Helen; Martins Ferry, Zoodochos Peghe Church (1929); Massillon, St. George (1931); Middletown, Sts. Constantine and Helen (1931); Springfield, Assumption (1935); Steubenville, Holy Trinity (1940s); Toledo, Holy Trinity (1915); Warren, St. Demetrios (1920); Youngstown (two parishes), St. John the Forerunner (1915) and St. Nicholas (1919).

In recent years, a number of Orthodox Christian monasteries have been established in the United States. There is one in Ohio, St. Gregory Palamas Monastery in Perrysville, which is under the jurisdiction of the Metropolis of Pittsburgh.

CONTACT INFORMATION

Greek Orthodox Archdiocese of America: *www.goarch.org*
Metropolis of Pittsburgh (covers eastern half of Ohio, including Columbus),

5201 Ellsworth Avenue, Pittsburgh, Pennsylvania, 15232–1421, 412-621-5529, *www.goarch.org/goa/pittsburg*

Metropolis of Detroit (covers western Ohio), 19405 Renfrew Road, Detroit, Michigan 48211–1835, 313-864-5433, *www.goarch.org/goa/detroit*

RESOURCES

Constantelos, Demetrios J. *The Greek Orthodox Church: Faith, History, and Practices.* New York: The Seabury Press, 1967.

Greek Orthodox Telecommunications. *History and Holy Sacraments of Orthodox Christianity* (three-part video documentary) and *Decades of Faith: The Greek Orthodox Church in America* (2000; video history of the Church in the United States since the 1920s). Address: 8 E. 79th St., New York, New York 10021.

The Orthodox Observer (monthly). Official newspaper of the Greek Orthodox Archdiocese of America. Offices at 8 E. 79th St., New York, New York 10021.

Ware, Kallistos. *The Orthodox Church.* London: Penguin Books, 1997.

COPTIC ORTHODOX CHURCH OF EGYPT

Anthony R. Zifer

HISTORY

COPTS ARE THE NATIVE CHRISTIANS OF EGYPT AND ARE DIRECT descendants of the ancient Egyptians. The word "Coptic" is derived from an ancient Egyptian name for Memphis, the first capital of ancient Egypt. Coptic not only describes Egyptian Christians, but also identifies their distinctive art, architecture, and the last stage of the ancient Egyptian language. The Coptic language and script is still in use today during all church services and is written using a combination of the Greek alphabet and Egyptian hieroglyphs. Copts feel blessed to live in the only land outside Israel that Jesus Christ visited during his lifetime. Soon after Jesus' birth the Holy Family fled from Bethlehem to Egypt, remaining there until King Herod's death.

The Church of Alexandria (Coptic Church) is one of the five most ancient churches of the world, along with the Churches of Jerusalem, Antioch, Rome, and Ephesus. The Coptic Church is an apostolic church founded by Saint Mark the Evangelist sometime between 48 and 61 C.E. St. Mark was one of the seventy apostles chosen by Jesus Christ and is credited as the first to write a New Testament Gospel. St. Mark also started the first Christian theological school—in Alexandria—and is regarded as the first pope of the Coptic Church in an unbroken succession of patriarchs. Today, the Coptic Orthodox Church is lead by His Holiness Pope Shenouda III, the 117th pope and patriarch of the great city of Alexandria and the See of Saint Mark. Pope Shenouda lives at his papal residence in Cairo, Egypt.

The Coptic Orthodox Church is a very young church in Ohio and the United States. In the early 1960s Copts started to identify themselves as communities in New York City and Los Angeles. In the spring of 1970 the Los Angeles congregation purchased a Lutheran church building that would become St. Mark's, the first Coptic Church in the United States.

It was not until the late 1960s that groups of Coptic Orthodox families started to form in Cleveland, Columbus, and Dayton. His Grace the late Bishop Samuel, Special Assistant to the late Pope Kyrillos (Cyril) VI, advised the largest group in Cleveland to contact Fr. Marcos Marcos, a pioneer priest in Toronto, Canada. Fr. Marcos responded to the group's call, coming to Cleveland and celebrating the first Divine Liturgy in September 1968. He continued Divine Liturgy services to the Cleveland group every three months, eventually increasing to once a month. Two years later, in 1970, the Cleveland group incorporated the first Coptic Orthodox Church in Ohio, Saint Mark. The number of Copts steadily increased in Cleveland from six families in 1968 to nearly sixty families by 1973. In 1975, with the blessings of Pope Shenouda III, the Cleveland parish received its first resident priest, Reverend Father Mikhail E. Mikhail.

Before coming to Ohio, Mounier Mikhail, as Fr. Mikhail was known before becoming a priest, attended the Coptic Orthodox Theological Seminary in Cairo, studying under Pope Shenouda III, who was then Bishop of Christian Education and Dean of the Seminary. After completing his studies, Mounier became the first consecrated deacon to serve in the United States, at the Coptic Church of St. Mary and St. Antonious in Queens, New York. In May 1974, Deacon Mounier married Seham Samuel, a Sunday school teacher from Masarra, Egypt, at the Coptic Orthodox Cathedral of St. Mark in Cairo. Later that same year, on August 23, the pope ordained Deacon Mounier as priest Fr. Mikhail Edward Mikhail. Fr. Mikhail and his wife arrived in Cleveland on April 30, 1975, to begin his new ministry at Saint Mark Coptic Orthodox Church.

The St. Mark congregation rented St. Paul's Episcopal Church in East Cleveland and by 1977 purchased its first church, in Parma. This small church would become home of the Cleveland congregation for nearly

Saint Mark Coptic Orthodox Church in the Cleveland suburb of Seven Hills (1988) is the first Coptic church in Ohio. Its design incorporates architectural traditions unique to the Coptic Orthodox cathedrals and monasteries of Egypt. (Courtesy of Saint Mark Coptic Orthodox Church)

eleven years. Also in 1977, Cleveland was one of several cities that hosted Pope Shenouda's first pastoral visit, the first ever by a Coptic pope to the United States. The Greater Cleveland community leadership recognized the Coptic Church as the official representative of the Egyptians in Cuyahoga County. Cleveland became a sister city to Alexandria, Egypt, which was announced during this visit. It was in 1988 that St. Mark completed construction of its new church complex, located in the Cleveland suburb of Seven Hills. The church was designed to resemble the Coptic architectural tradition seen in the Orthodox churches of Egypt.

St. Mark was blessed by the "Miracle of Oil" seeping from two icons, or religious paintings, hanging inside the new church. Oil poured from the icons "Our Lord Jesus Christ" and "Holy Virgin Mary, Mother of God." The miracle began on the Feast of St. Athanasius, May 15, 1990. The oil recurred several times and was witnessed by thousands of pilgrims to the church as well as television stations, newspapers, and by Pope Shenouda III, who, after personally seeing the icons, declared the phenomenon an official miracle in May 1991.

During this same period, Fr. Mikhail traveled to Columbus and Dayton to perform monthly Saturday services at rented churches in those cities. It was not until November 1992 that Ohio received its second priest, Fr. Shenouda Awadalla, to serve the parishes of St. Mary (in Columbus) and St. Mina and St. Abanoub (in the Dayton suburb of Miamisburg). Both congregations purchased church buildings in 1993. Fr. Shenouda served until 1995, when Fr. John Ragheb was assigned to both churches. When Fr. Sedarous A. Sedarous arrived in Columbus in 1998, Father John remained in charge of the Dayton church, allowing these parishes to have weekly Sunday services for the first time.

BELIEFS

The Coptic Church is recognized as "Orthodox," meaning it continues to use liturgical doctrine and church rituals that have gone nearly unchanged for almost two thousand years. The Nicene Creed, written in 325 C.E. by Saint Athanasius, the twentieth Pope of Alexandria, is what Copts recite as their declaration of faith. Saint Anthony (251–356 C.E.), who is considered the "Father of Monasticism," was another great Coptic contributor to Christianity.

There are seven canonical sacraments: baptism, chrismation, eucharist, confession, matrimony, priesthood, and anointing of the sick. Baptism is performed by full submersion of the infant or adult into consecrated, or blessed, water three times to symbolize the Holy Trinity. Chrismation is an anointing of holy oil performed immediately after baptism. Confession with a personal priest is necessary to receive the eucharist, or communion.

Copts celebrate seven major and seven minor holy feasts. The major feasts commemorate Annunciation, Christmas, Theophany, Palm Sunday, Easter, Ascension, and Pentecost. Most feasts are preceded by fasting. During fasts, no meat or dairy products are to be eaten. Lent, known as "the Great Fast," starts with a one-week pre-Lent fast. This is followed by a forty-day fast commemorating Christ's fasting on the mountain and culminating with the Holy Pascha, the most sacred week of the Coptic calendar, which ends on the Feast of the Resurrection (Easter).

The Coptic Church requires that bishops, from whom the pope is chosen, remain celibate and live as monks. They are all members of the Coptic Orthodox Holy Synod, which meets regularly to oversee matters of faith and pastoralship. Direct pastoral responsibility of congregations falls on priests, who must both be married and have attended catechetical school before being ordained.

CURRENT DEMOGRAPHICS

Approximately two thousand Coptic Americans call Ohio home and attend services at four churches across the state. Recent immigration to Ohio from Egypt, Canada, and Australia, as well as from other parts of the United States, has sparked growth in new Coptic communities such as Toledo and Youngstown.

CONTACT INFORMATION

Coptic papal residence: *www.CopticPope.org*

Coptic Orthodox Archdiocese of North America, 5 Woodstone Drive, Cedar Grove, New Jersey 07009, 973-857-0078.

St. George Coptic Orthodox Church, 4860 Waterville-Monclova Road, Monclova, Ohio 43542, 419-878-3800. Or: P.O. Box 730, Holland, Ohio 43528.

St. Mark Coptic Orthodox Church, 2100 East Pleasant Valley Road, Seven Hills, Ohio 44131, 216-642-7692, *www.stmarkcoccleveland.org*

St. Mary Coptic Orthodox Church, 200 Old Village Road, Columbus, Ohio 43228, 614-853-0566. Or: P.O. Box 282113, Columbus, Ohio 43228.

St. Mina and St. Abanoub Coptic Orthodox Church, 1531 King Richard Parkway, Miamisburg, Ohio 45342, 937-866-0622. Or: P.O. Box 595, Miamisburg, Ohio 45343.

RESOURCES

Atiya, Aziz Suryal. *The Coptic Encyclopedia.* 8 vols. New York: Macmillan, 1991.

El Masri, Iris Habib. *The Story of the Copts: The True Story of Christianity in Egypt.* Newberry Springs, Calif.: St. Anthony Coptic Orthodox Monastery, 1982.

Malaty, Tadros Y. *Introduction to the Coptic Orthodox Church.* Alexandria, Egypt: St. George's Coptic Orthodox Church, 1993.

Episcopal

Peter W. Williams

HISTORY

THE EPISCOPAL CHURCH IS THE DIRECT AMERICAN DESCENDANT of the Church of England. The latter came into being in the 1530s when King Henry VIII, at odds with the pope for refusing to grant Henry's request for an annulment of his marriage to Catherine of Aragon, persuaded Parliament to declare Christianity in England independent of the Roman Catholic Church. This formal break came after centuries of tension between the English monarchy and the Church in Rome and was built on long-standing traditions asserting that Christianity had been introduced into England in the time of the apostles and therefore had always enjoyed a certain independence from Roman domination. From the time of Henry until the present, therefore, the Church of England or Anglican church has been an independent national church, with authority vested in the queen or king and Parliament, as well as in the Archbishop of Canterbury and other bishops of the church.

With the achievement of independence from England at the end of the eighteenth century, residents of the new nation who belonged to the Church of England and who valued their religious tradition were faced with a dilemma. To be an Anglican involved pledging one's allegiance to the king—in this case, the thoroughly disliked George III. Obviously, a citizen of the new republic of the United States could not engage in such

St. John's Episcopal Church in Worthington, Ohio (congregation founded 1804; church constructed 1827–31), is the oldest Episcopal church in the state. (Courtesy of St. John's Episcopal Church)

an act, which was at once political and religious. As a result, church leaders agreed to begin anew, to reinvent their tradition in the new republic.

In order to establish an American episcopate or body of bishops separate from the Church of England, the Americans sent Samuel Seabury, a clergyman from Connecticut, to Scotland, where there were bishops willing to consecrate him. As a result the Episcopal Church has existed as an independent American denomination since 1784, carrying forward most of the traditions of the Church of England but completely free of governance of that church. After other British colonies became independent of the mother country (and church), bishops from these now independent national Anglican churches began to meet regularly in Canterbury in England and designated their churches collectively as the Worldwide Anglican Communion, which now consists of about three dozen members.

After the American Revolution Ohio was still frontier territory, and Episcopalians began to send missionaries to the area in 1817. The most important figure in the early history of the Episcopal Church in the state was Philander Chase, a convert from New Hampshire who became the state's first Episcopal bishop in 1818. Chase is also notable as the founder of Kenyon College in the town of Gambier in 1824. (The names of both college and town were taken from those of wealthy English benefactors whom Chase had cultivated during fund-raising tours abroad.) Kenyon continues to this day as one of Ohio's premier liberal arts colleges, although its connection with the Episcopal Church is no longer as close as it was in earlier years. Chase's successor, Charles Pettit McIlvaine, served as bishop of Ohio from 1832 until 1873.

McIlvaine continued in Chase's tradition as an advocate of "Low Church" Episcopalianism, that is, the faction within the broader denomination which stressed the Protestant character of Anglicanism and emphasized the roles of preaching and personal conversion. This position led McIlvaine into direct conflict with some parishes and clergy over the proper character of worship; in 1846, for example, he refused to consecrate a church in Columbus which had a stone altar as its centerpiece, insisting that a communion table of wood be substituted instead. As a "Low Churchman," McIlvaine was hostile to all aspects of Roman Catholicism and staunchly opposed what he saw as the "High Church" program for introducing elements of Catholic worship, such as stone altars, into the Episcopal Church. The enthusiasm for Gothic revival architecture, which had been introduced into the Episcopal Church during the 1840s and was at first closely associated with "High Churchmanship," prevailed in Ohio as well, however, and many of the state's parishes have fine examples of this style exhibited in their churches.

Leadership in the Episcopal Church of the twentieth century—divided in Ohio into two dioceses since 1875—was generally less colorful and combative than in the days of Chase and McIlvaine. Bishop Henry Wise Hobson of Southern Ohio was a firm champion of "Low Churchmanship" during the century's middle decades, and the denomination here as elsewhere appealed especially, though by no means exclusively, to the well educated, well-to-do, and socially prominent. During the latter half of the twentieth century, Episcopalians in Ohio became embroiled in the same issues that engaged the Church nationally, for example, the struggle for civil rights for minorities and the empowerment of women, the latter especially in the context of ordination to the Episcopal priesthood. Today, these issues are largely moot, as many parishes in the state's two dioceses now have women as priests, and the Bishop of Southern

Ohio at the turn of the millennium was an African American, Herbert Thompson. (A woman serves as bishop in nearby Indianapolis.) Membership regionally, as nationally, has declined somewhat from its heyday in the 1950s and '60s, but now has stabilized and may be on the rise again. Ohio Episcopalians remain staunch in their respect for a style of public worship at once traditional and adaptable; an individual quest for personal spirituality rooted in the traditions of Christian England; and, however much individual Episcopalians might differ on particular issues of political and economic policy, a firm commitment to social justice for all founded on the principles of scripture.

BELIEFS

The Episcopal Church in the United States maintains continuity with the Anglican tradition in several ways. Its public worship is based on the *Book of Common Prayer,* which was originally compiled in England in 1549 and has long since been adapted for American use. Its worship is also *sacramental,* and the Eucharist is now celebrated as a rule during most Sunday morning worship services. Its clergy are known as priests, since their central liturgical function is the celebration of the Eucharist. A good summary of the church's tradition is contained in the formula known as the "Anglican Triad," which states that religious truth can be known through the three divinely ordained means of scripture, church tradition, and human reason. Another formulation is contained in the Chicago-Lambeth Quadrilateral of the 1880s, a document adopted by the bishops of the Episcopal Church in the United States and subsequently by those of the Church of England. As its name implies, this document has four points, each of them a source through which Christian faith is transmitted: the two sacraments of baptism and the Eucharist, Holy Scripture, the creeds of the early churches, and the historic episcopate, or apostolic succession of bishops. These formulations have frequently been interpreted as allowing the individual believer a good deal of leeway in his or her interpretation of the Christian tradition, so that contemporary Episcopalians tend toward the liberal, or "mainline," end of the Christian spectrum in the United States.

CURRENT DEMOGRAPHICS

The Diocese of Ohio today consists of 112 parishes, more than two hundred clergy (not all of them active in parishes), and an active membership of about twenty-six thousand. The Diocese of Southern Ohio now has eighty-one parishes, somewhat fewer than two hundred clergy, and about twenty thousand lay members.

CONTACT INFORMATION

Since 1875 the state of Ohio has been divided into two Episcopal dioceses. The Diocese of Ohio, with its bishop resident in Cleveland, ends at a line just north of Columbus; the Diocese of Southern Ohio, with its bishop in Cincinnati, consists of the remainder of the state.

The Episcopal Church, USA: *www.ecusa.anglican.org*

Diocese of Ohio, Trinity Commons, 2230 Euclid Avenue, Cleveland, Ohio 44115–2405, 800-551-4815, *www.dohio.org/*

Diocese of Southern Ohio, 412 Sycamore Street, Cincinnati, Ohio 45202–4110, 513-421-0311, *www.episcopal-dso.org*

RESOURCES

Butler, Diana Hochstedt. *Standing against the Whirlwind: Evangelical Episcopalians in Nineteenth-Century America.* New York: Oxford University Press, 1995.

The Episcopal Church Annual (annual yearbook). Wilton, Conn.: Morehouse-Barlow.

Krumm, John. *Flowing Like a River.* Cincinnati: Christian Forward Movement, 1989.

Smythe, George Franklin. *A History of the Diocese of Ohio until the Year 1918.* Cleveland: Diocese of Ohio, 1931.

Friends (Quakers)

EVANGELICAL FRIENDS
CHURCH–EASTERN REGION

Wayne Evans

HISTORY

Westward expansion brought many people to Ohio in the early days of the state's history. This included Quakers, or Friends, from the eastern states. As more and more arrived to set up communities and churches, delegates from those local churches met in Mt. Pleasant to form the Ohio Yearly Meeting of Friends in 1812.

Friends trace their religious roots back to mid-seventeenth-century England, where George Fox, the group's founder, led a spiritual revival that spread rapidly—even to America. Friends pioneered a simple lifestyle. That is why they are known for their plain clothes and plain speech. Their services were called "meetings," and they met in "meetinghouses." Once several congregations could be identified in a state, they conducted common business at a "yearly meeting." Ohio's Mt. Pleasant Yearly Meeting House still stands and is managed by the Ohio Historical Society.

Friends' simplicity sowed the seeds of new problems. In their first two decades in Ohio, controversy arose (as it did in other parts of "Quaker-dom" worldwide) over theology. That controversy swelled until 1826,

Interior of the Friends yearly meetinghouse in Mount Pleasant (1814). This brick structure is capable of holding two thousand persons on the main floor and the galleries. The Ohio Historical Society currently administers the building. (Courtesy of the Historical Society of Mount Pleasant)

when the Ohio Yearly Meeting split into two groups. One group pursued its Christian calling (often going more by the name of Friends), while the other group pursued its universalist identity (often going more by the name of Quakers).

Prior to the Civil War, Friends in Ohio were active in the movement to abolish slavery. John Woolman spent years convincing all Friends/Quakers in America to end any involvement in the slave trade. After thirty years, he was successful. By the end of the Civil War not one Friend or Quaker in America owned any slaves. In fact, they were often involved in the Underground Railroad, helping runaway slaves find freedom in the northern United States and in Canada. Simultaneously, many Friends meetings began schools in their communities in order to provide education for themselves and the people around them.

By 1850 another controversy had arisen in the Friends' ranks. This time it was a controversy over passions within the faith. This became known as the Gurneyite-Wilburite dispute (named for Joseph John Gurney [d. 1847] and John Wilbur, leaders in the dispute). In 1854 Gurney's widow visited Mt. Pleasant during the summer yearly meeting sessions. Eliza Gurney's presence empowered her husband's followers to make another separation. The new group later called itself the Evangelical Friends Church–Eastern Region and chose Damascus for its headquarters due to the large number of Gurneyite Friends in that community.

These were the days of the revivalist movement in America. David B. Updegraff from Mt. Pleasant developed into a passionate evangelical himself and began a preaching ministry that took him to many parts of America. His ministry shaped many lives. He introduced the Ohio Friends to new practices of worship, namely baptism and communion, that were unusual for many Friends/Quakers.

If Updegraff's ministry introduced new practices to Ohio Friends, J. Walter Malone's ministry took a further step. During Malone's leadership, the Ohio Friends launched a modern missionary movement (first to China and then to India), began to make use of paid pastors, and started training those pastors at the school Malone founded with his wife, Emma, in Cleveland. What he called the Cleveland Bible Training Institute eventually moved to Canton in 1957. There it was renamed Malone College for its cofounders and led the move of the headquarters, called the World Outreach Center, to Canton in the 1970s.

During the twentieth century other leaders stepped forward. Women like Esther Butler, Esther Baird, Delia Fistler, and Isabella DeVol served in early missionary endeavors around the world—often as teachers, doctors, and nurses. They were joined by a number of men who often worked as teachers and preachers, men like George DeVol, Everett Cattell, Cliff Robinson, and Robert Hess.

As time passed and the movement's influence grew, the Ohio Friends made two major moves. One, the name was changed to the Evangelical Friends Church–Eastern Region (EFC–ER). Two, the EFC–ER began cooperating with other Friends around the country and formed an organization known as Evangelical Friends International (EFI), also based at the World Outreach Center in Canton. The six yearly meetings of EFI cooperate in publishing educational materials, as well as overseeing a missionary endeavor that now encompasses more than 150,000 attenders in more than twenty-five countries.

At the time of Ohio's bicentennial, Dr. John P. Williams Jr. entered his fifteenth year as the EFC–ER's general superintendent. Williams, a great-grandson of the Malones, and his wife Carol graduated from Malone

College and worked as pastors and college instructors before leading the EFC–ER. John—along with David Rawson, a former U.S. ambassador to Rwanda—were selected in the 1990s as Malone College's most outstanding alumni. Together they personify the spirit of the college's founders and that of the church they now serve.

BELIEFS

George Fox felt disappointment that the church he knew in England in the mid-seventeenth century made great use of religious forms but seemed to miss the heart of a vital relationship with Jesus Christ. The movement he founded thus sought to regain that vibrancy. Religious forms were nearly eliminated. Simplicity and honesty (whether in worldly possessions or missionary purpose) became the Quakers' banners of identity.

Since then, controversies and passions have continued to shape how those qualities would be expressed. The EFC–ER inherited the line of Friends that sought to remain distinctly Christian with an evangelical zeal and purpose. By the early 1900s Ohio Friends were seeking ways to express their faith through church ministry, medical missions, and education. Their preaching aim could be described as evangelical and holiness oriented. Purity of heart and life and ministry were their goals.

The same is true at this historical juncture. Today worship styles blend traditional hymns and contemporary choruses with preaching that aims to be practical and influential in order to move people closer to the Lord Jesus Christ. Local ministry has blossomed from education into meeting the needs of people in many ways: youth events, divorce recovery, marriage rebuilders, sports ministry, feeding and caring for the poor, caring for the aging, crisis pregnancies, preschools and academies, disaster relief, and more.

What summarizes the passion of evangelical Friends today has been called by Dr. John P. Williams Jr. "GC2," the Great Commission driven in the spirit of the Great Commandment. The two "GCs" bring together two of Jesus' core values. Matt. 28:19–20 is called the Great Commission because in it Jesus calls us to reach out to everyone with the Gospel. Matt. 22:36–39 is called the Great Commandment because in it Jesus ties together the love we have for the Lord with our love for our fellow human beings. We are not perfect at fulfilling that, but being driven in that spirit is certainly our passion today.

CURRENT DEMOGRAPHICS

Currently, the EFC–ER alone has an average attendance of almost seventeen thousand in ninety-three churches. In Ohio the greatest concentrations are found from Canton to Salem, around Cleveland, around St. Clairsville, and from Columbus to Van Wert. The EFC–ER does extend now beyond Ohio, but congregations are scattered from Rhode Island to Michigan to Florida. EFC–ER churches are largely Caucasian, but a growing number of ethnic and minority churches are surfacing.

The EFC–ER is only one of several Friends or Quaker groups in Ohio. The main connection between all of the groups in recent years has been through the national Friends Ministers Conference, held in various cities around the United States every six to seven years.

CONTACT INFORMATION

Evangelical Friends International: *www.evangelical-friends.org*
World Outreach Center, 5350 Broadmoor Circle NW, Canton, Ohio 44709, 800-334-8863.
Evangelical Friends Church–Eastern Region: *www.efcer.org*

RESOURCES

Bill, J. Brent. *David B. Updegraff: Quaker Holiness Preacher*. Richmond, Ind.: Friends United Press, 1983.
DeVol, Charles E. *Fruit that Remains*. Canton, Ohio: Evangelical Friends Church–Eastern Region, 1988.
Williams, Walter R. *The Rich Heritage of Quakerism*. Grand Rapids, Mich.: Eerdmans, 1962.

RELIGIOUS SOCIETY OF FRIENDS

Herbert R. Hicks

HISTORY

THE RELIGIOUS SOCIETY OF FRIENDS (QUAKERS) GREW OUT OF THE spiritual quest of George Fox (1624–91), an itinerant English preacher and reformer. Fox proclaimed a simple faith, based on the belief that people can have an immediate relationship with God without the aid of clergy. He rejected violence and proclaimed the equality of all people.

Friends have been a vital part of America's life since 1681, when William Penn, an English Quaker, received the charter from the king of England and founded the colony of Pennsylvania. Penn's "holy experiment" gave Friends a haven from religious persecution in England, and they migrated to the New World in great numbers. Their presence in Ohio was an early, natural result of the westward flow of the young nation. For more than 225 years Friends have enriched Ohio's spiritual tapestry.

The earliest recorded activity of Friends in Ohio came in 1775 in the form of a mission to the Shawnee and Delaware Indians by a recorded Friends minister, Thomas Beals. Beals recruited Bowater Sumner, William Hiatt, and David Ballard, who accompanied him on his expedition. In spite of their being arrested on suspicion of being allies with the Indians, their excursion provided an opening between Quakers and Native Americans, an opening that would produce rich relationships for decades to come.

Quaker migration into Ohio flowed in two main streams. One of these was from Pennsylvania. Another stream came out of the South. Friends actively sought the abolition of slavery. One consequence of this testimony was hostility toward them and, at times, actual persecution of Friends living in states where slavery was legal. The fact that the Northwest Territory, which included part of Ohio, was "free" territory meant that Quakers moving there could escape persecution over their views on slavery. Here again, Thomas Beals played an important role. In a communication with Friends in North Carolina, Beals pointed to the Ohio country as a pleasing site for Quaker settlement. It was good farmland and was free from the affliction of slavery.

Quakers' testimonies on peace and justice flourished in their new home. Friends, who had historically sympathized with the oppressed—and frequently experienced oppression themselves—sought justice for the Indians and assisted them in many ways. Their strong opposition to slavery continued with renewed vigor in Ohio. Friends were active in creating the Underground Railroad, and Quaker homes frequently sheltered fugitive slaves.

The general pattern of migration from the South saw Friends from Virginia moving into the region by crossing the Ohio River at Wheeling. Friends from the Carolinas and Georgia commonly came through the Kanawha River Valley, in what is now West Virginia, to the Ohio River. From the Ohio River they would travel up such tributaries as the Scioto and Miami Rivers.

The first known association of Friends for worship in what is now Ohio met in 1799 at Quaker Bottom in Lawrence County. Here Thomas Beals, who had followed his own advice and moved his family there, was once again in a leadership position. Several families from Quaker Bottom soon moved up the Scioto River and settled in the vicinity of Chillicothe. Thomas Beals died in this area in 1801 and was buried near Richmondale, south of Chillicothe, where his grave marker can still be found.

The honor of being the first Quaker family to settle in what would become Ohio belongs, however, to the family of George Harlan. The Harlan family moved to Deerfield in 1795. Deerfield was located on the Little Miami River, now in Warren County, near Cincinnati.

The region's first official organization of Friends was established in 1801 in what is now Belmont County, across the Ohio River from Wheeling. Concord Monthly Meeting (a local congregation with business meetings each month) was set up under the care of Redstone Quarterly Meeting (an area organization of several monthly meetings which held business sessions each quarter) in southwest Pennsylvania. Redstone Quarterly Meeting was a subdivision of Baltimore Yearly Meeting (a regional organization of several quarterly meetings which held an annual business session).

The Friends population in Ohio expanded rapidly, and in 1810 Friends in Ohio requested approval to have a yearly meeting of their own. Baltimore Yearly Meeting granted permission, and the Ohio Yearly Meeting was established in 1813 at Short Creek, near Mount Pleasant, with an estimated membership of twenty thousand. When the Ohio Yearly Meeting was established, men and women held separate business sessions in harmony with Quaker custom. The women met in the brick meetinghouse, while the men met in a nearby shed. In 1814 a larger brick meetinghouse was erected.

Another group of Friends was at work in Warren County near Waynesville, where Joseph Cloud, a Friends minister from North Carolina, began holding meetings for worship in 1800. The Miami Monthly Meeting was organized in 1803 and a brick meetinghouse was erected in 1811. This meetinghouse is still in use by the Miami Monthly Meeting.

The nineteenth century, which began with so much hope and promise, would also bring deep and lasting divisions among Friends. Much work has been done to heal these wounds and, as the twenty-first century begins, there is a renewed, growing sense of unity among Friends.

BELIEFS

Quakers are a part of the Protestant branch of the Christian faith and share the core beliefs of mainstream Christianity.

Because Friends believe that "there is that of God" in every person, they have always valued education and sought to educate males and females on an equal basis. A schoolhouse was typically the first thing to be built after the meetinghouse. High academic standards were the rule, and Quaker schools acquired a reputation for excellence.

These early Quaker schools and teachers played a significant role in shaping the development of the public school system in Ohio. The rise of public education, however, resulted in the decline of Friends' schools, and most of them were eventually closed.

The Friends yearly meetinghouse in Mount Pleasant was the first house of worship built by the Society of Friends west of the Allegheny mountains. The building, constructed in 1814 of handmade bricks, served as the center of the Quaker faith in Eastern Ohio for nearly a century. The building is now owned by the **Ohio Historical Society.** (Courtesy of Herbert R. Hicks)

Olney Friends School, a boarding school in Barnesville that was established in 1837, is the only Quaker school in operation in Ohio today. Two excellent colleges, Wilmington and Malone, continue the zeal for education begun by Ohio Quakers.

Traditional Quaker worship is unique in that it is based on an expectant, silent waiting for "openings" from God. In early Quaker history there were no ordained or trained professional pastors. Those who were called to preach were "recorded," or recognized as having a gift for ministry from God. The introduction of professional pastors, along with more "programmed" or structured forms of worship represented one area of division. Today Quaker worship varies widely from the classic "silent" or "unprogrammed" form to worship services very much like those of mainstream Protestant churches.

Another area of division is theology, which ranges from fundamentalist to evangelical to moderate to conservative to liberal. All groups believe in the presence of God in the lives of God's people, the sanctity of human life, and the rejection of all forms of violence.

CURRENT DEMOGRAPHICS

Today seven different bodies—Ohio Yearly Meeting, Wilmington Yearly Meeting, Indiana Yearly Meeting, Lake Erie Yearly Meeting, Ohio Valley Yearly Meeting, Central Yearly Meeting, and the Evangelical Friends Church–Eastern Region—represent five different branches of the Society of Friends in Ohio. The branches are Conservative Friends, Friends United Meeting, Friends General Conference, "Holiness" Friends, and Evangelical Friends.

As of 2003 the combined membership of all Quaker groups in Ohio is approximately eleven thousand, or just over one-half what it was nearly two hundred years ago. Ohio Friends are concentrated in northeastern and southwestern Ohio. Although the number of Quakers in Ohio has declined, Quakers' commitment to their traditional testimonies remains strong. Friends continue to seek peace, oppose violence, believe in the equality of all people, and have faith in a living God who speaks to them and actively leads them to ever-new horizons of adventure.

CONTACT INFORMATION

Wilmington Yearly Meeting, 251 Ludovic Street, Pyle Center, P.O. Box 1194, Wilmington, Ohio 45177–4194, 937-382-2491.

Friends United Meeting, 101 Quaker Hill Drive, Richmond, Indiana 47374–1980, 765-962-7573, *www.fum.org*

RESOURCES

Quaker Life (monthly magazine). Published by Friends United Press, Richmond, Indiana.

Weishart, Randy. *A Winding Road to Freedom*. Richmond, Ind.: Friends United Press, 1999.

Jehovah's Witnesses

James N. Pellechia

HISTORY

IN THE LATE NINETEENTH CENTURY, AN ARDENT STUDENT OF THE Bible named Charles Taze Russell launched what he called "a vigorous campaign for the Truth." Challenging the popularity of so-called higher criticism of the Bible and Darwin's theory of evolution, as well as non-Biblical church practices, Russell became a staunch advocate for the spreading of the good news of God's kingdom and for the Bible as the inspired word of God. Beginning in July 1879 in Allegheny, Pennsylvania, Russell published the Bible journal *Zion's Watch Tower and Herald of Christ's Presence,* a widely circulated and translated religious publication. He formed several corporations to facilitate the publishing of the good news. One, now known as the Watch Tower Bible and Tract Society of Pennsylvania, was formed in 1884. Another is the International Bible Students Association (IBSA), formed in 1914.

In August 1880 Russell traveled to Ohio, visiting *Watch Tower* readers in Elyria and starting small congregations there and in Cleveland. Bible Students, as Jehovah's Witnesses were called prior to 1931, gathered for Bible discussions, for the most part in small groups. Like Russell, many *Watch Tower* magazine readers joined the campaign to preach good news. Letters from enthusiastic Ohio readers appeared frequently in the *Watch Tower,* reporting that some were distributing copies of Watch Tower Society publications to interested persons throughout the state. During

1892, Bible Students in Ohio and neighboring states handed out more than five hundred thousand free copies of Russell's book *Food for Thinking Christians: Why Evil Was Permitted, and Kindred Topics,* first published in 1881. Two Bible Students undertook visits by boat to cities and towns along the Ohio River. On April 18, 1886, Bible Students from Ohio and six other states, as well as Canada, assembled in Pittsburgh to commemorate the anniversary of Jesus' last supper. In the next few decades, the Bible Students rapidly expanded their Bible education efforts to the four corners of the globe.

Although the Bible Students had several small congregations in the state, the first large one was in Cleveland. In 1919 that congregation met at the Market Square Theatre on Broadway Avenue. Esther Madzay of Brunswick remembers that her mother, Mary Pawlowski, was the organist. Beginning in 1926, the Bible Students also had a special contract for all the program time allotted to religion at radio station WHK, whose call letters stood for "We Herald the Kingdom."

Landmark Conventions

At the turn of the twentieth century, Ohio became a favorite location for annual conventions of the Bible Students. About forty-eight hundred met in Put-in-Bay in 1908 for Bible talks and fellowship. Russell Kurzen of Dalton, Ohio, who was present as a one-year-old at that convention, still serves on the volunteer staff at the World Headquarters of Jehovah's Witnesses in Brooklyn, New York. Charles Taze Russell, whose sermons regularly appeared in more than two thousand newspapers on four continents, died on October 31, 1916. Shortly after the United States entered World War I in 1917, eight leading Bible Students from world headquarters were prosecuted and convicted under the Espionage Act because their literature criticized clergymen who mixed religion and politics. All eight were later exonerated of the charges.

The first major IBSA convention after World War I took place at Cedar Point, Ohio, in September 1919. The auditorium of the Breakers Hotel, with a capacity of twenty-five hundred, proved far too small for the six thousand Bible Students and one thousand members of the public who attended the principal lecture, "The Hope for Distressed Humanity." So

The Bible Students' convention at Cedar Point, September 1922. (Copyright Watch Tower Bible and Tract Society of Pennsylvania; reprinted by permission)

the delegates moved outdoors and held their sessions in a grove of trees. The *Sandusky Register* of September 9, 1919, reported: "The annual convention of the International Bible Students Association, by far the biggest thing of its kind ever held in this part of the Great Lakes section, was concluded with a rousing open-air mass meeting at Cedar Point Sunday afternoon."

The 1922 Bible Students convention likewise came to Cedar Point, with ten thousand present to listen to a lecture with the provocative title "Millions Now Living Will Never Die." Sessions were held in ten languages. In July 1931 in Columbus, convention delegates adopted a historic resolution to take on a new name—Jehovah's Witnesses. The name, based on Isaiah chapter 43, verses 10 through 12, described the responsibility that the Bible Students took so seriously, that of witnessing, or preaching, about Jehovah, the God of the Bible. With the help of AT&T, the lecture "The Kingdom, the Hope of the World" went out to 163 radio stations in the United States, Canada, Mexico, and Cuba.

Educational Programs and Worship Services

World War II proved to be another stormy period for Jehovah's Witnesses in the United States, Europe, and Asia because they abstained from military service for reasons of conscience. While Witnesses in the United States were mobbed and accused of being Communists and Nazis, thousands of Witnesses in Nazi Germany were tortured and executed as "subversives" and "spies." At the height of the wartime turbulence, however, the Witnesses set up two new schools to better equip their members to teach love for God and fellow humans. The Watchtower Bible School of Gilead has trained more than seven thousand missionaries since its establishment in 1942. The Theocratic Ministry School is conducted weekly in congregations of Jehovah's Witnesses worldwide, including the 369 congregations in Ohio. Thousands of Ohio residents—men and women, young and old—have improved their reading, speaking, and teaching abilities by enrolling in this free course.

Jehovah's Witnesses in Ohio today continue the long tradition of Bible education and volunteer community service. Their teaching work includes personalized programs to provide Bible knowledge, along with family counseling, addiction counseling, literacy and other life skills to which scriptural principles can be applied. All members, young and old, receive training as ministers and Bible teachers. None receives a salary. Nearly thirty-five thousand active Witnesses in Ohio come from diverse ethnic and socioeconomic backgrounds. They worship together in "Kingdom Halls," a designation reflecting the Witnesses' belief that God's Kingdom is the main theme of the Bible. Local Kingdom Halls are financed and maintained by means of voluntary donations. Their Bible classes and worship services are all free and open to the public. No collections are taken, nor are attendees obligated to sign up for membership.

BELIEFS

- *God:* There is only one true God, the Creator of all things. His name is Jehovah and his outstanding qualities are love, justice, wisdom, and power.
- *Jesus:* He is the Son of God, who came to earth from heaven and sacri-

ficed his perfect human life as a ransom. His death and resurrection made salvation to eternal life possible for those exercising faith in him. He is now king of God's heavenly kingdom, which will soon bring peace to the earth. Jesus never claimed equality with God and thus is not part of a trinity.

- *The Bible:* It is God's infallible, inspired word. Some portions of the Bible are to be understood figuratively, or symbolically.

- *Sin, Death, and Resurrection:* Death is a result of sin inherited from the first man, Adam, who chose to disobey God. The original sin was a deliberate disobedient act of eating from "the tree of the knowledge of good and bad." The dead are conscious of nothing. God promises that in the future there will be a resurrection of the dead to a paradise on earth.

- *Judgment:* Jesus is God's appointed judge who determines what each one's future will be. Those judged as righteous will be given everlasting life on a paradise earth. Those judged as unrighteous will not be tormented but will die and cease to exist.

- *Baptism:* This act of complete immersion symbolizes one's dedication to God. This step is taken by those of responsible age who have made an informed decision.

- *Marriage:* Jehovah's Witnesses view marriage as a serious, lifelong commitment. They look to the Bible for guidance in resolving marital problems in a loving and respectful way.

- *Respect for Authority:* Jehovah's Witnesses believe that it is their Christian responsibility to be model citizens. For this reason, they honor and respect governmental authority. Only on those rare occasions when a government demands what is in direct conflict with what God commands do Jehovah's Witnesses decline to comply.

CURRENT DEMOGRAPHICS

The thirty-five thousand Jehovah's Witnesses in Ohio meet for worship and study at Kingdom Halls throughout the state. Congregations are located in large metropolitan areas such as Cincinnati (twenty-seven congregations), Cleveland (fifty), Columbus (twenty-six), Dayton (eighteen), and Toledo (thirteen), as well as in rural areas of the state, and total 369.

CONTACT INFORMATION

Official website of Jehovah's Witnesses: *www.watchtower.org*

Jehovah's Witnesses Assembly Hall, 38025 Vine Street, Willoughby, Ohio 44094, 440-942-3166.

RESOURCES

Jehovah's Witnesses—Proclaimers of God's Kingdom. Brooklyn: Watch Tower Bible and Tract Society of New York, Inc., 1993.

Jehovah's Witnesses Stand Firm against Nazi Assault (video). Brooklyn: Watch Tower Bible and Tract Society of New York, Inc., 1996.

Jehovah's Witnesses—The Organization behind the Name (video). Brooklyn: Watch Tower Bible and Tract Society of New York, Inc., 1990.

Peters, Shawn Francis. *Judging Jehovah's Witnesses—Religious Persecution and the Dawn of the Rights Revolution.* Lawrence: University Press of Kansas, 2000.

Latter-day Saints

COMMUNITY OF CHRIST (FORMERLY REORGANIZED CHURCH OF JESUS CHRIST OF LATTER DAY SAINTS)

Lachlan Mackay

HISTORY

THE COMMUNITY OF CHRIST TRACES ITS ORIGINS TO JOSEPH SMITH Jr. As a young person in western New York State, Smith was a seeker. His study of scripture and his encounters with other Christians awakened in him a desire to find God's love and guidance for his own life. His search eventually led to the publication of the Book of Mormon as an additional witness that Jesus is the Christ and to the founding of the "Church of Christ" on April 6, 1830.

Hoping to share the Book of Mormon with the Native Americans, Joseph Smith soon sent missionaries toward what is now the state of Kansas. One of the missionaries, Parley P. Pratt, persuaded his traveling companions to stop in northeastern Ohio to preach to his former spiritual mentor, Sidney Rigdon. Like Smith, Rigdon was a "restorationist."

He was inspired by the way this movement wanted to listen to and be led by the example of Jesus Christ and to emulate in particular the way the first Christians lived and died. Rigdon had attracted many followers throughout Ohio's Western Reserve. In fall 1830 the Church of Christ missionaries converted him and many of his followers. There were soon more members in Ohio than there were in New York. Joseph Smith and his wife, Emma, moved to Kirtland, Ohio, early in 1831.

A church community was soon established in Independence, Missouri, as well. Members were encouraged to "gather," or move, to one of the communities. The membership in northeastern Ohio grew rapidly, and in 1833 construction began on a temple to be used for worship and education.

Built of rough sandstone covered with stucco, the temple still stands. It is more than one hundred feet tall and has three floors. Distinctive design features include two large assembly rooms with tiers of elaborately carved pulpits at both ends and windows in every interior and exterior wall. When finished, the temple served as the center of community life for the thousands of members who came to live in and around Kirtland. Members and friends gathered on the first floor to worship on Sundays and Thursdays. The second floor was devoted to church leadership education and training. The third floor housed schoolrooms and administrative offices.

According to a local minister of that time, life for many members was difficult. They lived in what he described as an "assemblage of hovels and shanties and small houses." They overcame their hardships through great sacrifice, with some giving up "even the necessaries of life" in order to build what was then one of the largest buildings in northern Ohio ("Truman Coe's 1836 Description of Mormonism," ed. Milton V. Backman, Jr., *BYU Studies* 17 [spring 1977]: 352; text also at http://www.boap.org/LDS/Early-Saints/Coe.html).

In an attempt to build up the economy of Kirtland, church members opened a bank in 1837. However, the state legislature refused to recognize the bank, and it soon failed. The resulting financial problems led to lawsuits against Joseph Smith and others. Many members openly criticized church leaders, and some left the faith. The church community in Kirtland began to break apart. Smith and his family moved to Missouri in 1838, and most members followed.

Kirtland Temple, circa 1900. Construction of the temple began in 1833, and it was completed and dedicated in 1836. (Courtesy of Community of Christ)

To reflect the increasing emphasis on the belief that the 1830s were the latter days and that Jesus Christ would soon return to earth, the Church of Christ had in 1834 changed its name to the Church of the Latter Day Saints; in 1838 it became the Church of Jesus Christ of Latter-day Saints. Also in that year, the Ohio and Missouri church communities came together for the first time. A short stay in northern Missouri led to a clash of cultures between the church and the surrounding community that resulted in the Latter-day Saints being driven from the state. They established Nauvoo, Illinois, which soon grew into one of the largest cities in the state. Political, economic, and religious issues again led to problems with their neighbors. In 1844 the church founder, Joseph Smith, was killed by a mob in Carthage, Illinois.

With his death, the church fragmented. Some of those who chose to stay in the Midwest reorganized in 1860 under the leadership of Joseph Smith III, son of the founder. That same year members were once again worshiping in Kirtland Temple. Missionaries returned to Ohio to find members of the early church and to share their message with other potential converts. By the early 1870s these Midwesterners renamed themselves the Reorganized Church of Jesus Christ of Latter Day Saints to differentiate their church from others which shared the heritage. The temple was restored during the early 1880s so that it could be used to hold general church conferences. Family camps were held at the temple during the first half of the twentieth century. Members from Ohio and surrounding states gathered together annually for a week filled with worship and fellowship.

Declared a National Historic Landmark in 1977, Kirtland Temple is used for spiritual retreats and other special services and classes through-out the year. It symbolizes the empowerment that comes from spiritual preparation and dedicated stewardship while inspiring continuing efforts to build up the communities in which we live.

BELIEFS

Our mission is to proclaim Jesus Christ and promote communities of joy, hope, love, and peace. The church has no official creed that must be accepted by all members. However, the following statements, adapted from a publication titled "Faith & Beliefs," reflect the generally accepted beliefs of the church. The one eternal, living God is triune: one God in three persons. God is the Eternal Creator, the source of love, life, and truth. Jesus Christ is "God with us," the Son of God, and the living expression of God in the flesh. Jesus Christ lived, was crucified, died, and rose again. The Holy Spirit is the continuing presence of God in the world.

Through the ministry of Christ and the presence of the Holy Spirit, we are able to turn to God and to receive the gifts of salvation and eternal life. Those who accept the Gospel are called to respond to Christ through baptism and committed discipleship. Christian discipleship is most fully possible when it is pursued in a community of committed believers. The church, as part of the body of Christ, is the means through which the ministry of Christ continues in the world today.

The process through which God reveals divine will and love is called revelation. God continues to reveal today as in the past. God is revealed to us through scripture, the faith community, prayer, nature, and in human history. The scriptures provide divine guidance and inspired insight for life when responsibly interpreted and faithfully applied. With other Christians, we affirm the Bible as scripture for the church. In our tradition, the Book of Mormon and the Doctrine and Covenants are additional scriptural witnesses of God's love and Christ's ministry. God loves each of us equally and unconditionally. All persons have great worth and should be respected as creations of God with basic human rights. All men, women, youth, and children are given gifts and abilities to enhance life and to become involved in Christ's mission. Some men and women are called to particular responsibility as ordained ministers (priesthood) in the church. Because of our commitment to Christ and belief in the worth of all people and the value of community building, we dedicate our lives to the pursuit of peace and justice for all people.

CURRENT DEMOGRAPHICS

In an effort to more adequately express our mission, the Reorganized Church of Jesus Christ of Latter Day Saints took on a new name, Community of Christ, on April 6, 2001. The denomination, headquartered in Independence, Missouri, has about 250,000 members in fifty countries. Ohio is home to sixty-four hundred members of the Community of Christ who worship in more than thirty-five congregations. The membership is distributed fairly evenly throughout the state, with slightly larger concentrations in northeast and central Ohio.

CONTACT INFORMATION

For more information about the history or beliefs of the Community of Christ, please write to Kirtland Temple, 9020 Chillicothe Road, Kirtland, Ohio 44094, call 440-256-3318, or visit *www.kirtlandtemple.org*
Community of Christ official homepage: *www.cofchrist.org*

RESOURCES

Bolton, Andrew, and Anthony Chvala-Smith. *Seekers and Disciples.* Independence, Mo.: Herald Publishing House, 2001.
Edwards, Paul M. *Our Legacy of Faith: A Brief History of the Reorganized Church of Jesus Christ of Latter Day Saints.* Independence, Mo.: Herald Publishing House, 1991.

THE CHURCH OF JESUS CHRIST OF LATTER-DAY SAINTS

Ernie J. Shannon

HISTORY

WITH NEARLY 12 MILLION MEMBERS, SIXTY-FIVE THOUSAND missionaries, three universities, and countless chapels, temples, and other structures, the Church of Jesus Christ of Latter-day Saints spreads its influence into every state and virtually every region of the world today. Add to those figures approximately three hundred thousand new members annually, and the church is counted as one of the fastest-growing religions in the world. Yet this worldwide organization with congregations from Tokyo to Johannesburg traces its earliest expansion from a small, relatively unknown community in northeastern Ohio.

In 1831, Joseph Smith, considered by church members to be a prophet of God and the founder of the church, moved from upstate New York to Kirtland, Ohio, with several hundred others. Composed primarily of New York residents at the outset, the growing church soon baptized large numbers of Ohio settlers, and by 1838 congregations had been established throughout Ohio. At first, church members were received peacefully in the Kirtland region, but as the church's membership grew dramatically, longtime residents of the area began to fear the economic and political might of the church.

As the church grew, Joseph Smith received a commandment from God instructing the church to begin the seemingly impossible feat of building the Kirtland Temple—a modern "house of God." Construction of the temple, the main priority of the church between 1833 and 1836, presented huge challenges for the members, who lacked both manpower and money. Neither the church nor its poverty-stricken members had ever undertaken such a task. Fifty thousand dollars, the estimated cost of the building, was a staggering sum in the 1830s. Church members also faced opposition from the community. Nevertheless, on June 5, 1833, ground was broken for the temple, and three years later, on March 27, 1836, the Kirtland Temple was dedicated.

In 1837–38, the final years of the church in Kirtland, dissension and persecution engulfed the members. As violence escalated, it became unsafe for them to remain in Kirtland. The prophet was warned and decided to move immediately to Missouri. Most of the membership followed. In the first seven months of 1838, more than sixteen hundred members of the church left the city and headed west, most to Far West, Missouri. By 1839, only about a hundred church members remained in Kirtland. However, peace would elude church members for another eight years. Violence forced the church to move from Missouri to Illinois, where the city of Nauvoo became the headquarters from 1839 to 1840. Finally, when Illinois mobs killed Joseph Smith and his brother and injured others over many months of persecution, the Lord led his church west to the Salt Lake Valley in Utah in the summer of 1847. There members found peace at last.

By the 1870s, the church had reached a level of stability in Utah that allowed ever-increasing numbers of missionaries to be sent eastward to reestablish small branches in Ohio and elsewhere. During the next seventy-five years these branches grew slowly due to the depression and two world wars. However, by the 1950s Americans were enjoying sufficient peace and prosperity to allow the church to more firmly establish its presence in Ohio. One of the ways in which the church secured its presence in Ohio in the mid- to late 1950s was to organize what is called a "stake." Stakes include from three to five thousand members and are subdivided into congregations, otherwise known as wards, numbering approximately five hundred members each. Stakes are, in large part, self-sufficient and are able to provide for both the spiritual and the physical needs of their members. The first such stake in Ohio was organized in Cincinnati in 1958.

During the period from 1958 to 1986, the Church of Jesus Christ of Latter-day Saints experienced tremendous growth in Ohio with the creation of nine stakes and the construction of church buildings throughout the state. However, an even more significant event occurred as the twentieth century closed: the construction of another sacred temple. Modern temples, however, differ from the Kirtland structure in that today sacred ordinances are performed. These include sealing couples together in marriage for eternity rather than until death, sealing children to their parents for eternity so that families can be together forever, and conducting baptisms for the dead, in which the departed are baptized by proxy (a living relative or descendant is baptized in their stead). For these and other reasons, temples are considered sacred to members of the church.

In April 1998 church president Gordon B. Hinckley traveled to Ohio's capital and announced before a congregation of more than seven thousand that the church would build a new temple in Columbus. Construction began in September 1998 and was completed one year later. President Hinckley returned to Columbus for the 1999 dedication and promised church members that the temple would be a place of peace, of refuge from the pressures of the world, and of love where the Lord's spirit would be felt in great abundance. Today, the church stands complete in its organization in Ohio. Through 170 years of work and sacrifice, the church in Ohio has built temples and chapels, educational programs, and storehouses of food, clothing, and other goods for people in need. More importantly, however, the church has striven to make good people better, strengthen families in the midst of challenges, and serve people of all walks of life much as the Savior did during his mortal ministry. As a result, in the year 2002, nearly fifty thousand Ohioans call themselves members of the Church of Jesus Christ of Latter-day Saints.

BELIEFS

Following is a list of thirteen articles of faith originally penned by the church's first prophet, Joseph Smith, in response to a question posed by a newspaper reporter.

1. We believe in God the Eternal Father, and in His Son, Jesus Christ, and in the Holy Ghost.

The Columbus Ohio Temple (1999) features interior double doors that echo the Kirtland Temple's "Window Beautiful." Inside, Church members continue to worship and make covenants. (Courtesy of The Church of Jesus Christ of Latter-day Saints)

2. We believe that men will be punished for their own sin, and not for Adam's transgression.

3. We believe that through the Atonement of Christ, all mankind may be saved, by obedience to the laws and ordinances of the Gospel.

4. We believe that the first principles and ordinances of the Gospel are: first, faith in the Lord Jesus Christ; second, repentance; third, baptism by immersion for the remission of sins; fourth, laying on of hand for the gift of the Holy Ghost.

5. We believe that a man must be called of God by prophecy, and by the laying on of hands by those who are in authority, to preach the Gospel and administer in the ordinances thereof.

6. We believe in the same organization that existed in the primitive church, namely, apostles, prophets, pastors, teachers, evangelists, and so forth.

7. We believe in the gift of tongues, prophecy, revelation, visions, healing, interpretation of tongues, and so forth.

8. We believe the Bible to be the word of God as far as it is translated correctly; we also believe the Book of Mormon to be the word of God.

9. We believe all that God has revealed, all that He does now reveal, and we believe that He will yet reveal many great and important things pertaining to the Kingdom of God.

10. We believe in the literal gathering of Israel and in the restoration of the Ten Tribes; that Zion (the New Jerusalem) will be built upon this the American continent; that Christ will reign personally upon the earth; and, that the earth will be renewed and receive its paradisiacal glory.

11. We claim the privilege of worshiping Almighty God according to the dictates of our own conscience, and allow all men the same privilege, let them worship how, where, or what they may.

12. We believe in being subject to kings, presidents, rulers, and magistrates, in obeying, honoring, and sustaining the law.

13. We believe in being honest, true, chaste, benevolent, virtuous, and in doing good to all men; indeed, we may say that we follow the admonition of Paul—We believe all things, we hope all things, we have endured many things, and hope to be able to endure all things. If there is anything virtuous, lovely, or of good report or praiseworthy, we seek after these things.

CURRENT DEMOGRAPHICS

Ohio members: 49,000
Number of congregations in Ohio: 109

CONTACT INFORMATION

The Church of Jesus Christ of Latter-day Saints, 50 East North Temple Street, Salt Lake City, Utah 84150, 801-240-1000.

RESOURCES

Kimball, Spencer W. *Miracles of Forgiveness.* Salt Lake City: Deseret Book Company, 1956.

Richards, LeGrand. *A Marvelous Work and a Wonder.* Salt Lake City: Deseret Book Company, 1990.

Talmage, James E. *Jesus the Christ: A Study of the Messiah and His Mission According to Holy Scriptures, both Ancient and Modern.* Salt Lake City: The Deseret News, 1916.

———. *The Articles of Faith: A Series of Lectures on the Principal Doctrines of the Church of Jesus Christ of Latter-Day Saints.* Salt Lake City: The Deseret News, 1919.

Lutheran

Paul F. H. Reichert II

HISTORY

HAVING BEGUN IN 1517 AS A REFORM MOVEMENT WITHIN THE Roman Catholic Church in Germany spearheaded by Martin Luther, Lutheranism spread throughout northern Europe and into Scandinavia, eventually forming a separate "Protestant" denomination. The first Lutheran settlers from these areas and from the eastern United States brought their faith to Ohio. Lutherans arrived without pastors. They placed a high value on educated, properly ordained clergy, so they had to rely on traveling pastors from Pennsylvania or clergy of other denominations who were willing to lead their services. By 1805, three Lutheran clergymen, John Stauch, George William Forster, and Paul Heckel, had moved to Ohio and were serving the surrounding communities.

Organization of the Ohio Synod

The number of Lutherans continued to grow as more people of German and Scandinavian heritage made Ohio their home. As they grew, Lutheran congregations began to look forward to organizing themselves into administrative structures familiar to them from Europe and the eastern states. These were conferences, ministeriums, and synods, which were groups of congregations organized around common theological beliefs and usually geographical proximity (sometimes congregations would for

Sketch of an early group of Lutherans in Marietta being served by the first episcopal rector there in the "greenwood" place of worship. Date and artist unknown. (From *Churches in the Buckeye Country,* 1953; reprinted by permission of St.
Luke's Lutheran Church, Marietta, Ohio)

theological reasons opt to affiliate with a synod located in a different
area). Soon the Lutheran Church in Ohio was large enough to run its
own affairs rather than be a missionary outpost of the much older Pennsylvania Ministerium. This began in 1812 with the formation of the Western Conference as a subgroup within the Pennsylvania Ministerium. In
1814 the Ohio Conference gained the right to choose ministers for its
sixty congregations. In 1818 four pastors and six candidates met in Somerset, Ohio, and formed the Ohio Synod, which was still connected to the
Pennsylvania Ministerium by theological perspective, practice, and heritage. While the Ohio Synod continued to grow, including the creation
of Trinity Lutheran Seminary in Columbus in 1830, new conferences and
synods began to form as differences in theology and language motivated
people to create independent groups. Other synods were formed by new
immigrants from Europe, as was the case of the Missouri Synod. Though
Lutherans have a common set of confessional documents, different nu-
ances in understanding have often kept us apart.

Formation of the German Evangelical Lutheran Synod of Missouri, Ohio, and Other States

In 1838 a German Lutheran clergyman named Friedrich C. D. Wyneken made a preaching tour in Ohio, beginning near Wapakoneta. He then returned to Germany and inspired Lutherans there with the potential for the Good News of Jesus Christ in the "new world." This and other factors spurred a group of seven hundred from Saxony to move to St. Louis. Led by C. F. W. Walther, they were soon connected with the Ohio German Lutheran congregations Wyneken had met. When in 1845 the Saxon group was invited to join one of the western synods, author E. Clifford Nelson notes that they were concerned about the expanded use of English rather than German in worship and in the seminary in Columbus, the increasing Americanization of the Lutheran Church in the Midwest, and the change in confessional standards (*The Lutherans in North America*). Instead, together with several Ohio congregations, they in 1847 constituted the German Evangelical Lutheran Synod of Missouri, Ohio, and Other States.

Formation of the German Evangelical Ministerium of Wisconsin

The story of the Wisconsin Synod is similar to that of the Missouri Synod. In 1850 a group of congregations led by three clergymen, Muelhlhaeuser, Weinmann, and Wrede, constituted the German Evangelical Ministerium of Wisconsin. This group began in Wisconsin, but soon grew to include congregations in Minnesota, Michigan, and Ohio.

Lutherans Join Together

Most Lutherans have seen themselves as a part of something far larger than a single congregation. They were a part of a ministerium, a conference, a synod, a national church body. Over the years, congregations joined and left synods, and new synods formed along ethnic, linguistic, theological, or geographic lines. In the early 1900s Lutheran synods began to merge. By 1988 the majority of Lutherans in Ohio belonged to one of three national Lutheran church bodies: the Evangelical Lutheran Church in America (ELCA), the Lutheran Church–Missouri Synod (LCMS), or the Wisconsin Evangelical Lutheran Synod (WELS).

The Switch to English

Lutherans began their worship in Ohio in their native languages, primarily German but also Norwegian, Swedish, Finnish, Hungarian, and various Slavic languages. As the number of Lutherans continued to grow, and as they began to transform from European Lutherans living in Ohio into Ohio Lutherans, English was becoming the language of daily life. The younger generation's desire to make the language of worship contemporary and the older generation's desire to keep worship authentically Lutheran created a tense situation. Some congregations became English speaking in worship, and today one can find Lutheran congregations named "First English" in many communities. Other congregations continued in German or their own native language.

More Lutheran churches were established in cities as the populations moved from rural areas, and the pressure toward English grew. However, nothing changed Ohio Lutheranism as profoundly as World War I. Overnight, Lutherans went from being valued members of society to being potential enemies. All Lutherans were presumed guilty because of their association with German speakers. Church buildings were vandalized, and Lutherans faced many personal attacks. Lutherans responded by dramatically increasing their support of the war effort and rapidly transitioning to the use of English in most congregations. This change dramatically reduced the enmity against Lutherans, and the widespread use of English opened an opportunity for unity in worship that before had existed only in social-service projects.

Social Service

After their commitment to word and sacrament (see below), Lutherans have few expressions of faith they value more highly than social service. Ohio Lutherans have been involved in social service projects since our state's beginning. Lutherans, often LCMS and ELCA jointly, continue to serve Ohioans through Lutheran Social Services; campus ministries; camps; schools; homes for youth, the disabled, and the aged; and a host of other ministries. Serving together to share the Gospel of Jesus Christ through word and deed will continue to be a focus not only in our home state but also throughout our nation and our world.

BELIEFS

Lutheranism is a Christian denomination based not on structure or worship style but on confessions and theology. Lutherans are joined by a common way of viewing the Bible and Christianity through the lens of our confessional documents, which are gathered in *The Book of Concord*. This book contains the Apostles', Nicene, and Athanasian Creeds, as well as a number of writings by Martin Luther and Philip Melanchthon, including the Small Catechism, which sets out several tenets of the faith that Christians should know. Another document in *The Book of Concord* is the Augsburg Confession (1530), article VII of which states, "It is sufficient for the true unity of the Christian church that the Gospel be preached in conformity with a pure understanding of it and that the sacraments be administered in accordance with the divine word."

So Lutherans value word and sacrament. By *word*, Lutherans mean the word of God—the Bible—particularly the *law*—the disciplining, sin-revealing, life-directing—and the *gospel*—the Good News of Jesus Christ and his salvation. Lutherans believe there are two special ways, called *sacraments*, in which God shows signs of unmerited love and favor. The two Lutheran sacraments are Holy Baptism and Holy Communion. Lutherans welcome infants, children, and adults to the waters of baptism. Since baptism is understood to be God's action, forgiving sins and making one part of the community of faith, the amount of water is not prescribed and varies from sprinkling to immersion. Holy Communion is shared in both kinds, that is, bread and wine. The Lutheran understanding of Holy Communion is in the middle of the Christian spectrum of miracle to memorial. Lutherans believe that Christ's body and blood are "truly present" in the bread and wine. The phrase Luther used to describe this understanding was "in, with, and under." The sacraments are celebrated by everyone, usually in a worship setting rather than privately. Lutherans understand Christians to be a part of the priesthood of all believers. This means no one occupation, including that of pastor, is holier than another; all Christians are part of the Kingdom of God. If one had to point out the principal gift of Lutherans to the Christian church, it would be the focus on "justification by grace through faith." Lutherans believe we are set into a right relationship with God through Jesus Christ —his life, death, and resurrection—and not through any work of our own.

CURRENT DEMOGRAPHICS

You do not need to look very far to find a Lutheran church in Ohio. Most Lutherans in Ohio today are part of a national Lutheran body. Currently these number from around half a million (WELS) to 2.5 million (LCMS) to around 5 million (ELCA) nationally. All told, there are nearly four hundred thousand baptized Ohio Lutherans in more than 835 congregations. From congregations with fewer than twenty members to those with more than a thousand, from rural to urban, from brand-new congregations to those which trace their history back to the early 1800s, Lutherans are well represented throughout Ohio.

CONTACT INFORMATION

Evangelical Lutheran Church in America: *www.elca.org*

Lutheran Church Missouri Synod: *www.lcms.org*

Wisconsin Evangelical Lutheran Synod: *www.wels.org*

Ohio District (LCMS), P.O. Box 38277, Olmstead Falls, Ohio 44138–0277, 440-235-2297, *www.oh.lcms.org*

Northeastern Ohio Synod (ELCA), 1890 Bailey Road, Cuyahoga Falls, Ohio 44221–5259, 330-929-9022, *www.neos-elca.org*

Northwestern Ohio Synod (ELCA), 621 Bright Road, Findlay, Ohio 45840–6940, 419-423-3664, *www.nwos-elca.org*

Southern Ohio Synod (ELCA), 300 South Second Street, Columbus, Ohio 43215–5001, 614-464-3532, *www.southernohiosynod.org*

RESOURCES

Nelson, E. Clifford, ed. *The Lutherans in North America.* Rev. ed. Philadelphia: Fortress Press, 1980.

Tappert, Theodore, ed. and trans. *The Book of Concord: The Confessions of the Evangelical Lutheran Church.* Philadelphia: Fortress Press, 1959.

Methodist

UNITED METHODIST

Marvin D. Bean and L. Cean Wilson

HISTORY

F UELED BY THEIR ZEAL TO "SAVE SOULS" AND "SPREAD SCRIPTURAL holiness across the land" the Methodists moved from the East Coast westward with the frontier into the Northwest Territory, which would one day include the state of Ohio. The earliest recorded preaching by a Methodist in northeast Ohio was by circuit rider George Callahan in 1787. Another of the first Methodist circuit riders, John Kobler, was appointed by the first bishop in the United States, Francis Asbury, to southwestern Ohio on August 1, 1798. Kobler was known as "the man of the long road" for his many sacrifices on behalf of the Gospel of Jesus Christ. That Christmas (1798), the first quarterly conference was held in the Northwest Territory; the first-ever official report from an Ohio Methodist congregation, made to the 1799 Methodist General Conference, listed "ninety eight white and one colored member."

In those early days and continuing today, much preaching and teaching occurred in homes of Methodists. The first Methodist Meeting House was at Hopewell, in what is now Jefferson County, in 1798. In this place Bishop Asbury ordained Rev. John Wrinshall on September 10, 1803, and consecrated the building the following day. A second church,

Salem/Moore's Chapel is one of the oldest Methodist churches in Ohio and one of the first Methodist church buildings in the Northwest Territory. Salem/Moore's Chapel was dedicated in 1800 and is located in Adams County, twenty miles west of Portsmouth. (Courtesy of Sam Fillmore)

Salem Chapel, was begun in August 1799 and dedicated a year later. It was located in what is now Adams County, twenty miles west of Portsmouth. In 1880, the chapel was rebuilt on the same sacred ground and renamed Moore's Chapel, for Rev. Joseph Moore, who had built Salem Chapel. An authentic reconstruction, rededicated in 1976, exists today on the original site. The decoration of the simple cabin-style building includes stained-glass windows and interior painting of brown pastel fern leaves and an open Bible above the chancel. Famous pioneer preachers at the chapel included Philip Gatch, Peter Cartwright, James B. Finley, and Edward Tiffin, later elected the first governor of Ohio.

John Stewart, described as a "wandering, drunken mongrel," was converted through the witness of Methodists in Marietta. His passion was ministry among the Wyandotte Indians near Upper Sandusky; many were converted. A memorial chapel with Native American artifacts and a detailed history is located in the town cemetery of Upper Sandusky.

The General Conference of 1812 divided the Western Conference into the Tennessee and Ohio Conferences. The first session of the Ohio Conference was held October 1, 1812, in Chillicothe, with sixty-one traveling preachers in attendance, 23,644 members reported, and six districts spread across Ohio, Kentucky, portions of Indiana, and northwestern Pennsylvania.

By the time of the Civil War, the cities of Portsmouth, Ironton, Cincinnati, Dayton, and Middletown had grown along the Ohio and Great Miami Rivers. Methodism also grew in these emerging industrial centers, with downtown churches named Main Street, Market Street, and First Methodist. A significant part of Methodism in some of these cities was among the German-speaking immigrant population.

Schisms, unions, reunions, and mergers occurred in the Methodist family over the years. The Methodist Protestants pulled away in the early 1800s over issues of episcopal authority and lay representation. In 1844 the Methodists split into the Methodist Episcopal Church and the Methodist Episcopal Church, South because of disagreements over slavery. The Ohio River was the official dividing line between them, but Ohio Methodist churches in the river cities could choose which faction to follow. It was a heart-rending time for the denomination.

In 1939, with the Civil War long behind them, the Methodist Episcopal Church, the Methodist Episcopal Church, South, and the Methodist Protestants were reunited to form the Methodist Church. In 1964 the segregated African American Lexington Methodist Conference merged with the Methodist conferences, putting an end to the racial separation compromise that had allowed the 1939 reunion to take place between the northern and southern Methodists. The merger of the Methodist Church and the Evangelical United Brethren Church in 1968 united Christians with deep Wesleyan roots and long histories of similar faith and practice. The new church was today's United Methodist Church. The United Methodist Church in Ohio comprises the East Ohio Conference and the West Ohio Conference, each of which has a bishop and separate organizational structure and governance.

Historically, the Methodist family has shared a vision for humanity and its needs, resulting in the following priorities:

- Mission at home and abroad through preaching, teaching, farming, and medicine;
- Health care, including the establishment of hospitals and clinics all over the world (including Ohio Health and Flower, Bethesda, and Christ Hospitals in Ohio);

- Wholeness and quality of life for older adults in retirement communities (including Wesley Glen, Otterbein Homes, Hill View, Mary Scott, and Twin Towers in Ohio);
- Higher education through colleges, universities, and seminaries (including Otterbein College, Ohio Wesleyan University, and Methodist Theological School in Ohio);
- Diversity and inclusiveness, especially encouraging minorities and women to assume leadership positions as both lay people and clergy. The Methodist Protestants began ordaining women in 1880, thirty-nine years before women could vote and seventy-six years before the Methodist Church would ordain women. The first woman bishop in the United Methodist Church and perhaps all of Christendom, Marjorie Swank Matthews, was elected in Dayton in 1980.

BELIEFS

In the words of the founder, John Wesley (1703–91), "A Methodist is . . . one who loves the Lord his God with all his heart, with all his soul, with all his mind, and with all his strength." Wesley believed that people are saved by grace through faith alone—according to Romans 5—and that good works and striving toward perfection should naturally follow.

The United Methodist Church is grounded in the life, death, and resurrection of Jesus Christ. Truth and guidance are discerned through a reflective study of Scripture, tradition, reason, and experience, rather than through confessional doctrine. The United Methodist is distinguished by a commitment to the basics of Christianity and by a Christian lifestyle instead of by adherence to a particular set of beliefs. United Methodists share a common heritage with other Christians, including:

- Conviction that God has mercy and love for all people and creation
- Belief in the triune nature of God
- Faith in the mystery of salvation through Jesus Christ
- Celebration of the sacraments of baptism and communion (Eucharist, Last Supper)

Traditional and contemporary Methodists affirm the primacy of the grace of God through Jesus Christ; holiness, both personal and social; the worth of all persons; the possibility of conversion and new birth; the pre-venient grace of invitation; welcome and urging; and tolerance of different points of view. "Though we cannot think alike, may we not love alike? May we not be of one heart, though we are not of one opinion? Without all doubt, we may" (John Wesley, *Catholic Spirit*, 1872; text at http://umaffirm.org/cornet/catholic.html#oneheart).

CURRENT DEMOGRAPHICS

Ohio Membership:

East Ohio Conference	190,000
West Ohio Conference	264,209
Total	454,209

There are more United Methodist Churches in Ohio than there are post offices! The vast majority of churches own a parsonage where the appointed minister lives. Providing housing makes it easier to maintain a United Methodist presence in every city, town, and rural area.

CONTACT INFORMATION

East Ohio Conference, 8800 Cleveland Avenue NW, North Canton, Ohio 44720, 800-831-3972, 330-499-3972, *www.eocumc.com*

West Ohio Conference, 32 Wesley Boulevard, Worthington, Ohio 43085, 800-437-0028, 614-844-6200, *www.westohioumc.org*

Archives of Ohio United Methodism, Ohio Wesleyan University, Beeghly Library, 740-368-3285, *aoum@owu.edu*

RESOURCES

Barker, John Marshall. *History of Ohio Methodism.* Cincinnati: Curts & Jennings, 1898.

Gaston, Fred, and Alice Cromwell. *Journey: Streams of Faith.* Acton, Mass.: Tapestry Press, 1995.

Leedy, Roy B. *The Evangelical Church in Ohio: Being a History of the Ohio Conference and Merged Conferences of the Evangelical Church in Ohio, Now the Evangelical United Brethren Church, 1816–1951*. Cleveland: Ohio Conference of the Evangelical United Brethren Church, 1959.

Versteeg, John. *Methodism: Ohio Area (1812–1962)*. Cincinnati: Ohio Area Sesquicentennial Committee, 1962.

Whitlock, Elias, Nathaniel B. C. Love, and Elwood O. Crist. *History of the Central Ohio Conference: 1856–1913*. Cincinnati: Press of the Methodist Book Concern, 1914.

AFRICAN METHODIST EPISCOPAL

Earl G. Harris

HISTORY

THE AFRICAN METHODIST EPISCOPAL CHURCH IS PART OF THE Methodist family of churches, which marked its American beginning in the gathering of Wesleyan Methodists in Baltimore on December 24, 1784. Richard Allen, a former slave, was an observer at that initial gathering of Methodists. He would three years later lead a group of black Methodists out of St. George's Methodist Episcopal Church in Philadelphia to protest the insulting and degrading treatment they had received at the hands of white Methodists. The exodus of black Methodists was the sociological response to the theological issue of racism. They understood that the attitudes and actions of their white brethren did not conform to Scripture. In the Acts of the Apostles, chapter 10, Peter addresses the racism of his Jewish brethren: "I now realize how true it is that God does not show favoritism but accepts men from every nation who fear him and do what is right" (Acts 10:34–5 NIV).

African Methodists founded their church in the year 1787, however, formal recognition of their independence would not come until 1815. In 1816 the compact between the Philadelphia, Baltimore, and Delaware African Methodist churches was established, and Richard Allen was consecrated as the first bishop.

From its inception, the African Methodist Episcopal (AME) Church fanned out in all directions. The westward expansion of the AME Church is due in large part to the work and genius of William Paul Quinn, who was just ten years old when the AME Church was organized in 1816. It is William Quinn who would be credited with the establishment of forty-seven congregations and fifty Sunday schools with a combined membership of more than two thousand souls stretching from Pittsburgh, Pennsylvania, to California.

The AME Church would officially enter the state of Ohio in the early 1820s. The earliest Ohio congregations (c. 1824) would be found at Chillicothe (Quinn Chapel), Columbus (St. Paul), Cincinnati (Allen Temple), and Cleveland (St. John). All of these congregations are still in operation today. The Ohio Annual Conference was organized in 1830 to oversee the development of missionary work "west of Ohio." The work and witness of William Paul Quinn, who would be elected bishop in 1844, is all the more significant when viewed against the backdrop of "black laws" adopted in the state of Ohio. Although Ohio was a *free state,* Ohio enacted laws that discouraged the immigration and settlement of blacks within its boundaries.

Howard D. Gregg, in his *History of the African Methodist Episcopal Church,* observed that the Ohio Annual Conference was the first to advance the subject of "organized education." As a result, an educational conference was convened in 1845 that would lead to the church's first venture into higher education. In 1856 Wilberforce University was established on a one-hundred-fifty-two-acre track of land in Greene County near Xenia. Richard Allen and most of his colleagues were not educated men and women. In fact there was some real resistance to the notion of an educated clergy for the AME Church. However, it would be Daniel Alexander Payne who would be the guiding force, not only for the founding of Wilberforce, but also in the political effort which insisted on an educated clergy. In 1844 the Ohio Annual Conference would fail in its attempt to establish Union Theological Seminary near Columbus. Yet, it would be out of those ashes that the AME Church would in 1894 establish, Payne Theological Seminary, named in honor of the father of education, Bishop Daniel Alexander Payne. Wilberforce and Payne would be, respectively, the first of nine colleges and universities and the first of five theological seminaries established by Methodists in Ohio. Collectively the colleges, universities, and seminaries in Ohio and throughout the country would represent the efforts of an oppressed people to train and educate themselves.

Wilberforce University was founded in 1856 by the African Methodist Episcopal Church near Xenia in Greene County. Wilberforce is the first institution of higher education in America established and operated by African Americans. (Courtesy of the Ohio Historical Society)

For 216 years the AME Church has been the spiritual home and platform of some prominent African Americans who have had a profound impact upon the country. Among the notables are Fredrick Douglass, nineteenth-century abolitionist; Hiram Revels, first black to serve in the U.S. Congress (during Reconstruction); Rosa Parks, mother of the modern civil rights movement; and Floyd Flake, former U.S. Congressman and the current president of Wilberforce University. Some notable Ohioans on that list would include Paul Laurence Dunbar, poet (Wayman Chapel, Dayton); Perry B. Jackson, first common pleas court judge (St. John, Cleveland); William McClain, common pleas judge (Allen Temple, Cincinnati); Charity Adams Earley (Col. Ret.), highest ranking commissioned WAC officer serving in a combat theater in World War II (Greater Allen, Dayton), and Kathleen Battle, international opera star (Allen Chapel, Portsmouth). These are some of the personalities who have been and continue to be part of the fabric of the African Methodist Episcopal Church.

BELIEFS

Two historic documents, the Apostles' Creed and the twenty-five Methodist Articles of Religion frame the faith and witness of the African Methodist Episcopal Church.

The Apostles' Creed is used as a confessional in our worship services today. The Apostles' Creed is that single statement of faith to which many Christian traditions subscribe and by which they declare themselves Christian. In the Apostles' Creed one finds Christian declarations about God, Jesus Christ, and the Holy Spirit. The creed speaks of the virgin birth of Jesus, his suffering, his death and resurrection, and our hope of his second coming. In the Apostles' Creed, African Methodism shares a common confession with all Christians.

The second historic document to which the African Methodist Church subscribes is the twenty-five Articles of Religion. The Articles of Religion of the AME Church are drawn from the thirty-nine Articles of Religion of the Church of England. These doctrinal statements of faith would define the Protestant movement and thereby separate those who accepted them from Roman Catholicism and the Anabaptists of the sixteenth century.

The twenty-five Methodist Articles of Religion define seven areas of doctrinal difference in terms of what Methodists believe about God, scripture and sin, justification and works, the sacraments, rites, and rituals, and about the church as it relates to community and country.

It is these two historic documents that inform the faith and polity of the African Methodist Episcopal Church and give rise to the church's motto, "God our Father, Christ our Redeemer, Man our Brother." The third part of this motto is the most startling and striking. For a people whose history is born of slavery and oppression to have a theology absent of malice which declares that those who have enslaved and oppressed them are, in fact, their brothers and sisters is a statement surpassed only by Jesus' words from the cross: "Father forgive them for they know not what they do."

CURRENT DEMOGRAPHICS

Today in Ohio there are 115 AME congregations with twenty thousand members.

CONTACT INFORMATION

The African Methodist Episcopal Church national website: *www.amecnet.org*

Third Episcopal District, 5300 E. Main Street, Suite 101, Columbus, Ohio 43213–2580, 614-575-2279.

RESOURCES

The Doctrine and Discipline of the African Methodist Episcopal Church, 1992. Nashville: AMEC Sunday School Union, 1993.

Gomez, J. *Polity of the African Methodist Episcopal Church.* Nashville: Abingdon Press, 1971.

Gonzalez, Justo L. *From the Protestant Reformation to the Twentieth Century.* Vol. 3 of *A History of Christian Thought.* Nashville: Abingdon Press, 1975.

Gregg, Howard D. *History of the African Methodist Episcopal Church: The Black Church in Action.* Nashville: AMEC Sunday School Union, 1980.

AFRICAN METHODIST EPISCOPAL ZION

Vincent T. Frosh

HISTORY

T HE AFRICAN METHODIST EPISCOPAL (AME) ZION CHURCH HAD its embryonic start in the city of New York about the year 1765. The John Street Church (1768) was the first Methodist church built in that city. There were several black members in this church from its first organization, but the church was still part of the Methodist Episcopal Church, which was primarily white. Between the years 1765 and 1796 the number of "colored" members increased greatly—so much so that caste prejudice took hold, and they were forbidden to take the Sacrament until all the white families had been served. This and the desire for other church privileges denied to them induced black members to organize themselves, which they did in 1796. This was the first African Methodist Episcopal church of which we have any account. In 1880 they built a church and called it Zion. This church, unlike the other black Methodist Churches formed about the same period, was from the first financially and administratively separate from the Methodist Episcopal Church. Members of Zion drew up articles of agreement with the Methodist Episcopal Church, which supplied them with ministers for about twenty years. Later the denomination added the name Zion out of respect for the mother church.

The Ohio Conference was organized September 16, 1891, at Cambria Chapel, Johnstown, Pennsylvania, by Bishop James W. Hood. It was the offspring of the Allegheny Conference, which originally included the part of Pennsylvania lying west of the Allegheny River and the entire state of Ohio. The only AME Zion churches in the state of Ohio when the Ohio Conference was organized were in Akron, Salem, and Massillon.

The first presiding elder of the Ohio Conference, Rev. J. H. Trimble, began organizing churches faster than the bishop could find preachers to hold the points he had taken in for Zion. This shortage of missionary preachers posed a problem for Zion in that territory. The growth became gradual and many problems were encountered. Rev. George W. Lewis was one of the faithful pioneers, serving as first secretary of the conference and pastoring several mission points. The people, however, kept the faith, and after several strenuous efforts to start churches in the metropolitan cities of Cleveland, Columbus, Dayton, Youngstown and others, success, which had come the long, hard way, was realized. Zion was quite successful, however, in establishing her first major church in Cincinnati. A large number had withdrawn from the Methodist Episcopal Church and built an independent church. Through the hard work of Presiding Bishop Hood and Bishop Alexander Walters, the entire group voted to join Zion, and its leader and people were a big asset to the conference and connection. In 1894 Rev. M. A. Mason started the first mission effort in Cleveland with twelve members. It took a while for Zion to become firmly established in this city.

In 1896 Bishop C. C. Pettey was assigned to the Ohio Conference and reported the purchase of a church property in Cleveland, which was occupied November 15, 1899, led by Presiding Elder G. W. Lewis. The membership, however, had not grown strong enough to sustain this venture, and the property apparently was soon lost. Under the charge of Bishop Small, Rev. Mrs. M. C. Brown maintained a mission group in the city in her house until 1905. Rev. Pero Williams, who had a unique talent for constructing congregations, was sent there by Bishop Caldwell. Rev. S. C. Harris followed Williams; he held services in a storefront with his residence above it. The mission continued its growth. This consistently growing membership, led by Rev. E. D. W. Bell and Bishop George C. Clement and assisted by the Tercentenary Fund, acquired the present edifice at 2393 E. 55th Street, which would be known as one of the finest plants in the denomination, around 1921. The membership increased manifold, and Zion began to blossom with other congregations and churches in and around the city of Cleveland. Like a number of churches throughout the connection, St. Paul, our mother church of Cleveland, has given us some of the country's most outstanding citizens, including Carl B. Stokes, who became the first black mayor of Cleveland, and his brother Louis Stokes, presently serving as a U.S. Congressman.

The Ohio Conference at first developed so slowly that the 1900 General Conference combined it again with the Allegheny Conference. It was known as the Allegheny-Ohio Conference until 1915, when Bishop Caldwell set it off again from the Allegheny Conference, after the Ohio District had grown sufficiently. During the early 1900s, Bishop Caldwell transferred the Cincinnati District of the Kentucky Conference back into the Ohio Conference, and the work in this state began to grow rapidly. The conference flourished and presently consists of three districts: Akron, Cleveland, and Columbus-Cincinnati.

BELIEFS

The AME Zion Church holds fast to the tenants of true Methodism: 1) methodical in study and life, and 2) systematic in study, prayer, and worship. We claim John Wesley (1703–91) as our founder and hold to the attributes of true holiness.

The mission of the African Methodist Episcopal Zion Church is to increase our love for God and to help meet the needs of humankind by loving God with all our hearts, with all our souls, and with all our minds, and loving our neighbors as ourselves. We embrace two sacraments, the Eucharist (Lord's Supper) and baptism. The Apostles' Creed remains our statement of faith, and our twenty-five Articles of Religion serve as our doctrine of witness.

CURRENT DEMOGRAPHICS

There are twenty-eight churches with a total membership of more than ten thousand in the Ohio Conference.

CONTACT INFORMATION

African Methodist Episcopal Zion Church: *www.theamezionchurch.org*

Mid-Atlantic District, AME Zion Church, 2000 Cedar Circle Drive, Catonsville, Maryland 21228–3743, 410-744-7330.

RESOURCES

The Book of Discipline of the A.M.E. Zion Church 2000. Charlotte, N.C.: AME Zion Publishing House.

Hoggard, Bishop James Clinton, ed. *The African Methodist Episcopal Zion Church: A Bicentennial Commemorative History, 1972–1996*. Charlotte, N.C.: AME Zion Publishing House, 1998.

Walls, Bishop William J. *The African Methodist Episcopal Zion Church—Reality of the Black Church*. Charlotte, N.C.: AME Zion Publishing House, 1974.

CHRISTIAN METHODIST EPISCOPAL

Juanita Bryant

HISTORY

T HOSE WHO FOUNDED THE CHRISTIAN METHODIST EPISCOPAL (CME) Church were members of the Methodist Episcopal Church, South (ME Church, South) while they were slaves. In 1860 more than 207,000 slaves were members of the ME Church, South. At the close of the Civil War, seventy-eight thousand of them were still members of that church. After the Civil War, they realized that continued membership in their former masters' church was neither desirable nor practical. They requested their own separate and independent church. In 1866 the General Conference of the ME Church, South meeting in New Orleans granted the request of the "colored" members and authorized the establishment of a separate jurisdiction. In 1870 forty-one African American men representing eight annual conferences of the Methodist Episcopal Church, South organized the Colored Methodist Episcopal Church in America. That conference adopted portions of the Discipline of the Methodist Episcopal Church, South as its polity and set the boundaries of ten annual conferences. In 1954 the term "Colored" in the denomination's name was changed to "Christian." From these humble beginnings, the CME Church has become a major denomination. One of its most significant witnessing arenas has been the education of African Americans. As slaves won freedom, more than twenty-one schools were founded under the auspices of the CME Church.

The Christian Methodist Episcopal Church's presence in Ohio began shortly after the church's organization in 1870. A few African American families began migrating to the northern states in search of a better life for themselves and their children. Two church congregations were among the first to bring the Christian Methodist Episcopal Church to the great state of Ohio. These congregations were begun in Ripley in 1892 and in Cleveland in 1902.

The oldest CME Church in Ohio is Beebe Chapel CME Church located in Ripley. It was organized by Rev. Pop Jackson in 1892 after a split in the local Wesleyan Church. The church building was started in 1899. It was dedicated by and named after Bishop Joseph A. Beebe, who was the presiding bishop for this area. The original church building has undergone many repairs and restoration projects in its 110-year history. The church has established a scholarship that supports first-year college students who graduated from the Ripley Union Lewis Huntington Schools. Beebe Chapel CME has often been referred to as the Mother Church in the Ohio region of the Christian Methodist Episcopal Church.

The second oldest church in Ohio is the Lane Metropolitan CME Church in Cleveland, which was organized in 1902. At the turn of the twentieth century, Isaiah T. Shy, a young local preacher, arrived in Cleveland. Upon learning that there was no CME church in Cleveland, Shy immediately began enlisting the CMEs from house to house. He inspired them to begin prayer meetings and worship services in the homes of Richard A. Wilson, John Carr, and Peter Shy. The group soon asked the Reverend Lucius E. Shy, an ordained minister from Atlanta, Georgia, to help them organize a CME Church in Cleveland. Then they met and decided to implore Bishop L. H. Holsey, the senior bishop of the CME Church, to come to Cleveland and organize a church for them. The United Brethren Church at the corner of Cedar Avenue and Newton Street (now East 31st Street) was purchased for thirty-three hundred dollars. Bishop Isaac Lane guaranteed to the United Brethren Church the purchase price and pledged to pay three hundred dollars down. He subsequently induced the CME Church to levy three cents per capita upon the membership in order to pay for the property. Lane Memorial Colored Methodist Episcopal Church was born. Bishop Lane came to Cleveland and preached the dedicatory sermon on March 14, 1902. The original building still stands, now under a different denominational banner, as a beacon of light to wayward men and women.

From 1902 to 1918 the church's growth was slow and arduous. Many blacks who had migrated to Cleveland prior to 1902 had become members of existing churches of other denominations. In 1918 the church began to explore the possibility of finding a more desirable location. Lane's dream of finding and possessing a new and better home led him to the beautiful Christian Science church at the corner of East 46th and Cedar Avenue. This was an exquisitely beautiful edifice of sandstone constructed in the spring of 1900. Practically new, it was simply awe-inspiring inside and out. It was the first church in Cleveland to be air-cooled. On July 1, 1919, the church was purchased by and transferred to the Colored Methodist Episcopal Connection. On Sunday, July 20, 1919, Lane Memorial Colored Methodist Episcopal Church became Lane Metropolitan Christian Methodist Episcopal Church as the group of worshipers marched up Cedar Avenue from East 31st Street to East 46th Street singing "Onward Christian Soldiers."

BELIEFS

The heritage of the CME Church is fully Methodist. Its history, doctrine, and polity are an unbroken link with American Methodism. It claims John Wesley (1703–91) as its founder, the Methodist Episcopal Church as its progenitor, and the ME Church, South as it parent. The CME Church is proud to be an integral part of "the People Called Methodist" around the world. As with all Methodist churches, the CME Church has sought to spread "Scriptural holiness" and "social righteousness" throughout the land.

There is but one living and true God, everlasting, without body or parts, of infinite power, wisdom, and goodness, the maker and preserver or all things, both visible and invisible. And in unity of this Godhead there are three persons of one substance, power, and eternity—the Father, the Son, and the Holy Ghost. The holy scriptures contain all things necessary to salvation. No one is required to believe anything that is neither contained in the Bible nor proved by it, and such things cannot be requisite or necessary to salvation. There are two sacraments ordained of Christ our Lord in the Gospel: baptism and the Supper of our Lord. Lay people and clergy alike partake of the Eucharist, which Christ commanded ought to be administered to all Christians.

We believe that the Christian Methodist Episcopal Church is a part of the body of Christ and that it must express itself in the world in the light of the life and teachings of Jesus Christ. Jesus taught us many things by both word and example—to be concerned for the welfare and well-being of others, to love our neighbors as ourselves, to be concerned for justice. For the church to be silent in the face of need, injustice, and exploitation is to deny the Lord of the church.

CURRENT DEMOGRAPHICS

Currently there are more than thirty-five CME church congregations in Ohio with over thirteen thousand communicant members. Many are in urban areas, but there are also many churches in the less-populated regions of Ohio.

CONTACT INFORMATION

Christian Methodist Episcopal Church, First Memphis Plaza, 4466 Elvis Presley Boulevard, Memphis, Tennessee 38116, *www.c-m-e.org*

Second District, 7030 Reading Road, Cincinnati, Ohio 45237, 513-772-8622, *www.secondepiscopaldistrict.com/*

RESOURCES

Lakey, Othal Hawthorne. *The History of the CME Church.* Memphis: CME Publishing House, 1996.

Smith, Rev. Frank A., and Charles L. Helton. *A Pilgrimage in Faith: The History of Lane Metropolitan CME Church, 1902–1984.* Cleveland: The Church, 1984.

Pentecostal

ASSEMBLIES OF GOD

Roger L. Culbertson

HISTORY

THE ASSEMBLIES OF GOD, WITH ITS EMPHASIS ON BEING FILLED with the Holy Spirit and its distinctive Pentecostal testimony, has a beginning that is easy to find. It begins in the last decade of the nineteenth century, in a time period secular historians commonly refer to as the Gay Nineties. For most Americans, however, thirty-five years was not enough time to erase the horrors of the Civil War from their minds.

The nineteenth century found America in the midst of a genuine spiritual paradox. Newspapers all across America carried weekly accounts of the "tent" revivals conducted by evangelists such as Rev. D. L. Moody (1837–99). These articles record the large number of people who responded to Rev. Moody when he gave his "altar calls." At the same time Charles Darwin's (1809–82) theory of evolution was making great inroads into the educational community. History shows this theory appealed to many Catholic and Protestant leaders, who began preaching what they called "biblical higher criticism." Any move of God in their religious services was openly shunned, while reports of spiritual awakenings were labeled "fanaticism."

This hostile atmosphere led Rev. Charles F. Parham and his forty Bible students in Topeka, Kansas, to come together for the purpose of figuring out how to meet the challenges of the coming century. These students met in an old stone mansion that eventually became known as Bethel College. Built in the form of a medieval castle, Bethel College is the birthplace of modern Pentecostalism.

There is documented evidence of believers being filled with the Holy Spirit in every century. Testimonies of people speaking in tongues ring with authenticity. What made the group in Kansas unique was the decision they made after doing independent research on the Pentecostal experience during their Christmas vacation in December 1900. Before leaving on a trip to Kansas City to conduct meetings, Rev. Parham challenged the group to diligently study the Bible, especially the Book of Acts, to discover what constitutes proof or evidence of the baptism of the Holy Ghost. Upon returning to school the students made an interesting discovery. Although they had studied alone, they had all reached the same conclusion. The indisputable proof of the Pentecostal experience was speaking in other tongues. After agreeing on this conclusion, they immediately began seeking God for a new outpouring of His spirit. At about eleven o'clock on the evening of January 1, 1901, Agnes N. Ozman asked her friends to "lay hands" on her that she might receive the gift of the Holy Spirit. As they began praying together, Miss Ozman began speaking in other tongues. Thus, on the first day of 1901, we have the first recorded experience of someone who actually expected to speak in tongues as she was baptized in the Holy Spirit.

Believers were enjoying the Pentecostal experience long before records were kept. Sometime during January 1890 Rev. Daniel Awrey was baptized in the Holy Spirit at his church in Delaware, Ohio. Fifteen years later Rev. T. K. Leonard, who had pastored three small Christian churches near Findlay, received the Pentecostal experience and became a pioneer for the movement. In the spring of 1907 Miss Ivy Campbell returned from California, where she had received the Holy Spirit and spoke in tongues. She went to Akron and Youngstown, where she preached the Pentecostal message. In the summer of that same year Pentecostal believers held a camp meeting in Alliance, Ohio. This camp, sponsored by Levi R. Lupton, was attended by several ministers who later became leaders of the Assemblies of God. Among them was J. Roswell Flower, who later became the first general secretary of the denomination.

Many of Ohio's Pentecostal churches, missions, and assemblies were

The Gospel School Publishing House, Findlay. This picture was taken around 1910. The building was used for many purposes during the formative years of the Assemblies of God, including serving as their national headquarters and as a Bible school to train ministers. (Courtesy of Assemblies of God)

in existence before there was any denominational organization. They operated as independent churches and might have remained independent except for one thing. In the early 1900s almost all intercity and interstate travel was done by train, and ordained clergy were permitted to travel at half fare. To prevent unscrupulous people from taking advantage of this, the railroads required each denomination to be certified at the Clergy Bureau and each ordained minister to be certified by his or her denomination.

In April 1914 the national Assemblies of God organized in Hot Springs, Arkansas. From June to November of that year, the first national headquarters of the Assemblies of God was located in Findlay, Ohio. At that time the Ohio District Council did not exist. It was not until October 26, 1920, that representatives from Michigan, Ohio, Indiana, and Illinois met to form the Central District of the Assemblies of God. This meeting took place at the Pentecostal church in Cleveland, with twenty-four ministers and delegates present. They represented sixteen churches from four different states. Of the sixteen churches represented, eight were from Ohio. They were from Cleveland, Akron, Findlay, Dayton, Toledo, Conneaut, Warren, and Elyria.

The organization these ministers and delegates established was a very simple one. Pentecostal in doctrine and congregational in government, the purpose of the organization was to carry out the idea of a cooperative fellowship. The movement was intensely evangelical and missionary. It has grown from a handful of cooperative churches to a full-fledged denomination of thriving congregations in every part of the state.

BELIEFS

While the Pentecostal experience does set the Assemblies of God apart, it is very similar to all other Bible-believing churches. We accept the Bible as the inspired and only infallible written word of God. For our congregants there is one God, eternally existent in three persons: God the Father, God the Son, and God the Holy Spirit. We believe in the deity of Jesus Christ, his virgin birth, his sinless life, and his miracles.

In addition to this, we believe in Christ's vicarious and atoning death, followed by his bodily resurrection and ascension to the right hand of the Father. Finally, we believe in Christ's personal return to earth in power and glory commonly referred to as the "rapture of the church." After this all mankind will appear before the judgment seat of Christ. We believe that those who have accepted Jesus Christ as their personal savior will be saved and receive God's gift of everlasting life and that those who have rejected God's gift of salvation will be lost and receive eternal damnation.

CURRENT DEMOGRAPHICS

At the end of 2000, the number of Assemblies of God churches in Ohio was 266. The number of credentialed ministers of all categories combined was 756. And the average number of people attending the morning worship service at Assemblies of God churches across the state on any given Sunday was 41,654.

CONTACT INFORMATION

Assemblies of God, national office, 1445 North Boonville Avenue, Springfield, Missouri 65802, 417-862-2781, *www.ag.org/top/*

Assemblies of God in Ohio, 3021 East Dublin-Granville Road, Columbus, Ohio 43231–4031.

PENTECOSTAL ASSEMBLIES OF THE WORLD

Howard Collier

HISTORY

Early records of the Ohio District Council show that it was organized on October 7, 1925, in Cleveland. Its first office was at 2564 East 38th Street, site of a church pastored by Rev. A. R. Schooler. From September 1917 to April 1925, more than four thousand people had been baptized and filled with the Holy Spirit in and around the city of Cleveland and the state of Ohio. In approximately seven months, the original place of worship (33rd and Central Streets, Cleveland) became too crowded, and they relocated to 2641 East 40th Street, Cleveland. Most of those converted had no central place that held to the oneness doctrine; therefore it became necessary to form an organization. No organizational name was chosen at that time, but meetings were held quarterly with Rev. A. R. Schooler and his congregation until more organizational structure was final. Rev. Schooler, founder of the Ohio District Council, allowed the organization to serve under his church's name, Church of Christ, in its early beginnings.

More people came, and that church became too small. Rev. Schooler and the members organized a district council to help small churches around the state. Many assemblies were set up directly from that assembly in Cleveland, namely: Akron, Oberlin, Youngstown, Canton, Paulding,

Xenia, and some churches in cities in other states, such as Pittsburgh, Chicago, and New York.

The Ohio District Council is affiliated with the Pentecostal Assemblies of the World, Inc., with headquarters in Indianapolis, Indiana. Included in its present geographical boundaries are small portions of the states of Pennsylvania and West Virginia. The main auxiliaries of the Ohio District Council are the Ohio District Council Campground Department and the Ohio District Council Nursing Home.

Ohio District Council Campground Department

In 1944, Bishop Arthur William Lewis, who was pastoring in Cleveland, was traveling along State Route 40 and came across the Washington Heights Motor Hotel, which had been formerly known as the Wick Hotel. An older facility located three miles east of Zanesville, it was for sale. Money to buy the property was raised by asking council churches to set aside ten cents per member each week to be turned in at each council session. This plan was executed with great success, and the property was purchased in July 1944. In 1947 Rev. and Mrs. Jarvis moved to Zanesville from Oberlin and became the managers of the property. In 1955 plans were put in motion to start a campground on the site, and a one-story frame tabernacle (temporary shelter) was erected. Each July session of the Ohio District Council was held there. In 1958 a metal pole building was erected beside the tabernacle. The Ohio District Council's attendance flourished, and after the sessions were over there were two weeks of camping for young people and children. The numbers continued to grow until it became necessary to expand. Another tabernacle was built to seat six hundred. In the late 1970s a new tabernacle was erected high above all of the other buildings. The July sessions of the Ohio District Council were held in the campground, and in later months, hundreds of young people came to attend camp. In the 1980s, the council built a four-hundred-seat cafeteria, and today the six-million-dollar complex is known as Hallowed Hills.

Ohio District Council Nursing Home

In 1938 Bishop Fred Clark visited some church members who had been put in an "old folks home," and he was appalled at the humiliating conditions. Many church members, including Mrs. Lottie Medcalf of Wellsburg, traveled all over the state asking for dimes to be brought to each conference. Mrs. Gertrude Spellman was very inspired and gave a small farm, which was located in the town of Green, just outside Warren. Several days later, while driving along State Route 40 two mile east of Zanesville, Bishop Arthur William Lewis noticed that the Washington Heights Motor Hotel was for sale. The property was purchased, renovated, and over time converted into a rest home. In July 1944 the doors opened to the Ohio District Council Rest Home, capable of housing twenty-three residents.

From 1944 to 1963 the home was run by five "matrons," each of whom served for several years. In 1963 Rev. Royal Haines of Warren took control of the home and served as its first superintendent. Because the facility was equipped to provide skilled care, it was licensed by the state of Ohio as a nursing home in 1963 and became the Ohio District Council Nursing Home. Haines served as superintendent until his death in May 1969. Rev. Frank McDonald, the first licensed administrator, replaced him. His son Rev. Nathan McDonald trained as an intern and in February 1974 became the facility's second administrator. He further expanded the facilities, a project completed in July 1978. The addition made it possible to properly care for a total of one hundred patients. At that time, the state of Ohio licensed the nursing home as a skilled nursing facility, the highest license any nursing home can receive.

BELIEFS

The chief aim of the Pentecostal Assemblies of the World, Inc., is to glorify the Savior, Jesus Christ, who gave himself for us that he might redeem us from all iniquity and purify unto himself a peculiar people, zealous of good works. Our duty is to lift the fallen, visit the sick, strengthen the weak, encourage the faint-hearted, comfort the feebleminded, point the lost to the way of salvation, and urge all believers to seek a spirit-filled life (Eph. 5:18; Acts 19:1–16) and prepare for the coming of the Lord (James 1:27; I Thess. 5:4; Mark 16:15–18; Matt. 25:1–13).

Moreover it is our indispensable duty as partakers of the "royal priesthood" (I Pet. 2:9; Rev. 1:6, 5:10) to offer supplications, prayer, and intercessions and give thanks for all humanity. We must also obey human laws for the Lord's sake, as long as those laws do not infringe upon the liberty of service towards God according to the dictates of the heart or conscience.

CURRENT DEMOGRAPHICS

The Ohio District Council includes 106 churches in Ohio, three churches outside the state, and a total of about 150,000 members.

CONTACT INFORMATION

Pentecostal Assemblies of the World, Inc., 3939 Meadows Drive, Indianapolis, Indiana 46205, 317-547-9541.

Ohio District Council, 3125 East Pike, Zanesville, Ohio. Present mailing address is P.O. Box 628, Piqua, Ohio 45356, 513-522-1150.

RESOURCES

Burgess, Stanley M., Patrick H. Alexander, and Gary B. McGee, eds. *Dictionary of Pentecostal and Charismatic Movements*. Grand Rapids, Mich.: Zondervan Publishing House, 1993.

Lawson, Robert C. *The Anthropology of Jesus Christ Our Kinsman*. Piqua, Ohio: Ohio Ministries, 1925.

Paddock, Ross P. *Apostolic Roots: A Goodly Heritage*. Piqua, Ohio: Ohio Ministries, 1992.

Pietist and Holiness

MORAVIAN

Albert H. Frank

HISTORY

THE MORAVIAN CHURCH IN AMERICA TRACES ITS ROOTS BACK TO Bohemian reformer John Hus, who was burned at the stake at the Council of Constance in 1415. Some Hussites founded the Unitas Fratrum (Unity of Brethren) in 1457, and the church grew in its homelands of Bohemia and Moravia to a membership of two hundred thousand. Forced into a clandestine existence by the Thirty Years War (1618–48)1, its future life was connected with the work and dreams of John Amos Comenius (1592–1670), whose educational work was known throughout Europe. Small cell groups continued to meet and preserve the teachings and worship practices of the Unity until relocation was possible in the 1720s. At that time several groups of refugees went to Saxony, where they founded the community of Herrnhut on the lands of Count Nicolaus Ludwig von Zinzendorf. Following a renewal experience in 1727, the Brethren's Church (called the Moravian Church because many members were from Moravia) began an extensive mission movement that led to its first North American work—in Georgia in 1735 and then in Pennsylvania in 1740. The work among Native Americans began in New York in 1740, then moved across Pennsylvania and into the Northwest Territory.

The first Moravians in Ohio were Christian Frederick Post and John Heckewelder, who visited the Bolivar area in Tuscarawas County in 1763. The purpose of their visit was to establish contacts with the Indians. This visit led to a settlement of Christian Indians in 1772 under the leadership of David Zeisberger at Schoenbrunn ("beautiful spring") near what is now New Philadelphia. Here they built a village of twenty-eight buildings, including the first school and church in Ohio. Other settlements were founded nearby, but all were abandoned after 1782.

On March 8, 1782, ninety Christian Indians were killed at Gnadenhutten ("tents of grace"). They were attacked by American militia under Colonel David Williamson. This ended the settlement and the Moravian Indian mission in Ohio. After years of wandering in northern Ohio and Ontario, Moravians established a settlement at Goshen (1798), near the original site of Schoenbrunn. The Goshen congregation lasted until 1821.

The Revolutionary War had been a hard time for the missions. The missionaries were accused of helping the Americans and the British. After the time of wandering, the U.S. government granted a large tract of land to the Moravian Church in trust for the Native Americans, which encouraged a return to Ohio. The decision was made to establish churches for the white settlers and to work for harmony and understanding among all people of eastern Ohio.

The present Moravian congregations in Ohio are centered in Tuscarawas County. A second congregation was organized by Heckewelder at Gnadenhutten in 1799. Beersheba was established at Lock Seventeen in the early 1800s. It served the English-speaking settlers until 1827, when it was merged with Gnadenhutten. Work in nearby Tuscarawas led to the organization of the Sharon congregation in 1815. Canal Dover (now Dover) was organized in 1842, Fry's Valley in 1857, Uhrichsville in 1874, and New Philadelphia (Schoenbrunn) in 1947. An earlier work near New Philadelphia had not been successful and was abandoned in 1907. A congregation existed at Port Washington from 1882 to 1973. A second congregation was present in Dover from 1925 to 1988, when it merged back into the First Church.

These congregations have formed a strong center for Moravian work that has included a mission society and a summer camping program. Youth ministry and outreach have been united concerns.

In 1985 a congregation named Redeemer was established at Dublin, in

The Moravian Church at Schoenbrunn in Tuscarawas County, constructed in 1772, was the first Christian church building in Ohio. It was destroyed by the Moravians in April 1777 during the turmoil of the American Revolution. This reconstruction was completed in the 1920s, on the original foundations of the church. (Courtesy of the Ohio Historical Society)

the northern suburbs of Columbus. This congregation erected its own building in 1989. A new congregation, The Promise Moravian Church, was established as an outgrowth of Redeemer in 2001. The eight current Ohio Moravian congregations are part of the international Moravian Church, which engages in educational and mission work throughout the world. With a total membership of two thousand, the Ohio congregations are a small part of the worldwide church, which has 780,000 members, yet they are an integral part of its global ministries.

BELIEFS

A mainline Protestant denomination, the Moravian Church accepts the Apostles' Creed and the Nicene Creed, as well as other ecumenical statements of belief. Moravians have always been more interested in living a Christian life than in debating theology. The official seal of the Moravian Church contains the motto "Our Lamb has conquered, let us follow Him."

Worship materials—hymns and liturgies—also contain expressions of belief.

One of the most expressive hymns is:

> 'Tis the most blessed and needful part
> To have in Christ a share,
> And to commit our way and heart
> Unto His faithful care,
> This done, our steps are safe and sure
> Our hearts' desires are rendered pure
> And naught can pluck us from His hand
> Which leads us to the end.
>
> —C. R. von Zinzendorf (1727–52)

CURRENT DEMOGRAPHICS

The eight Moravian congregations in Ohio have a total membership of approximately two thousand. Of these 1,628 are confirmed communicants. The congregations' geographical locations—six in Tuscarawas County and two in Fulton County—are indicative of the method of church growth among Ohio Moravians. The Tuscarawas County congregations developed around the center, which had been established during the Indian mission work. Spreading north to Dover and as far south as Gnadenhutten, these congregations form a group which can readily meet for programs and worship occasions. The two newer congregations, in Fulton County, began as an outreach to Moravians who had settled around the state capitol. These eight congregations are part of the Eastern District of the Northern Province of the Moravian Church in America, which has its headquarters in Bethlehem, Pennsylvania.

CONTACT INFORMATION

Moravian Church in America: *www.moravian.org*
Eastern District, Northern Province, Moravian Church in America: 1021 Center Street, Betblehern, Pennsylvania 18016, 610-867-7566.

Ohio congregations: Dover First: 330-364-8831; Church of the Redeemer
(Dublin): 614-766-5030; Gnadenhutten: 740-254-4374; Fry's Valley (New
Philadelphia): 740-254-9373; Schoenbrunn (New Philadelphia): 330-339-1940;
Sharon Church (Tuscarawas): 740-922-5507; Uhrichsville: 740-922-0886.

RESOURCES

Hamilton, J. Taylor, and Kenneth G. Hamilton. *A History of the Moravian
Church.* Bethlehem, Penn.: The Moravian Church in America, 1967.

Moravian Daily Texts, 2003. Bethlehem, Penn.: The Moravian Church in America.

Schattschneider, Allen W., and Albert H. Frank. *Through Five Hundred Years.*
Bethlehem, Penn.: The Moravian Church in America, 1996.

Weinlick, John R., and Albert H. Frank. *The Moravian Church through the Ages.*
Bethlehem, Penn.: The Moravian Church in America, 1996.

CHURCHES OF GOD, GENERAL CONFERENCE

Jonathan A. Binkley

HISTORY

UNDER THE INSPIRED LEADERSHIP OF THE REVEREND JOHN Winebrenner, an estranged pastor from the German Reformed Church in eastern Pennsylvania, the denomination began under the name "Church of God" in 1825–26. By 1830 an eldership (consisting of a pastor and two "ruling elders") had been organized, enabling the energetic new leadership to send "western missionaries" to Ohio to hold services among new arrivals from Pennsylvania. Mostly rural and of Germanic heritage, these Ohio settlers helped organize preaching stops and services for the arriving "circuit-riding" pastors. Wayne County became an early focus for denominational success. By 1834 the East Pennsylvania Eldership had appointed the Reverends Thomas Hickernell and Jacob Keller to the Ohio circuit. In just two successful years, this team established enough pastoral locations to justify an Ohio eldership.

Meeting in September 1836 at the home of John Beidler in Holmes County, the ministers of the Church of God in Ohio held their first annual eldership. The next year the efforts were expanded, and other elderships partially involving Ohio territory were created. In 1857 the original 1836 Ohio Eldership was formally split into the East and West Ohio Elderships. These continued until 1875, when they were rejoined. (In 2001

Former home of Brother John Beidler in Holmes County. The first eldership of the Church of God in Ohio was held here in September 1836. Photo by Esther M. Thomas. (From *History of the Ohio Conference of the Churches of God: General Conference, 1836–1986*, ed. Richard Kern, 1986; reprinted by permission of Richard Kern)

the Ohio Conference was combined with the Michigan Conference to form the present Great Lakes Conference of the Churches of God.)

In the early years of the denomination, many energetic, talented, and spiritually inspired ministers gave great momentum to the movement's efforts and beliefs. Leaders agreed in deed and practice to keep beliefs as close to biblical simplicity as possible. Besides circuit-riding preaching stops, camp meetings built up local churches.

Early Church of God leaders were active in the antislavery movement, against the use of alcoholic beverages and the organized liquor traffic, for moderation in life, and concerned over the Mexican War of 1846–48. They backed President Lincoln and the war effort to preserve the Union and rejoiced in the Union's victory in the Civil War. However, the war did slow down the denomination's growth, as so many of its pastors and members were involved.

The period from 1868 to 1925 saw a renewed thrust of the organization —its most rapid growth occurred during this period. The denomination would eventually establish church efforts in nearly fifty Ohio counties. During this period the denomination's name, "Church of God in North America," was changed to "Churches of God in North America" (1896) and again to "General Eldership of the Churches of God in North America" (1903). The name changes—first the plural "Churches" and then the addition of "North America"—reflect the movement's rapid growth.

During the late nineteenth century the national denomination, headquartered in Harrisburg, Pennsylvania, launched a number of educational efforts, including Findlay College (1882), now the University of Findlay. By the 1880s camp meetings were becoming a thing of the past in Ohio. Instead, permanent church buildings—almost all of them in northern Ohio—replaced preaching stops, borrowed facilities, and camp meetings.

Upon entering the twentieth century, the Ohio Churches of God movement was ending its rapid early rural growth with new moves to more urban areas. The Ohio Eldership also joined the growing movement to establish youth church camps. By 1946–47 it had its own camp, Camp Otyokwah near Butler. Existing rural preaching circuits and churches were also consolidated and new ones were being established, especially in the post–World War II era. Today, the denomination remains basically a rural and urban northern Ohio movement. The Ohio Eldership changed its name to "Ohio Conference" in 1964, in part to acknowledge that its annual meetings included many active nonminister church workers. It also launched its own home for the aged in Findlay.

The national denomination, renamed "Churches of God, General Conference (CGGC)" in 1974, focused on Ohio during this period. It established what is now the Winebrenner Theological Seminary at Findlay in 1942. In 1970 it made Findlay its second national headquarters (along with its original Harrisburg, Pennsylvania, site). Findlay became the administrative headquarters and Harrisburg the headquarters for publishing. By 1979 Findlay had become the sole national headquarters for all functions. To accomplish this, a new national Church Center for Christian Ministries was built in the years 1980–81 in northern Findlay. Here denomination's foreign mission efforts, along with all other national business, are conducted. The Great Lakes Conference has had its offices in this national headquarters since the building's dedication in 1981.

BELIEFS

In 1983 and 1986 CGGC reformulated its original tenets of faith in a publication called "We Believe." Basically, the denomination believes:

- That we keep faith and practices as close to the simple messages of spiritual truth in the Bible as is possible;
- Similarly, since the New Testament name for the body of believers was cited twelve times as "church of God," that was adopted as the original name for the denomination;
- That the initial, primary focus of spiritual thrust should be the acceptance of God's son, Jesus Christ, as one's personal savior—and the Bible as one's "rule of faith and practice" in the newfound Christian life;
- That single-immersion baptism resembles Christ's biblical example most closely and that it reflects the inward spiritual change of salvation and commitment in one's spiritual life;
- That the Lord's Supper (communion) should be used sparingly to preserve full consciousness of its spiritual meaning. And since Christ by example—in spiritual humbleness of servitude—washed his disciples' feet afterward, this too can be a meaningful spiritual example and experience;
- That three things are recognized as divine ordinances of the church: baptism, feet-washing, and the Lord's Supper;
- And, that we recognize the Trinity; the Bible as an inspired, infallible authority—the word of God—our only rule of faith and practice; free moral agency; justification by faith in Christ; the healing power of faith for the whole person; and the need for redeemed Christians to fulfill the biblical Great Commission (see Mark 16:15–18) as their postsalvation mission in life.

CURRENT DEMOGRAPHICS

In 2001 the Great Lakes Conference had approximately three thousand members. In Ohio, members are clustered mainly in the north, around Celina, Findlay, and Wooster. The Churches of God, General Conference had an estimated 32,500 members in 2001. Its world headquarters, national seminary, and main university are all in Findlay, Ohio.

CONTACT INFORMATION

Churches of God, General Conference, Center for Christian Ministries, 700 E. Melrose Avenue, P.O. Box 926, Findlay, Ohio 45839, 419-424-1961, *www.cggc.org*

Great Lakes Conference, 700 East Melrose Avenue, P.O. Box 1132, Findlay, Ohio 45839, 419-423-7694, *green.occg@juno.com*

The Historical Society of the Churches of God, General Conference, 700 E. Melrose Avenue, P.O. Box 926, Findlay, Ohio 45839, 419-424-1961, *leathersj@mail.findlay.edu, www.cggc.org*

University of Findlay: *www.findlay.edu*

Winebrenner Theological Seminary: *www.winebrenner.edu*

RESOURCES

Forney, C. H. *History of the Churches of God in the United States of North America.* Harrisburg, Penn.: The Gospel Publishing House, 1914.

Kern, Richard, ed. *History of the Ohio Conference of the Churches of God: General Conference, 1836–1986.* Nappanee, Ind.: Evangel Press, 1986.

THE WESLEYAN CHURCH

Jeffrey Mansell

HISTORY

THE CHRISTIAN CHURCH KNOWN AS THE WESLEYAN CHURCH GREW out of a rich heritage whose roots run deeply in Ohio history. The church was birthed out of national struggle and a religious revival intended to reawaken a passion for Christlikeness.

The Wesleyan Church had its earliest expression in the Wesleyan Methodist Connection of America, an offshoot of the Methodist Episcopal Church. In the early 1800s a growing number of United States citizens, called abolitionists, were crying out against the evils of slavery, and dissension was growing in the Methodist Episcopal Church between opposing parties on this issue. In the early 1840s abolitionists within the church initiated a break from the Methodist Episcopal Church. The organizational meeting for the Wesleyan Methodist Connection was held in Utica, New York, from May 31 to June 7, 1843. The first general conference was held in October 1844 in Cleveland.

One of the early leaders of the Wesleyan Methodist Connection was Rev. Orange Scott, a Methodist minister born in Vermont. Rev. Scott found a receptive audience to his preaching in Ohio, which had already established itself as strongly opposed to slavery. States like New York, Michigan, and Ohio had become storm centers for the abolition movement. Congregations in Troy, Leesville, and Dayton were primed to join the movement that was growing under Scott's preaching.

Critical to the antislavery movement was the establishment of the Underground Railroad. This system of escape routes and safe houses was responsible for the safe passage of thousands of slaves out of the slave-holding states of the south to the more hospitable environment of the north. Numerous Wesleyan Methodist churches in Ohio were active in this system. These included the Fargo Wesleyan Methodist Church and the Africa Wesleyan Methodist Church, both just north of Columbus.

The story is told of Ephraim Eastman, a layman in the Harrison Wesleyan Methodist Church, whose cunning allowed for the safe escape of a slave in his care. An officer arrived at his home and insisted that Eastman turn over the slave, known to be hiding there. Eastman replied that he would oblige, but that he must first lead the family in worship. He invited the officer to join them for worship, which included a lengthy scripture reading and a very long prayer. By the time family worship was concluded, the slave was well on his way to safety.

After emancipation many churches that had previously aligned themselves with the Wesleyan Methodist Connection of America on the abolitionist cause returned to the Methodist Episcopal Church. Others, however, chose to remain separate because of their belief in John Wesley's teaching of Christian perfection. The Wesleyan Methodist Connection continued to grow throughout Ohio and across the United States. An international presence was established through the development of foreign missions.

In the late 1800s a spiritual awakening occurred in America that was labeled the "Holiness movement" due to its emphasis on the doctrine of Christian perfection and the experience of holiness. This awakening had far-reaching consequences and brought about another stream that would eventually merge with the Wesleyan Methodist Connection of America. Two preachers, Martin Wells Knapp and Seth C. Rees, were affected by the preaching of the Holiness movement. Their paths crossed in Cincinnati at the end of the nineteenth century. Recognizing the kindred spirit that existed between them, they inaugurated the International Holiness Union and Prayer League in September 1897. "The purpose of the union was to rally holiness people for a more vigorous soul-winning effort with worldwide holiness evangelism as the primary goal" (Relly et al., *The Discipline of The Wesleyan Church,* 2000 [Indianapolis: Wesleyan Publishing

The Africa Wesleyan Methodist Church in Africa (north of Columbus) was a part of the Underground Railroad, providing safe passage for escaping slaves on their way north. (Courtesy of Leroy A. Wilcox)

House, 2001], 28). The International Holiness Union and Prayer League, with its origins in Ohio, experienced a series of mergers with other like-minded churches over the next twenty-five or so years, eventually arriving at the name Pilgrim Holiness Church.

Both the Pilgrim Holiness Church and the Wesleyan Methodist Connection of America had a strong presence in Ohio. As early as the 1940s informal and formal talks were conducted about the possibility of merging these two bodies into one denomination. The next twenty years brought additional conversations, which eventually resulted in votes by both denominations to unite as The Wesleyan Church. The merger occurred in 1968.

Consolidation of individual churches in Ohio under The Wesleyan Church was accomplished by the creation of two districts, known as the Eastern Ohio District of The Wesleyan Church and the Western Ohio District of The Wesleyan Church. The first district superintendents of the merged denomination were Rev. Roy Ankrim (Eastern) and Rev. Melroy Ward (Western). These men were followed by Revs. John Minsker

III, C. E. Hanks, and David Holdren, and Jeffrey Mansell in the Eastern Ohio District and by Revs. Walter Jeffries and James Vermilya in the Western Ohio District.

The resignation of Rev. Vermilya in 1999 prompted a discussion between the districts about the possibility of uniting the state under one district. Extensive studies were completed on the creation of not only a new district but a new model of district ministry for The Wesleyan Church. The plan for merger was enthusiastically adopted by delegates from both districts meeting at the Dayspring Wesleyan Church in Marion on March 4, 2000. The new district was named the Greater Ohio District of The Wesleyan Church.

The mission statement adopted by the Greater Ohio District states, "The mission of the Greater Ohio District is to equip and empower its local churches to fulfill the Great Commission in the spirit of the Great Commandment." Aggressive church planting and active development of local and district leaders characterize the district's present ministry. In a growing, ethnically diverse culture, ministry to the Hispanic community in the state is being pursued through the establishment of churches with Spanish-speaking pastors and the development of a Bible institute for the training of Hispanic pastors and local church workers. The district also supports international ministries in India, Mexico, and Central and South America.

BELIEFS

The Wesleyan Church, like its parent bodies, ascribed many of its tenets of faith to the teachings of John Wesley (1703–91), an Anglican priest in England. The "Methodists," as they became known, made their way to the colonies during and after the Revolutionary War. Under the leadership of such men as Francis Asbury and Thomas Coke a strong movement in the United States was established. Unique to the doctrines of the Methodist Church was the teaching of Christian perfection, in which Wesley taught that the heart of man could be so changed by the work of the Holy Spirit as not to will to sin any longer. This did not rule out the possibility of future transgressions against God, but implied a dominant disposition of sinless obedience to God made possible by the believer's being completely controlled by the Holy Spirit.

A fuller statement of Wesleyan beliefs includes belief in one God who is Father, Son, and Holy Spirit and the savior of all men and women who put their faith in Him alone for eternal life. Wesleyans believe that those who receive new life in Christ are called to be holy in character and conduct and can live this way only by being filled with the Lord's Spirit. They believe in the Bible as the inerrant word of God and seek to establish their faith and actions on its teachings. Wesleyans believe that God wills for people everywhere to know Him and that the purpose of the church is to tell the world about Christ through worship, witness, and loving deeds.

CURRENT DEMOGRAPHICS

At the time of Ohio's bicentennial the Greater Ohio District of the Wesleyan Church consists of ninety-six local congregations. Three of these congregations are located in West Virginia. On any given Sunday, more than eight thousand persons can be found worshiping in Wesleyan congregations across Ohio. Churches are evenly distributed across the state of Ohio, with the exception of the far northeast corner of the state. The largest churches are found in Galloway, Athens, Chillicothe, Greenville, Newark, and Marion.

The Wesleyan Church as a whole numbers approximately seventeen hundred congregations throughout North America, with more than two thousand additional congregations under its foreign mission's ministries. Its international center is located in Indianapolis, Indiana.

CONTACT INFORMATION

The Wesleyan Church: *www.wesleyan.org*

Wesleyan Ministry Center, P.O. Box 508, Galloway, Ohio 43119, 614-870-6962, *www.gowesleyan.org*

RESOURCES

McLeister, Ira Ford, and Roy S. Nicholson. *Conscience and Commitment: The History of the Wesleyan Methodist Church of America.* Marion, Ind.: The Wesley Press, 1976.

Relly, Ron, et al. *The Discipline of The Wesleyan Church, 2000.* Indianapolis: Wesleyan Publishing House, 2001.

Thomas, Paul Westphal, and Paul William Thomas. *The Days of Our Pilgrimage: The History of the Pilgrim Holiness Church.* Marion, Ind.: The Wesley Press, 1976.

CHURCH OF GOD
(ANDERSON, INDIANA)

John A. McFarland

HISTORY

T HE CHURCH OF GOD REFORMATION MOVEMENT BEGAN IN OHIO
around 1880 as a result of efforts by Daniel Sidney Warner (1842–95)
and others to reform Christianity from all the bitter divisions among the
many Christian denominations. Warner came to active faith in Jesus
Christ in February 1865 during winter revival services conducted by the
general eldership of the Churches of God in North America (founded by
John Winebrenner and based in Findlay, Ohio). While attending Oberlin
College, he felt a call to ministry. He turned to private study, and his
spiritual journey led him to become an avid student of the Bible. Warner
eagerly embraced the great truths restored during the Protestant Reformation, such as (a) one is made acceptable to God through one's faith
rather than one's good deeds, (b) all believers are priests, and (c) God
causes believers to be godly in their hearts and daily living and then
works to enable them to be Christlike in all things. During his time with
the Winebrennerian Churches of God, he believed this group of churches
to be the most like the New Testament pattern for the church, especially
since they used the biblical name Church of God. But his preaching on
the experience of godly living brought him into conflict with the leadership of the Winebrennerians, and they ultimately asked him to leave.

Warner saw the biblical church not as a collection of much divided denominations but as a fellowship of believers united under God's name, Christlike in its life and service, and free from denominational restrictions and authority. In addition to his preaching, he promoted this view through the *Gospel Trumpet,* a magazine he published. His Gospel Trumpet Company, later located in Anderson, Indiana, ultimately was renamed Warner Press in 1963. The evangelistic efforts, articles, and hymns he wrote contributed greatly toward establishing the movement.

Music played an important part in gathering an audience when Warner and others went out to preach. The message of the Church of God movement penned in song by Warner, Barney Warren, Charles Naylor, and others called for believers to "come out" of denominational structures and man-made rules and to demonstrate and declare the unity of God's church. Catchy slogans such as "We reach our hands in fellowship to every blood-washed one" and "A united church for a divided world" helped to express their emphasis on unity. The leadership of the movement identified itself as neither denominational nor Protestant, instead tracing its roots back to New Testament times without going through the lineage of the Roman Catholic Church. These, then, were some of the things that enabled the Church of God Reformation Movement to establish itself.

The movement started in Northwest Ohio and rapidly expanded throughout the state and beyond. Congregations seemed to spring up everywhere following evangelistic meetings. The first camp meeting of the Church of God (1895) was located just west of Payne, Ohio. Since then the state has grown into five districts, each with its own campgrounds. A state camp was established near Marengo for youth camping and retreats. In addition, the movement within Ohio has changed from a personality-driven ministry to a more formally structured organization. During the transition, strong voices of conservatism helped to guide the process so the work of the church could become strengthened without empowering any leader or group with governing authority. As a result, the Church of God remains a voluntary association of congregations with governing authority at the local level rather than with the district or state structures that can thus model unity while calling the church at large to conform to New Testament standards.

The Church of God is alive and well in Ohio with about 224 congregations (thirty-seven of which are African American), around 650 li-

First Church of God in Wauseon was established in 1890 and is the oldest existing Church of God congregation in Ohio. (Courtesy of John McFarland and the First Church of God at Wauseon, Ohio)

censed or ordained ministers (including a significant portion of women), and a wealth of programs at the local, district, and state levels. Some of these programs have general appeal, while others are age specific (youth, senior adults) or gender based (Women of the Church of God, Churchmen). Ministers and church representatives gather for district as well as statewide meetings each year. Voluntary support by congregations as well as fees from camping and various events help to fund the ministry of the Church of God in Ohio. Efforts are currently underway to promote growth through natural church development principles, structured restarts, and church planting.

Over the last several years the movement has made great strides toward balancing its structure and program. Efforts toward racial reconciliation have ensured a more balanced racial representation in district and state ministry structures as well as cooperative ministry events. Special programs have been promoted to support and encourage women in ministry.

In fulfilling the great commission, the Church of God not only maintains an evangelistic focus within the state but also fully funds eight missionary households (Argentina, Australia, Ecuador, Eurasia, Hong Kong,

Japan, Tanzania, and Zambia). This support is in addition to the North American and global missionary projects in more than ninety countries around the world financially assisted by the many congregations of the Church of God in Ohio. Besides the monetary gifts, many congregations and state groups promote work camps to minister to the needy by providing medical supplies and education and constructing worship facilities. Thus, the Reformation Movement of the Church of God, in both its proclamation and practice, is providing a good model of what a New Testament church should be.

BELIEFS

Trinitarian View of God

We believe in the one true and eternal God, creator and sustainer of all things, who expresses Himself as Father, Son, and Holy Spirit.

Salvation

We preach Christ Jesus—God's eternal Son, born of a virgin, savior of the whole world, crucified, risen, and ascended back to heaven—as the only means of obtaining from God eternal salvation (forgiveness for sins, being saved from going to hell). Salvation is a free gift from God and involves believing, asking, and receiving; it in no way depends on any good works on our part.

Bible

With highest regard, we hold the Bible to be the inspired word of God. Although we have no formal creed and keep ourselves open to all truth, we look to God's word as the ultimate authority for beliefs and practices.

Church

We promote unity among all believers by lifting up the New Testament pattern of the church as the family of God. The church comprises only those who have accepted Jesus as their personal savior and has no denominational requirements for membership or other barriers that divide what should be a united fellowship of God's people. All believers in Jesus should present a unified witness to the redemptive work of God in the world.

Holiness

Holiness is the experience of belonging to God, living daily above sin, and being used by God to serve others. This lifestyle is made possible by a second work of grace, following one's decision to become a follower of Christ. It is a commitment to allow the Holy Spirit free influence over one's daily life.

Kingdom

We view the Kingdom of God as a present reality, spiritual in nature, and expressed as the ongoing battle against evil spiritual forces. Through this battle, believers free others overcome by sin and learn to reign over sin and Satan as Jesus did.

Eschatology

We proclaim that the end of the earth will occur when Jesus appears, ushers in eternity, raises all the dead, and separates during the final judgment those who accepted his offer of salvation from those who rejected his offer of love and forgiveness. Those who rejected him will spend eternity apart from God in a literal hell; those who accepted him will be taken home to heaven.

Ordinances

We practice three ordinances: believer's baptism, communion, and footwashing. All three are regarded as symbolic expressions of spiritual experiences without sacramental grace being bestowed during their observance.

CURRENT DEMOGRAPHICS

2001:

Number of congregations:	223
Number of districts:	5
Congregations per district:	
Northwest	20
Northeast	61
Central	59
Southwest	53
Southeast	30
Total Sunday morning attendance:	330,635

Although most congregations are found in small towns and rural areas, about two-thirds of Church of God attendees are located in large cities and metropolitan areas. Almost 60 percent of the congregations average less than a hundred in attendance, while 5 percent average more than five hundred.

Membership (in the denominational understanding) does not exist in the Church of God, so figures are not available.

CONTACT INFORMATION

Church of God national website: *www.chog.org*

Ohio Ministries Center, 3438 Township Road 221, P.O. Box 276, Marengo, Ohio 43334, 740-747-2916, *ohiochog@bright.net, bdeel@rrohio.com*

RESOURCES

Byers, Andrew. *Birth of a Reformation: Life and Labors of D. S. Warner.* Guthrie, Okla.: Faith Publishing House, 1966.

Callen, Barry. *It's God's Church! The Life and Legacy of Daniel Sidney Warner.* Anderson, Ind.: Warner Press, 1995.

From Heaven to Earth (video reenactment of the early days of the movement and how it grew). Produced by Church of God Ministries (Anderson, Indiana) in the 1950s. Available from Warner Press, P.O. Box 2499, Anderson, Indiana 46018–9988.

THE SALVATION ARMY

Linda D. Johnson

HISTORY

IN 1871 CABINET MAKER AND LAY PREACHER JAMES JERMY MOVED TO what he called "the beautiful City of Clevleand [*sic*]." He had emigrated from England to Canada the year before with the blessing of William and Catherine Booth, the leaders of London's Christian Mission. The Mission, which would become The Salvation Army in 1878, had been formed in 1865 by the Booths to reach out to sinners in the bars and slums of the city.

In Cleveland Jermy happened into a small African American church led by a young minister, James Fakler. When Jermy told Fakler about the Christian Mission, Fakler said, "Brother, that is what I have been waiting for." By 1872 the city had four "mission stations" and seven preachers, who often conducted open-air meetings that drew large crowds, especially in the "Whiskey Hill" district of Haymarket.

When Jermy and Fakler left Cleveland, the work died out there, but they had paved the way for The Salvation Army, with William Booth as its first general. In 1882 Steubenville became the first city in Ohio to have a Salvation Army corps (church).

The pioneering years for the Army in Ohio were turbulent. Nine Salvationists were jailed for conducting street services in Dayton. Sympathetic townspeople brought provisions to the jailed Salvationists. In Cleveland, Salvationists sold yellow hymnbooks for ten cents and played tambourines to attract attention. One officer, Lieutenant Blackburn, was quoted in the *Plain Dealer* as saying, "We will hold meetings here and in the low and degraded parts of the city and try to save the souls of men and women that the churches never reach" (October 29, 1883).

Established in 1884, the East Liverpool Salvation Army church became known as the "corps of the gallant 600." Despite intense persecution from authorities and even other Christians, these six hundred people had accepted Jesus as savior during the corps's first six months. Here, Tom Manton also organized the first Salvation Army band in the United States; it included African American as well as white members.

From the outset the Army was multicultural in nature. Early ministries in Ohio reached out to German and Scandinavian immigrants; today, the Army in Ohio has a fast-growing number of Hispanic congregations. Following the example of cofounder Catherine Booth as a theologian and powerful preacher, the Army has also always welcomed women as leaders. In Cincinnati the local newspaper noted that an equal number of men and women made up the team of evangelists that opened the work.

From its beginnings The Salvation Army has always set out to meet people's physical as well as spiritual needs. In 1897 Army "slum sisters" began cleaning the homes of poverty-stricken women in Cincinnati. A children's camp opened on a two-acre plot in the village of Glendale, and the Army established programs for alcoholics. In 1917 the Evangeline Home (named for U.S. Commander Evangeline Booth, William and Catherine's daughter) became the only home for unwed mothers in greater Cincinnati to serve black women and the only hospital in which black doctors could practice surgery.

During World War I the Army provided doughnuts, letter writing, and chapel services for soldiers in France. In the United States, including Ohio, the Army operated service centers known as "huts" or "hostels" that provided food, recreation rooms, libraries, and small chapels for soldiers on their way to war.

The Great Depression brought hard times for the Army, but it never stopped serving people. In Canton, for example, when the banks failed, the Army enlisted volunteers and businesses to provide food, shelter, and help to desperate people.

During World War II, the Army set up canteens throughout Ohio. In Denison, Lucille Mussdorfer established a canteen that served more than

The East Liverpool Citadel, the first Salvation Army building in Ohio, was built in 1884. It is being used today as a credit union. The first Salvation Army band in the United States was formed at East Liverpool. (Courtesy of the Heritage Museum, the Salvation Army USA Eastern Territory)

two hundred thousand servicemen on their way to war. In 1949 the Cleveland Harbor Light program opened to help down-and-out men. Today, the award-winning program provides more than $5 million in community-based services, especially for homeless adults who suffer from chemical dependency and mental illness. The Army's thrift stories support six Ohio Adult Rehabilitation Centers, which provide a comprehensive recovery and work therapy program that also includes Bible study, worship, and spiritual counseling.

The Salvation Army is also known for its rapid response and comprehensive service in time of disaster. During the great flood of 1937, when more than a hundred thousand Cincinnatians lost their homes, a commentator reported, "I passed The Salvation Army's doors often during the flood and saw long lines of hungry being fed. . . . And I saw God" (the

War Cry, February 13 and 20, 1937). Most recently, the Army in Ohio pitched in with fundraising, in-kind donations, and personnel following the September 11, 2001, terrorist attacks on the World Trade Center and Pentagon.

Today The Salvation Army has a strong presence throughout Ohio. Ohio corps are part of two divisions in the Army's USA Eastern Territory, the Northeast Ohio (NEOSA) Division and the Southwest Ohio and Northeast Kentucky (SWONEKY) Division. The Army in Ohio has a strong commitment to youth. NEOSA recently hired and trained more a dozen new youth pastors and established twenty-three learning centers to help children break free of the cycle of poverty. Many new programs are reaching children in innovative ways as part of a SONday'SCOOL™ initiative. For example, in Springfield the Army has the SonShine Club™, an evangelistic after-school program that meets in city schools. And in keeping with the Army's "street ministry" heritage, the Sandusky corps is actually a church on wheels that travels to four at-risk neighborhoods each week, bringing meals and the message of Jesus to children.

BELIEFS

The Salvation Army's mission statement is: "The Salvation Army, an international movement, is an evangelical part of the universal Christian church. Its message is based on the Bible. Its ministry is motivated by the love of God. Its mission is to preach the gospel of Jesus Christ and to meet human needs in His name without discrimination."

The Army is part of the Holiness movement of the evangelical Christian church. Army doctrines affirm that justification is possible only through Jesus Christ; that believers can be made pure, or sanctified, through the work of the Holy Spirit; that the Bible is the inspired word of God and the only divine rule of Christian faith and practice; that Jesus Christ was fully human and fully divine and that he is part of a holy trinity of Father, Son, and Holy Spirit; and that all people will be judged by God.

Based in London, England, The Salvation Army has churches and ministries in 108 countries. Its quasi-military structure is headed by a general; all officers wear uniforms and are ordained clergy. In nearly all cases of officer couples, both partners are ordained and are officers in their own right. Members, called *soldiers*, are believers in Jesus Christ; they may also wear uniforms. When they are enrolled, soldiers sign the Articles of War, in which they affirm belief in the Army's doctrines and agree not to participate in any practices that might harm mind or body. These include drinking alcohol, taking illegal drugs, and dabbling in the occult. *Adherents* are believers who attend Salvation Army churches but do not feel they can commit to all of the Articles of War. Each Army church has an *advisory board* composed of community leaders. Most corps are not self-sufficient; they are supported by territorial and divisional funds raised through donations and capital campaigns. All corps are churches; many offer social services as well.

CURRENT DEMOGRAPHICS

In Ohio, the Army has about 180 officers (ordained clergy), four thousand soldiers (full members), and nine hundred adherents (attenders). The largest concentrations of soldiers are found in Cleveland, Columbus, Dayton, Cincinnati, Akron, Coshocton, and Canton. There are about eighty corps, or churches, in Ohio. The Army's more than one thousand employees and 119,000 volunteers help in the many programs, including emergency shelters, soup kitchens, day-care centers, literacy programs, after-school clubs, nursing homes, family assistance, and camping ministries.

CONTACT INFORMATION

Salvation Army International: *www.salvationarmy.org*

Salvation Army USA: *www.salvationarmyusa.org/www_usn.nsf*

Northeast Ohio Division, 2507 East 22nd Street, Cleveland, Ohio 44115–3202. Mail: P.O. Box 5847, Cleveland, Ohio 44101–0847.

Southwest Ohio and Northeast Kentucky Division, 114 East Central Parkway, Cincinnati, Ohio 45210. Mail: P.O. Box 596, Cincinnati, Ohio 45201, *www.swoneky.org*

RESOURCES

Good News! and *Priority!* From USA East Publications: *www.prioritypeople.org*

McKinley, Edward H. *Marching to Glory: The History of The Salvation Army in the United States, 1880–1992.* Grand Rapids, Mich.: William B. Eerdmans Publishing Co., 1995.

Winston, Diane H. *Red-Hot and Righteous: The Urban Religion of The Salvation Army.* Cambridge, Mass.: Harvard University Press, 2000.

ACKNOWLEDGMENT

The author wishes to thank Colonel Paul M. Kelly for sharing his research on the history of the Salvation Army in Ohio.

CHURCHES OF CHRIST
IN CHRISTIAN UNION

James Schroeder

Members of the Churches of Christ in Christian Union (CCCU) are Christian believers with their roots firmly planted in Ohio soil. Though much smaller than many other denominations described in this book, there are a few facts which make the CCCU important to the student of Ohio history. Every student should be aware that the Churches of Christ in Christian Union is a denomination founded in Ohio, headquartered in Ohio, and having the majority of its churches in Ohio.

HISTORY

The Churches of Christ in Christian Union trace their heritage chiefly through Methodist and Christian Church traditions, especially that of Rev. Barton Stone and the revival held at Cane Ridge, Kentucky, in 1801. Many years later, many Christians were in search of a better way to live with each other and before God after the atrocities of the Civil War. Some of these believers gathered in July 1865, to form the Christian Union in Terre Haute, Indiana. At that conference was a strong Ohio delegation, and it was soon clear that the new group had its largest presence in the Buckeye state.

By the 1880s Holiness Camp Meetings originating in southern New Jersey had spread to Ohio. It is evident that these meetings back East, along with God's Bible School meetings in Cincinnati, had a great impact on the founding of the CCCU. Camp meetings were a gathering of persons who stayed on the grounds overnight in wagons or tents and spent their days in community fellowship, attending preaching meetings led by some of the most renowned orators of the day.

In September 1909, in the sanctuary of the Christian Union Church of Marshall, Ohio (located in Highland County, ten miles southeast of Hillsboro), Rev. James McKibban led a group out from the Southern Ohio Convention of the Christian Union to form a new denomination. The group no longer felt at home in the Christian Union, and on September 25, 1909, the articles of incorporation for the Churches of Christ in Christian Union were signed. The new churches located their headquarters in Washington Court House, Fayette County.

From these beginnings the group experienced tremendous growth in its membership and work among the Ohio churches. By 1915 there were forty churches in the fellowship, and by 1925 the group had grown to sixty churches. It was during these early years that the Churches of Christ in Christian Union began to evangelize and start churches beyond the state of Ohio. One of the most noteworthy of these endeavors was the formation of a church in Pall Mall, Tennessee. The second elder of this church was Sgt. Alvin York, the greatest American war hero of World War I. Sgt. York helped start the church after an Ohio evangelist from the Churches of Christ in Christian Union held services near Pall Mall.

In 1917 Rev. O. L. Ferguson was walking across a field to get a drink from a well when he heard God tell him the land where he was standing should be used to hold camp meeting. Donations were solicited and the land was purchased from the owner. By the next summer a tabernacle had been constructed and the Mount of Praise Camp Meeting was held on the grounds, located on East Ohio Street in Circleville. In recent years the Mount of Praise Camp Meeting has been moved to the new campus for the denominational headquarters and Circleville Bible College. It remains one of the strongest Holiness camp meetings in the United States today. Plans for the near future include building a large tabernacle or auditorium for the meetings.

From the beginning, the leaders of the Churches of Christ in Christian

The international headquarters of the Churches of Christ in Christian Union is located on State Route 22, east of Circleville. (Property of Circleville Bible College. Used with permission)

Union have sensed a need for education among their youth and adults. In the early days a house was purchased in Washington Court House to be used, among other purposes, for a Bible school. From 1910 to 1917 the school operated, teaching classes in bible, theology, and music. Although the school failed, the dream of having a Bible college was not completely forgotten.

On October 12, 1948, Rev. Everett Keaton welcomed ten students to the first day of class at the Mount of Praise Bible College, which was located on the campgrounds in Circleville. Circleville Bible College, as it is known today, remains one of the premier Bible colleges in the country. Recently the school dedicated the Melvin and Laura Maxwell Library in honor of its former president. The school has grown in size. Under the direction of President John Conley (1995–) it has added programs for working adults who wish to continue their education. Through this growth the college has continued to be primarily a school dedicated to training Christians in the understanding of the Bible. While still affiliated with the mother denomination, it welcomes students from many different church backgrounds.

The Churches of Christ in Christian Union remain a vital part of many communities across our state. Some of our churches are timeless and historical—in them people worship in the same way they have since before the formation of the CCCU. Other churches are as progressive and modern as any in the world, with multimedia presentations built into their Sunday worship services. Regardless of style, these churches remain anchors in their local communities, places of fellowship and celebration, as well as safe havens in times of natural disaster and crisis. The local congregations, the Bible college, the missionaries, the denominational leaders, and the camps are all interesting and important parts of our history. With God's assistance they will continue to serve others and glorify God for many years to come.

BELIEFS

The people of the Churches of Christ in Christian Union share beliefs similar to the historic Methodist teachings of John Wesley, Charles Wesley, and Francis Asbury. These beliefs, often described as "Wesleyan Holiness" state that a person can have his or her life completely cleansed from sin. This state of "entire sanctification" is possible for every believer and is the goal of the Christian life. This doctrine is the hallmark of our faith.

From the beginning the church also clearly established its position on four social issues. The church favored women's suffrage; one of the nine original ministers who signed its charter was a woman, Eliza Wamsley. Second, the church was a firm supporter of the Temperance movement, which was also born in southern Ohio. Tobacco was an important issue in these southern Ohio barley-growing communities, and in 1912 the council of the church passed a strong resolution against ministers using tobacco or joining secret societies. The fourth issue the churches faced head on was the Ku Klux Klan; in 1924 it passed a special resolution banning Klan activities in the church and by its pastors and leaders.

CURRENT DEMOGRAPHICS

As of 2002 the denomination had at least fifty active missionaries and supported countless others through its missions department. There are two hundred churches affiliated with the Churches of Christ in Christian

Union. The majority are still in Ohio, though the group includes congregations in thirteen other states and the West Indies.

CONTACT INFORMATION

Churches of Christ in Christian Union: *www.cccuhq.org*

Churches of Christ in Christian Union, World Gospel Mission: *www.wgm.org*

Circleville Bible College, 1426 Lancaster Pike, Circleville, Ohio 43113, 740-474-8896, *www.biblecollege.edu*

RESOURCES

Brown, Kenneth, and Louis Brevard. *Our Goodly Heritage.* Circleville, Ohio: Circle Printing, 1970.

Case, David. *What We Believe: A Layperson's Guide to Wesleyan Holiness Theology.* Circleville, Ohio: D. A. Case, 2000.

CHRISTIAN AND MISSIONARY ALLIANCE

Arnold R. Fleagle

HISTORY

A CANADIAN MINISTER NAMED ALBERT BENJAMIN SIMPSON MOVED to the United States, and after successful pastorates in Louisville, Kentucky, and New York City formed the Christian and Missionary Alliance in 1887. Dr. Harry M. Shuman assessed the founder's legacy in these terms: "To A. B. Simpson must go the chief honor, for he was the instrument used of God to bring into evidence this missionary movement through which have flowed streams of blessing to the whole world" (*All for Jesus,* xii). This movement was not initially a denomination, but a group of societies or "branches" that committed to spread the good news of Jesus Christ around the world and stress the fullness of Jesus Christ in personal experience.

In 1909 the leaders of the Christian and Missionary Alliance first designated the societies or branches in Ohio and West Virginia as the Central District. A report in 1916/17 stated that there were twenty-five organized branches (churches) and eight unorganized branches. On May 6, 1918, the Central District took another growth step and became incorporated. This incorporation encompassed the states of Ohio, West Virginia, Indiana, Michigan, and Kentucky and the southern parts of Illinois and Missouri.

Under the direction of District Superintendent Rev. H. E. Nelson

The Union Avenue Christian and Missionary Alliance Church, Cleveland, the oldest church in the Central District, is an African American congregation started in 1890. (Courtesy of Central District Archives)

(1928–41), the work of the Central District grew. This period of expansion translated into increased missionary giving, the opening of new churches, and the retiring of the district's heavy financial debts. The Central District did not escape the adverse affects of the Great Depression in the 1930s, however, many new missionaries were appointed and sent out to various countries across the globe. Numerical growth occurred in the United States and across the world, and intensive prayer and significant sacrifice became trademarks of the movement.

In 1965 the General Council of the Christian and Missionary Alliance voted to change the boundaries of its districts. Rev. Neil E. Fye was elected district superintendent of a redefined Central District that included eastern Ohio and West Virginia. A new heartbeat for expansion led to a series of consultations that laid the basis for church growth and new church planting. An important part of this expansion involved the organization and ministry of newly planted African American churches. In 1979 the Central District purchased land in Wadsworth, Ohio. Under the leadership of District Superintendent Rev. Charles Holmes, a new office complex was completed and the district headquarters, previously located in Beulah Beach and Norton, Ohio, moved in.

The 1990s witnessed the team of Rev. Howard D. Bowers, district superintendent, and Dr. Gordon Meier, director of development, assuming leadership of the district. Church growth increased dramatically, and sixteen churches were planted, bringing the total number of churches to seventy-three.

Currently Dr. Gordon Meier is the district superintendent, and he has cast a vision that by 2007 the Central District will have one hundred churches, twenty-five thousand people, one hundred new missionaries, and a million-dollar annual district budget. The Central District leadership team now includes a director of church planting, Rev. Terry D. Smith, a director of church development, Dr. Arnold R. Fleagle, and directors of missions' mobilization, Drs. Woodford C. and Charlotte Stemple. The vision statement for the Central District is "A Revived Church . . . Planting and Growing Healthy Great Commission Churches."

BELIEFS

There is one God, who is infinitely perfect, existing eternally in three persons: Father, Son, and Holy Spirit. Jesus Christ is true God and true man. He was conceived by the Holy Spirit and born of the Virgin Mary. He died upon the cross, the just for the unjust, as a substitutionary sacrifice, and all who believe in him are justified on the ground of his shed blood. He arose from the dead according to the scriptures. He is now at the right hand of the Majesty on high as our great high priest. The Holy Spirit is a divine person, sent to indwell, guide, teach, empower the believer, and convince the world of sin, of righteousness, and of judgment. The Old and New Testaments, inerrant as originally given, were verbally inspired by God and are a complete revelation of His will for the salvation of men. Man was originally created in the image and likeness of God; he fell through disobedience, incurring thereby both physical and spiritual death. All men are born with a sinful nature, are separated from the life of God, and can be saved only through the atoning work of the Lord Jesus Christ. Salvation has been provided through Jesus Christ for all people, and those who repent and believe in him are born again of the Holy Spirit, receive the gift of eternal life, and become the children of God.

It is the will of God that each believer should be filled with the Holy Spirit and be sanctified wholly, being separated from sin and the world and fully dedicated to the will of God, thereby receiving power for holy living and effective service. Provision is made in the redemptive work of the Lord Jesus Christ for the healing of the mortal body.

Prayer for the sick and anointing with oil are taught in the scriptures and are privileges for the church in this present age.

CURRENT DEMOGRAPHICS

Churches in Ohio: 118
Members in Ohio: 33,453

CONTACT INFORMATION

Christian and Missionary Alliance: *www.cmalliance.org*
Central District of the Christian and Missionary Alliance, 1218 High Street, Wadsworth, Ohio 44281, 330-336-2911, *CDCMA@Wadsnet.com*

RESOURCES

Fye, Neil E. *A Story of God's Working: Central District History.* Wadsworth, Ohio: Central District Publishing, 1995.
Mead, Frank Spencer. *A Handbook of Denominations.* Nashville: Abingdon Press, 2001.

Presbyterian and Reformed

PRESBYTERIAN CHURCH (U.S.A.)

L. Gordon Tait

HISTORY

OHIO PRESBYTERIANS, ALONG WITH OTHER PROTESTANTS, WOULD claim that the history of their church goes straight back to the New Testament church founded by Jesus Christ. They would further say that the Catholic Church in Europe in the sixteenth century was in great need of a reformation. John Calvin in Geneva and John Knox in Scotland were two outstanding reformers who helped to purify the Church and bring the Reformed or Presbyterian Churches into being.

Their spiritual descendents came from Europe and Scotland to America. One of them, the Reverend Francis Makemie, an Irish-educated Scot, settled on the shore of Virginia. In the late 1600s he established Presbyterian churches in Maryland and Virginia. From these beginnings in the east, Presbyterian ministers, missionaries, and lay people moved across the Allegheny Mountains and down the Ohio River, settling churches as they went.

The first Presbyterians in Ohio were two ministers from eastern Pennsylvania, the Reverends Charles Beatty and George Duffield, who came to explore the possibility of starting a mission station. They preached to a group of Native Americans on September 21, 1766, near present-day New-

William Lucas painting of the Reverend Charles Beatty and the Reverend George Duffield, Presbyterian ministers from eastern Pennsylvania, preaching to Native Americans beside the Tuscarawas River in 1766. Date unknown. (Courtesy of The Presbyterian Church, Coshocton, Ohio)

comerstown. Their sermons were undoubtedly the first ever heard in what was to become the state of Ohio.

The first Presbyterian church in Ohio was organized in 1790 in what was then a small village that, in the same year, took the name of Cincinnati. The Reverend David Rice, known as "Father Rice," had come from Kentucky to preach in the area. On October 16, 1790, he organized the "mother church" of Presbyterians in the area. Those early Presbyterians worshipped for a year without a regular minister until the Reverend James Kemper moved with his wife, Judith, and their ten children from Danville, Kentucky, to Cincinnati in October 1791. That trip was considered to be so dangerous, especially because of possible Native American attacks, that Cincinnati Presbyterians sent a military escort to protect the Kempers as they traveled overland and then across the Ohio River in a flatboat to their new home.

Before becoming a minister, James Kemper had been a farmer, a school-teacher, and a theological student who studied with Father Rice. He now preached regularly in Cincinnati and elsewhere, usually riding from place to place on horseback, often many miles from home. His usual clothing, we are told, included knee breeches, silver knee and shoe buckles, a coat with three high collars, and a large white scarf.

The first Presbyterian worship services were held outdoors beneath the trees, with worshippers seated on split logs placed across stumps. Each man brought his rifle to church to guard against Native American attacks. In 1792 the congregation cleared the land at Main and Fourth Streets and built a rough frame house of worship, thirty feet by forty feet. Church members sat on planks taken from river flatboats. The pulpit was made out of rough cherrywood. During the week the church sometimes served as a courthouse. The first congregation that worshipped there continues today in downtown Cincinnati as the Covenant–First Presbyterian Church, at the corner of Eighth and Elm Streets.

In 1796 a group left the original congregation in the village and started a new church in what was then called Duck Creek. In 1818 the name changed and this congregation became the Pleasant Ridge Presbyterian Church. It continues to this day on Montgomery Road in the Pleasant Ridge section of Cincinnati. These two Cincinnati churches are proud of their long history, which began in 1790 when the city was still a tiny village and Ohio was not yet a state.

A few years after 1790, Presbyterians moved into Ohio from western Pennsylvania, New Jersey, and the Carolinas. Some settled in a large area of nearly four million acres in northeastern Ohio called the Western Reserve. Another religious group, the Congregationalists, also came to this area. They cooperated with the Presbyterians in a Plan of Union (1801), a blueprint for founding churches and supplying them with pastors. Those who participated in the plan were known as "Presbygationalists."

By the middle of the nineteenth century there were Presbyterian churches in most parts of Ohio. In 1861 Presbyterians, by then a national church, split over the issue of slavery into a Northern and a Southern church. These two churches were finally reunited in 1983.

However, in 1858 two smaller Presbyterian groups, the General Synod of the Associate Reformed Church and the Synod of the Associate Presbyterian Church, joined to form the United Presbyterian Church of North America. This denomination established its own churches in many parts of Ohio until 1958 when it merged with the Northern Presbyterian Church. Today throughout Ohio and the rest of the nation, the vast majority of Presbyterians belong to the Presbyterian Church (U.S.A.), which was formed in 1983. Other small Presbyterian denominations in Ohio include the Presbyterian Church in America (sixteen churches) and the Orthodox Presbyterian Church (five churches).

From the time of Calvin to the present, Presbyterians have believed in the importance of education for both laity and clergy. The laity had to be able to read and understand the Bible. Ministers were required to have a broad college-level education and then be trained in many religious subjects, such as Hebrew and Greek, the original languages of the Bible. Thus, Presbyterians were quick to start schools, colleges, and seminaries. Today there are two colleges in Ohio that are related by agreement to the Presbyterian Church (U.S.A.)—the College of Wooster in Wooster and Muskingum College in New Concord. Lane Theological Seminary in Cincinnati was founded in 1829 and later merged with McCormick Theological Seminary in Chicago.

What is surprising is how influential the Presbyterians were in creating what are now state universities. When Ohio University was founded in 1804, its first president was the Reverend Jacob Lindley, a Presbyterian. The next four presidents were also Presbyterian ministers. For several decades after Miami University was chartered in 1818, all the presidents were Presbyterians. The first of these was the Reverend Robert Bishop.

Famous Ohio Presbyterians include U.S. president Benjamin Harrison, William H. McGuffey of McGuffey Readers fame, Nobel Prize winner (physics) Arthur H. Compton, and astronaut and U.S. senator John Glenn.

BELIEFS

Presbyterian beliefs are to be found in the Book of Confessions. This book includes creeds and statements of faith from earliest times (Apostles' Creed) to the twentieth century (Confession of 1967).

Presbyterians see God in Jesus Christ, who is fully human yet fully divine. God is majestic and powerful, the Lord of all creation, and yet totally loving. Human beings are sinful and guilty of pride and wrongdoing, but are forgiven and made new through the death and resurrection of Jesus. God is spirit, and through that Holy Spirit works in our world. God is mystery and holiness, and in some sense more wonderful than we can ever imagine. As we live from day to day, God inspires us to love and to work for justice and peace.

Like other Protestants, Presbyterians observe and find special meaning in two sacraments: baptism and communion, or the Lord's Supper.

The word *presbyterian* is the New Testament term for *elder*. Lay elders are important in Presbyterian church government. Church members belong to local congregations led by a session, which is made up of the minister and elders. Churches in a region are organized into a presbytery.

The presbyteries elect members to large regional bodies called synods, and to the national organization called a general assembly, which makes decisions and discusses issues for the whole church. Presbyterians believe that this representative form of government, which includes ministers and elders on every level, remains faithful to the New Testament.

CURRENT DEMOGRAPHICS

There are eight presbyteries in Ohio and 625 churches, with more than 130,000 church members. Presbyterian churches are to be found in major cities, towns, and rural areas in Ohio.

CONTACT INFORMATION

Synod of the Covenant, 1911 Indianwood Circle, Suite B, Maumee, Ohio 43537, 800-848-1030, *www.synodofthecovenant.org*

Presbyterian Church (U.S.A.), 100 Witherspoon Street, Louisville, Kentucky 40202–1396, 888-728-7228, *www.pcusa.org*

RESOURCES

Committee on History. *One Hundred and Fifty Years of Presbyterianism in the Ohio Valley, 1790–1940*. Cincinnati: N.p., 1941.

Nutt, Rick. *Contending for the Faith: The First Two Centuries of the Presbyterian Church in the Cincinnati Area*. Cincinnati: Presbytery of Cincinnati, 1991.

Smylie, James H. *A Brief History of the Presbyterians*. Louisville, Ky.: Geneva Press, 1996.

Weeks, Louis B. *To Be a Presbyterian*. Atlanta: John Knox Press, 1983.

Welsh, E. B., ed. *Buckeye Presbyterianism*. Wooster, Ohio: Collier Printing Co., 1968.

CHRISTIAN REFORMED CHURCH IN NORTH AMERICA

Richard H. Harms

HISTORY

THE OLDEST CHRISTIAN REFORMED CONGREGATION IN OHIO WAS formed when immigrants from the southern part of the Netherlands, traveling westward along the Ohio River, settled in Cincinnati beginning in 1843. These immigrants were the beginning of a larger migration of European people to the United States during the nineteenth century. They came seeking economic opportunity not available in their homelands. For the Dutch in the 1840s, one particular cause for leaving was the hunger resulting from the potato blight.

Most of the Dutch immigrants were deeply religious and sought to join Christian churches theologically similar to the Reformed tradition that had been practiced in the Netherlands since the sixteenth century. At first, this was not possible in Cincinnati since too few from that tradition had settled there. Instead, most of the immigrants continued westward to farm. The small group that did settle in Cincinnati found a leader in Anthonie Van Agthoven, who opened a cooperage. They began worshiping in the basement of the Ninth Street Baptist Church, which aided the Dutch-speaking settlers. In 1853 the Baptist congregation called Jacobus De Rooy, also from the Netherlands, to be a missionary to the Dutch group. De Rooy's leadership allowed the congregation to worship in its own building. When De Rooy left two years later to work in New Jersey,

Rev. Gerrit J. Raidt came to organize a formal congregation. Because of theological similarity and the offer of financial support, the congregation joined the Presbyterian rather than the Baptist church.

The congregation grew slowly during the Civil War. Some newcomers were immigrants arriving from the Netherlands; some had initially lived in western Michigan. In 1867 two recent immigrants who wished to become ministers felt that Presbyterian doctrine was too different from Reformed doctrine. They convinced several other church members to leave the congregation and organize a Christian Reformed congregation. The Christian Reformed denomination had been formed in western Michigan in 1857 by immigrants seeking to maintain direct ties to their former churches in the Netherlands. The Cincinnati group that joined the Christian Reformed Church subsequently moved into its own facility on Hughes Street.

In the early 1850s another group from the southern Netherlands, primarily the province of Zeeland, immigrated to Ohio, settling in Cleveland's east side, which was then a small community. As more immigrants arrived, a congregation was organized that joined what is now the Reformed Church in America, whose theological roots also reach into the Dutch Reformed tradition. Believing their concerns and complaints about doctrine and some practices in this denomination were not satisfactorily addressed, a group of members left to form an independent congregation in 1871. At the same time, another small Dutch settlement, from the province of Gelderland, formed on the west side of the city. These immigrants also organized a church and erected a small building on West 58th Street. A short time later the eastside group bought a building from the Episcopalians and moved it to a lot on Calvert Street.

Because of the problems that the eastside Dutch church had experienced, the westside church decided not to join the Reformed Church in America. Instead the two congregations looked to join another denomination. One of the westside members, who was from Cincinnati, suggested the Christian Reformed Church. Although both congregations were small, in April 1872 they joined the Christian Reformed Church as separate churches sharing one set of officers. About ten years later, further dissent within the Reformed Church in America congregation caused several more families to join each of the Christian Reformed churches. This growth allowed the two to form two completely separate congregations.

Initially determined to remain Dutch in character, particularly through the use of the Dutch language in worship, the outreach efforts of the individual congregations were primarily directed to newly arrived Dutch immigrants. Since the number of Dutch settling in Ohio was modest compared to places in Michigan, Illinois, and Iowa, the growth of the Christian Reformed churches in Ohio was also modest.

A fourth congregation—in Willard, Huron County—resulted from a decision by nine families and several single men in Kalamazoo, Michigan, during the mid-1890s to leave the muck fields that had made Kalamazoo synonymous with celery for similar opportunities in the marshy land in New Haven and Richmond Townships in Ohio. The congregation, known successively as Sharon, Chicago Junction, and now Willard (but popularly as Celeryville for much of the time), was formed in 1896. Because of the difficulties in cultivating the land and bringing produce to market, the members could not afford to build a church and met in each other's homes for the first ten years. The first structure was erected in 1906 at what is now 4263 Broadway Road. The current structure was completed in 1952.

Following World War I the denomination began to use English instead of Dutch, and after World War II—in spite of a new wave of Dutch immigrants, particularly in Canada, that again added a strong element of Dutch ethnicity to the membership—the denomination began to focus on becoming more multiethnic. Efforts resulting from these decisions led to the organization of several other churches in Ohio. Maple Heights began in 1943 and was discontinued in 1993, while Calvary Chapel in Willard was open from 1955 to 1979 and Calvary Community Church in Dayton served that community from 1960 to 1986. Churches from these post–World War II efforts still serving are Olentangy in Columbus (1957), Akron (1963), and Community in Toledo (1963). The Akron and Olentangy congregations have active ministry programs to Kent State University and the Ohio State University, respectively.

Currently the denomination has ministries in more than thirty countries. Its U.S. services are conducted in fourteen languages. Its 991 North American congregations are located in thirty-eight states and the District of Columbia and nine of Canada's thirteen provinces and territories. The congregations are particularly numerous in Michigan, Ontario, California, and Iowa.

1893 photograph of First Holland Christian Reformed Church, Mulberry Street, Cincinnati (1891). (Courtesy of Archives, Calvin College, Grand Rapids, Michigan)

BELIEFS

The beliefs and doctrine of the Christian Reformed Church in North America are based on the Holy Bible, God's infallible written word contained in the sixty-six books of the Old and New Testaments. They believe that it was uniquely, verbally, and fully inspired by the Holy Spirit and that it was written without error (inerrant) in the original manuscripts. It is the supreme and final authority in all matters on which it speaks. With many other Christians, the denomination subscribes to the Apostles' Creed, the Athanasian Creed, and the Nicene Creed. The Christian Reformed Church is part of the Christian church that follows the teachings of sixteenth-century reformer John Calvin and is rooted in the Reformed churches in the Netherlands that subscribe to the Belgic Confession, the Canons of Dordt, and the Heidelberg Catechism.

The denomination's ecclesiastical structure involves local, regional, and binational (Canada and the U.S.) levels. Local congregations, which provide a variety of ministries, are administered by a council—a meeting of the elders, deacons, and minister(s)—which has responsibilities detailed in the church order. Classis, a regional group of congregations within a geographical area, has the authority to deal with matters that concern its congregations. A minister and an elder from each congregation are delegated to attend each classis meeting. A classis's decisions are binding on the congregations in its region. There are forty-seven classes in the denomination: twelve in Canada and thirty-five in the United States. The annual synod is a binational gathering that represents all the congregations with delegates from each classis. The tasks of synod include adopting creeds, liturgical forms, hymnals, principles of worship, and moral/ethical positions. Synod also provides general oversight for the joint ministries undertaken among congregations.

CURRENT DEMOGRAPHICS

The Christian Reformed Church in North America (this name was adopted in 1974) is a denomination of 279,000 members in 991 local congregations. Seven congregations with a total of nine hundred members are located in Ohio. With their years of organization, these are: Akron (1963); Crosspoint (1997) in Cincinnati; East Side (1872) and West Park (1872), both in Cleveland; Olentangy (1957) in Columbus; Community (1963) in Toledo; and Willard (1896). Willard has the largest membership (190).

CONTACT INFORMATION

The Christian Reformed Church in North America has two administrative offices, one in the United States and one in Canada:

2850 Kalamazoo Avenue, SE, Grand Rapids, Michigan 49560, 616-224-0744, *crcna@crcna.org, www.crcna.org*

3475 Mainway, P.O. Box 5070, STN LCD 1, Burlington, Ontario L7R 3Y8, 905-336-2920, *crcna@crcna.ca, www.crcna.ca*

RESOURCES

Beets, Henry. *The Christian Reformed Church in North America: Its History, Schools, Missions, Creed and Liturgy, Distinctive Principles and Practices and Its Church Government.* Grand Rapids, Mich.: Eastern Avenue Book Store, 1923.

Bratt, James D. *Dutch Calvinism in Modern America: A History of a Conservative Subculture.* Grand Rapids, Mich.: William B. Eerdmans Publishing Co., 1984.

Christian Reformed Church: *www.crcna.org/crcr/crcr_aboutthecrc.htm*

Kromminga, John. *The Christian Reformed Church: A Study in Orthodoxy.* Grand Rapids Mich.: Baker Book House, 1949.

Schaap, James C. *Our Family Album: The Unfinished Story of the Christian Reformed Church.* Grand Rapids, Mich.: CRC Publications, 1998.

REFORMED CHURCH IN AMERICA

Stephen M. Norden

HISTORY

How is it that the Protestant denomination with the longest uninterrupted ministry in North America is one of the smallest denominations in the state of Ohio? The Reformed Church in America (previously known as the Reformed Protestant Dutch Church) began when the Dutch colonized New Amsterdam, now New York. In April 1628 a group of Dutch colonists gathered for worship in the loft of a mill on the southern tip of Manhattan Island. Since that spring Sunday there has been at least one worship service of the Reformed Church in America every Sunday somewhere in North America. Still, at the beginning of the twenty-first century, there are only seven congregations of the Reformed Church in America in the state of Ohio.

The Reformed faith was brought to this continent by Dutch colonists whose faith had been formed by the teachings of John Calvin. During the Protestant Reformation in Europe, John Calvin preached and taught in Geneva, Switzerland. French Huguenots, in their pursuit of religious freedom, spent some time in Geneva and were significantly influenced by John Calvin. As their journey toward religious and political freedom continued, the Huguenots went to the Netherlands and on to the "new world" of North America. While in the Netherlands the Huguenots promoted the religious teachings of John Calvin, and in 1568 William of Orange declared the Reformed faith to be the official faith of that country. Six years later the Dutch Reformed Church became the state church of the Nether-lands.

As Dutch colonists came to North America in the seventeenth and eigh-teenth centuries, many congregations developed in New York and New Jer-sey. Nineteenth-century Dutch immigrants helped spread the Reformed Church in America to Michigan, Wisconsin, Illinois, and Iowa. After World War II, as the population of the United States began to shift toward the west and southwest, several Reformed Church congregations began in that region of our country, most notably in the state of California.

Until the middle of the twentieth century, most Reformed Church in America congregations were developed around a nucleus of persons whose ethnic background was Dutch. This, in large measure, explains why there are so few Reformed Church congregations in Ohio. In 1855 the first Reformed Church in America congregation in Ohio was organized near Sandusky, but it lasted only a year. Nine years later the First (Hol-land) Reformed Church of Cleveland was organized on the east side of the city. This congregation had a vital ministry for approximately sixty-five years but then was disbanded in 1929. However, this congregation was the mother church of what began as the Second Reformed Church of Cleveland, today known as Calvary Reformed Church, on the city's near westside. A group of members from the First Reformed Church desired to worship in a style that was more "American." No longer did they wish to worship in the Dutch language; they wanted to sing hymns as well as the Dutch Psalter and particularly to have their children incorporated into the mainstream of American life.

Not until the middle of the twentieth century did the Reformed Church in America begin to establish new congregations in Ohio. The late 1940s, the '50s, and the '60s saw the beginning of six new Reformed churches, many of which were given their birth by the Calvary Reformed Church in Cleveland. Riverside Community Church of Cleveland began in 1946. During the 1950s congregations were organized in Brooklyn, Brunswick, and Fairview Park. The Church in the Woods of Parma Park began in 1961, and a congregation was established in Gahanna in 1967. Seventeen years would pass before the next Reformed congregation was begun in the state of Ohio. New Hope Reformed Church began worshiping in an ele-mentary school in Dublin in 1984 and moved into its facility in Powell in

The New Hope Reformed Church in Powell (1991). (Courtesy of Stephen M. Norden)

1991. During the summer of 2002 a new congregation was begun in Lewis Center, a rapidly growing suburb in southern Delaware County.

While the number of congregations and members of the Reformed Church in America in the state of Ohio is quite small, Ohio can be proud of its contribution to the religious history of the United States through some of the Reformed clergy born in the Buckeye state. Chaplain Clark Poling, one of the four chaplains on the USS *Dorchester* during World War II who chose to go down with the sinking vessel while giving their life jackets to men on board, was a Reformed Church minister born in Columbus in 1910. The late Dr. Norman Vincent Peale, pastor of Marble Collegiate Church in New York (the oldest congregation of the Reformed Church in America), noted author and speaker, and arguably one of the best-known clergy of the Reformed Church, was born in Bowersville, Ohio, in 1898.

As the state of Ohio celebrates its bicentennial, the congregations of the Reformed Church in America in this state celebrate also. While small in number, these churches are involved in many vital, thriving programs that make substantial contributions to the spiritual, emotional, and physical well-being of their communities. Visitors to congregations of the Reformed Church in Ohio and other states will find churches that care about them and their families, churches that care about others, churches with a biblical faith, churches they can trust, churches with a solid history, and churches that are interested in meeting their needs.

BELIEFS

In addition to the major tenets of the Christian faith held in common with several other Christian communions and expressed in the creeds of the church (Apostles' Creed, Nicene Creed), certain distinctive elements of Reformed belief emerge. Basic to a Reformed understanding of the Christian faith is the belief that there is no higher authority than the Bible. Reformed people are "people of the Word," as is evidenced by a major theme of the Protestant Reformation: *sola scriptura* (by scripture alone). Additionally, the Reformed Church believes that it is by God's sovereign grace that one comes to faith in God through Jesus Christ. While human response is necessary and important, that response comes as a result of God's initiative and gift of faith. The Reformed faith understands that all of life is under God's rule and that therefore there is no division between sacred and secular. All of life is a gift of God and all of life is to be lived to the glory of God. Therefore, Reformed Christians believe that we have a responsibility to meaningfully engage the world in which we live.

CURRENT DEMOGRAPHICS

Today the seven Ohio congregations of the Reformed Church in America—Brunswick, Brooklyn, Calvary (Cleveland), Good Samaritan (Gahanna), New Hope (Fairview Park), New Hope (Powell), and Parma Park (Cleveland)—are home to approximately twelve hundred persons.

CONTACT INFORMATION

Reformed Church in America, Interchurch Center, 475 Riverside Drive, New York, New York 10115, 212-870-2841, *www.rca.org*

Synod of the Great Lakes, 4500 60th Street SE, Grand Rapids, Michigan, 49512, 616-698-7071.

New Hope Reformed Church, Powell, Ohio: *www.nhrcoh.org*

RESOURCES

Gathered from Many Nations: The Early Years of the Reformed Church in America, 1628–1776 (video). Produced by John Grooters. RCA Distribution Center, 4500 60th Street S.E., Grand Rapids, Michigan 49512.

Hesselink, I. John. *On Being Reformed: Distinctive Characteristics and Common Misunderstandings.* Ann Arbor, Mich.: Servant Publications, 1983.

Roman Catholic

Patrick Mooney

HISTORY

IN THE TWO DECADES FOLLOWING THE FOUNDING OF THE UNITED States, Catholics numbered only about thirty thousand in a nation of four million, more than a million of whom were black slaves. Nearly all Catholics in the young country were of English, Irish, German, or French background; they lived mostly in Maryland and Pennsylvania, where they had been part of the population for several generations. Catholics make up about 23 percent of today's U.S. population and are of diverse ethnic and racial origins. From its beginning as the Ohio Country of the Old Northwest Territory, Ohio has been a leader in the development of the United States. The story of the Catholic Church in Ohio in many ways parallels the development of Ohio and our nation.

The earliest documented presence of Catholics in what is now Ohio was in 1749, when French Jesuit missionary priests from Detroit visited Catholic Native Americans in the Sandusky area. In the same year another Jesuit, Father Joseph Pierre de Bonnecamps, accompanied the expedition of Celeron de Bienville into the Ohio Country and ministered to Miami Indians in the southern part of Ohio.

The earliest migrations of Catholic settlers into Ohio occurred just after 1800, as Ohio entered the Union. Their routes were the Ohio River and Zane's Trace, which had been laid out in 1796 as a trail across southeastern Ohio to connect Wheeling, Virginia (now West Virginia), with

The meeting of Father Edward Fenwick of Kentucky with the Dittoe and Fink families in 1808 near Somerset marked the beginning of the Catholic Church in Ohio. This painting by W. Lamprecht is in St. Joseph's Church near Somerset. (Courtesy of Catholic Record Society, Diocese of Columbus)

the Kentucky settlements. Most of these earliest Ohio Catholics were from the various eighteenth-century Pennsylvania Catholic settlements. After these small beginnings, Ohio's Catholic population grew in a succession of waves of immigration from Europe. The first Catholic immigrants, from the 1800s to the 1830s, were from Ireland. By the 1830s other Catholic immigrants came from the German states, escaping the effects of various adverse conditions occurring there. The Great Irish Potato Famine, which began in 1845, and the failed revolutions of 1848 in the German states brought a much larger immigration of Irish and German Catholics to Ohio.

During the Civil War, Ohio began a period of rapid industrialization and development as a railroad center. Its role as a major agricultural state continued. These changes, along with Ohio's geographical position as the "Gateway State" through which moved much of America's nineteenth-century traffic to the West, ushered in several decades of rapid internal growth and rising national political influence. The need for industrial workers in parts of the state brought about exceptionally large immigration into Ohio of Catholics from Eastern Europe and the Mediterranean in the last decades of the nineteenth century and the first decades of the twentieth. Most of this immigration fed the growth of Ohio's more industrialized urban centers, particularly in the northeastern part of the state. In 2003 one in every five Ohioans was a member of the Catholic Church, and Ohio's most Catholic areas are still those parts of the state that originally attracted industrial workers.

Ohio's earliest Catholics were without clergy to bring them the sacraments of their faith, and in 1804 they petitioned Archbishop John Carroll, who in 1789 had been appointed the first Catholic bishop of the United States, to send priests to Ohio. Carroll's Diocese of Baltimore consisted of the entire United States, and he had only about thirty priests under his jurisdiction. A number of Maryland Catholic families who had moved to central Kentucky beginning in 1785 were being served by a single priest. In 1805 Rev. Edward D. Fenwick, a Dominican priest trained in Europe and a Maryland native, established at the request of Bishop Carroll the Dominican Order in Kentucky and became an itinerant minister to Catholics in Kentucky and Ohio. In 1808, the same year that Bardstown, Kentucky, became the first Catholic diocese west of the Alleghenies, Fenwick made contact with Catholic settlers in southeastern Ohio. In 1818 he blessed the first Catholic Church in Ohio, St. Joseph's near Somerset in Perry County.

Increasing numbers of Catholics in Ohio settlements led to the establishment of the Diocese of Cincinnati in 1821, with Fenwick as bishop. The new diocese stretched as far as Green Bay, Wisconsin, and in the ten years before his death of cholera in 1832, Fenwick continued his itinerant travels by horseback through his vast diocese, traveled to Europe to seek priests and material assistance for Catholics in the West, founded Ohio's first Catholic schools and first institution of higher education (the Athenaeum of Ohio) and newspaper (the *Catholic Telegraph* of Cincinnati, still being published). He brought the Dominican Sisters from Kentucky to Somerset, Ohio, in 1830 to found the first academy for girls and the first congregation of Catholic sisters in Ohio. In addition to preparing young men for the priesthood, the Dominican priests of the Province of St. Joseph, established by Fenwick near Somerset, served as itinerant clergy

St. Joseph's Church (Roman Catholic) near Somerset in Perry County, taken circa 1940. Father Edward Fenwick oversaw the building of a small log-and-stone church at this site. On December 6, 1818, St. Joseph's, the first Catholic Church in Ohio, was dedicated. This 1846 church is on the site of the original building. The adjacent priory was razed in the 1970s. (Courtesy of Catholic Record Society, Diocese of Columbus)

throughout southeastern and central Ohio and ranged as far as Canton and beyond, founding more than twenty parishes by the 1840s. St. Joseph's came to be called "Cradle of the Faith in Ohio." In addition to the contributions of Fenwick and the Dominicans within Ohio, a number of the young priests recruited from throughout Europe to serve in the developing state of Ohio in the first half of the nineteenth century became the first bishops of significant Catholic centers—including Santa Fe, San Francisco, Nashville, Memphis, Galveston, and Milwaukee—in the developing American West.

The Diocese of Cleveland, comprising the northern third of the state, was established in 1847 as a result of very rapid growth of northern parts of Ohio during the second quarter of the nineteenth century. This growth was due in large part to the completion of Ohio's canal system, which connected the Great Lakes and the Ohio River in both eastern and western Ohio. The creation in 1868 of the Diocese of Columbus, with jurisdiction over more than 40 percent of Ohio's eighty-eight counties, was the third and last of the nineteenth-century Catholic jurisdictional divisions. The division of the Diocese of Cleveland to form the Diocese of Toledo in 1910 and that of Youngstown in 1943 reflect large Catholic immigration into the heavily industrialized Lake Erie and Upper Ohio Valley regions. In 1943 thirteen counties in east central and southeastern Ohio were separated from the Diocese of Columbus to form the Diocese of Steubenville.

While Cincinnati remained a strongly German Catholic city, and Columbus mostly German and Irish Catholic, other Ohio urban centers became notable for a multiplicity of ethnic parishes, including German and Irish, but also Italian, Polish, Slovenian, and others. The rapid rise of the Catholic population in Ohio during the nineteenth and twentieth centuries was accompanied by episodes of anti-Catholic feeling, including Know-Nothingism in the 1850s, the American Protective Association movement in the 1890s, and Ku Klux Klan activities directed against Catholics and Jews in the 1920s. Ethnic parishes provided mutual support during these times, but also served as centers for the Americanization of immigrant Catholics. In the 1880s the bishops of the United States first called for extension of the fledgling Catholic school system into every parish where it was possible. By the mid-twentieth century nearly every Ohio Catholic parish had an elementary school, supported entirely by financial and other contributions of Catholic Church members, with no state support. Also in Ohio were a large number of Catholic schools—mainly high schools and academies—operated by religious orders of men and women.

By the mid-twentieth century, Ohio Catholics were also moving into every aspect of Ohio life. The end of the Great Depression, the rising affluence of the post–World War II period, and increased opportunities for higher education changed the lives of all Ohioans, including Ohio Catholics, who were increasingly found in every profession, occupation, and sphere of influence. Ethnic heritage was remembered and valued, but in many ways the American Dream was being realized. The mid-twentieth century was a "bricks and mortar" period of Ohio Catholicism, in which increasing Catholic population and affluence brought about the construction of large numbers of Catholic churches and schools in the developing suburbs.

The Second Vatican Council, a meeting in Rome of all the world's Catholic bishops, which occurred during several years of the 1960s, brought changes to the lives of Catholics around the world. The full effect of council documents, which called for reform and renewal of Catholic liturgy and practice, is not yet felt, and their influence will certainly continue into the twenty-first century. The last quarter of the twentieth century saw a marked decline in the number of ordained male clergy and of women committed to celibate life in community, and a corresponding rise in the number of lay members of the Catholic Church involved in teaching in Catholic schools and colleges and in serving their fellow Catholics in diocesan, parish, and social ministries and in administrative roles within church governance.

Among challenges faced by Ohio Catholics as we celebrate Ohio's bicentennial are demographic shifts as suburban populations mature and significant numbers of Hispanic, Asian, and African Catholics immigrate to Ohio's urban centers, and the need to deal with internal concerns of church life and governance. Despite current challenges, and those yet unknown, Ohio Catholics trust in their future as full and vital participants in a leading state of one of the world's great democratic nations.

BELIEFS

During the celebration of a Catholic mass (service), participants profess their faith by reciting the Nicene Creed:

> We believe in one God, the Father, the Almighty, maker of heaven and earth, of all that is, seen and unseen.
>
> We believe in one Lord, Jesus Christ, the only Son of God, eternally begotten of the Father, God from God, Light from Light, true God from true God, begotten, not made, one in Being with the Father. Through him all things were made. For us [men] and for our salvation he came down from heaven: by the power of the Holy Spirit he was born of the Virgin Mary, and became man.
>
> For our sake he was crucified under Pontius Pilate; he suffered, died and was buried. On the third day he rose again in fulfillment of the Scriptures; he ascended into heaven and is seated at the right hand of the Fa-

ther. He will come again in glory to judge the living and the dead, and his kingdom will have no end.

We believe in the Holy Spirit, the Lord, the giver of life, who proceeds from the Father and the Son. With the Father and the Son he is worshiped and glorified. He has spoken through the Prophets. We believe in one holy, catholic and apostolic Church. We acknowledge one baptism for the forgiveness of sins. We look for the resurrection of the dead, and the life of the world to come.

For the organization and hierarchical structure of the Roman Catholic Church, see *The Catechism of the Catholic Church* (Liguori, Mo.: Liguori Press, 1997), paragraphs 871–933. For the same in brief, see paragraphs 934–45. The Catholic Conference of Ohio is the official representative of the Catholic Church in public matters affecting the church and the general welfare of the citizens of Ohio. Established in 1945, The Catholic Conference of Ohio is the second oldest state bishops' conference in the United States.

CURRENT DEMOGRAPHICS

In 2001 there were more than 2.2 million Catholics in Ohio. Catholics make up 19 percent of Ohio's 11 million people, and Catholics are 23 percent of the population of the United States. The Catholics of Ohio belong to more than nine hundred parishes and missions, are served by more than twenty-five hundred priests and permanent deacons, operate schools and colleges attended by more than 230,000 students, and have twenty-nine hospitals with Catholic affiliation. The Catholic schools and colleges of Ohio are staffed by nearly eleven thousand teachers, 94 percent of whom are lay persons (not priests, permanent deacons, or members of religious orders). Catholic parishes and institutions in Ohio are staffed by many thousands of lay women and men whose responsibilities include nearly every category of institutional and ordinary life (except those functions reserved to ordained clergy) and who provide service of every sort to church members and other citizens of the state. The geographical distribution of Catholic Church members in Ohio varies widely, reflecting the history of Ohio's industrial and urban development and patterns of immigration:

Diocese	No. counties	No. parishes	Members	% of area population
Cleveland	8	235	816,000	29
Toledo	19	161	336,000	23
Youngstown	6	116	262,000	22
Cincinnati	19	230	513,000	18
Columbus	23	107	198,000	9
Steubenville	13	73	41,000	8

CONTACT INFORMATION

United States Conference of Catholic Bishops, 3211 4th Street, NE, Washington, D.C. 20017–1194, 202-541-3000.

Catholic Conference of Ohio, 9 East Long Street, Suite 201, Columbus, Ohio 43215, *www.cdeducation.org/cco*

Archdiocese of Cincinnati: *www.catholiccincinnati.org*

Diocese of Cleveland: *www.dioceseofcleveland.org*

Diocese of Columbus: *www.colsdioc.org*

Diocese of Steubenville: *www.diosteub.org*

Diocese of Toledo: *www.toledodiocese.org*

Diocese of Youngstown: *www.doy.org*

RESOURCES

No single source for the history of Catholics in Ohio is available. Many parts of the story have been published over the years. Several recent diocesan histories are available, and others may be in process. Contact the sources listed above for information. For comprehensive information about the Catholic Church and its beliefs and practices, see *The Catechism of the Catholic Church* (Liguori, Mo.: Liguori Press, 1997). Complete text is available online at *www.usccb.org/catechism/*

Seventh-day Adventist

Kris Stevenson

HISTORY

ADVENTIST HISTORY STARTED WITH THE MILLERITE MOVEMENT. William Miller, who came out of a Baptist background, began to preach in the 1830s and early 1840s that Jesus would return to earth on October 22, 1844. Both Miller and other "Millerite" preachers penetrated the heartland of the newly formed state of Ohio, moving about the state by wagon roads and by canal.

Miller's message started a wave of fervor that swept across America, and a large group of "advent" believers waited in vain for Christ's return on October 22. After the "Great Disappointment" a small group spent time in earnest prayer and study, trying to understand what had gone wrong. Eventually they became impressed that Miller had been correct in his date, but incorrect about what would happen on that day. They believed that Christ was coming soon, but that no one knew the exact time. In their intense study of the Bible, they were also convinced to keep the seventh-day Sabbath as instituted at Creation and as practiced by Jesus here on earth.

This fledgling group eventually chose the name "Seventh-day Adventist" (SDA). They formed small companies in New England, Michigan, and Ohio. Adventist pioneers traveled extensively, sharing the gospel message. At the center of the group were Ellen and James White. Seventh-day Adventists believe that Ellen White was chosen to receive a special manifestation of the spiritual gift of prophecy. Starting at age seventeen she had numerous visions where God gave messages of encouragement and instruction to the fledgling group. One of her earliest and most important visions occurred in Lovett's Grove, Ohio, in 1858. After standing up to preach, she fell into vision for some time. This vision was a comprehensive picture of the great controversy between Christ and Satan, concluding with the triumphant return of Christ. It was recorded in the book *The Great Controversy,* which has circulated around the world.

In 1860 the believers in Lovett's Grove (near Bowling Green) were organized into a company of about thirty. This company was officially recognized as a church—the first Seventh-day Adventist church in Ohio—on February 8, 1862. On May 31, 1863, the Ohio Conference of Seventh-day Adventists was officially formed. It elected Oliver Mears its first president. Elder Mears faithfully traveled the state in his lumber wagon— preaching, organizing, and raising money to help spread the Gospel —while his family kept the farm near Bowling Green running. Other early Adventist pioneers active in Ohio were H. S. Case, J. N. Andrews, who later became the first Adventist overseas missionary, and Joseph Bates, a converted sea captain.

Money for church buildings was scarce, so the newly formed churches met at first in homes, tents, and rented halls. In keeping with the farming communities of the time, camp meeting were held after the crops were harvested. Families would come with wagons full of belongings to enjoy several weeks of fellowship and good preaching. The first Ohio Adventist camp meeting was held in 1869 in Clyde.

In the 1870s the church began organizing parochial grade schools. Eventually (1893) a college was started on the grounds of the old Mount Vernon Sanitarium. Today this school operates as a four-year boarding high school—Mount Vernon Academy.

The Adventist church in Ohio was a vibrant community that initiated several ideas that the world Adventist church later adopted. It was in Mount Vernon that the SDA Missionary Volunteer society, known as MV, was launched. Local MV societies planned programs and activities for Adventist young people.

By 1920 there were sixty-five Seventh-day Adventist churches in Ohio, with 2,860 members. By 1944 the number of churches had grown to eighty-nine. A regular camp meeting was officially established on the grounds of Mount Vernon Academy and continues to meet there the second week of June every year. The Ohio conference headquarters also

The Clyde Seventh-day Adventist church is the second-oldest Adventist church established in Ohio. The first church was established at Lovett's Grove and is no longer standing. The Clyde church was damaged by fire in 1928. This photograph was taken after the church was rebuilt. (Courtesy of James B. King)

moved to Mount Vernon in 1959, and Camp Mohaven, a Christian summer youth camp located on the Mohican River near Danville, was operating by summer 1962.

Adventist work in Ohio also includes the Charles F. Kettering Memorial Hospital, now called Kettering Medical Center, which opened in the early 1960s in Dayton. The hospital operates the Kettering College of Medical Arts. Worthington Foods, which produces healthy vegetarian meat substitutes, was also Adventist owned and operated until recently.

Seventh-day Adventists are also active in publishing, with fifty-five publishing houses worldwide producing books and literature in 310 languages. SDA radio programs reach up to 70 percent of the world's population, and recently a satellite television network was established to help share the Gospel around the world. For young children there are Pathfinder clubs, modeled on the Boy Scout organization, which teach children how to serve God and man.

Ohio Adventists have been and are an integral part of this worldwide mission, from their charter membership in the original General Conference of Seventh-day Adventists in 1863 to their initiation of organized work for young people to their focus on Christian education. And most importantly Ohio Adventists still use their local resources in a substantial way—by giving tithe and offerings, volunteering their time and skills to go on short-term mission projects, and helping with disaster relief and humanitarian aid both here in Ohio and all over the world. Ohio Adventists are vital not only to their own world church but also to the development of Christianity and humanitarian relief across the world.

The Ohio Seventh-day Adventist church is proud to be part of the worldwide church now numbering more than 12 million in 204 countries. The worldwide church operates six thousand parochial schools, including approximately ninety colleges and universities. The Adventist Development and Relief Agency (ADRA) provides aid in more than 120 different countries, and disaster relief and community-based humanitarian aid is available all across North America.

BELIEFS

We believe,

1. That the Holy Scriptures are the written Word of God, given by divine inspiration.

2. In the Trinity. There is one God: Father, Son, and Holy Spirit.

3. In the scriptural account of creation in six days and God resting on the seventh.

4. That all humanity is involved in a great controversy between Christ and Satan regarding the character of God, His law, and His sovereignty over the universe.

5. In Christ's suffering, death, and resurrection as the only means of atonement for human sin, so that Christ, who knew no sin, was sin for us.

6. That the church is a community of believers.

7. In baptism by immersion as a way to confess our faith in Jesus Christ.

8. In the Lord's Supper as well as the service of foot washing.

9. In the spiritual gifts of all members to use in loving ministry for the common good of the church and humanity. This includes the gift of prophecy as exhibited by Ellen White.

10. In the law of God as listed in the ten commandments and exhibited in Christ's life.

11. In the Sabbath as the seventh day in honor of the seventh day of Creation, when God rested and instituted the Sabbath for all people. This is also the fourth commandment.

12. In being good stewards of God's blessings—time, abilities, possessions, resources—and in being godly people in harmony with heaven's principles, especially purity, health, and joy.

13. That marriage was divinely set up as a lifelong union between man and woman.

14. That there is a sanctuary in heaven in which Christ ministers on our behalf.

15. That Christ's coming will be literal, personal, visible, and world-wide. Those of his redeemed who die will lie in an unconscious state until Christ appears to take them to heaven. Those alive at Christ's coming will be taken up to the Lord along with the resurrected dead.

CURRENT DEMOGRAPHICS

Today the Seventh-day Adventist church in Ohio has ninety-two churches and companies with a total membership of 11,582. This includes twenty parochial grade schools and two academies—Mount Vernon Academy and Spring Valley Academy in Dayton. Churches in Ohio include a Spanish-speaking church, a Hungarian church, a Yugoslavian church, and a Ghanaian church.

CONTACT INFORMATION

General Conference of Seventh-day Adventists: *www.adventist.org*

Columbia Union Conference of Seventh-day Adventists: *www.columbiaunion. org*

Ohio Conference of Seventh-day Adventists: P.O. Box 1230, 2 Fairgrounds Road, Mt. Vernon, Ohio 43050, 740-397-4665, *www.ohioadventist.org*

RESOURCES

Maxwell, C. Mervyn. *Tell It to the World: The Story of Seventh-day Adventists.* Nampa, Idaho: Pacific Press Publishing Association, 1976.

Seventh-day Adventists Believe . . . A Biblical Exposition of Twenty-seven Fundamental Doctrines. Hagerstown, Md.: Review and Herald Publishing Association, 1988.

Unitarian Universalist Association

Susan Ritchie and Linda L. Thompson

HISTORY

Unitarian Universalism (UU) combines two religious traditions (Unitarianism and Universalism) that appeared early in our country and in our state. It is a liberal religion that "affirms the worth of human beings, advocates freedom of belief and the search for advancing truth, and tries to provide a warm, open, supportive community for people who believe that ethical living is the supreme witness of religion" (UUA Congregational Handbook, 1995).

Unitarianism

Some of the earliest Unitarian congregations in Ohio were ethnic community churches that only gradually made a specific embrace of Unitarianism. Most congregations, however, were intentionally established with the assistance of the Boston-headquartered American Unitarian Association (AUA), often with the intention of serving transplanted New Englanders who were familiar with American Unitarianism from its Massachusetts origins. Cincinnati saw the origin of the oldest churches of both varieties. St. John's Church was formed in 1814 as an ethnic German congregation, and while largely Unitarian in theology, the church did not affiliate with the AUA until 1924. The First Congregational Church was the result of an 1828 visit there by the Reverend John Pierpont of Boston.

The First Universalist Society of Belpre church was built in 1832. (From *Churches in the Buckeye Country*, 1953)

The congregation dedicated its first building in 1830. In 1852, Cincinnati hosted the organizational meeting of the Western Unitarian Conference (WUC), thereby becoming the center for Unitarian expansion into the Midwest. The WUC had a significant influence on Unitarianism as a whole through its early stress on the importance of ethical living, a strategy which other regions would later adopt as a means of uniting persons and congregations that represented a wide range of theologies.

Nineteenth-century Unitarians were also instrumental in the development of Antioch College, located in Yellow Springs. Although not a Unitarian school, it was repeatedly bailed out of financial trouble by the denomination, which first responded to a request from the school's Unitarian president, Horace Mann, in 1854.

Other early Unitarian churches had appeared in the Ohio River Valley and on the shores of the Great Lakes. Inspired by a visit from the Reverend Moses Thomas, transplanted New Englanders had long wished to organize in Marietta. Nahum Ward achieved this in 1855, organizing the First Unitarian Society of Marietta and then building a church at his own expense. A congregation in Cleveland was established as a result of the visit of the Reverend George Hosmer to New England families in the area in 1836. Meeting from the 1860s on in public meeting halls, the Cleveland group built its first structure in 1880. Especially notable there was the early joint pastorate of two women, Revs. Florence Buck and Marion Murdock, who served from 1893 to 1899. Currently more than half of all UU ministers are women.

As western Unitarianism grew beyond its New England inheritance and took on its own distinctive and often humanist character, some churches that had early disappointments were able to reestablish themselves more solidly. These included the First Unitarian Churches of Youngstown (1904), the re-established Unitarian Society of Youngstown (1892); Dayton (1910), formerly the First Unitarian Society of Dayton (1846); and Columbus (1940), which followed an earlier group of the same name (1896) and an independent German church.

Universalism

Individual preachers teaching Universalism, or universal salvation without any external support or explicit institutional sanction, began appearing in Ohio as early as 1800, when the Reverend Abel Morgan Sargent traveled in the area of Marietta and Belpre. The Universalist "mother church" in Belpre was established in 1823 and erected a building in 1832. Other groups in the area were formed later in Newbury, Watertown, Fairfield, Vincent, Lower Salem, and Frost.

Similarly, churches organized in the Western Reserve were prompted by some of the early preaching in the area by the Reverend Thomas Bigelow. These churches included Akron, Ravenna, Brimfield, Parkman, Sharon Center, LeRoy, North Olmstead, and others. Rev. Jonathan Kidwell's presence in the 1820s in southwest Ohio inspired later gatherings in Eldorado, Palestine, and New Madison. Cincinnati was visited by a number of prominent ministers, and through the efforts of one, the Reverend Eliphalet Case, the church there was organized in 1827.

A chief concern of the early Universalists in Ohio was education. In 1832 the "First Universalist Religious Library Association of Marietta," was established in order to provide the public with nonsectarian educational materials. That same group went on to form a church in 1850. In an early example of a Unitarian and Universalist merger, that group merged with the Unitarian Society in 1869. Concerned about the lack of nonsectarian public schooling, early Universalists also established a number of schools: the Madison Liberal Institute, Hamilton County (1836), the Sharon Academy, Medina County (1836), the Universalist Institute of Ohio City (1839), the Western Liberal Institution of Marietta (1850), and a school in Springfield. In 1870 the state Universalist Convention established

Buchtel College in Akron. In 1914, due to lack of funding, Buchtel College was transferred to the city of Akron to serve as the base of its plan for a municipal university, now the University of Akron (and the location of the Ohio Universalist Archives).

In the period between 1840 and 1850, Universalism boasted its greatest number of churches in Ohio, claiming 163 congregations. By 1923 only fifty-seven churches still existed. Today, existing churches of Universalist origin are to be found in North Olmstead, Bellville, Jersey, Eldorado, Lyons, Akron, Westfield Center, New Madison, Kent, and Cincinnati. As mainstream churches began to liberalize in the late nineteenth and twentieth centuries, the need for the message of the Universalist Church was felt less keenly than it once had been.

Unitarian Universalism

Merger between these two theologically similar denominations had been discussed as early as 1848, but differences in polity and focus prevented their joining until 1961, when the Unitarian Universalist Association (UUA) was formed.

BELIEFS

The following statements ("Purposes and Principles") were adopted by the 1984, 1985, and 1995 General Assemblies (the annual gathering of congregational representatives).

We, the member congregations of the Unitarian Universalist Association, covenant to affirm and promote:

- The inherent worth and dignity of every person
- Justice, equity, and compassion in human relations
- Acceptance of one another and encouragement to spiritual growth in our congregations
- A free and responsible search for truth and meaning
- The right of conscience and the use of the democratic process within our congregations and in society at large

- The goal of world community with peace, liberty, and justice for all
- Respect for the interdependent web of all existence of which we are a part

  The living tradition we share draws from many sources:

- Direct experience of that transcending mystery and wonder, affirmed in all cultures, which moves us to a renewal of the spirit and an openness to the forces which create and uphold life,
- Words and deeds of prophetic women and men which challenge us to confront powers and structures of evil with justice, compassion and the transforming power of love,
- Wisdom from the world's religions which inspires us in our ethical and spiritual life,
- Jewish and Christian teachings which call us to respond to God's love by loving our neighbors as ourselves,
- Humanist teachings which counsel us to heed the guidance of reason and the results of science, and warn us against idolatries of the mind and spirit,
- Spiritual teachings of Earth-centered traditions which celebrate the sacred circle of life and instruct us to live in harmony with the rhythms of nature.

CURRENT DEMOGRAPHICS

The UUA is divided into geographical districts that provide services to member congregations. Each congregation is democratic in polity and operation, governs itself, and through representation has a voice in governing its district and the UUA.

Ohio Congregations	36	(27 in the Ohio Meadville District; 9 in the Heartland District)
Certified Members	4,906	
Sunday School Enrollment	1,909	
Total Membership	6,815	
Ministers	24	(13 male, 11 female)

CONTACT INFORMATION

The Unitarian Universalist Association, 25 Bean Street, Boston, Massachusetts 02108, 617-742-2100, *www.uua.org*

Heartland District, 445 N. Pennsylvania Street, Suite 330, Indianapolis, Indiana 46204, 317-634-5384.

Ohio Meadville District, 611 West Market Street, Suite B, Akron, Ohio 44303, 330-762-8860.

RESOURCES

Lyttle, Charles H. *Freedom Moves West: A History of the Western Unitarian Conference, 1852–1952*. Boston: The Beacon Press, 1952.

Robinson, Elmo Arnold. *The Universalist Church in Ohio*. Akron: Ohio Universalist Convention, 1923.

Ross, Warren R. *The Premise and the Promise: The Story of the Unitarian Universalist Association*. Boston: Skinner House Books, 2001.

Unitarian Universalist Association Directory, 2002–2003. Boston: The Unitarian Universalist Association.

United Church of Christ

Pamela Brown

HISTORY

T HE ROOTS OF THE UNITED CHURCH OF CHRIST (UCC) IN OHIO
go back to the early U.S. history of the four denominations from
which the UCC was formed. The UCC came into being in 1957 with the
union of two Protestant denominations: the Evangelical and Reformed
Church and the Congregational Christian Churches. Each of these denominations was in turn the result of a union of two earlier traditions.

The Congregational Christian Churches was a union between the Congregational Churches, organized when the Pilgrims of Plymouth Plantation (1620) and the Puritans of the Massachusetts Bay Colony (1629)
acknowledged their essential unity in the Cambridge Platform of 1648,
and the Christian Churches, which sprang up in the late 1700s and early
1800s in reaction to the rigid theology and organization of the Methodist,
Presbyterian, and Baptist Churches.

The Evangelical and Reformed Church was formed when the Evangelical Synod of North America, which traced its beginnings to an 1841 association of German Evangelical pastors in Missouri, and the Reformed
Church in the United States, which traced its beginnings to congregations of German settlers in Pennsylvania later joined by Reformed immigrants from Switzerland, Hungary, and other countries, merged.

Most UCC churches in Ohio today were founded before 1900 by one

First Congregational Church in Marietta was the first UCC church in Ohio and is the oldest continuously worshipping fellowship west of the Alleghenies. The congregation was established in 1796 and laid the cornerstone of its first building in 1805. This building was erected in 1906, after a fire destroyed the original building. (Courtesy of First Congregational Church—Archives)

of these four original denominations. The first New England Congregational colony in the Northwest Territory was established at Marietta in 1788. In 1796 First Congregational Church in Marietta was founded by these colonists. This congregation, still thriving today, is the oldest UCC church in Ohio and the oldest continuously worshipping fellowship west of the Alleghenies.

Other congregations followed soon after Marietta; many are UCC congregations still worshipping in Ohio today. First UCC, Austinburg (1801); First Congregational UCC, Hudson (1802); Springboro UCC (1802); Old Springfield UCC, New Middletown (1803); Congregational UCC, Shandon (1803); and First Congregational UCC, Newton Falls (1804) are modern descendants of the oldest of these congregations.

The UCC's "ancestor denominations" were pioneers in health care and education. The Evangelical Synod of North America founded Christian hospitals in Cleveland: Fairview Park (1896) and Evangelical Deaconess (1923). The Marietta colony opened Muskingum Academy early in its history; in 1835 it became Marietta College. The Reformed Church founded Heidelberg College in Tiffin in 1850. The Christian Church founded Defiance College in 1850 and Antioch College in Yellow Springs in 1852.

Congregationalists and Presbyterians founded Oberlin College in 1833. Oberlin was the first college to grant undergraduate degrees to women and has been a leader in education for African Americans.

In 1835 the Reverend Dr. Charles Finney, the foremost evangelist in the pre–Civil War United States, was hired to head Oberlin's theological department and serve as pastor of the First Congregational Church of Oberlin. Finney also continued his career as an evangelist, holding revivals in New England, New York, Ohio, and England. He became Oberlin's president in 1851. His fame and reputation increased knowledge of and respect for Oberlin College and the church.

The first mergers that eventually formed the United Church of Christ began in 1925, when members of the German-speaking Evangelical Protestant Church, with several congregations around Cincinnati, united with the National Council of Congregational Churches. By 1947 they were fully integrated into the Ohio Congregational Christian Conference.

The Reformed Church extended its ministry to the large numbers of Hungarians who began arriving in the States in the late 1800s. Hungarian congregations were formed in Cleveland, Columbus, Conneaut, Dayton, Fairport Harbor, and Lorain.

The Evangelical and the Reformed Churches formally united in a worship service in Cleveland in 1934. The national Congregational and Christian merger in 1931 was preceded by the 1930 union of the Congregational Conference and the five Christian Conferences in Ohio.

Not long thereafter (around 1937) discussions began about a merger of the two denominations. In June 1957 the union was complete. The United Church of Christ was born.

A number of community churches that came into being in the early 1900s were part of the development of the UCC in Ohio. A keystone of the community church movement in Ohio for many years has been First Community Church in Columbus, itself a mission planting from the downtown First Congregational Church.

The pastor who led First Congregational in establishing First Community Church, Dublin Community Church, and four others was the Reverend Dr. Washington Gladden. Pastor of First Congregational from 1882 to 1918, Dr. Gladden was one of America's leading religious figures in the late 1800s. He significantly influenced many turn-of-the-century Christians and their views of society. He is best known as an advocate of the Social Gospel, which states that the Gospel is intended not merely for the salvation of individuals but also for the transformation of society.

Gladden's ministry reflected his views. His support of labor's right to strike; his opposition to the death penalty, to injustices in the public schools, and to inequities in health care; and his views on race, religion, and civic fairness were legendary and prophetic.

The UCC's commitment to social justice stems from ancestors like Gladden and from abolitionists who operated an Underground Railroad stop in Oberlin, Congregationalists who supported the African people held captive on the slave ship *La Amistad* as they fought for their freedom, and activists who pushed for education and voting rights for women and people of color.

Through the years, other groups such as American Indians, African Americans, Asian Americans, Pacific Islanders, Volga Germans, Armenians, and Hispanic Americans have joined with the four groups that formed the United Church of Christ. In recent years Christians from other traditions have found a home in the UCC, as have gay and lesbian Christians who have not been welcome in some other churches. Thus the UCC celebrates and continues a variety of traditions.

UCC congregations in Ohio represent the broad diversity of the UCC as a whole. People from a wide variety of backgrounds and beliefs have organized themselves into local churches, five associations, and a conference through which they cooperate to carry out their ministries in Ohio, the United States, and around the world.

BELIEFS

There are seven phrases from scripture and tradition that express the commitments of the United Church of Christ:

- *That they may all be one.* The UCC is based on a spirit of unity and looks toward future efforts to heal the divisions in the body of Christ.
- *In essentials unity, in nonessentials diversity, in all things charity.* The unity that we seek requires mutual agreement about the essentials of the Christian faith and life, not uncritical acceptance of any point of view or rigid doctrine.

- *The unity of the church is not of its own making. It is a gift of God.* Expressions of that unity are as diverse as there are individuals. The common thread that runs through all is love.

- *Testimonies of faith rather than tests of faith.* The UCC embraces a theological heritage that affirms the Bible as the authoritative witness to the word of God. The UCC has roots in the "covenantal" tradition, meaning there is no centralized authority that can impose any doctrine or form of worship on its members. Christ alone is head of the church. We seek a balance between freedom of conscience and accountability to the apostolic faith. The UCC therefore receives the historic creeds and confessions of our ancestors as testimonies to, but not tests of, the faith.

- *There is yet more light and truth to break forth from God's holy word.* We believe that the Bible is the primary source for understanding the Good News. The study of the scriptures is not limited by past interpretations but is pursued with the expectation of new insights and God's help for living today.

- *The priesthood of all believers.* All UCC members are called to minister to others and to participate as equals in the worship of God, each with access to the mercies of God through personal prayer and devotion. We recognize those who have received special training, but these persons are regarded as servants rather than as persons in authority. Their task is to guide, instruct, and enable the ministry of all, rather than to do the work of ministry for us.

- *Responsible freedom.* As individual members of the Body of Christ, we are free to believe and act in accordance with our perception of God's will for our lives. But we are called to live in loving, covenantal relationships with one another—within our local churches and among our local churches.

(Source: United Church of Christ website: *www.ucc.org*)

CURRENT DEMOGRAPHICS

The Ohio Conference of the United Church of Christ includes 424 churches, totaling about 127,000 members. The majority of these are former Congregational Christian or Evangelical Reformed congregations that were organized in the 1800s and early 1900s. About twenty-five Ohio congregations have been organized by the United Church of Christ since its creation in 1957. The highest concentration of UCC members in Ohio is in the Cleveland-Akron-Canton area. There are also many members around Toledo, Columbus, Dayton, and Cincinnati.

CONTACT INFORMATION

United Church of Christ, National Office, 700 Prospect Avenue East, Cleveland, Ohio 44115, 216-736-2100, *www.ucc.org*

Ohio Conference, United Church of Christ, 6161 Busch Boulevard, Suite 95, Columbus, Ohio 43229, 800-282-0740 or 614-885-0722, *ohioucc@ocucc.org, www.ocucc.org*

RESOURCES

Celebration Part One: Who Do We Say We Are? and *Celebration Part Two: Where All Are Welcome* (videos). These UCC videos can be viewed online at *www.ucc.org*

Zikmund, Barbara Brown, ed. *Hidden Histories in the United Church of Christ.* Cleveland: United Church Press, 1984. Available online at *www.ucc.org/aboutus/histories*

Zikmund, Barbara Brown, gen. ed. *The Living Theological Heritage of the United Church of Christ.* 7 vols. Cleveland: The Pilgrim Press, 1997.

JUDAISM

Jane A. Avner

HISTORY

AMERICAN JEWISH HISTORY IS THE STORY OF DIFFERENT WAVES OF immigration. Each period described below includes the Jewish immigrants who came to Ohio.

1817–1880

The earliest Jewish settlers who came during the colonial period were from the Netherlands and England. Like their non-Jewish counterparts, they sought religious freedom and economic opportunity. Their numbers were small, and they settled mostly in New York; Philadelphia; Newport, Rhode Island; Charleston; and Savannah. After the establishment of the United States in 1776, small numbers of Jews moved to unsettled areas such as Ohio. When Ohio became a state in 1803 there may have been individual Jews present, but no community has been documented. In the early years of the nineteenth century, immigration was curtailed by revolution and war in Europe. But after 1815 normal transportation was restored across the Atlantic Ocean and immigration resumed.

Ohio's first identified permanent Jewish settler was Joseph Jonas, an English watchmaker who made his home in Cincinnati in 1817. He was something of a curiosity to the locals, who had never before seen a Jew.

Finding himself accepted there, he sent word to his family about Cincinnati's advantages and was joined by his brother and sister and their spouses several years later. By 1824 there were twenty Jewish families, enough to establish a congregation they called Bene Israel and build Ohio's first synagogue in 1836.

The organization of Cincinnati's Jewish community coincided with a marked increase in Jewish immigration from Central Europe. From the 1830s until about 1880, German-speaking Jews looked to America to provide them with personal freedom and economic opportunities that were unavailable in Europe. During this period, Jewish communities were established in a number of Ohio's major cities.

In Cleveland, physician Benjamin Peixotto arrived in 1836 to teach at the Willoughby Medical College. Simson Thorman, a fur trader who had lived in Cleveland briefly, returned in 1837 and sent word to family and friends in Unsleben, Bavaria, to join him. Of the nineteen Unsleben Jews who came to America in 1839, fifteen settled in Cleveland. They carried with them the "Alsbacher Document," which listed their names and included a request by their Bavarian teacher to remember their religion when facing the "tempting freedom" of noncompulsory religion in the United States. This group formed the nucleus of Cleveland's first congregation, the Israelitische Society, founded in 1839. Joseph Labensburger arrived in Dayton in 1842. Previously from Cincinnati, his success encouraged others from Cincinnati to follow, and they established the Dayton Hebrew Society in 1850.

Before the Civil War, Jewish communities were established in four other Ohio towns and settlements: Columbus (1838), Hamilton (1855), Piqua (1858), and Portsmouth (1858). Several others were founded after 1865. Youngstown, which had Jewish settlers as early as 1837, established Rodef Sholom Congregation in 1867. Akron had Jewish merchants working in the area by 1845. They founded the Akron Hebrew Association in 1865. A permanent Jewish settlement began in Toledo in the 1850s, with religious services beginning in the 1860s. Its first Jewish organization was a benevolent society established in 1867 to provide a cemetery for the community. Canton had a small Jewish community by 1869.

The general pattern during this German Jewish immigration period was for men to arrive on their own and send for family members and potential wives once they were settled. Typical occupations were peddling

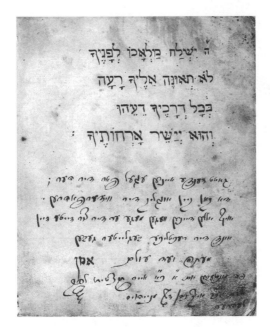

A page from the Alsbacher Document, written in 1839 for the founders of Cleveland's Jewish community. The four-line prayer, in Hebrew and German (the latter transliterated into Hebrew characters), states: "May God send His angels before you / May no ill befall you / In all your ways know Him / And He will make your paths straight." (Courtesy of the Western Reserve Historical Society, Cleveland, Ohio)

and clothing manufacturing and sales. People also worked as grocers, butchers, tobacco manufacturers, in wine and liquor sales, and as bakers. Women worked alongside their husbands and parents in stores while raising their children.

Most Ohio Jewish communities were well organized by the 1880s, when Ohio experienced a large influx of immigrants from Russia and Eastern Europe. Consistent with patterns of American Jewish settlement in other states, organized Jewish communities established synagogues, burial grounds, and cemetery societies; charitable organizations serving the poor, widowed, and orphaned; and educational institutions to instruct children in the basics of Judaism. On the whole, Ohio's Jews felt comfortable enough in their larger communities to be active in social and civic affairs. Columbus merchant Marcus Frankel served on the city council during this period, and William Kraus and Guido Marx both served as mayors of Toledo.

The period from the 1840s to the 1880s was one of great change in American Judaism. Ohio's Jewish communities played an important part in this change. This was the period when the Reform movement was developing its uniquely American version of Judaism.

The early synagogues were all Orthodox. The prayer service was in

Built in 1866, the Plum Street Temple in Cincinnati is the oldest synagogue building in Ohio still used for Jewish religious services. It is now one of the sanctuaries of the Isaac M. Wise Synagogue. (Courtesy of Jacob Rader Marcus Center of the American Jewish Archives, Cincinnati Campus, Hebrew Union College, Jewish Institute of Religion)

Hebrew, men and women sat separately, and men covered their heads and used a *tallit* (prayer shawl). In both Cleveland and Cincinnati, the first congregations argued internally about ritual. In 1839 several members left Cincinnati's Bene Israel and formed B'nai Jeshurun. Cleveland's Israelitische Society divided into two congregations that still are in existence today, Anshe Chesed and Tifereth Israel. Rabbis Isaac Mayer Wise and Max Lilienthal in Cincinnati and Rabbi Isadore Kalish in Cleveland all favored reforms, which included increased use of German and English in the service, using organs and choirs, and allowing men and women to sit together.

Rabbi Wise was particularly interested in unifying congregations in America. In 1854 he founded *The Israelite,* the first English-language Jewish newspaper west of the Allegheny Mountains. In 1855 he organized a conference in Cleveland calling for a revised prayer book, a union of synagogues, and the establishment of a rabbinical college to train American rabbis. *Minhag America,* the revised prayer book, was first published in 1857. The Union of American Hebrew Congregations was established in 1873, and Hebrew Union College was founded in Cincinnati in 1875. It was the first rabbinical college in America. Ohio therefore became the center of Reform Judaism in America.

Yet not all agreed to the changes instituted in Reform synagogues. In Cleveland, a group from Poland established Anshe Emeth in 1850 and Hungarians created B'nai Jeshurun in 1866. Both were traditional Orthodox synagogues. Between 1846 and 1860, five Orthodox synagogues were established in Cincinnati. Youngstown's first synagogue, Rodef Sholom (f. 1867), retained many Orthodox features even though founded in a Reform context.

From the 1830s through the 1870s, Ohio Jews brought family and friends to their chosen towns and established and organized their communities. Many synagogues affiliated with the developing Reform movement. It was a period of economic growth, with many individuals who began as peddlers becoming shop owners in various trades, including clothing, groceries and bakeries, and cigar making. Jewish population growth was slow and steady, reaching 14,500 by 1878.

Russian and Eastern European Migrations, 1880–1920

As economic conditions worsened and violent anti-Semitism increased in Russia and Eastern Europe, all major American cities were faced with an enormous influx of Jewish immigrants. In 1880 there were 7.7 million Jews worldwide. Of these, close to 6 million lived in Eastern Europe. Between 1880 and 1920 two million Jews settled in the United States. The Ohio Jewish population increased to 50,000 by 1900 and to 166,000 by

1917 (this and previous paragraph: figures from Jacob Rader Marcus, *To Count a People: American Jewish Population Data, 1585–1984* [Lanham, Md.: University Press of America, 1990] and Gerald Sorin, *A Time for Building: The Third Migration, 1880–1920* [Baltimore: Johns Hopkins University Press, 1992]).

Unlike German Jewish immigration, where unmarried men arrived first and then wrote home for relatives, fiancées, and wives to follow, Eastern European Jewish immigrants often came as families and had fewer economic opportunities in the United States. Single women came as well, just as anxious as were men to leave difficult economic conditions and religious and social persecution in Europe. Existing Jewish American communities looked at these Eastern European newcomers with some concern. Not all Americans welcomed newcomers. It was a time of increased anti-Semitism. Would these people, who spoke Yiddish (a mixture of German and Hebrew) and looked so different, fit in?

The network of Jewish charitable institutions already in place turned its attention to the new Eastern European settlers. Women joined the National Council of Jewish Women, which helped build settlement houses to "Americanize" the Eastern Europeans. Council House in Columbus, Council Educational Alliance in Cleveland, the Council Cottage in Youngstown, and the Jewish Settlement in Cincinnati provided vocational, educational, and social activities for the new immigrants. Jewish hospitals like Mt. Sinai in Cleveland and Jewish Hospital in Cincinnati not only treated Jewish patients but also provided employment for Jewish doctors. Homes for the aged, orphanages, residences for transients, and free loan societies made their services available. In time, as the Eastern Europeans became more established and economically comfortable, they began their own charitable, social, educational, and religious institutions. Jewish communities were established in more Ohio cities: East Liverpool, Lima, and Lorain (about 1880), Canton (1885), Bellaire and Warren (about 1890), Steubenville (1891), and Alliance (1898).

The existing Reform synagogues did not appeal to the newcomers, who instead established smaller congregations that followed Orthodox traditions (although the new immigrants did not always follow Orthodox practice) and maintained the melodies and traditions of their Eastern European hometowns. In neighborhoods like the Woodland area of

Cleveland or the eastern side of Columbus, one could find several tiny synagogues following Russian, Hungarian, Polish, or Lithuanian traditions interspersed with kosher butchers, bakeries, groceries, cigar stores, clothing stores, and many other small businesses where the immigrants worked and shopped. Yiddish newspapers and theater and *landsman-shaften* (friendly associations of Jews from the same city or country of origin), together with the synagogues and stores, gave the appearance of a Jewish neighborhood, although in most Ohio cities these neighborhoods also had Italians, non-Jewish Eastern Europeans, and African Americans.

At the very end of this period, the developing Conservative movement of Judaism became appealing to Eastern European immigrants. It retained many traditions of Orthodoxy, yet embraced modernity. Conservative Judaism embraced Zionism, a movement which promoted the establishment of a Jewish homeland in Israel and ties between Jews all over the world. Zionist groups sprang up all over Ohio, including Hadassah, a women's organization committed to providing medical services in Israel. In 1913, Hadassah sent a Cleveland nurse, Rae Landy, to what was then Palestine to begin health-care programs for the Jewish population there.

A massive immigration of Eastern European Jews to Ohio cities changed Jewish demographics. The new immigrants faced economic challenges, yet learned trades, established businesses, and became American citizens. Ohio Jewish life was primarily in cities, although there were a few farming communities, like Geneva.

Consolidation, the Depression, and World War II (1920–1945)

The Johnson-Reid Act of 1924 slowed the flow of immigration to the United States. Eastern European immigrants already in Ohio became more comfortable as Americans, and they followed the earlier Jewish community to neighborhoods beyond the city centers. In Cincinnati they moved to Avondale, in Cleveland to Glenville and Kinsman, and in Columbus they moved farther east along Livingstone Avenue and Broad and Main Streets. Occupations changed, too, as the children of unskilled and semi-skilled laborers and shopkeepers joined the professions and became doctors, dentists, lawyers, schoolteachers, bookkeepers, accountants, and social workers. The women's suffrage movement of the early twentieth century attracted some Jewish women, including Pauline Steinem, who was also the first woman elected to public office in Toledo, and Cleveland resident Mary Belle Grossman, the first woman municipal judge in America.

The depression of the 1930s was a severe economic blow to all Americans. In the Jewish communities of Ohio, existing charitable agencies worked to assist the jobless, homeless, and hungry. Some Jewish institutions, like the Jewish Center of Youngstown, had to close their doors due to lack of funding. To prevent duplication of efforts, the agencies formed "federations." In larger communities like Cincinnati and Cleveland, federations had already been established earlier in the century. But in smaller cities like Akron, Canton, Steubenville, and Youngstown, Jewish federations were formed during the Depression.

In addition to economic depression, Ohio Jews were increasingly concerned about anti-Semitism and discriminatory laws against Jews in Germany. In general, Americans were concerned about Nazi Germany's warlike politics. However, there was some support for the Nazis in the 1930s. In Cincinnati and Dayton, for example, the German American Bund held pro-Nazi, anti-Semitic rallies and meetings. Ohio Jewish communities responded in several ways. In Cleveland, Rabbi Abba Hillel Silver helped to organize a boycott against German-made goods, and Jews throughout Ohio opened their communities to any German Jews who were able to leave Germany.

Following the German invasion of Poland in 1939 and the United States' declaration of war against the Axis powers in 1941, Ohio Jews joined the United States armed forces to fight against this tyranny. Nationally, 550,000 Jews joined up, which made the proportion of Jews fighting in World War II much higher than their proportion of the general population. The close of the war in 1945 brought the horrible revelation that more than 6 million European Jewish men, women, and children had been slaughtered by the Nazis. Although so many died, some were saved due to Ohio Jewish efforts, like the students and faculty of the Telshe Yeshiva, a famous European center of Jewish learning, which was brought to Cleveland in 1941. Holocaust survivors made up the next wave of Jewish immigrants to the United States. Approximately 140,000 came to America, some to Ohio cities.

Ohio Jews Since World War II (1945 to the present)

When servicemen and women returned from World War II, the United States experienced a time of greater prosperity. Like many other city dwellers, Jews bought homes in the newly developing suburbs. In Cleveland, the Jewish population moved east to Cleveland Heights and Shaker Heights; in Cincinnati it moved farther north to Roselawn, Golf Manor, and Amberley Village; in Toledo it moved farther west. The communities built new synagogues, community centers, and schools. In Cleveland, Cincinnati, Akron, Toledo, and Youngstown, all-day Jewish schools, which offered a double curriculum of general and Judaic studies, were established.

The 1960s and 1970s were more turbulent times. Civil rights for African Americans, women's rights, and the controversies surrounding the Vietnam War all called for participation by Ohio Jewish communities. Rabbis Arthur Lelyveld of Cleveland and Sylvan Ruslander of Dayton were active in the civil rights movement. In 1972 a Cleveland-born and Hebrew Union College–educated woman, Sally Priesand, became the first woman rabbi in the United States. Jerry Rubin of Cincinnati was a radical opponent of the Vietnam War and cofounder of the Youth International Party.

In a small Cleveland synagogue, Louis Rosenblum, Herb Caron, and Rabbi Daniel Litt founded the Cleveland Council on Soviet Anti-Semitism. This organization galvanized an international effort to allow Jews to escape from persecution in the Soviet Union. This created the most recent wave of Jewish immigration to Ohio. Each Ohio city with a sizable Jewish population absorbed a number of Soviet Jewish families by supplying them with housing, food, jobs, education, and counseling until they could be self-sufficient. When the Soviet Union dissolved in 1989, Jews from the former republics continued to emigrate to the United States.

As Ohio enters the twenty-first century, the Jewish communities of Ohio are an integral part of their respective cities. Individual Jews have moved to the forefront of civic participation, contributing in the arts, in education, and in politics. Ohio Jewry, which now numbers about 149,000, is religiously diverse, ranging from secular and unaffiliated to ultra-Orthodox. Through Jewish federations and individual efforts, support is strong for Israel and for local Jewish charitable and educational institutions.

BELIEFS

Three Concepts

Judaism is one of the world's oldest religious traditions. Although there are currently many interpretations of this tradition, three ideas are common to almost all Jews: belief in a single God, in the existence of a covenant between God and the Jewish people, and in the common heritage of the Jewish people.

First, Jews believe that a single God created the universe and continues to govern it. This belief is known as *monotheism.*

Second, Jews believe that there is a unique covenant, or contract, between God and the Jewish people. Jews believe that approximately four thousand years ago, God told Abraham that he and his descendents had been chosen to become a great nation that would live in a promised land (Israel). Jews also believe that God revealed his expectations of ideal human behavior to Moses at Mount Sinai as *mitzvot,* or commandments. These commandments are contained in written form in the Tanach, the Hebrew Bible, which includes the Torah (the five books of Moses), Nevi'im (prophets), and Ketuvim (writings). In later years rabbis, or teachers, added commentaries to the Bible which make up what is known as the oral tradition. These oral teachings were passed down from generation to generation, and eventually written down as well in such books as the Mishnah and the Talmud.

A third idea common to Jews is that they are not bound by geographic borders and are responsible for one another. There are more than 12 million Jews living all over the world who share the beliefs and religious literature mentioned above. Because Judaism began over four thousand years ago in the land of Israel and has been practiced there continuously ever since, most Jews, wherever they live, feel a special relationship to Israel and the Hebrew language.

THE JEWISH CALENDAR

The mitzvot that Jews observe relate to every aspect of life, including specific daily rituals, celebration of holidays and life-cycle events, earning a living, interpersonal relationships, and social justice. We can get a sense of Jewish life by looking at the Jewish calendar. The Jewish week is the same as the secular week—seven days long—but it begins on Sunday. The seventh day (Saturday) is celebrated as the Sabbath, a day of rest. All Jewish Sabbaths and holidays begin at sundown on the night before, so the Sabbath begins on Friday night. The Jewish year is divided into months based on the cycles of the moon. The Jewish year begins in September with Rosh Hashanah (new year), and the holidays that follow in the fall are: Yom Kippur (day of atonement), Succoth (festival of booths), Shemini Atzeret (the eighth festival day after Succoth), and Simchat Torah (rejoicing in the Torah). Winter holidays include Hanukkah and Tu B'Shvat (new year of the trees); spring holidays are Purim (feast of lots), Passover, and Shavuot (festival of weeks); and there is a fast day in the summer, Tisha B'Av (commemorating the destruction of the temples in Jerusalem). There is also a day celebrating the founding of the state of Israel and a Holocaust memorial day, as well as several minor fast days.

LIFE-CYCLE EVENTS

In addition to the Sabbath and holidays, certain life-cycle events are celebrated through Jewish practice and custom. On the eighth day of life infant boys have a *brit milah* (circumcision); infant girls have a naming ceremony soon after birth. When children reach the age of thirteen, a boy becomes a *bar mitzvah* (son of the commandment) and a girl a *bat mitzvah* (daughter of the commandment) through a special religious ceremony. They are then considered adults and participate fully in all aspects of Jewish communal and religious life. There are also specific Jewish ceremonies for weddings and funerals. Belief in life after death is present in Judaism, but much of Jewish law and tradition concerns itself with everyday life.

PERFECTING THE WORLD

An important goal in Judaism is *tikkun olam,* or perfecting the world. Acts of benevolence and loving-kindness are required. An example of benevolence is *tzedakah* (charity). Sizable Jewish communities have communal organizations that coordinate charitable giving to local, national, and international causes. Acts of loving-kindness are good deeds performed personally. Many Jews interpret this obligation by actively engaging themselves in activities promoting civil rights and equality among all people.

THE DIVERSITY OF AMERICAN JEWS

Jewish communities in other parts of the world were usually isolated from their non-Jewish neighbors. In America religious freedom, particularly the separation of church and state, led to new developments in the expression of Judaism. Denominations common in America are Orthodox, Reform, Conservative, and Reconstructionist. Orthodox Jews strictly observe both the written laws and laws derived from the oral tradition. Reform Jews disagree with the idea that Jewish law is unchanging. They believe that traditional beliefs and practices, while not necessarily rejected, must be adapted to present-day conditions. Conservative Judaism emerged as a reaction to both Reform and Orthodox Judaism. This group upholds Jewish law and ritual, but believes that the law is flexible enough to evolve to meet the needs of modern life. Recently a fourth movement, the Reconstructionist movement, has emerged. It sees Judaism as a continually evolving civilization. All four movements have training programs for rabbis and houses of prayer, called synagogues or temples. All four have prayer services that have similar basic structures but that vary in length and in the balance of Hebrew used in the service. There are also people who consider themselves Jews solely through cultural or ethnic identification with the Jewish people.

The varieties of Jewish experience can be confusing to non-Jews. An example is the mitzvah of *kashrut*. Kashrut is the observance of laws regarding food. The Torah states that dairy and meat products should not be mixed and that it is forbidden to eat certain animals, including pigs and shellfish. The oral tradition further dictates that kosher animals must be slaughtered in specific ways and that households should have separate sets of dishes and cookware for meat and dairy dishes. Orthodox Jews follow these regulations, both in their own homes and when eating outside their homes. Reform Jews consider these practices voluntary. Conservative Judaism upholds the concept of kashrut, but its rabbis have made some modifications based on modern scientific knowledge. Reconstructionist Jews may follow some or all of these practices. The interpretation of the Sabbath as a day of rest also varies among the denominations.

ATTENDING JEWISH · WORSHIP SERVICES

Anyone can attend a Jewish Sabbath or holiday service. Sabbath services are held Friday evening and/or Saturday morning. There are synagogues in many Ohio cities, and services are also held at campus centers run by Hillel, the Foundation for Jewish Campus Life, at many Ohio colleges and universities. The only times tickets may be required are during the high holidays of Rosh Hashanah and Yom Kippur. It is advisable to check during the week for starting times, which can vary.

Jewish worship services can be in rooms ranging from simple to elaborate. Those attending sit on chairs that face east—the direction of Jerusalem. In an Orthodox service, men and women sit separately, while in all other denominations mixed seating is acceptable. Although not strictly required at a Reform gathering, men generally cover their heads with a *kippah* (also called a *yarmulke*), which are usually provided in bins outside the sanctuary. Non-Jewish guests are not expected to wear a tallit. Prayer books and books containing the Bible readings are provided either at the back of the sanctuary or near the seats. As in all houses of worship, modest dress and a quiet demeanor are expected. In Orthodox synagogues, women do not wear pants. Typical "nos" are photography and smoking. Just watching the congregation will tell the visitor when to stand up and when to sit down. There are no collection plates and there is no kneeling.

Sabbath services last from one to three hours, are conducted in both Hebrew and English, and often end with wine, grape juice, and snacks.

CURRENT DEMOGRAPHICS

According to the *American Jewish Yearbook,* published by the American Jewish Committee in 2002, the Ohio Jewish population is 149,000. The largest numbers of Jews live in Cleveland (81,500), Cincinnati (22,500), Columbus (22,000), Toledo (5,900), Dayton (5,000), Akron (4,000), Youngstown (3,200), and Canton (1,450).

CONTACT INFORMATION

When Jewish communities become large enough, they usually establish a Jewish federation to coordinate charitable giving and other community efforts. For information about a particular community, its federation is often the best place to start. Each federation keeps lists of synagogues, schools, service organizations, and kosher butchers, bakeries, and restaurants. Ohio's federations are listed below alphabetically by city:

Jewish Community Board of Akron (f. 1935), 750 White Pond Drive, Akron, Ohio 44320–1129, 330-869-2424, *www.jewishakron.org*

Canton Jewish Community Federation (f. 1935), 2631 Harvard Avenue NW, Canton, Ohio 44709–3147, 330-452-6444, *www.jewishcanton.org*

Jewish Federation of Cincinnati (f. 1896), 4380 Malsbary Road, Suite 200, Cincinnati, Ohio 45242–5644, 513-985-1500, *www.jewishcincinnati.org*

Jewish Community Federation of Cleveland (f. 1903), 1750 Euclid Avenue, Cleveland, Ohio 44115–2106, 216-566-9200, *www.jewishcleveland.org*

Columbus Jewish Federation (f. 1926), 1175 College Avenue, Columbus, Ohio 43209, 614-237-7686, *www.jewishcolumbus.org*

Jewish Federation of Greater Dayton (f. 1910), 4501 Denlinger Road, Dayton, Ohio 45426–2395, 937-854-4150, *www.jewishdayton.org*

Jewish Community Council of Steubenville (f. 1938), 300 Lovers Lane, Steubenville, Ohio 43952, 614-264-5514.

United Jewish Council of Greater Toledo (f. 1907), 6505 Sylvania Avenue, Sylvania, Ohio 43560–3918, 419-885-4461, *www.jewishtoledo.org*

Youngstown Area Jewish Federation (f. 1935), 505 Gypsy Lane, Youngstown, Ohio 44504–1314, 330-746-3251.

RESOURCES

But Don't Forget to Dream: Stories of Jewish Dayton. Videotape produced for ThinkTV, 2001.

Diner, Hasia R. *Jews in America.* New York: Oxford University Press, 1999.

Heritage: Civilization and the Jews. Nine-episode series on videocassette covering Jewish history from 3500 B.C.E. to the present. Produced by WNET/ Thirteen, New York. Also available in DVD format.

Jewish Federation of Greater Toledo. *Eightieth Anniversary, From Generation to Generation: 1907–1987.* Toledo: Jewish Federation of Greater Toledo, 1987.

Kaplan, Helga. "Century of Adjustment: A History of the Akron Jewish Community, 1865–1975." Ph.D. diss., Kent State University, 1978.

Ozer, Irving E. *These Are the Names: The History of the Jews of Greater Youngstown, Ohio, 1865–1990.* Youngstown: I. E. Ozer, 1994.

Raphael, Marc Lee. *Jews and Judaism in a Midwestern Community: Columbus, Ohio, 1840–1975.* Columbus: Ohio Historical Society, 1979.

Sarna, Jonathan D., and Nancy H. Klein. *The Jews of Cincinnati.* Cincinnati: Hebrew Union College, 1989.

Scharfstein, Sol. *Understanding Jewish Holidays and Customs: Historical and Contemporary.* Hoboken, N.J.: Ktav Publishing House, Inc., 1999.

Vincent, Sidney, and Judah Rubinstein. *Merging Traditions: Jewish Life in Cleveland.* Cleveland: Western Reserve Historical Society, 1978. (Second edition to be published in 2004.)

ISLAM

Meena Khan

HISTORY

Muslims in the United States

CONTRARY TO POPULAR BELIEF, ISLAM IS NOT NEW TO THE AMERICAS. Muslim adventurers and explorers are believed to have landed in South America before Christopher Columbus arrived in 1492. However, historians have often ignored the strong presence of Muslims. Some of the first slaves arriving in the United States in 1717 were Arabic speaking and had names like Omar Ibn Said, Ben Ali, and Prince Omar. It is documented that they used words such as Allah and Muhammad and refused to consume pork. According to a conservative estimate, about thirty thousand Muslim slaves came from Muslim-dominated West Africa. There are reports of Muslim slaves in the state of Ohio dating back to the late 1700s. However, in spite of the much larger presence of African Muslims in America than previously thought, the Islamic influence did not survive beyond the slavery period. Muslims continued to be active in the United States up to the Emancipation Proclamation.

Immigration of Muslims to the United States occurred in several waves. The first wave took place from 1875 to 1912 and consisted of uneducated and unskilled young Arab men from countries under Ottoman rule. The second wave occurred from 1918 to 1922 and included friends, relatives, and acquaintances of the earlier immigrants. The third wave of Muslim immigration occurred from 1930 to 1938 and was spurred by

American immigration laws confining immigration to relatives of those already in the country. The fourth wave, from 1947 to 1960, comprised immigrants from the Middle East as well as from South Asia, Eastern Europe, the Soviet Union, and other parts of the Islamic world. These immigrants were the children of the upper class in various countries. They were for the most part urban and educated and had been Westernized prior to their arrival in the United States. They came to America for various reasons, including higher education, technical training, work opportunities, and ideological fulfillment.

Eventually Muslims began to settle down and establish organizations and houses of worship. In the early 1900s, a small community of Muslims in Ross, North Dakota, conducted communal prayers in private homes. In Michigan, Islamic associations were established in Highland Park in 1919 and in Detroit in 1922. In 1925, Muslim immigrants in Cedar Rapids, Iowa, rented a building to serve as a mosque. In 1934, they established the first Muslim place of worship in North America specifically built as a mosque.

Muslims began to take part in all facets of American life, from educational institutions to the military. In 1949, Dr. Majid Khadduri, an authority on Islamic law, became a professor at the Johns Hopkins University. In 1952, staff sergeant Abdullah Igram, a World War II veteran, established the Federation of Islamic Associations–U.S./Canada. The federation held its first convention that year in Cedar Rapids, Iowa, attracting more than four hundred Muslims from across the United States. The second convention was held in Toledo, Ohio, in 1953. While Muslims had migrated to Ohio earlier in the century, this convention marked the official emergence of a Muslim presence in Ohio.

Muslims in Ohio

There are about 150,000 Muslims in Ohio. Most live in Toledo, Columbus, Dayton, Springfield, Cincinnati, Cleveland, Youngstown, Akron, and Kent. Currently there are more than a hundred Islamic centers, mosques, and other Islamic organizations and four full-time Islamic schools in the state.

Toledo
The history of Islam in Ohio begins with the history of the faith in Toledo. While there were few Muslim families in Toledo at the beginning of the

The first Islamic center of Toledo, at Bancroft and Cherry Streets, built in 1954. (Courtesy of the Islamic Center of Greater Toledo)

twentieth century, their number slowly grew to about one dozen after World War I, and then steadily increased as Muslim immigration increased. By 1939, the community, made up mostly of immigrants from the Middle East, organized the first Muslim society in Toledo. On November 15, 1943, the state of Ohio granted the society an official charter.

The first society dissolved because of lack of funding and participation. In 1951, a second society was formed. The new society was called the Syrian American Muslim Society, descriptive of the local Syrian and Lebanese Muslims. Soon the community became aware of the need for a permanent home for religious worship and social gatherings. In the first week of June 1953, the society hosted the second Federation of Islamic Associations convention in Toledo at the Commodore Perry Hotel. Speakers at the convention included Iran's official representative to the United Nations and the director of the Islamic center in Washington, D.C.

The enthusiasm generated from the convention provided the impetus for the Toledo community's drive for a new mosque. On October 5, 1953, the Muslim society held a general meeting to discuss the site of a mosque. A committee headed by Abdul Jalil Abdo Fakih (Eddie Simon) presented a proposal to buy a lot on Bancroft Street for thirty-three hundred dollars. The motion passed and construction began on October 20, 1953, when mayor Lloyd Roulet broke ground in the presence of the new Imam, Muhammad Yusuf Al-Abdoney. The mosque was dedicated on April 4,

Dedication ceremony for the first Islamic center of Toledo, April 1954. Attendees included the Imams of Toledo and Detroit, Christian clergy, and the mayor of Toledo. (Courtesy of the Islamic Center of Greater Toledo)

1954. With a newly built mosque, a number of second-generation Muslim Americans from other parts of the country started moving to Toledo. The first Indian Muslim brothers arrived in 1954. On January 8, 1955, the society held its first meeting in the new edifice. At that meeting, under the leadership of Yehiya (John) Shousher, the society voted to change its name to the American Muslim Society, thus omitting the Syrian descriptor, which did not accurately depict the changing demographics of the new community.

As the community grew, the mosque was unable to accommodate all of the religious, educational, and social needs of its members. The ever-increasing membership led to the decision to build a bigger and better facility. The present Islamic Center of Greater Toledo, located in Perrysburg Township, took more than a decade to plan and construct. In 1978, forty-eight acres of land were purchased at the junction of Interstates 475 and 75. The late Talat Itil of Toledo, a notable Turkish architect, designed the center in the style of traditional Islamic architecture. The foundation of the center was laid in October 1980 and construction began in September 1982. The building was completed within a year. The center consists of a forty-thousand-square-foot covered area flanked by two 135-foot-tall minarets. A sixty-foot dome sits on a carpeted octagonal prayer area that can accommodate about a thousand persons. The upper floor contains a five-hundred-seat sermon hall, and the basement contains classrooms and a dining area. Made of faceted glass, seventy-two windows adorn the building. There are thirty-two small windows in the dome, with the attributes of God inscribed in Arabic calligraphy. The large windows in the prayer area and on the front display verses from the Quran, the Muslim holy book. The new building is one of a kind in North America because of its size and its classical Islamic architecture. The center was also the first in the United States to elect a female president, which it did in 2000. It presently has a membership of more than four hundred families from more than thirty different ethnicities and nationalities. Nearly five thousand Muslims live in the greater Toledo area. With the active participation and contribution of the local Muslim community, the University of Toledo established the Imam Khattab Endowed Chair of Islamic Studies in 1999.

Since the establishment of the Islamic Center in Perrysburg, a number of new mosques have been established in the Toledo area, namely Masjid Saad Foundation, Imam Ali Mosque, Masjid Al-Islam, and Masjid Qur'an wa Sunnah.

Columbus

Historically, the majority of Muslims migrated to central Ohio in pursuit of higher education and for economic reasons. In the last thirty-five years, the Muslim community has come a long way from a tiny, unrecognizable group mostly pursuing academic excellence in the mid-1960s, to a community of professionals and business entrepreneurs that numbered more than twenty-five thousand in 2002. The three major civil and ethnic disturbances—Afghanistan, the Balkans, and particularly Somalia— contributed to a dramatic influx of refugee immigrants during the 1990s.

The Islamic Foundation of Central Ohio was first established in 1972 and began its formal activities in 1976 at its current location on East Broad Street. The foundation came to be known locally as the Islamic

The Islamic Center of Greater Toledo, a striking mosque designed by Talat Itil and constructed in 1982–83, overlooks the junction of Interstates 75 and 475 at Perrysburg in Wood County. It is the first mosque in North America constructed in classical Islamic architectural style. (Courtesy of the Islamic Center of Greater Toledo)

Center. The center became the nucleus for the Muslim community. Its facilities accommodated an Islamic school and adult education lectures. The center regularly received visitors from city hall and the statehouse. The state of Ohio was one of the first states in the Union to proclaim an Islamic Day (second Saturday of October each year). Unfortunately, following September 11, 2001 (on December 28, 2001), the center was severely vandalized. It was reopened in January 2003.

As the Muslim population has increased in Columbus, several additional organizations and mosques have developed. These include the Islamic Society of Greater Columbus, the Sunrise Academy, the Council on American Islamic Relations–Ohio Chapter, Masjid Al-Islam, Omar Ibn-el-khattab Mosque, and American Islamic Waqf. A mosque serving the needs of African American Muslims has been established on Oak Street near the Franklin Park Conservatory, and an Islamic Center on Cooke Road serves the Somalian Muslim community. The most ambitious project undertaken by the central Ohio Muslim community, the Masjid-e-Aenour, is under construction and is due to open in 2004. It is expected to cater to the social and cultural needs of the more than twenty-five thousands Muslims who call Central Ohio their home.

Dayton and Springfield

The earliest documented record of a Muslim presence in Clark County is the 1910 census, which listed more than a hundred persons from Turkey. At that time, Turkey was the home of the then-dominant Muslim Ottoman Empire, and it is likely that the majority of these Turkish residents were Muslims. During the 1950s and 1960s a number of Muslim professional started moving into the Miami Valley region. The ethnicity of the population at that time was predominantly Arab, Iranian, and Turkish, with a minority from South Asia. Around the same time, indigenous Muslims, mainly African American, began organizing their own communities.

With the close proximity of Dayton and Springfield, Muslim families from the two cities joined together for prayer services in a donated single-family home. The Miami Valley Islamic Association built the first mosque in the area in Springfield in 1978. In 1971 the African American community, at that time a part of the Nation of Islam, created Temple Number 71 in Springfield by purchasing an old church and converting it to a mosque called Masjid-e-Nur. At the same time, the African American community of Dayton purchased a house on the west side of the city and converted it to a mosque called Masjid-e-Taqwa.

Young Muslims on college campuses were also organizing themselves. A group of Libyan students rented a house, which served as a mosque, near the campus of the University of Dayton. The group then purchased a small church in the historic district of St. Ann and established a mosque called the Islamic Center of Dayton. In 1985 the center established a part-time Islamic school; within ten years a full-time school was established. This initiated the formation in 1993 of the Greater Dayton Islamic Foundation, which would eventually build a new Muslim community center on five acres of land in the city of Beavercreek in 1996. Plans are currently under way to add a separate mosque to the center.

During the 1970s, the Springfield community rented property near the community hospital for congregational events. In 1981, the Miami Valley

Islamic Association purchased land to build an Islamic community center on South Burnett Road. Today, this mosque is known as Masjid Al-Madinah and is attended by more than sixty-five families.

Currently, about ten thousand Muslims live in the greater Dayton area, and more than five hundred Muslims have chosen Springfield to be their home. The three Muslim communities of Dayton, Springfield, and Cincinnati formed the American Muslim Council–Southwest Ohio Chapter in November 2001.

Cincinnati

The presence of Muslims of African descent in Ohio dates back to the slave period. There are documented reports of Muslim African slaves who lived in the Cincinnati area who earned the respect of their slave owners to such an extent that they were often recipients of gifts from their native lands. If the slave owner visited the land in which his slaves were born, he would bring them a copy of the Quran. Cincinnati was also one of the first cities in Ohio to establish an African American Muslim community under the teaching of Elijah Mohammed, who later took over the reins of what became known as the Nation of Islam. This community was known as Mohammed Mosque No. 5, being the fifth mosque to be established in America under his leadership in the 1950s.

Many immigrant Muslims came to Cincinnati as exchange students and as visiting professionals in the mid-1950s. Until then, the number of Muslims was very small. Religious functions were typically celebrated in homes. Community members represented their country and not necessarily their religion in the annual International Festival. The first efforts to organize the community occurred in the late 1960s, when some Muslim men got permission to meet for Friday prayer in the basement of the Clifton YMCA. By the early 1970s there was large influx of Muslims into the area. A small house was purchased on Fairview Avenue close to the University of Cincinnati and converted into a mosque. Soon the mosque was full on Sundays and appeared to be too small to accommodate new arrivals. A bigger building was bought on Clifton Avenue, but within five years the need for a new Islamic center became apparent. Built by Ahmed Samavi, a generous local contractor, the sprawling new Islamic Center of Greater Cincinnati stands on eighteen acres on Plantation Drive. A smaller community center has been built at the Clifton Avenue location.

The Cincinnati community of ten thousand is proud to have two Islamic centers to serve its religious needs.

Cleveland

Historically Cleveland had a small community of Muslim African Americans whose ancestors were brought as slaves from different countries in Africa. Immigrant Muslims began moving to Cleveland in the 1950s and 1960s. Most worked in local factories, but a few were professionals—doctors, teachers, and engineers. In the early 1960s, El Hajj Wali Akram established the first mosque in the city, First Cleveland Mosque. In the late 1960s another mosque was established on Superior Avenue, but it closed after a few months.

In 1966 Muslim immigrants from India, Pakistan, Yugoslavia, Lebanon, and the former Palestine formed the present organization, Islamic Center of Cleveland. The organization arranged Sunday prayers in homes, hotels, and the downtown YMCA. It held its first Eid dinner celebration at Case Western Reserve University's student union hall. Soon the number of Muslims moving into Cleveland increased significantly. The organization purchased a house at 9400 Detroit Avenue and used it for community prayers. In the late 1970s and early 1980s the Muslim population of the city increased quite significantly and mosques started appearing in many different parts of the city. An example is the Masjid Bilal at East Seventy-fourth Street and Euclid Avenue, which was the first mosque built in the city according to Islamic architecture. The Detroit Avenue mosque of the Islamic Center of Cleveland was by now clearly too small for the ever-increasing community. In 1989 the center began construction of a new mosque in Parma, and it was completed and dedicated on March 15, 1995. At the same time, Masjid Uqba, used mainly by university students, was completed near Case Western Reserve University.

At the present time, the Muslim population in Greater Cleveland area is approximately thirty thousand, and it has established about fifteen mosques and Islamic community centers in the region.

Youngstown

Muslims arrived in Youngstown soon after World War I. By the mid-1920s a significant number of them had settled there. The vast majority of these were from North Yemen and Palestine, and they found work in steel mills. The Muslim community did not increase significantly until immigration patterns changed in the 1950s. The postwar period (1949–53) saw a resurgence of Muslim immigration into the city, and by 1955 there were hundreds of Muslims in Youngstown and the towns surrounding it. Like those who came before them, they too were from the Middle East and became steel workers. They did not establish permanent roots in the city but remained transient. This changed in the 1960s with an increasing number of South Asians from India and Pakistan moving into the area. Today, approximately two thousand Muslims reside in the greater Youngstown area, which includes East Liverpool, Salem, and Warren.

The present-day Islamic Society of Greater Youngstown and its Islamic center—Masjid Al Khair—are the culmination of planning that occurred in 1973. Initially some members of the community expressed doubts about building an Islamic center because they felt that the Muslim community in the city was still transient. This perspective changed as more immigrants felt secure enough to consider Youngstown their permanent home. In 1979 the Islamic Society of Greater Youngstown was formally established. In 1980 the American Muslim Society of North America donated a house at 535 Harmon Street for the purpose of establishing a mosque, the Masjid Al Khair. By 1985 the society had acquired sufficient land to accommodate a new structure. In the summer of 1988 construction of a new building was begun, and it was completed in January 1989. The mosque and the establishment of a university professorship in Islamic studies at Youngstown State University testify to the permanent roots this Muslim community of nearly two thousand has put down in the greater Youngstown area.

Akron and Kent

Muslims began arriving in the Akron and Kent area in the 1960s and 1970s, mainly as students. In September 1979 Muslim students at Kent State University organized themselves into an Islamic society and established a small mosque in an apartment on Rhodes Avenue in Kent. Soon Muslims from adjoining areas joined them. A Sunday Islamic school was started shortly thereafter. The mosque was moved to Williams Street in 1980, and the Islamic Society of Greater Kent was established in 1981. In

1982 the mosque was moved to a rented apartment in the Silver Oaks complex. Then in 1985 an old church on Crain Avenue was purchased and renovated into a mosque, which was completed in May 1986. Soon that facility as well grew too small for community activities, and more than seventeen acres were purchased in Cuyahoga Falls in June 1995. The new Islamic center was built on this site at a cost of $2.8 million. It consists of a mosque, an Islamic school, and a community hall.

In the meantime, Muslim students at the nearby University of Akron had started holding Friday prayers at the Gardner Student Center. In 1985 they established a mosque in a rented house on Powers Street in Akron. Local Muslims in the Akron area joined them, and the Islamic Society of Akron was established in June 1989. In 1991 the mosque was moved to another rented location on Sherman Street in Akron. In 1995, the Islamic Society of Akron and Islamic Society of Greater Kent merged to form the Islamic Society of Akron and Kent. The Sherman Street house was then vacated.

In the early 1980s the African American Muslim community had established a mosque on Garth Avenue in Akron. In 1995 an old theater on Old South Main Street in Akron was converted to a mosque and it became the focus of community activities. The Shia Muslims also have a mosque on Manchester Road. It is commonly referred to as Jaffery Union Mosque. In addition, the Canton Muslim community, established in the mid-1980s, holds prayer services in a medical office building. About two thousand Muslims currently reside in Summit, Stark, Portage, and Medina counties.

BELIEFS

What Is Islam?

Islam means submission to the will of God. It also means peace with God, with one's self, and with all humankind. The will of God is universal and unchanging in that it requires all human beings to worship Him and do good for humanity. Islam is an Abrahamic religion and incorporates the same truths revealed by God through the prophets to all peoples of all times. Islam is not only a set of beliefs; it is a complete way of life.

What Are Muslims?

The people who believe in Islam are called Muslims. Worldwide, there are about 1.5 billion Muslims of different nationalities, races, and cultures. Islam is the second largest religion in the world and is composed of various nationalities. An estimated 7 million Muslims live in the United States today.

Who Is Allah?

Muslims believe in the one, unique, and incomparable God. Allah is the Arabic name for God and is preferred by Muslims for it cannot be pluralized and is gender neutral. Allah (God) alone is to be worshiped.

Who Was Muhammad?

Muhammad was the messenger of God. He was born in Makkah, present-day Saudi Arabia, in 570 c.e. At age forty, he received his first revelation through the Angel Gabriel. Muslims believe in a chain of prophets starting with Adam and including Noah, Abraham, Ishmael, Isaac, Jacob, Joseph, Job, Moses, Aaron, David, Solomon, Elias, Jonah, John the Baptist, Jesus, and Muhammad. It is important to understand that Muslims do not worship Muhammad in any way. Muhammad was a prophet. Islam views Adam, Noah, Abraham, Moses, Jesus, and Muhammad as prophets of God, with Muhammad being the last messenger.

The Quran and the Hadith

Muslims believe the Quran is one of four revealed scriptures: the Torah to Moses, the Psalms to David, the Gospel to Jesus, and the Quran to Muhammad. The earliest copies of the Quran are preserved in the museums and libraries of Egypt and Turkey. The Quran is the prime and divine source of Islamic faith and practice. It is like a manual for human life, dealing with all aspects of wisdom, doctrine, worship, and law. It provides guidelines for a just society, proper social conduct, and an equitable economic system. Along with the Quran, the sayings and practices of the Prophet (Hadith and Sunnah) are the second source of law. Hadith and Sunnah are transmitted reports of what the Prophet said, did, or approved. Hadith and Sunnah are an integral part of Islamic teaching but are not considered to be of divine origin.

The Five Pillars of Islam

Among the specific duties set forth in the Quran and spelled out in the traditions are the Five Pillars of Islam. The first pillar is the profession of faith (*shahada*): "There is no god but God and Muhammad is the messenger of God." The statement contains the essence of Islam: the unity and uniqueness of God and the role of Muhammad in bringing the message of God to humankind. It is so central to Islam that in order for one to accept Islam, one must profess this creed. The second pillar is prayer (*salat*). Prayer is offered five times a day at prescribed times. It has the effect of reminding the faithful to adhere to the path of righteousness and to refrain from indecency and evil. The third pillar is fasting (*sawm*). A fast is observed every day from dawn until sunset during the lunar month of Ramadan. It involves abstinence from eating, drinking, smoking, and sexual and sensual activities while fasting. While fasting in Ramadan serves many purposes, two of the main objectives are to teach self-discipline throughout all aspects of a Muslim's life and to teach a sense of compassion and true understanding for those less fortunate than oneself. The fourth pillar is obligatory giving (*zakat*, the share of the needy). This requires giving each year a fixed amount of personal assets for the benefit of the poor and the welfare of the community. It serves to remind Muslims that all beneficence comes from the bounty of God and is enjoyed only by God's mercy. Sharing becomes an act of purification both of the wealth and of the giver, whose soul is disciplined against greed by the virtue of selflessness. The fifth pillar is the pilgrimage (*hajj*) to Makkah, which all Muslims should perform at least once in a lifetime, if physically and financially able. The pilgrimage brings believers together into a single community. Pilgrims are required to dress alike, in simple garments that strip away distinctions of class and culture.

How Do Muslims View the Nature of Man, the Purpose of Life, and the Hereafter?

In the Holy Quran, God teaches human beings that they were created in order to worship Him, and that the basis of all true worship is God-consciousness. Islam makes clear that all human acts are acts of worship if they are done in accordance with His divine law. The teachings of Islam act as a mercy and a healing for the human soul, and such qualities as humility, sincerity, patience, and charity are strongly encouraged. Additionally, Islam condemns pride and self-righteousness.

The Islamic view of the nature of man is that human beings are not inherently sinful but equally capable of good and evil. There is no doctrine comparable to the Christian idea of Original Sin. Humans are God's representatives on earth. Islam considers itself to be the primordial religion—it seeks to return humanity to its original, true nature in which human beings are in harmony with creation, inspired to do good, and confirming the oneness of God. There is no priesthood in Islam, and every Muslim is required to do good and avoid evil. Islam teaches that faith and action go hand in hand. God has given people free will, and the measure of one's faith is in one's deeds and actions. However, human beings have also been created weak and regularly fall into disfavor. The avenue of repentance is always open to all human beings, and the almighty God loves the repentant sinner as much as the one who does not sin at all. The true balance of an Islamic life is established by having a God-consciousness as well as a sincere belief in His infinite mercy.

Upon death, Muslims believe that God judges every soul for its beliefs and actions in its earthly life; God will be merciful and just. Islam teaches that life is a test, and that all beings will be accountable before God on the Day of Judgement. A sincere belief in the hereafter is the key to leading a well-balanced, moral life.

How Does Islam View Other Faiths?

In Islam, those who follow the faiths of Judaism and Christianity are called People of the Book. Islam further believes that other prophets were sent to other nations. All the prophets are messengers of the same one

God. The Quran mentions the names of twenty-five prophets and indicates that there have been others who were not mentioned to the Prophet Muhammad. The Quran's account of Jesus rejects his divine sonship and presents him as one of the great prophets of God. The Quran makes it clear that the birth of Jesus without a father does not make him the son of God and mentions in this respect Adam, who was created by God without a father or mother. Like other prophets, Jesus also performed miracles. For example, he raised the dead and cured the blind and lepers, but always made it clear that these miracles were performed with the permission of God. According to the Quran, he was sent to the children of Israel; he confirmed the validity of the Torah, which was revealed to Moses; and he also brought the glad tidings of a final messenger (Muhammad). Neither Muhammad nor Jesus came to change the basic doctrine of the belief in God, brought by earlier prophets, but rather to confirm and renew it.

Justice, Peace, and Equality in Islam

The Quran states, "And act justly. Truly, God loves those who are just" (49:9). When we speak of human rights in Islam we really mean that these rights have been granted by God. No one has the right to abrogate or withdraw them. Human blood is sacred and cannot be spilled without justification. If anyone violates this sanctity of human blood by killing a soul without justification, the Quran equates it to the killing of all of humankind. "Whoso slays a soul not to retaliate for a soul slain, nor for corruption done in the land, should be as if he had slain mankind altogether" (5:32). It is not permissible to oppress women, children, old people, the sick, or the wounded. Women's honor and chastity are to be respected under all circumstances. The hungry person must be fed, the naked clothed, and the wounded or diseased treated medically, irrespective of whether they belong to the Islamic community.

Islam is by nature a religion of peace that emphasizes respect for the sanctity of human life. Islam does not promote violence, aggression, terrorism, or oppression. The Quran is clear on this: "[Allah] does not love the aggressor" (2:190). Every human being is related to all others and all become one community of brotherhood in their honorable and pleasant servitude to the most compassionate God of the universe. There is no distinction made among human beings based on differences in nationality, color, or race. Islam promotes human rights regardless of social status or geographical limits. Islam's fundamental human rights include: security of life and property, protection of honor, sanctity and security of private life, security of personal freedom, right to protest against tyranny, freedom of expression, freedom of association, freedom of conscience and conviction, protection of religious sentiments, protection from arbitrary imprisonment, the right to basic necessities of life, equality before the rule of law, and the idea that rulers are not above the law (Quran, 4:75).

Other Sects of Islam

Technically speaking, Islam has no sects. However, there are two major schools of thought that prevail in today's Islamic world: the Sunni and the Shia. They have many things in common. Both schools follow the Quran and the teachings of the Prophet Muhammad. The Shia sect comprises approximately 15 percent of the world's Muslim population.

The Spread of Islam

The simplicity of Islamic doctrine (one God, one message, and one humanity), which calls for faith in one God and values reason, intelligence, and observation, was among the reasons for the rapid and peaceful spread of Islam in the centuries following its birth. The Prophet said, "Seeking knowledge is an obligation for every Muslim man and woman" (Hadith). Taking their cue from the Quran, Muslims made great advances in the universities of Baghdad, Samarkand, Cordova, and Cairo in medicine, mathematics, physics, astronomy, geography, architecture, art, literature, and history. Many crucial disciplines, such as algebra, the Arabic numerals, the concept of zero, and optics, were developed and transmitted to medieval Europe from the Muslim world. European voyagers used the astrolabe, the quadrant and the sextant, the compass and navigational maps—all developed by Muslims—up until the development of the Global Positioning System.

The success of Islam owed a lot to the faith's tolerance of other religious beliefs and to the fact that Muslims are not allowed to force conversion of any kind. The Quran says, "There is no compulsion in religion"

(2:256). In fact, Prophet Muhammad forbade the destruction of churches and synagogues. Christians and Jews flourished under Islamic rulers. The Jews often refer to their period under the Moors (Muslims who ruled Spain) as a golden era. Christians living within Islamic empires found themselves in high-level government positions. They were also free to establish churches and operate hospitals as they saw fit.

VISITING A MOSQUE

If one wishes to visit a mosque, one need only call the Imam of that particular mosque to arrange a visit. One must dress conservatively when visiting a mosque, covering one's arms and legs. Shoes are always left outside of the prayer area so as to not trample the prayer space. Women may be asked to cover their heads with a scarf before entering the prayer room. Visitors to a mosque should behave as they would when visiting any religious institution, but should feel free to ask any questions regarding the mosque and Islam.

CURRENT DEMOGRAPHICS

It is estimated that more than 150,000 Muslims call Ohio their home. Of these, some thirty thousand reside in the Greater Cleveland area, twenty-five thousand in the Columbus Metropolitan area, ten thousand each in the Greater Cincinnati and Dayton areas, five thousand in the Toledo area, two thousand each in the Youngstown and Akron/Kent areas, and about five hundred in Springfield. There are approximately one hundred Islamic Centers, mosques, and other Islamic organizations spread throughout the state in every major metropolitan city. In addition, there are four full-time Islamic schools in Ohio.

CONTACT INFORMATION

There is no central office for the Islamic faith in Ohio. However, information on Islam and Muslims in Ohio can obtained from the following:

Council on American-Islamic Relations (CAIR): *www.cair-net.org;* Ohio Chapter (CAIR–Ohio), 4700 Reed Road, Suite B, Columbus, Ohio 43220, 614-451-3232, *info@cair-ohio.com, www.cair-ohio.com*

First Islamic Web: *www.islamicweb.com*

Islamic Society of North America: *www.isna.net*

Religious Tolerance in Islam: *www.religioustolerance.org/islam.htm*

The Islamic Council of Ohio, 25877 Scheider Road, Perrysburg, Ohio 43551, 419-874-3509.

RESOURCES

Ibrahim, I. A. *A Brief Illustrated Guide to Understanding Islam.* Houston: Darussalam, 1997.

Islam: Empire of Faith (video). Produced and directed by Robert Gardner. Distributed by PBS Home Video, 2000.

Islamic Horizon (magazine published by Islamic Society of North America, Plainfield, Indiana), online at *www.isna.net/Horizons/*

The Message: The Story of Islam (video). Produced and directed by Moustapha Akkad. Troy, Mich.: Anchor Bay Entertainment, 1998.

Minaret (magazine published by Islamic Center of Southern California, Los Angeles, Calif.), online at *www.minaretonline.com/*

Sarwar, Ghulam. *Islam: Beliefs and Teachings.* London: Muslim Educational Trust, 1998.

ACKNOWLEDGMENTS

The author wishes to thank the following for providing information about the Muslim community in Ohio: Mohamed Ismail and Imam Emile Bashir of Columbus, Bashir Ahmed of Dayton, Naseem Rahim of Springfield, Majid A. Qureshi of Cincinnati, Ahmad Saeed Ansari of Cleveland, Ikram Khawaja of Youngstown, and Ihsan-ul-Haque of Akron. In particular, sincere appreciation is expressed to Mazhar Jalil of Columbus for providing much-needed encouragement and contacts. Finally, Habib Khan of Toledo and T. O. Shahnavas of Adrian, Michigan, are acknowledged for their valuable suggestions and final review of this essay.

HINDU DHARMA

Shive K. Chaturvedi and Bishun D. Pandey

HISTORY

Hindus began to arrive in Ohio around the early 1950s. It was not until the 1970s and 1980s that the community became significant in number and started organizing spiritual and religious activities.

As the Hindu population in metropolitan areas across the state increased, a few devoted families started meeting together regularly in private homes. These activities continue to not only bring these communities together but also transmit and inculcate religious, moral, ethical, and spiritual values into Hindu children and teenagers. These groups started growing bigger in size as well as in their degree of commitment. This gradual process of growth and evolution created an urgent need for larger prayer and community spaces and financial resources. These needs gave rise to the momentum for building temples, and the initial commitments for the required funds came mostly from the families and groups that had initiated these activities. Gradually, the active participation and financial commitments by large sections of the community contributed to the development of temples and associated institutions in cities across Ohio.

In 2001–2, the authors contacted all the known Hindu temples and organizations in Ohio to collect factual information about the history of their religious, educational, and other associated activities. Some of these temples and organizations provided enough information, while others provided only a short history or no information at all. The information gathered on Hindu temples and organizations across Ohio is presented here.

Cincinnati

The idea of starting religious activities in the Cincinnati area was conceived on Basant Panchami day (spring festival day) 1978. Right after this beginning, several families started hosting religious services (*puja*) in their homes. The first official puja was organized in March 1978 at Dr. Gangadhar Choudhury's residence. Dr. Choudhury also acted as the priest. After this religious service, the community showed keen interest and as a result the religious and spiritual activities moved to the basement of First National Bank (now Firstar Bank), Ludlow Branch, in Cincinnati. Later, in order to formalize this group as a religious organization, it was named the Hindu Society of Greater Cincinnati, and its constitution was adopted in March 1979. It was officially registered with the State of Ohio on April 17, 1980.

An old house was purchased with the help of Ram Jindal at Martin Luther King Drive on September 16, 1982. It was renovated and used as a temple until November 1995. Swami Bhashyanand of Vivekanand Vedanta Society of Chicago performed the inaugural puja for the temple on January 2, 1983. In August 1985, Acharya Ravindra Nagar joined as the first resident priest of the temple.

On September 17, 1986, approximately one hundred acres were purchased in the city. Swami Jyotirmayanand, from Miami, Florida, performed the *bhumi puja* (religious ritual for Mother Earth) on October 12, 1986. He also laid the foundation for the new temple in a ceremony on June 13, 1992. With God's grace, the Hindu Temple of Greater Cincinnati was inaugurated on November 18 and 19, 1995, at the current site. The installation and consecration of deities was performed during a ceremony on May 22 through 26, 1997.

This was the first Hindu temple where there is no central deity. Instead, a sign reading "OM" was installed, indicating the equal significance of all deities. This special glass crystal "OM" is unique in concept and structure. It was carved by the world-renowned Italian master glass sculptor Maestro Pino Signoretto. This generous contribution was from the family of Satgur and Usha Srivastava.

Cleveland

The Greater Cleveland Shiva Vishnu Temple, a magnificent edifice, serves as a Hindu religious center in the sylvan surroundings of Parma, Ohio. The temple caters to the spiritual, cultural, and social needs of the Hindu community of Cleveland and the surrounding areas. The temple started about seventeen years ago in an old rented building at the intersection of West 120th Street and Lorain Road. Today it has its own beautiful and spacious building on thirty-three acres, land surrounded by tall trees that provide a serene atmosphere for devotees.

In autumn 1983 Professor J. L. Sharma of Cleveland State University organized a meeting of the Indian community of Cleveland and surrounding areas, and the attendees decided to build a Hindu temple in Cleveland. The name Greater Cleveland Shiva Vishnu Temple was chosen. The Greater Cleveland Shiva Vishnu Temple came into existence on paper in early 1984. But J. L. Sharma was looking for a temporary building to house the temple though he did not have any financial commitment. Sharma and Darshan Mahajan decided to rent a closed Moose Lodge building at West 120th and Lorain Road. Volunteers cleaned up this rented facility and sanctified it in early 1985. On an auspicious Sunday morning, B. Dattatreya and A. V. Srinivasan performed the first puja and inaugurated the temple. In this way, the Shiva Vishnu Temple came into being. Two weeks later, Ramakrishnan, an engineer by profession, volunteered his priestly services and started the weekly puja in a very systematic manner, which inspired the devotees and then they started donating money more generously toward building a temple.

After the temple came into operation, the temple board started to look for a permanent location, and in 1988 it purchased a thirty-three-acre wooded lot with a burned-out warehouse on it on Ridge Road in Parma. In March 1989, Ramakrishnan performed the bhumi puja at the Parma location. Chandu Patel Construction Company remodeled the building, and finally the Shiva Vishnu Temple was inaugurated on September 10, 1989.

The board of trustees was still hard at work, planning the third important phase of the master plan, that is, building a new Shiva Vishnu Temple at the Parma location. In January 1994 the board engaged the services of architect Ganapathi Stapathi of Chennai (Madras, India), the

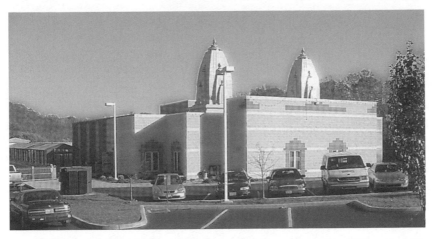

The Shiva Vishnu Temple in Parma, built in 1997. (Courtesy of Shiva Vishnu Temple)

Cleveland firm of Collins, Reimer, and Gordon, and Shashi Patel and Associates of Pittsburgh to design a plan for the new temple according to Hindu architecture. The plan consisted of building the new temple with the Shiva and Vishnu sanctums in the sanctorum and with twelve subsidiary sanctums—four behind the primary sanctums, four on the north side, and four on the south side on the upper level—and a big hall at the lower level. The bhumi puja ceremony for the new temple took place on November 10, 1996, and the East-West Construction company started building the temple in February 1997. The construction was completed within ten months, in October 1997.

A grand inauguration ceremony was planned October 24 through 26, 1997, and the *vigraha* (consecrated statue or idol) of Lord Ganesha was installed. After this, the vigraha of Lord Jagannath was installed in April 1998, Radha Krishna and Sri Nathji deities were installed in June 1998, Somanatheswara (Shiva) and Parvathi were installed in June 1998, Badri Narayana (Vishnu), Lakshmi, and Saraswati was installed in July 1998, Devi Durga was installed in April 1999, Sri Aiyappan was installed in May 1999, Sri Rama Parivar was installed on June 20, 1999, and the final installation ceremony for Sri Subrahmania (Kartikeya) was held on June 30, 2000. Most of the deities are made out of either granite or marble, and all were custom ordered from India. A "bridge to the future" from the parking lot to the temple door was covered with a glass canopy in the year

2000. In 2001 the priests' quarters were constructed and the front door was beautifully decorated with Indian architectural elements.

The temple currently has five priests who provide religious services to the community. The temple conducts regular puja on Sundays and also celebrates all Hindu festivals and holy days. To fulfill the community's cultural and social needs, the temple has established an India Cultural and Educational Center (ICEC), which presents music concerts, classical dance programs, religious discourses, and so forth. A small library is available for children and adults. For educational purposes, the temple runs two Sunday-school classes—Vedic Heritage class by Arsha Gurukula Vidyalaya and Bala Vihar (elementary level) class by Chinmaya Mission. The temple also provides various community services to help the needy and senior citizens.

A second temple in the Cleveland area also exists, the Shree Swaminarayan Mandir.

Columbus

When, in 1975, Manu Bhatt started *bhajans* (prayers and devotional songs) at his house every Friday evening, no one could have guessed that the program would keep growing and ultimately result in the establishment of a temple in central Ohio. Soon interest in attending grew, and on many days more than a hundred people would gather to recite the bhajans. After several years, Subhash and Shanta Bhatia, Manu and Bharati Bhatt, Haren and Mrudula Mehta, Bhupendra and Nayan Parekh, Niranjan and Chhaya Shah, Bhupen and Raksha Trivedi, and others in the bhajan group decided to form a study circle and meet on Sunday mornings to study Bhagavad Gita, Upanishads, and other Hindu scriptures. Later, this group learned that Jagdish and Kamala Rustagi were conducting a similar study circle at their home. The two groups merged, and study continued with more vigor. Harish Chinai, Sarvabhaum and Jyotsana Parikh, Kunj Rastogi, and Jagdev Singh were other members of the larger group.

In the early 1980s, the study circle was incorporated as the Vedanta Society of Central Ohio, which started a monthly lecture series in which many distinguished saints, thinkers, and scholars were invited to speak. These lectures were usually held at various churches. Sometimes several

The Bharatiya Hindu Temple moved in July 1994 to its present location on Hyatts Road in Powell. The temple was originally located on Westerville Road in Columbus (1984–94). (Courtesy of Anish Doshi)

hundred people attended these lectures. In order to conduct these programs in a more regular and dependable manner, the community felt the need for a permanent place. So, starting in late 1984, Manu Bhatt, Harish Chinai, Jagdish Rustagi, and Jagdev Singh started looking for a property where a temple could be established. Thirteen families, known as "Founding Benefactor Members," pledged financial assistance. In June 1985, a property consisting of an old building on a 3.4-acre parcel on Westerville Road was purchased. After six months of repairs and renovations, the temple was inaugurated on December 6, 1985. For the first five years, volunteers performed most of the priestly duties. Then Suresh Deshmukh joined as a full-time priest in 1990. Gopi Tejwani started Hindi classes, which are going strong even today.

A huge growth in temple attendance made it necessary to plan a larger facility. In 1991 the temple purchased a twenty-two-acre parcel at 3671 Hyatt Road in Powell, Delaware County. Architect Shashi Patel designed a temple with six shrines—Ganesh, Durga, Radha-Krishna, Shiva, Venkateshwara, and Sita Ram. Seven members of the community, Krishna Choudhary, Raju and Rajesh Gaglani, Dalsukh Madia, Bishun Pandey, C. K. Satyapriya, Gopi Tejwani, and Raj Tripathi, guaranteed a loan, and the construction of the Bharatiya Hindu Temple started in late 1993. The inauguration of the temple and the installation of Ganesha *murti* (statue or idol) took place on July 9 and 10, 1994. In 1998 the temple purchased two houses on Liberty Road to provide accommodation to its

This deity of Lord Ganesha, the Lord for removing obstacles, was the first to be installed in July 1994 at the opening of the Bharatiya Hindu Temple at its present site in Powell. (Courtesy of Bharatiya Hindu Temple)

priests. Plans are underway to construct a community center near the temple.

The temple celebrates Hindu festivals and provides religious and spiritual services to the Hindu community in central Ohio. Religion, Hindi language, music, and dance classes are provided free of cost. The temple also organizes discourses by well-known scholars, dance drama, and concerts. Currently, the temple has more than three hundred families who are formal members. In addition, the temple is also involved in outreach activities, such as a Red Cross blood drive, summer youth camp, health fair, and other community service activities, which are open to the general public.

Several other Hindu organizations and temples are active in the Columbus area, including:

- *Spiritual Sadhna Society:* In 1975 Dr. Sneh Jindal, a clinical psychologist initially located in Chillicothe, along with Dr. J. S. Jindal of Columbus, started religious, educational, and spiritual activities, which are being continued under the above nonprofit organization. The first religious program arranged in Columbus—on August 20, 1983—was attended by then-governor Richard F. Celeste and K. R. Narayanan, then Indian ambassador to the United States, along with other dignitaries. The society also arranged *ramayan katha* (a discourse on the epic story of Lord Rama) programs in major Ohio cities during 1983. Dr. Sneh Jindal is still continuing her teaching of Vipassana meditation as the senior teacher. This society is further engaged in various social services as well as in interfaith activities for promoting mutual understanding, respect, and spiritual relationships.

- *Krishna House:* On May 12, 1968, the founder Acharya of the International Society for Krishna Consciousness (ISKCON), A. C. Bhaktivedanta Swami Prabhupada, along with poet Allen Ginsberg, had addressed an audience in Hitchcock Hall at the Ohio State University in Columbus. Within a few months of this event, the first Hare Krishna temple was opened in Columbus near the University Hospitals. The Ohio Historical Society recently awarded the Columbus Krishna House a historical marker as the "Oldest Hindu Temple in the State of Ohio."

- *Shree Swaminarayan Mandir.*

Toledo

The idea of constructing a Hindu temple in Toledo came into the picture in December 1981. It was created to provide a place where Hindus and Jains could worship together and the growing religious and spiritual needs of the community could be fulfilled. At the time, the size of the Indian community was roughly 150 Hindu families and about ten or twelve Jain families. The temple organization was formed in 1982. The temple hired an Indian architect to design a traditional Hindu temple on a fifteen-acre parcel it purchased in 1983. A Hindu and Jain religious function was organized in 1984 in a house that came with the land. The construction of the temple was completed in August 1989, and the inauguration and *murti prana pratishtha* (religious rituals to invoke the presence of deity in the idol) of Hindu and Jain deities Mahavir, Rama, Sita, Krishna, Radha, Vishnu, Lakshmi, and Ganesha were performed.

The temple has become the center of religious, spiritual, and social activities for the Hindu community of Toledo and other cities within a radius of about fifty miles. It serves about four hundred families in these areas and about three hundred Hindu Indian students attending two universities, the University of Toledo and Bowling Green State University.

The temple is open daily for worship and prayers conducted by the priests. Every Sunday the temple has about three hours of religious programs, consisting of rituals, worship, prayers, and sermons and discourses, followed by lunch. The temple celebrates religious festivals and auspicious days throughout the year. The temple also organizes classes on Hindu scriptures and heritage for children and adults. In addition, the temple celebrates the "festival of India" and makes its premises available to the Red Cross and the local interfaith association for an annual blood drive.

Akron, Dayton, and Youngstown

Neither the Vedic Foundation of Akron nor the Indian Association of Greater Akron is currently active, but both occasionally arrange spiritual programs. In general, Hindus from the greater Akron area attend Hindu temples in Parma and/or Youngstown. Youngstown (Shri Lakshmi Narayan Temple) and Dayton (Hindu Temple of Dayton) are also home to Hindu temples.

HINDU WORLDVIEW: BASIC IDEAS

"The Whole World Is One Family"
—Hitopadesh, a Hindu scripture

The term "religion" can be described as those modes of thinking and acting which are directed toward goodness and justice (George Sarton, introduction to *Science, Religion, and Reality*, ed. Joseph Needham [New York: George Braziller 1955], 5). Of course, these ideas may entail enquiry into the concepts of God, immortality, sin, and salvation. In Hinduism, the term *dharma* is comprehensive and includes all orders and harmonies (social, moral, aesthetic, religious, scientific, spiritual, natural, cosmic, etc.) that can manifest through arts, sciences, and spiritual disciplines. Therefore, it is also known as the *sanatana dharma,* or eternal order and harmony within the totality of existence, nonmaterial as well as material. The ideas, principles, and traditions that foster a wide variety of disorders and discords within an individual, society, and world have been characterized as the fields of *adharma* (antonym of dharma). For example, untruthfulness, false ego, lust, anger, hatred, violence, greed, enviousness, sexual indulgence before marriage, theft, absurd and offensive behavior, and talk are called *adharmic*. They are real sources of miseries for humanity, and therefore must be controlled and annihilated.

The term "Hindu" refers to the people of Vedic civilization. The term probably came from ancient Persian and Greek. Hinduism can best be described as a civilization whose ancient sages and seers received revealed multifaceted wisdom during deep meditation and fashioned their living traditions based on this revealed wisdom, which encompassed all aspects and mysteries of the cosmos and life. Its many social customs, traditions, and ideas are not to be thought of as engraved in stone to be preserved intact for future generations, but rather as living organisms which must change and grow with new times and surroundings. However, this change and growth cannot be arbitrary but must be within the framework of the eternal and universal web of dharmic principles.

Scriptures

The fundamental concepts, ideas, and practices within the Vedic or Hindu Dharma came to be known through the first books of wisdom, known as the Vedas (Rigveda, Samaveda, Yajurveda, and Atharvaveda). These scriptures, set to musical meters, were transmitted orally from one generation to another by the seers over many centuries before they were put into written form around 3000 B.C.E. In relentless pursuit of the whole truth, the Hindu sages and seers further contributed to the evolution and growth of wisdom through numerous volumes dealing with all aspects of divinity, humanity, and the natural world. These scriptures include the entire field of arts and humanities; sciences such as medicine (*ayurveda*), astronomy (*jyotish*), and architecture (*sthapatyaveda*); philosophy and Yoga sciences (Upanishads and Yoga-Shastras); epic poems and histories (Puranas, Ramayana, Mahabharata); as well as the essence of vedantic philosophies such as Bhagavata and Bhagavadgita, Lord Krishna's celestial song. The Bhagavadgita, the best-known scripture, has been translated into most major languages and has deeply influenced many famous scholars and thinkers, such as transcendentalists Ralph Waldo Emerson and Henry David Thoreau. The language of these scriptures is Sanskrit, which is recognized by linguists as one of the most perfect, melodious, and scientific languages of humanity.

Concept of God, the Cosmos, and the Individual

The concept of God, the ultimate reality, is central to the Hindu world-view. The self-existing and indefinable God is expressed variously as the Brahman (all-pervading, being, bliss), Paramatman (eternal divine whole), Bhagawan (transcendental personality of Godhead), and Parameshwara (Supreme Lord). He is transcendent as well as immanent, all pervading, omnipresent, omnipotent, omniscient. He dwells in all things and beings, and all things and beings dwell within Him, yet He is transcendental to all the potential existence. The one supreme personality of Godhead desired to become many with the result that He unfolded Himself to become the whole cosmos (living as well as nonliving) and yet remained above and beyond it. The Supreme Lord also descends in this world in various forms from time to time to reestablish righteousness, to annihilate evil, to reestablish His relationship with humanity, and to shower His grace on human as well nonhuman beings. Possessing unlimited compassion and mercy, the Supreme Lord can manifest as male or female, and yet is believed to be beyond and above gender categories.

According to the Hindu Dharma our cosmos is more than thirty trillion years old. The Supreme Lord brings forth the cosmos with all its variety, complexity, and diversity through His own creative power, known as Maya. This entire manifestation goes through infinite cycles of creation, sustenance, and dissolution. And to govern all these aspects of the cosmos, the One Supreme Lord takes three primary forms: Lord Brahma, Lord of creation; Lord Vishnu, Lord of preservation; and Lord Shiva, Lord of dissolution.

According to Hindu scriptures, human beings (male and female) and all other beings are recognized to be part and parcel of the One, the Supreme God. Thus, we are all one family irrespective of color, race, religion, sexual orientation, geographical origin, country, culture, or philosophy. Every human being is a composite entity consisting of *atman* (a nonmaterial entity) and *sarira* (a material body). The atman is unchanging, non-decaying, deathless, all pervading, eternal, and blissful, while the material body is by its very nature ever mutable and goes through cycles of birth, growth, old age, and death.

Each individual's personality is different, and so is his or her capacity to visualize and relate to God. Hindu traditions, therefore, allow each person to worship God in a form he or she can relate to and in a manner best suited to his or her own mental makeup and propensities. Lord Rama and Lord Krishna are recognized to be the fullest manifestations of the Godhead on this earth. Human beings can relate to Lord through their relationships as father, mother, brother, sister, son, daughter, spouse, friend, and teacher. The presence of a real spiritual sage or teacher (guru) is recognized to be very important for spiritual growth. The guru (male or female), whose life radiates the light of wisdom, compassion, and love for all human and nonhuman beings, is revered as the most visible manifestation of divinity.

In the Hindu view, the human condition in this world is the result of a complex dynamic web operating through various forces such as the natural, social, political, and spiritual, as well as one's own deeds (*karma*), good or bad, from the present life and many past lives. In every moment we are engaged in some kind of action or karma. Breathing, for example, is a karma. The karmic field includes all the actions performed externally or internally through our mind, words, and deeds. All our actions, in any form, produce some reaction in others as well as on our own deepest psychic core. These reactions accumulate and bear fruit, either good or bad, at proper times and circumstances. This central idea has come to be known as the "Law of Karma" or the universal law of justice.

Life after Death and Liberation

The Hindu worldview believes in life after death. Death comes only to the material body and not to the eternal and immortal atman. After leaving the physical body, the nonliberated atman can continue to live in a variety of modes and in regions unlike this world. The virtuous can go to higher and more prosperous regions (like heavens), the nonvirtuous to lower regions (like hells), and others can come back to earth to go through more cycles of birth and death. This process of endless cycles can continue till one attains liberation (*moksha*) and union with God through achieving purity and perfection of virtuous living and acting in this world. The process by which purification and liberation can be achieved includes prayers, chanting the holy names of God, worshiping God, meditation, selfless service to humanity, performing good deeds, practice of any of the yogas, visiting holy places and cleansing in holy waters, and other spiritual disciplines.

Hindu Temple: Meaning and Significance

A Hindu temple is a house of God (*devagriham*). There devotees offer prayers and worship to God and His various deity forms and meditate to experience direct vision of and communion with the deity. The temple also provides resources needed to perform religious rites and ceremonies, to provide social and cultural activities, and to educate children, teenagers, and adults in spiritual and other disciplines such as anthropology, history, visual and performing arts, recitation, and understanding of scripture and ritual. The temple also acts as a center for charitable activities like collecting and distributing food and other necessities to needy people and social services such as family counseling.

Attitude toward Other Faiths

Hindu sages discovered that there are many ways of knowing and reaching the Supreme Lord, and hence they proclaimed several thousand years ago, as the *Rig-Veda* states, that "the field of Truth is one unified whole, the wise proclaim it in manifold ways." Consequently, a true follower of Hindu dharma is bound to respect religious diversity and plurality, does not hate anyone, and is able to live in peace and harmony with people of all faiths and traditions. Furthermore, there is no room in the Hindu Dharma for conversion or evangelical activities. Belief in religious tolerance, respect for the whole world as one family, and love of humankind have been the ideals of Hindu traditions throughout the ages.

On Justice, Peace, and Equality

The complex interplay of innate nature, nurture, and karmic law that a human being is subject to makes equality in human propensities and habits of mind hard to establish. However, amid the external diversity there exists equality at the core or spiritual level of the human personality. In the Hindu view, for example, women and men have the same potential. Therefore, Hindu traditions focus on giving equal opportunity and justice to all human beings in pursuit of their physical, mental, intellectual, social, and spiritual progress and growth toward achieving complete spiritual freedom and real happiness. It is also recognized that with equal opportunities and rights, persons can bring out their hidden potential and thereby achieve the maximum good for themselves, their society, and the world. The Hindu view of justice also affirms the sacredness of Mother Earth, the value of ecological diversity, the interdependence of all species, and the right to be free from all forms of ecological destruction.

For attainment of universal peace, Hindus are required to pray to the Supreme Lord for achieving peace within each of us, within natural forces, within Mother Nature, within society, within the world, and within the cosmos.

ATTENDING A TEMPLE WORSHIP SERVICE

Hindu temples are open to everyone regardless of color, race, sexual orientation, religious faith, or culture. Guests are advised to have clean and modest attire and are required to observe cleanliness by removing their shoes before entering the worship areas. Attendees are encouraged to participate in the religious and spiritual services and to eat food served as the blessing of God.

CURRENT DEMOGRAPHICS

Based on the recent information provided by the Hindu temples and organizations in Ohio, it appears that approximately sixty thousand Hindus reside in the state. The largest concentration is in the greater Cleveland area.

CONTACT INFORMATION

Bharatiya Hindu Temple, 3671 Hyatts Road, P.O. Box 1466, Powell, Ohio 43302–1466, 740-369-0717, *www.bharatiyahindutemple.org*

Hindu Temple of Dayton, 2615 Lillian Lane, Fairborn, Ohio 45324, 937-429-4455.

Hindu Temple of Greater Cincinnati, 4920 Klatte Road, Cincinnati, Ohio 45244, 513-528-3714, *www.cintitemple.org*

Hindu Temple of Toledo, 4336 King Road, Sylvania, Ohio 43560, *www.hindutempleoftoledo.org*

Krishna House (International Society for Krishna Consciousness), 379 West 8th Avenue, Columbus, Ohio 54310, 614-421-1661.

Shiva Vishnu Temple, 7733 Ridge Road, Parma, Ohio 44129, 440-888-9433, *www.shivavishnutemple.org*

Shree Swaminarayan Mandir, 2195 Laurel Road, Brunswick, Ohio 44212, 330-220-4020, *www.swaminarayan.org*

Shree Swaminarayan Mandir, 2699 Farmers Drive, Columbus, Ohio 43235, 614-760-7672, *www.swaminarayan.org*

Spiritual Sadhna Society, P.O. Box 14830, Columbus, Ohio 43214, 614-975-6669.

Shri Lakshmi Narayan Temple, 6464 Sodomhutchings Road, Girard, Ohio 44420, 330-539-4077, *www.slntemple.org*

Hindu Traditions: *www.esamskriti.com*

RESOURCES

Bhaktivedanta Swami Prabhupada, A. C. *Srimad Bhagavatam.* New York: The Bhaktivedanta Book Trust, 1978.

Eck, Diana L. *A New Religious America: How a "Christian Country" Has Now Become the World's Most Religiously Diverse Nation.* San Francisco: Harper San Francisco, 2001.

Klostermaier, Klaus K. *A Survey of Hinduism.* Albany: State University of New York Press, 1989.

Organ, Troy Wilson. *The Hindu Quest for the Perfection of Man.* Athens: Ohio University Press, 1980.

Pandit, Bansi. *The Hindu Mind: Fundamentals of Hindu Religion and Philosophy for All Ages.* Glen Ellyn, Ill.: B & V Enterprises, 1998.

Panikkar, Raimundo. *The Vedic Experience: Mantramanjari.* Berkeley: University of California Press, 1977.

Smith, Huston. *The World's Religions: Our Great Wisdom Traditions.* San Francisco: Harper, 1991.

Zaehner, R. C. *The Bhagavad-Gita.* London: Oxford University Press, 1973.

BUDDHISM

Charles J. Dawes, C. Robert Pryor,
and Winifred C. Wirth

TRACING BUDDHISM IN OHIO

B UDDHISM, A RELIGION THAT BEGAN IN SOUTH ASIA MORE THAN
twenty-five hundred years ago and grew to dominate much of Asia,
was largely absent from Ohio until the 1940s. Buddhism has always been
a religion of nonviolence and tolerance, and many Asian Buddhist groups
came to Ohio in the twentieth century seeking refuge from war and persecution. A parallel development has been an increase in Buddhist influences in popular American culture, as well as in the serious study and
practice of Buddhism by non-Asian Ohioans. Together, these factors resulted in the presence of about fifty Buddhist groups in Ohio by the beginning of the twenty-first century.

The first Buddhists to set foot on Ohio soil were probably Asian laborers, including the more than eight hundred Chinese and Japanese men
who passed through Ohio in the mid-nineteenth century while building
the transcontinental railroad. In the late nineteenth century, at a time
when traditional Buddhist texts such as the Dhammapada and the Lotus
Sutra were translated for the first time into English, the first recorded Buddhist public event in Ohio was the visit of Anagarika Dharmapala, a monk
from Ceylon (now Sri Lanka), to Dayton and Columbus in 1896. The visit,
sponsored by the Theosophical Society, followed his acclaimed appearance
at the Parliament of the World's Religions held in Chicago in 1893.

In the twentieth century, the first Buddhist communities in Ohio were
established by about three hundred Japanese Americans released from

May 1970 dedication of the Cleveland Buddhist Temple in Euclid, site of the historical marker for the oldest continuously meeting Buddhist organization in Ohio. (Courtesy of Cleveland Buddhist Temple)

United States government internment camps in 1943. The first Buddhist temple in Ohio, the Cleveland Buddhist Temple, opened in 1945 under the auspices of the Buddhist Churches of America, the oldest institutional form of Buddhism in the United States, for the practice of Jodo Shinshu, a school of Pure Land Buddhism in the Mahayana tradition (the northern branch of Buddhism). Because the original temple, a house in the Hough section of Cleveland, burned during the civil rights riots in the late 1960s, the Ohio Historical Society marker for "Oldest Continually Meeting Buddhist Group in Ohio" is currently maintained in Euclid, the site of the current facility, which was dedicated in 1970. Members in other cities travel to Cleveland for services. In 1965 a Shin minister, Reverend Yurii Kyogoku, started a smaller congregation, called Mahamaya Society, that met in homes in Columbus. It was renamed Columbus Buddhist Sangha in the late 1970s, when it came under the direction of the Cleveland Buddhist Temple.

Another group of Japanese Buddhists also came to Ohio under circumstances relating to war in Asia. A handful of Japanese wives of American servicemen began meeting for mutual support in 1960 in homes throughout the state, and with the encouragement of Soka Gakkai Inter-

national (SGI)–USA, began to study, practice, and teach the Mahayana Nichiren Buddhist values of inclusion, individual cultivation, nonviolence, and world peace. This lay organization had grown to a notably diverse membership in Ohio of more than eleven hundred by the year 2000, with regional community centers in Cleveland and Columbus and more than two dozen in-home discussion groups around the state.

In the spirit of the Civil Rights Act of 1964, the Immigration Act of 1965 allowed increased immigration to the United States at a time when armed conflicts in Asia created a multitude of refugees, including more than ten thousand predominately Buddhist Vietnamese, Cambodians, and Laotians who resettled in Ohio in the 1970s and 1980s. Many non-refugee Asian groups have also immigrated to Ohio. The difficulty of their struggle to reestablish their communities and maintain their Buddhist religious traditions in a foreign culture echoes the story of European immigrants who came to America in preceding centuries, seeking a better life.

Within a few years of arrival, each community had established a temple despite extreme economic hardship. Temples served the crucial needs of community building and cultural preservation. They were especially critical for elderly refugees, who, having suffered so much from war, were now suffering culture shock. To this day, on the major Buddhist holidays as many as one thousand refugees travel from all over the state to their respective temples in Columbus. In Asia, special services are held on full and new moon days, but in Ohio, celebrations are also held on weekends to accommodate the American work schedule. In the 1990s, additional temples began to be established in other cities in Ohio; however, a scarcity of resident monks has been an obstacle. Another task of these temples in America has been to teach immigrants' American-born children not only Buddhist doctrine but also traditional languages and cultural identity.

An influx of about six thousand Vietnamese refugees began in 1975 and continued through 1993. A Vietnamese Mahayana temple, Linh Son Pagoda of Ohio, under the direction of the World Linh Son Pagoda Buddhist Congregation in France, began in Columbus in 1977 as a small group meeting in the home of Chuy Van Nguyen and later shared space with a group of American Buddhists. In 1996 the group was able to establish its own temple with a resident monk. Four other Mahayana temples in Ohio are associated with a national organization in California called the Vietnamese-American Unified Buddhist Congress in the United States of America, and the monk of the Dayton temple, Thich Tri Chon, is its vice-president. Chua Vien Quang was established in Cleveland in 1987, Tu Quang Temple in Dayton and Thuong Quang Temple in Columbus were established in the early 1990s, and Phat Bao Tu Temple was established in Cincinnati in 1999.

Beginning in 1980, some twenty-five hundred Laotians were resettled in Ohio. The Buddhamamaka Society, led by Khamsing Rajamountry, established a Theravadin (the older, Southeast Asian branch of Buddhism) temple in Columbus called Watlao Buddhamamakaran in 1987, under the direction of a national organization, Buddhist Monks of America. A second Laotian temple was established in Akron in the late 1990s called Wat Sirivathanaram. In Ohio, Buddhists from Burma and Thailand also attend these temples.

In the early 1980s some fifty-five hundred Cambodians were resettled in Ohio, of whom about two thousand remained in 2002. The Cambodian Buddhist Society, led by Yan Ke, established a Theravadin temple in Columbus in 1983 that served the entire state. In 1995, however, a controversy disrupted the Cambodian community, precipitating the establishment of a new temple, Wat Khmer Puthipreak, on fifty-eight acres in

Plain City. Subsequently, Cambodians in Cleveland and Cincinnati have, to borrow Thoreau's phrase, concluded to build their own temples.

Other immigrant (nonrefugee) Buddhist groups in Ohio include a community of more than five hundred Chinese people who left Hong Kong in 1991 and established a temple called Sam Tak in Cleveland in 1994, led by Master Hilton Tam. In Columbus, Master Judy Maa established the Taiwan-based Ching Ter Maitreya Buddha Temple in 1990, which moved into a newly built facility in the year 2000 and attracts a diverse community of students and others from Malaysia, Taiwan, Indonesia, Hong Kong, People's Republic of China, and Vietnam. Both of these temples have doctrines that have syncretized Pure Land Buddhism with other elements, such as Taoism, and a belief in a creator god, Laomu. Master Sheri Liaw taught Chi-gong meditation at the Shangri-La Meditation Center in Columbus in the mid-1990s.

Even with the presence of these Asian groups, most Ohioans have had little direct contact with Buddhism. Yet during the last fifty years, the sustained interest in Buddhism on the part of artists and intellectuals has had a profound and highly visible impact on popular American culture. The widespread availability of books on Buddhism, starting with those by D. T. Suzuki, has been key in the American embrace of Buddhism. Writers like the "beat" poets, musicians like Tina Turner, Herbie Hancock, and the Beastie Boys, other celebrities like actor Richard Gere and L.A. Lakers coach Phil Jackson, television shows like *Kung Fu* and *Shogun,* movies like *Kundun* and *Seven Years in Tibet,* and popular Asian arts such as feng shui, bonsai, ikebana, and the myriad forms of martial arts, to name a few, have also introduced many to Buddhist principles.

Buddhist influence has taken many forms in Ohio, including Buddhist collections at the Cleveland Museum of Art, Dayton Art Institute, Toledo Museum of Art, Denison University, and Johnson-Humrickhouse Museum in Coshocton. The Huntington Photographic Archive of Buddhist and Related Art at the Ohio State University, Columbus, the work of John C. Huntington and Susan Huntington, is an electronic archive of more than three hundred thousand original slides and photographs documenting the art and architecture of Asia. In the 1960s, The Dawes Arboretum in Newark unveiled a premier example of a Japanese garden based on principles which historically were influenced by Zen Buddhism; in 1980 it honored the sixteenth Gyalwa Karmapa (head of the Kagyu lineage of Tibetan Buddhism) as one of its famous tree dedicators. Later in the 1980s Nichiren monks stopped to pray at the arboretum while on a march across America for world peace.

In a departure from tradition, many Asian monks have recently embraced the new role of international spokespersons for human rights and the environment. Groups of antinuclear Buddhist monks walked across Ohio for world peace in 1981, 1988, and 1992. The Dalai Lama, winner of the 1989 Nobel Peace Prize, spoke at the University of Findlay in 1991. Starting in 1994 Tibetan monks have presented liturgical dances and constructed liturgical sand "paintings" called *mandalas* to sellout crowds at the Cincinnati Art Museum and at schools, colleges, rock concerts, and festivals in Ohio, while promoting the Tibetan cause. They also conducted joint "earth-healing" ceremonies with Native Americans in Ohio in 1994 and 2002.

Another development in recent decades has been an increase in the number of courses in Buddhist studies and Asian religions offered at many of Ohio's institutions of higher learning. An interesting example is the Antioch College Buddhist Studies Program started in 1979. In this program, students travel to the village of Bodh Gaya in northern India, where they spend the fall semester studying a variety of Buddhist traditions and living in a Burmese monastery near the site of the Buddha's enlightenment. Buddhist groups can also be found at some Ohio colleges, serving the needs of international students. For instance, in the 1990s Han-Ma-Um Seon Center served Korean students at the Ohio State University, and the Buddhist Association of Wisdom and Compassion served Chinese-speaking students at Case Western Reserve University; both groups became inactive as students returned overseas. In Columbus, the Buddhist Bodhi Association of Columbus (led by Katherine Lu and Jenny Lo-Shu) and a chapter of the international Buddhist humanitarian aid society Tzu Chi (led locally by Su-eng Choong) attract international students at the Ohio State University as well as members of the nonstudent community.

This burgeoning presence of Buddhist influences laid the foundation for Buddhism to attract practitioners in Ohio. In the journey from East to West, Buddhism has come to a major crossroads. Buddhist organizations in America, although associated with traditional lineages, have taken new forms accessible to lay people and are mostly led by lay people. A program of teachings, workshops, and retreats of various lengths allows lay people to work on personal spiritual transformation in everyday life rather than in a monastic setting. An indication of this change is that most facilities are called "centers" rather than "temples." Also, these centers do not serve the same social and cultural functions as Asian temples, as American converts to Buddhism have continued to celebrate "American" holidays with their families rather than the major Buddhist holidays that draw Asian communities together.

In Ohio, dozens of such small Buddhist centers have developed over the past thirty-five years. Often starting as small groups meeting simply for meditation in private homes, they tend to move to public spaces in churches or universities as they grow. Only a few have progressed to owning their own space. Many members do not think of themselves as exclusively Buddhist; however, as individuals begin to attend teachings or residential retreats at major meditation centers, they tend to become more committed to an affiliation with a particular tradition, lineage, and teacher, in the traditional Buddhist way. Most of the Buddhist centers in Ohio are affiliated with a practice lineage, either Vipassana, from southeast Asia; Zen, from east Asia; or Vajrayana, from Tibet, and some centers support practice in more than one lineage, an American invention.

The various centers in Ohio that focus on the Vipassana meditation of the Theravadin tradition are primarily affiliated with the Insight Meditation Society of Barre, Massachusetts, Spirit Rock Center in California, and Bhavana Society in West Virginia. Examples include: Tri-State Dharma, which hosts retreats in Kentucky, Ohio, and Indiana (at Grailville in Loveland 1990–98, then in Cincinnati since 1998), Athens Center for Mindfulness Practice (since 1990), Bowling Green Meditation Group, Insight Meditation of Cleveland, Mindfulness Meditation of Columbus (all three since 1992), and Buddhist Cincinnati (since 1999). A founding member of Mindfulness Meditation of Columbus, Ed Sweeney, developed stress-reduction and anger-management exercises based on Vipassana techniques for inclusion in the nationally distributed handbook of the Alternatives to Violence Project in 1997. These have been used for conflict resolution workshops at prisons and residential alcohol rehabilitation programs in Ohio. Dr. S. N. Goenka, an internationally renowned teacher of Vipassana meditation from India, visited Columbus in 1984. His student, Dr. Sneh

Jindal of Columbus, has taught meditation to more than thirty-five hundred inmates at Chillicothe Correctional Institute (1975–86) and at Vipassana meditation centers on three continents (1986–present).

Other Buddhist centers in Ohio are affiliated with Zen traditions. An example that illustrates the changing demographics of Buddhism in Ohio is the later history of the Cleveland Buddhist Temple. By 1977, the congregation had shrunk from about 180 families to twenty-five families, as members returned to the West Coast. This trend reversed, however, with the advent of a minister, Koshin Ogui (a trustee of the Parliament of the World's Religions and an eighteenth-generation Buddhist priest), who has ordination in both the Jodo Shinshu and Zen traditions. He instituted a subgroup of the Cleveland Buddhist Temple in 1978 called the Zen Shin Sangha, which has attracted a diverse group of people who practice meditation and attend teachings and services in English. One of his western students, Mike Shu Ho Bonasso, was ordained as a Buddhist priest by Reverend Ogui and was later fully ordained as a Ch'an monk. Shih Ying-Fa is dharma heir of Shih Shen-Lung. Shih Ying-Fa founded the Zen Society of Cleveland in 1992, and directs his order of monks, the Nien-Fo Ch'an order, as well as CloudWater Zendo, with affiliate groups in Wooster, Canton, Pittsburgh, and at the North Central Correctional Institute in Marion, where some inmates have taken vows.

Another westerner who has a transmission from an Asian Zen master is Robert Genthner, or Dae Gak, dharma heir of Seung Sahn of the Korean Chogye order. He established the Cincinnati Zen Center in 1994. Tim McCarthy, student of Kobun Chino Otogawa Roshi in the Japanese Soto Zen school, founded the Kent Zendo in 1984. The Cleveland Zazen Group, started in the late 1960s by students of Roshi Philip Kapleau, is now studying with his dharma heir, Bodhin Kjolhede of the Rochester Zen Center in New York. The Cleveland Zen Sangha and Mansfield Zen Sangha study with a student of Suzuki Roshi, Diane Martin of the Udumbara Zen Center in Evanston, Illinois. Members of the Columbus Zen Corner study with Daniel Terrango of the Diamond Sangha, California. Other groups following Zen traditions are the Milford Sitting Group and the Ohio Sitting Group in Macedonia. The Cleveland Heights Sangha, Cincinnati Sangha, and Toledo Sangha are associated with the Vietnamese Zen master and peace activist Thich Nhat Hanh.

A third set of Buddhist centers in Ohio is affiliated with Tibetan Vaj-

The November 1990 dedication of the Karma Thegsum Choling in Columbus. The center has an Asian teacher with an American congregation and a Tibetan Buddhist shrine in a former church building. (Courtesy of Karma Thegsum Choling Columbus)

rayana lineages. In another indication of the changing face of Buddhism, Tibetan refugees have established not only temples and monasteries to serve their own needs but a worldwide network of Buddhist centers to teach the dharma to lay people of many nationalities. In turn, these centers serve to support the Tibetan community in exile. An early example is Karma Thegsum Choling Columbus (KTC), a Tibetan Buddhist meditation center established in 1977 under the aegis of Karma Triyana Dharmachakra, a Karma Kagyu monastery in Woodstock, New York. In 1990 members purchased a church building near downtown, where they have been the most visible American Buddhist group in central Ohio. A founding member, Kathy Wesley, has the distinction of being one of the first women in America to complete the traditional three-year retreat of Tibetan Buddhism. She is now the resident *lama*, or teacher, of KTC Columbus.

Shambhala is a spiritual program inspired by Tibetan Buddhism with groups in Akron, Cleveland, Columbus, and Cincinnati. Developed especially for westerners in the 1960s and 1970s by Chogyam Trungpa, it combines aspects of Tibetan Vajrayana, Japanese Zen, and the Shambhala warrior tradition, with a unique focus on contemplative arts such as archery, horsemanship, calligraphy, and ikebana.

After 1990, increasing numbers of Tibetan Buddhist groups have appeared in Ohio, including the Jewel Heart Cleveland Chapter (Gelugpa), Palyul Changchub Dargyeling (Nyingma) in Chagrin Falls, Gar Drolma Choling (Drikong Kagyu) in Dayton, and Pema Tsal (Nyingma) in Yellow Springs.

Finally, several dharma centers in Ohio support the study and practice of more than one of the major Buddhist lineages. These include groups like the Buddhist Bodhi Association of Columbus, the Unitarian Universalist Buddhists of Columbus, the Dharma Study Group of Granville, and the Mila Retreat Center of Frankfort. At the Buddhist Dharma Center in Cincinnati, members have gathered together Vipassana, Zen, or meditative inquiry practice since the mid-1980s. Another example is the Yellow Springs Dharma Center, founded in 1993. Members meet in separate groups to follow the distinct practices of three major lineages (Vipassana, Zen, and Tibetan), but there are also common periods for silent meditation, a weekly family hour, discussion groups, and social events for the entire community. Each year in June the center hosts a seven-day residential meditation retreat that is led by an outstanding teacher from one of the lineages followed at the center.

It is an auspicious time in world history, indeed, when many traditions of Buddhism are present in Ohio, making possible dialogue among them, as well as with other religions. The Toledo Sangha welcomes meditators of all faiths, and the Buddhist Council of Ohio (Columbus) and the Northeast Ohio Buddhist Council (Cleveland), as well as Buddhist Cincinnati, made efforts in the 1990s to draw together different ethnic groups and denominations of Buddhism for teachings, practice, and celebration.

For Asian immigrants, the challenge of maintaining and transmitting traditional culture in a foreign setting has given a new significance and purpose to Buddhist institutions. For many of the refugees, the journey from East to West has also been an experience of interfaith solidarity, as some were sponsored for immigration by Christians. In turn, leaders in the Buddhist community have given back in the decades that followed to wave after wave of refugees from Somalia, Bosnia, Kurdistan, and Sudan, through their continued work with refugee service organizations in Ohio. For the western converts to Buddhism, each individual is a meeting ground of two or more different faiths and cultures. Despite the assault on Buddhism in Asia in the mid-twentieth century, Buddhism is experiencing a revival as the vitality of new forms instituted by westerners breathes new life into these ancient traditions and into the cultural life of Ohio in the twenty-first century.

BASIC BUDDHIST PHILOSOPHY AND PRACTICE

Buddhism is based on the teachings of Siddhartha Gautama, who was born in what is now Nepal in 563 B.C.E., twenty-five hundred years ago. He was the son of a king and led a protected, privileged life. He was well educated and accomplished and had a wife and an infant son. At age twenty-nine, however, when confronted with the suffering of the common people of his day, he was motivated by compassion to leave the palace to seek a way for humans to overcome suffering. At age thirty-five, after six years as a wandering ascetic, he had a transforming experience called "enlightenment," uncovering a state of mind beyond suffering while meditating under a tree at what is now Bodh Gaya. Thereafter he was known as Shakyamuni Buddha ("sage of the Shakya clan, the Awakened One"). For the next forty-five years, until his death at age eighty, he traveled and taught the dharma, a method that others can apply to achieve the same liberation from suffering. He founded one of the world's first monastic orders (the *sangha,* or community of practitioners), open to both men and women regardless of social position or hereditary caste, and taught a path that lay people, too, from princes to paupers, can follow to purify body, speech, and mind, a path that leads to enlightenment.

The essence of the Buddha's enlightenment experience is described in his first teaching, known as the Four Noble Truths: the truth of suffering, the truth of the cause of suffering, the truth of cessation of suffering, and the truth of the path to the cessation of suffering. When the Buddha pointed out the truth of suffering, he simply called attention to the unsatisfactoriness of life—birth, old age, sickness, and death. All things are impermanent. We cannot get what we want; we get what we do not want; we lose what we have. The Four Noble Truths, however, teach that our suffering is caused not by the ups and downs of life but by our response to them. We crave pleasure, hate pain, and in general are lost in denial (the Three Poisons) as we labor under the delusion that we are independent and unchanging. Our obsessive concern for our own happiness does not bring happiness because we are at the mercy of ever-changing circumstances and our own unconscious patterns of thoughts and actions (our *karma*) in an endless round of suffering called *samsara*.

Thus, the Second Noble Truth attributes the cause of suffering to attachment, and the Third Noble Truth is the good news that there is an option, a method that individuals can follow to experience life differently. The Fourth Noble Truth delineates that method, the Noble Eightfold Path, a path that leads to the experience of nirvana, the cessation of suffering, and has three aspects: 1) discipline or morality, consisting of right speech, right conduct, and right livelihood; 2) meditation, consisting of right effort, right mindfulness, and right concentration, and 3) wisdom, consisting of right view and right resolve.

The Four Noble Truths and the Noble Eightfold Path illustrate that Buddhism is a religion based on a science of the mind. Like other religions, Buddhism recognizes morality as the foundation of human happiness, but since our past behavior and experiences create our mental state and inclination to act in the present, the Buddha emphasized meditation practice as key to unconditioning and disciplining the mind so that conscious, positive choices about behavior can be made and implemented. Once the mind and behavior are purified, humans will spontaneously experience their inherent wisdom and compassion, or the true, sacred nature of all beings. Right view and right resolve express a commitment to this higher religious goal, not just for pleasure but also for enlightenment, and not just for self but also for others. This teaching continues to be fresh and relevant after twenty-five hundred years.

Over the centuries, many different types of Buddhism have evolved, many of which incorporated outer forms and symbols of other traditions while remaining faithful to the core message of liberation from samsara and the realization of nirvana for self and others. The Theravadin (Teachings of the elders) tradition is predominant in Southeast Asian countries such as Thailand, Burma, Sri Lanka, Cambodia, and

Laos. In Theravada, the emphasis is on individual effort to diligently practice the Buddha's teaching in order to achieve liberation as the Buddha did—by renouncing samsara and attaining nirvana.

The Mahayana (Great vehicle) tradition is practiced in China, Tibet, Nepal, Bhutan, Mongolia, Korea, Taiwan, Vietnam, and Japan. Among the most important Mahayana schools are Ch'an/Zen, Pure Land, Nichiren, and Vajrayana, also called Tantric, which is found primarily in Tibet, Mongolia, Nepal, and Bhutan. In Mahayana, the inherent equal purity of all beings (called Buddha Nature) and compassion (concern for liberation of all beings from suffering) are emphasized. In this tradition, enlightenment is realizing that the true, underlying nature of samsara is nirvana. Some Mahayana schools emphasize faith in enlightened beings embodying perfect wisdom and compassion who can aid beings seeking enlightenment.

Buddhists have many practices to train the body, speech, and mind in morality, meditation, wisdom, and compassion. These practices vary from the plainest of the plain, such as sitting and meditating on emptiness, to the most elaborate and colorful, such as Tibetan monks' liturgical dances. Some practices in various schools of Buddhism include: offering incense, candles, flowers, water, and food at a temple or home shrine; daily food offerings for the needs of monks and nuns; reciting the Buddha's teachings and the Five Precepts (vow of morality) daily; not eating meat on full and new moon days; releasing animals slated to die (such as earthworms); chanting short prayers (*mantras*) in Sanskrit using *malas* (prayer beads with 108 beads); meditation practice of concentrating on the breath; meditation practice of visualizing love flowing to friend and foe alike; circumambulating *stupas* (sacred sites); spinning prayer wheels; hanging strings of colorful prayer flags; painting or carving prayers on rocks; and practicing patience, generosity, and nonviolence every day.

Nature of God

Buddhism does not posit a definite beginning to the universe, nor that a deity created it. Rather, the Buddhist cosmology describes "six realms of existence" present since "beginningless time." These include humans, animals, and spirit beings such as ghosts, gods, and hell-beings, the latter three seen both as existing in fact and as metaphors for troubled human psychological states. The Buddha therefore emphasized practice leading to enlightenment rather than beliefs about God. The Buddha himself was neither a god nor a prophet. After his enlightenment, the Buddha was so transformed that people asked him if he were a god, but throughout his years of teaching he repeatedly emphasized that he was a human being like everyone else and that others could achieve what he had achieved through diligent application of his methods. The qualities that other religions might ascribe to God, that is, perfection, infinite wisdom, and compassion, are described in Buddhism as the true nature of every being, and therefore possible for each person to experience, not as a separate being but as the state of nirvana. When Buddhists offer incense or bow to a statue of the Buddha, they are not worshiping him but simply acknowledging the inspiration they get from his example.

Purpose of Life

The Dalai Lama of Tibet has said that the purpose of life is happiness (*An Open Heart: Practicing Compassion in Everyday Life,* ed. Nicholas Vreeland [Boston: Little, Brown, 2001]). All beings want happiness, but Buddhists speak of the "precious human birth," because we have the unique opportunity to seek happiness through spiritual development. In Buddhism, the true source of happiness is direct experience of awakened mind, beyond the pain and suffering of normal conditioned existence. Therefore the essential task of a human being is to seek to attain enlightenment, or the uncovering of the mind's inherent qualities of wisdom and compassion. Note that after attaining enlightenment himself, the Buddha decided that he had to go forth and rescue others from their suffering by teaching what he had learned. In this way, even the suffering of the world described in the First Noble Truth becomes instead a source of joy inasmuch as we can use our precious human birth not only to liberate ourselves and experience the happiness we want but also to help others to do the same. That is why the Dalai Lama also says that his religion is kindness (*The Dalai Lama, A Policy of Kindness: An Anthology of Writings by and about the Dalai Lama,* comp. and ed. Sidney Piburn [Ithaca, N.Y.: Snow Lion Publications, 1990]).

Life after Death

Buddhists believe in the law of karma (cause and effect) and a series of lifetimes through which all beings transmigrate. Our birth in the next life depends on the karma that we create in the present life through our thoughts, words, and actions. Depending on the force of this accumulated positive or negative karma, one may be reborn as a human, animal, spirit, or divine being. In the next life one may find oneself in a heaven or a hell, but not permanently. Buddhists believe that after some time even a being in a hell or a heaven passes from that realm and again transmigrates to a new existence. This process of rebirth is endless unless one is liberated through the experience of enlightenment, as was the Buddha.

View of Other Faiths

In his Nobel Peace Prize acceptance speech in 1989, the Dalai Lama said, "I believe all religions pursue the same goals, that of cultivating human goodness and bringing happiness to all human beings. Though the means might appear different, the ends are the same" (the Dalai Lama et al., *Ocean of Wisdom: Guidelines for Living* [Santa Fe: Clear Light Publishers, 1989], xi). In the Zen image of the finger pointing to the moon, religions are guides pointing the way to spiritual experience, not the spiritual experience itself, which is owned by no one and available to all. For this reason, the Buddha emphasized cultivation leading to experience, rather than belief, and Buddhists respect the beliefs and practices of any religion if they lead to an increase in wisdom and compassion in those who follow them.

Equality, Justice, and Peace

Equality is a fundamental Buddhist value. Buddha instituted equality in his teachings and the sangha. He left his caste, and accepted people of all castes and genders, even repentant murderers, as practitioners, as the expression of his belief in the inherent equality of all beings, including animals. His last words to his followers reiterate this respect of the individual: "Be lamps unto yourselves. Work out your own salvation with diligence" (Maha Parinibbana Sutta 2.26).

In Buddhism, justice is a natural process of the law of karma, as we experience the effects of our actions. "Speak or act with an impure mind, and trouble will follow you. Speak or act with a pure mind, and happiness will follow you" (Dhammapada 1.2 and 1.3). Real justice, however, is not punishment for some and reward for others, but enlightenment for all, because rehabilitation is always possible. Indeed, since all things are interdependent, real compassion is equal concern for perpetrator and victim, stranger and relative, foe and friend.

Likewise, cultivation of inner peace and a boundless mind of compassion is the first and best way to help create peace in the world. Peace is not an end, but rather a means, that is, a way of living. The Buddha advocated peaceful resolution of disputes, as illustrated in this beloved teaching from the Dhammapada: "Hatred never ceases with hatred, but by love alone is healed. This is the ancient and eternal law" (1.5).

VISITOR INFORMATION

It is not a Buddhist value to proselytize, so non-Buddhists are free to study Buddhist philosophy and meditation without converting. Many events at Buddhist temples and centers are open to the public. Visitors are welcome at New Year's celebrations (occurring at various times in January and February). Throughout the year, temples and centers often offer orientation sessions or free beginning classes for visitors. Services, meditation sessions, or teachings may be held in the evening or on weekends. Periodically, special workshops or lectures by a visiting teacher that are open to the public may be advertised. Private instruction and materials for students of comparative religion are sometimes available. Some Asian temples have instruction and materials available in English.

Most, but not all, Buddhist organizations follow the Asian customs of removing shoes before entering the shrine room and sitting on the floor on cushions; however, chairs are usually available if the latter presents a difficulty. Buddhists typically bow to the shrine or teacher when entering the room, but that is not expected of visitors.

CURRENT DEMOGRAPHICS

Accurate figures are not available on the number of Buddhists in Ohio. Informally, in the process of interviewing the leaders of the groups mentioned in this chapter, fewer than twenty thousand people are estimated to be actively associated with Ohio's Buddhist organizations at the start of the twenty-first century. Most are located in the major cities of Cleveland, Columbus, and Cincinnati, or near universities. The number of persons who self-identify as Buddhist may be much higher, however, as many Ohioans study the dharma on their own and the latest census figures show that more than eighty thousand Ohio residents are originally from predominately Buddhist countries.

CONTACT INFORMATION

Each Buddhist center or temple is administered independently. The Buddhist Council of Ohio, formed in 1992, serves as a contact organization: *www.buddhistcouncilofohio.org*. See also DharmaNet International (*www. dharmanet.org*), which has links to many Buddhist sites.

RESOURCES

Bercholz, Samuel, and Sherab Chödzin Kohn, eds. *Entering the Stream: An Introduction to the Buddha and His Teachings*. Boston: Shambhala, 1993.

Goldstein, Joseph. *The Experience of Insight: A Simple and Direct Guide to Buddhist Meditation*. Boston: Shambhala, 1987.

Khenpo Karthar Rinpoche. *Dharma Paths*. Ithaca, N.Y.: Snow Lion Publications, 1992.

Rahula, Walpola. *What the Buddha Taught*. New York: Grove Press, 1987.

Seager, Richard. *Buddhism in America*. New York: Columbia University Press, 1999.

Shambhala Sun (bimonthly periodical). 1345 Spruce Street, Boulder, Colorado 80302.

Suzuki, Shunryu. *Zen Mind, Beginner's Mind*. New York: Weatherhill, 1970.

Tricycle: The Buddhist Review (quarterly periodical). P.O. Box 3000, Denville, New Jersey 07834.

Van De Weyer, Robert, ed. *366 Readings from Buddhism: Global Spirit Library*. Cleveland: The Pilgrim Press, 2000. All selections from the Dhammapada and Sutta are from this edition.

ACKNOWLEDGMENTS

The authors wish to extend their thanks to each person who contributed research, suggestions, prayers, and effort, including Amanda Bilecki, Pam Free, Donna Hamilton, Donald Hardy, Derek Heyman, Sarah Levitt, Joseph Marshall, Aimee Maruyama, Sue Roy, Shary Scott Ratliff, Carol Tyler, Diana Wanicek, and many others. Our sincere apologies for errors and omissions. May all beings benefit.

THE SIKH FAITH

Ranbir Singh

THE SIKH RELIGIOUS PRESENCE IN OHIO IS A RECENT ONE. UNTIL about 1960 there were few Sikhs in the state. Now (2003) they number a few thousand and have five *gurdwaras* (Sikh places for congregational worship). A large majority of Ohio Sikhs are immigrants from Punjab, one of the states in India. Sikh immigrants have also come from other states in India as well as from other countries. With the passage of time, as Sikh families have grown, the younger generation of American-born Sikhs has become a strong, active, and vocal component of the Sikh community. A number of persons of Christian and Jewish background have also converted to the Sikh faith.

In this chapter we discuss the religious experience of Sikhs as they have settled in Ohio. In order to place these experiences in context, it is necessary to study some of their religious beliefs and practices and to briefly look at the history of immigration to the United States.

HISTORY

The Founder and His Successors

The Sikh faith originated in the fifteenth century in Punjab (lit., "the land of five rivers") in South Asia. At that time Punjab covered the present states of Punjab, Haryana, and Himachal Pradesh in India and the state of Punjab in Pakistan. The word *sikh* in Punjabi (the language of the people

Nearly a thousand Sikh families like this one have immigrated from South Asia to Ohio for better educational and economic opportunities and more religious freedom. The father is wearing a turban, the mother and daughter are wearing scarves, and the son is covering his hair with a tightly wrapped scarf, November 2002, Columbus. (Courtesy of Lifetouch Portrait Studios, Inc.).

of Punjab) means "disciple." Sikhs are disciples of Nanak (1469–1539), whom they refer to as Guru Nanak Sahib. The word *sahib* (lit., "master") is added as a mark of respect. The word *guru* means "teacher." When applied by Sikhs to Guru Nanak Sahib and his successors, it represents the "perfect teacher" who is in complete union with God and is sent by God for the benefit of mankind to tell people about God's greatness and to unite them with God.

Before he passed away, Guru Nanak Sahib appointed a successor. In all there were ten gurus up to Guru Gobind Singh Sahib (1666–1708). The fifth guru, Guru Arjan Sahib (1563–1606), compiled his own compositions with the compositions of his predecessors and selections from the work of several Hindu and Muslim religious teachers. The collection was called Granth Sahib (*granth* means "book"). Later, hymns by the ninth guru, Guru Tegh Bahadar Sahib (1621–1675), were added. All the gurus attributed their writings to "Nanak." This was symbolic of the continuity of the divine message. Guru Gobind Singh Sahib declared that after him not a person but the Granth Sahib would be the guru for all time. Sikhs refer to it as Guru Granth Sahib and regard it as the living word of God brought to mankind by Guru Nanak Sahib. It consists mostly of songs in praise of God and guru and prayers seeking divine mercy and guidance. Guru's word is synonymous with the Guru and it is Guru Nanak Sahib's eternal spirit providing instruction from Guru Granth Sahib.

A Turbulent Period

The new religion flourished and its following grew in the sixteenth century. Construction of Harmandar Sahib (popularly known as the "Golden Temple") in the city of Amritsar was completed during Guru Arjan Sahib's time. Starting early in the seventeenth century, religious extremists were able to persuade the Mughal emperors of India to suppress the new and growing faith. Guru Arjan Sahib was tortured to death in 1606 and, after a period of relative calm, the ninth guru, Guru Tegh Bahadar Sahib was publicly executed in 1675 for his support of the Hindus' right to free worship. The tenth guru, Guru Gobind Singh Sahib, had to defend himself against attacks by local Hindu chiefs supported at times by imperial troops. After Guru Gobind Singh Sahib's passing, Banda Singh organized a bold revolt but was defeated and, along with several hundred companions, publicly executed. Orders were given to kill all followers of Guru Nanak Sahib wherever they were to be found. Thousands were rounded up and massacred. However, the hold of the imperial government over distant provinces gradually weakened, and by 1760 Sikhs had emerged as the paramount military power in the Punjab region. In 1799 Maharaja Ranjit Singh (*maharaja* means "great ruler") founded the kingdom of Punjab. His rule lasted forty years. After his death, the Sikh kingdom rapidly unraveled. The British took advantage of the situation and after two bloody wars, annexed Punjab to British India in 1848.

Sikhs were ruthlessly suppressed and thoroughly disarmed during the early days of British occupation. Sikh places of worship were taken under government control or handed over to non-Sikh appointees. Later, noting Sikh pride in their history of warfare, the British declared them a "martial race" and recruited them heavily to the Indian army.

Sikhs were in the forefront of India's struggle for freedom from British rule. From 1857 until India's freedom in 1947, nearly 80 percent of those executed or sentenced to life in prison or exile for opposing British rule came from this 2 percent of India's population.

In 1947, India was split into Pakistan, an Islamic state, and India, a Hindu-dominated country. During this partition, Sikhs were forced to migrate to India. India's reorganization of states on the basis of language resulted in Punjab being reduced in area but having a majority Sikh population. The Sikhs wanted a measure of state autonomy in order to preserve Sikh identity and Sikh interests in the largely Hindu India. The national political parties described this demand as antinational and equated it with political separatism and treason. In June 1984, the Indian army attacked the Darbar Sahib complex (which includes Harmandar Sahib). The Indian government claimed that this was done to "remove terrorists, criminals, and their weapons from sacred places of worship" (Government of India, White Paper on the Punjab Agitation, July 10, 1984, 26). According to Professor Joyce Pettigrew of the University of Belfast, "The army went into Darbar Sahib not to eliminate a political figure or a political movement but to suppress the culture of a people, to attack their heart, to strike a blow at their spirit and self-confidence" (*The Sikhs of the Punjab* [London: Zed Books, Ltd., 1995], 8). During the oppression that followed thousands of Sikhs were jailed without trial, tortured, and killed while in police custody. Countless others sought shelter in countries of the free world, including the United States. Many came to the state of Ohio.

Sikhs in the United States and Ohio

In colonial times, the British took many Sikhs from Punjab to other colonies under their control to serve as policemen, security guards, soldiers, and so forth. Some enterprising Sikhs came to western Canada and California about the end of the nineteenth century. The first Sikh institution, the Pacific Coast Khalsa Diwan ("free divine communion") Society was incorporated in May 1912 in California, and the first gurdwara in this country was established in Stockton in 1915.

A few Sikhs came to the United States for advanced studies after World War I. Among them was Dalip Singh Saund (Ph.D., University of California at Berkeley, 1924), who became a citizen of the United States and the first Asian American to be elected to the U.S. Congress (in 1956). He served three terms representing the twenty-ninth district in California before his death in 1964. Partap Singh Kairon obtained his master's from the University of Michigan in 1929, went back to Punjab, became involved in politics, and was chief minister of his state from 1956 to 1964.

In the 1950s, the Ohio State University joined a consortium set up to support the Punjab Agricultural University. Many scholars, the majority of them Sikhs, came to Ohio for graduate or postdoctoral study. Most of them returned to Punjab to become professors, administrators, and leaders in Punjab's development. A notable example is Bishan Singh Sandhu (also known as Bishan Singh Samundri), who received his Ph.D. in 1957 and went on to become president of Guru Nanak Dev University in Punjab. His wife, Jagjit Kaur Sandhu, received her Ph.D. at the Ohio State University in 1958. Sardara Singh Johal, another Ohio State scholar, served as president of the Punjab Agricultural University. Several others went on to serve as deans of colleges in the United States or in India.

Liberalization of immigration rules in the 1960s removed the quota system and allowed highly qualified persons from around the world to seek immigration to the United States. Many Sikhs took advantage of this opportunity. Most of these immigrants were doctors, engineers, nurses, university and college professors, and scientists. Narinder Singh Kapany of California, a pioneer in the field of fiber optics, is one of them.

Job security was a primary consideration for first-generation immigrants. They started with "safe" professions like medicine, nursing, engineering, computer sciences, and allied fields. With increasing awareness and acceptance of diversity in the American population, many have moved on to other fields. Because Sikhs emphasized education, their children, the first generation of U.S.-born Sikhs, have excelled in school. Many have followed their parents into "safe" professions. However, quite a few among the new generation of Sikhs are venturing into fields that require extensive interaction with the public, like law, business management, public health, journalism, art, and literature, among others.

Later, close relatives of the early immigrants came to the United States, and over the last forty years the number of Sikhs in the United States has grown dramatically. There are now about half a million Sikhs in the country.

Unlike the immigrants of the 1960s, not all of these later immigrants were highly educated. The less educated have sought careers in business and industry. There are now many Sikhs working in the transportation, construction, service, and food industries.

Most of the first-generation Sikh immigrants in Ohio settled in the major metropolitan areas of Cleveland, Columbus, Cincinnati, and Dayton. In the 1960s the few Sikh families in Ohio used to meet at each other's homes for prayer. As their numbers grew they set up the Guru Nanak Foundation of Greater Cleveland Area and the Sikh Religious Society of Central Ohio, incorporated in 1969 and 1978, respectively. The first gurdwara in Ohio was established on West 25th Street in Cleveland in 1975. In order to accommodate the increasing size of the congregation, the gurdwara was moved to its present site in Richfield in 1991. It has undergone several renovations and expansions. Upon recommendation by the Ohio Bicentennial Commission's Religious Experience Advisory Council, the Ohio Historical Society designated it a historical site. A historical marker was dedicated on April 27, 2003.

Ohio Sikhs have been involved in affairs affecting their community at national and international levels. In the late 1970s they were prominently involved in the formation of the Sikh Council of North America. Later, in 1984, they played leadership roles in the establishment of the World Sikh Organization and the Sikh Association of America. When the World Sikh Council was constituted in 1997, the chairperson and the secretary for the American Region were both from Ohio.

Sikhs in the United States have been active in the interfaith movement for over two decades, working with numerous local and national interfaith organizations. Their role in the Parliament of the World's Religions held in Chicago in 1993 was quite significant. In Ohio, they actively participated in the "A World of Difference Campaign" organized by the Anti-Defamation League in 1992. Sikhs have supported the Interfaith Association of Central Ohio and have participated in seminars, vigils, concerts, and activities undertaken throughout Ohio jointly with other faiths in order to promote interfaith understanding, peace, and justice. This commitment was visible in the aftermath of the tragedy of September 11, 2001. The Ohio Sikh community stood shoulder to shoulder with others in that hour of grief and worked with local, state, and national leaders to promote understanding, minimize profiling, and reduce tensions.

The Guru Nanak Foundation of Greater Cleveland was the first gurdwara, or Sikh place of worship, established in Ohio (1975). In order to accommodate the increasing size of the congregation, the gurdwara was moved to its present site in Richfield in 1991. (Courtesy of Rajinder Singh)

Sikh Identity Issues

Unlike that of European immigrants to the United States, Asian immigrants' appearance makes them clearly visible as "different." Sikhs are even more visible because they do not cut their hair, and because Sikh men wear turbans. Like other "visible" minorities in many societies, Sikh immigrants have had to face discrimination, social ostracization, public harassment, and conflict with the law.

Many employers assumed that their "different" appearance disqualified them for jobs requiring significant interaction with the public or for jobs involving supervision of a large workforce. Most of the early immigrant Sikhs gave up the external symbols of their faith, believing that doing so was necessary for employment or for promotion, or simply for avoiding harassment and unwanted attention. Until 1980 there were hardly a dozen Sikh families in Ohio observing their traditional symbols. The situation has improved somewhat with the increase in the Sikh population and the greater public awareness of their presence. However, problems persist.

In the early 1970s a Sikh engineer in Cleveland trained several younger persons, and some of them were eventually promoted and became his supervisors. He was told that he could not be promoted to a managerial position because of his appearance. He finally left the company, set up his own construction business, and achieved considerable professional success and recognition.

In November 1978 a U.S. District Court judge in Columbus ordered a turbaned Sikh out of his court for not removing his "hat." It was only when this incident appeared in the news media that the judge called the victim to his office and offered a personal apology. More than two decades later, this problem persists. In November 2002, a Sikh student at the Ohio State University was refused appearance before a Columbus traffic court judge because the student was wearing a turban.

In March 1984, a Sikh aerospace engineer at the Wright-Patterson Air Force Base was refused renewal of his driver's license unless he agreed to have his photograph taken without the turban. A state representative had to persuade the Bureau of Motor Vehicles to make an exception.

In 1994 a Cincinnati veterinarian was arrested when a judge found him in contempt of court. While he was being searched, he was found to be wearing his *kirpaan* (a special type of sword; carrying one at all times is one of the Sikh religious requirements) and was cited for possession of a concealed weapon. He was sentenced to six month's probation and fined four hundred dollars. On appeal, the First Appellate District, Hamilton County, ruled that a Sikh's right to carry the kirpaan was protected by the Constitution and the federal Religious Freedom Restoration Act. Judge Mark Painter wrote: "I cannot understand the purpose for this prosecution which, if successful, would have the effect of banishing the members of one religious sect from the state of Ohio for its mandatory wear" (Court of Appeals of Ohio, Appeal no. C-950777, December 31, 1996). The harassment lasted two years and cost the victim thousands of dollars.

In September 1999 a Sikh was involved in a minor traffic accident in Mentor, Ohio. Because of his kirpaan the police charged him with carrying a concealed weapon. In this instance the Sikh received considerable public support. The Interfaith Association of Central Ohio wrote to the Mentor city prosecutor, to former Ohio governor Richard Celeste, and to the then U.S. Ambassador to India, who wrote to the mayor of Mentor. Eventually the charges were dropped.

After the tragic events of September 11, 2001, Sikhs were the targets of misdirected rage. People, out of ignorance, associated the Sikh turban and beard with Osama bin Laden and Al Qaeda. There were cases of verbal and physical abuse, arrests by law enforcement officers for possession of kirpaan, and even a murder in Mesa, Arizona. There was no physical violence in Ohio, but there were numerous cases of verbal abuse and obscene gestures.

Sikh children have had to face discrimination, discouragement, and harassment in school. Sikh families have had great difficulty in bringing up their children with their religious symbols. The situation is aggravated by the absence from school curricula of instruction about religious diversity in the state.

Despite the problems described above, there have been positive and encouraging developments over the last several years. Sikhs and other minority groups have received support from religious groups like the Interfaith Association of Central Ohio and the Columbus Metropolitan Area Church Council. The city of Columbus, the state of Ohio, the Ohio State University, the *Columbus Dispatch,* WBNS TV, and others have assisted in reaching out to the public and educating them after the September 2001 terrorist attacks. WKYC/NBC TV in Cleveland showed a video documenting the post–September 11, 2001, experience of two Sikh students in the Cleveland area. This award-winning documentary has been shown across the state to promote understanding and reduce prejudice and the tendency to stereotype. There is hope that with proper education there will be greater acceptance of religious diversity and that Sikhs, along with members of other faiths, will be perceived as an integral and enriching part of the multifaith and multicultural tapestry of the state.

BELIEFS

Sikh beliefs are documented in Guru Granth Sahib, the Sikh scripture and eternal guru. Sikhs believe in one God. God is the eternal reality, the creator and doer, all-pervading, omnipresent, omniscient, without fear or rancor, unchanging, unincarnate, and self-existent. God is the benevolent provider and the forgiving father. God creates the universe and sustains it. The entire creation is a manifestation of God. God pervades all and yet transcends all. The relationship between God and Creation is analogous to that between the ocean and the wave. Everything created must end and merge into God at God's will. The entire universe—inanimate creation as well as all life including plants, insects, birds, and animals—serves God's will.

Sikh religion teaches that of all forms of life, human life is supreme and is God's gift. It is an opportunity to understand God through love. This understanding liberates a person from the influences of lust, anger, greed, attachment, and pride, which lead only to suffering, pain, and separation from God. This understanding helps one lead a life marked by devotion, love, contentment, selfless sharing, and humility.

The individual soul is part of God and does not die. It is only the body that withers. At death, the individual soul, if it has used the opportunity of life in the human form to understand God, merges into God. If not, it continues in the cycle of birth and death in various life-forms. Death for a Sikh is either a passage from human form to union with formless God or a continuance of life in human or other form until God, in divine mercy, provides the opportunity to learn from the Guru and be liberated from the cycle of birth and death.

The role of the Guru is central. No one can understand God except through the Guru. The Sikh receives instruction from the Guru and thanks God and Guru for the enlightenment. Guru Granth Sahib assigns many divine attributes to the Guru. In essence, the Guru is the perfect being sent by God for the benefit of mankind and is not in the cycle of birth and death.

Tolerance and understanding of other religions is an integral part of the Sikh faith. The Gurus taught that all religions worship the same God and differ only in form. However, the Sikh religion rejects hypocrisy, idol worship, and empty rituals.

SIKH RELIGIOUS PRACTICE

The ideal lifestyle for a Sikh is that of "saint-soldier" exemplified by the gurus during their lifetimes. At the personal level, a Sikh is to constantly remember God, engage in honest labor, share the fruits of that labor, seek the company of others who love God, and rejoice in shared love of the divinity. As a member of the community, a Sikh participates in congregational prayer and service to humanity at large. A Sikh is committed to peace, but when all peaceful means have failed and tyranny over the weak and the oppressed continues, a Sikh is to be a soldier fighting for justice.

Any person may join the Sikh faith by going through the initiation ceremony introduced by Guru Gobind Singh Sahib in 1699. It is called the *amrit* (lit., "nectar of immortality") ceremony. Guru Granth Sahib defines God's name as amrit. Thus, initiation into the Sikh faith implies dedication to the worship of God. Those who have gone through the ceremony are often referred to as *khalsa,* meaning "Guru's own," or as *amritdhari.* Initiated Sikhs are instructed to regard all of humanity as a brotherhood of equals, regardless of race, color, creed, social class, caste, gender, or any other consideration. They adopt the last name Singh for men and Kaur for women. The word *singh* means lion; *kaur* means prince.

All Sikhs are required to wear the five *k*s. The most visible of these is the uncut hair (*kes* in Punjabi). The others are the *kachch* (a special type of shorts), *karaa* (an iron bangle, worn usually on the right wrist), *kangha* (a wooden comb), and kirpaan. The *kangha* serves to keep the hair clean and neat. The kirpaan, meaning "bringer of mercy," is symbolic of the Sikh pledge to keep weapons and to be ready to resist oppression but never to use weapons to attack anyone or to initiate a confrontation. The Sikh turban serves to cover and protect the kes. It is also a mark of honor. In the Gurus' times in South Asia, only kings and nobles typically wore the turban. By requiring his Sikhs to wear the turban, Guru Gobind Singh Sahib made the lowest of social classes feel equal to the most respected in society. The collection of all amritdharis is the Guru Panth. At the time of his passing away, Guru Gobind Singh Sahib vested his worldly authority in the Guru Panth. The Guru Panth alone has the authority to make decisions applicable to the entire faith.

There are no priests in the Sikh religion. Any Sikh who has been formally initiated (an amritdhari), regardless of gender, race, or social status, can officiate at any ceremony.

Sikh men tie their hair in a knot at the top of their head. Most women comb their hair to the back of the head and keep it tidy in a bun or braid. Many Sikhs wear a short version of the kirpaan slung in a sash called a *gaatraa.* In Punjab most Sikhs wear the sash over their shirts. However, in the United States, most wear it under the shirt to avoid undue attention. The turban, the kirpaan, and the karaa are never taken off in public. The photo on page 338 shows an Ohio Sikh family. The father is wearing a turban, the mother and daughter are wearing scarves, and the son is covering his hair with a tightly wrapped scarf.

Sikh women are equal to their male counterparts in every way and participate in all religious affairs as equals. The Sikh Rehit Maryada (Principles of Sikh living, a code by which all Sikhs are expected to live) requires Sikh men to regard women who are not members of their immediate family as mothers or sisters.

Sikh worship consists of reading, writing, reciting, singing, or listening to verses from Guru Granth Sahib. This can be done individually, as a family, or as a congregation. Sikh prayer consists of praising God, remembering that God provides for all beings, noting our human weaknesses and ignorance, and in humility seeking divine mercy and the Guru's guidance. A Sikh does not renounce the world to seek God. God is present within all. We have only to look inside our own hearts to find God.

Although pilgrimage and bathing in holy places is considered irrelevant to the practice of the faith, many Sikhs like to visit historical shrines and gurdwaras associated with the lives of the ten Gurus. The most important of these is Harmandar Sahib.

Sikhs observe the birthday of each guru, the day of his ascension to guruship, and the day of his passing. The birthdays of the first and tenth gurus and the anniversaries of the martyrdoms of the fifth and ninth gurus are the most prominent observances. All observances consist of congregational worship. In cities with sizable Sikh populations, there are also public processions and parades, for example, in New York City and in Los Angeles and Yuba City in California.

VISITING A GURDWARA

A gurdwara is the Sikh place for congregational worship, prayer, and learning. It offers a religious sanctuary where worshipers can gather. Some of the gurdwaras act also as community and educational centers. The gurdwara is open to all.

In congregational worship, Sikhs install Guru Granth Sahib beneath a canopy on an appropriate seat. A Sikh waves a *chowr* (a special type of whisk) over Guru Granth Sahib continuously. The service consists of a reverential reading from Guru Granth Sahib, followed by singing of hymns by professional musicians or by members of the congregation. Congregational worship must begin and end with *ardaas,* a formal prayer thanking God for mercy, seeking God's blessing and Guru's guidance, and rejoicing in belonging to the Guru Panth. After the ending ardaas, a hymn is again read from Guru Granth Sahib. Finally, *parshaad,* a special type of pudding, is distributed to the congregation.

Upon entering a gurdwara, the faithful remove their shoes and cover their heads before entering the presence of Guru Granth Sahib. They show respect by bowing before the Guru. Scarves are provided for non-Sikh visitors. Any person may visit a gurdwara. However, no visitor may have tobacco, alcohol, or drugs in his or her possession.

All gurdwaras also have a *langar* room where people sit on the floor in lines and share a meal. Any person, Sikh or not, regardless of gender, nationality, race, social rank, or faith, can partake of the meal. At smaller congregations, the langar is open after the prayer service. However, at larger gurdwaras, the langar is open at all times.

CURRENT DEMOGRAPHICS

Sikhs number about 25 million worldwide. There are about half a million Sikhs living in the United States of America. Nearly a thousand Sikh families live in Ohio. The Ohio Sikh community is concentrated within the metropolitan areas of Cleveland, Columbus, Cincinnati, and Dayton. There are five gurdwaras (Sikh places of worship) in Ohio.

CONTACT INFORMATION

As of early 2003, there were five gurdwaras in Ohio:

Guru Nanak Religious Society of Central Ohio, 2580 Dublin-Granville Road, Columbus, Ohio 43235, 614-761-0007.

Guru Nanak Society Gurdwara of Greater Cincinnati, 4394 Tylersville Road, Hamilton, Ohio 45011.

Guru Gobind Singh Sikh Society of Cleveland, 38 Tarbell Avenue, Bedford, Ohio 44146, 440-232-1702.

Guru Nanak Foundation of Greater Cleveland Area, 4220 Broadview Road, Richfield, Ohio 44286, 330-659-3748.

Sikh Society of Dayton, 1038 Forest Drive, Beavercreek, Ohio 45434, 937-427-1868.

Most of these *gurdwaras* are members of the World Sikh Council–America Region (*www.worldsikhcouncil.org*). Other Sikh organizations in the state include:

Sikh Educational and Religious Foundation (SERF), P.O. Box 1553, Dublin, Ohio 43017, 614-210-0591.

Sikh Youth Federation (SYF), 6863 Cloister Road, Toledo, Ohio 43617, 419-841-7178.

Websites:

Institute of Sikh Studies: *www.sikhstudies.org*

Sikh Educational and Religious Foundation: *www.serf.ws*

Sikhism website: *www.sikhs.org*

RESOURCES

Abstracts of Sikh Studies. Chandigarh, India: Institute of Sikh Studies.

Singh, I. J. *Sikhs and Sikhism: A View with a Bias.* Columbia, Mo.: South Asia Publications, 1995.

Singh, Kapur. *Sikhism: An Oecumenical Religion.* Chandigarh, India: Institute of Sikh Studies, 1993.

Singh, Khushwant. *A History of the Sikhs.* 2 vols. New York: Oxford University Press, 1999.

Singh, Ranbir, trans. *Principles of Sikh Living* . Dublin, Ohio: Sikh Educational and Religious Foundation, 1996.

Targets of Abuse—A Video Documentary. Produced by WKYC/NBC TV Cleveland, 2001.

THE BAHA'I FAITH

Cynthia Rickard

HISTORY

T HE BAHÁ'Í FAITH FIRST BECAME KNOWN IN OHIO BY WAY OF A
Chicago insurance salesman named Thornton Chase, who men-
tioned his new religion to two colleagues in Union Mutual Life Insurance
Company's Cincinnati office during a visit in 1898 or 1899.

Chase, one of the first four Americans to study the faith, enrolled in
1895. His hometown Bahá'í community of Chicago dispatched another
Bahá'í back to Cincinnati after Chase's visit there. That teacher offered a
class in January 1899, and five people enrolled in the faith, giving birth to
the first Bahá'í community in Ohio.

Cincinnati had been a population, economic, and antislavery strong-
hold in the Midwest before the Civil War, and it remained a center of
intellectual activity at the end of the nineteenth century. So it was not
surprising the Bahá'í faith first took hold in Ohio there.

Acceptance of the faith required then, and today, belief in Bahá'u'lláh
as God's messenger for this age and in his teachings that there is one God
who has educated mankind continuously through the ages, that humanity
in all its diversity is but one race, that men and women are equal in the
eyes of God, that science and religion are in harmony, and that every
human soul progresses toward God through life and after death.

The Cincinnati group's acceptance of those tenets and others made
it the eleventh Bahá'í community in North America. The others were
Chicago; Enterprise, Kansas; Kenosha, Wisconsin; New York City; Hudson

County, New Jersey; Philadelphia; Washington, D.C.; Baltimore; Princess Anne, Maryland; and London, Ontario. A Cleveland resident, Alice Davidson, actually embraced the faith earlier than did the Cincinnati residents —earlier than Chase even—in 1894. But she enrolled in Chicago, after visiting with Ibrahim Kheiralla, a Syrian physician who brought the faith to North America. And the Bahá'í group in Cleveland did not form until 1903, several years after Cincinnati's.

By 1909, Cleveland had its first Bahá'í wedding; it is the first ceremony on the continent known to have included Bahá'í scriptures. A year later, Cleveland began recording its observance of the Nineteen Day Feast, the monthly Bahá'í worship service. It was these two cities, Cincinnati and Cleveland, that had the privilege of a visit in 1912 by 'Abdu'l-Bahá, Bahá'u'lláh's eldest son and appointed successor. 'Abdu'l-Bahá is known to Bahá'ís as "the Master and the Center of the Covenant." During his eight-month North American tour, this gentle soul, whose name means "Servant of God," laid the cornerstone for the magnificent North American House of Worship on Lake Michigan in Wilmette, Illinois.

News accounts of his visit, like those marking the 1953 dedication of the completed House of Worship, infused the faith with seekers eager to learn more of its teachings about the unity of mankind, the common foundation of religions and the way to a world without war. In Cleveland, speaking to a large crowd at the Euclid Hotel, 'Abdu'l-Bahá stunned his listeners by advocating interracial marriage and pointed to the need for a spiritual civilization, a renewal of religion, and equality of the sexes. His visit spurred the Ohio Bahá'ís to great heights of study and teaching, while the forty-year effort to erect the Bahá'í temple galvanized the community, not only in the state, but on the North American continent and around the world. The names of more and more Ohio cities—Akron, Kent, Sandusky, Dayton, Toledo, Newark, Urbana, LaGrange, Fremont, Wellington, Xenia, Youngstown, Lithopolis, Galena, Gaysport, Wilberforce —began to appear in newspaper accounts and community records as sites of talks about the faith or community events.

Contributions for the House of Worship project poured in from Bahá'ís all over the world during the four decades of its construction, as the majestic structure of lacey concrete rose on Chicago's northern skyline. News of the building's progress was sent out to the community through the first North American periodical, *Bahá'í Bulletin,* in 1909,

'Abdu'l-Bahá, son of the founder of the Bahá'í faith, visited Cleveland in 1912. He is pictured here with several Persian Bahá'ís who traveled with him across the United States. (Courtesy of Houshang Ma'ani)

then a year later through its successor, *Bahá'í News*. That publication became bilingual, adding Farsi (Persian), Iran's native tongue, for its Iranian readers about five months later, and soon became known as *Star of the West*. The periodical, mailed to both North American and Persian Bahá'ís, served to further expand and strengthen the community and draw continents of believers to their common focus and goals.

The results in Ohio were sometimes startling:

- Dayton formed a Local Spiritual Assembly around 1930, the same time as Columbus. The next year the Dayton assembly sponsored an interracial banquet, rare for the time, "attended by about 60 prominent and professional people." The day after the banquet, the visiting Bahá'í speaker, Juliet Thompson, spoke to "the entire student body and faculty of Dayton's new Art Institute" (both, *Bahá'í News,* August 1931, edition 54, 2).

- In 1938 Dayton and several other Bahá'í communities were trying to stir interest in the development of Esperanto—an international language devised in 1887 in Poland by Dr. Ludwig Zamenhof—as a potential candidate for the universal language urged by Bahá'í teachings. Zamenhof's daughter, Lidia, a Polish Jew, became a Bahá'í in 1926 and spoke in several Ohio Bahá'í communities—including Lima, a center of Bahá'í teaching and growth—during the 1930s. She was later murdered during World War II in the gas chambers of Treblinka, a Nazi death camp in Poland.

- The Columbus community quickly began children's classes and radio commentary in the 1930s, started an archive in 1940, hosted the annual state convention seven times between 1946 and 1968, and was the site of an international Bahá'í youth convention in 1985. During World War II, the community sought additional ration coupons for gas and sugar to assist in their teaching work. And in 1955, it sent telegrams to the Shah of Iran, his minister of state, and President Dwight D. Eisenhower, asking for their assistance in ending the intense persecution of Bahá'ís in Iran at that time.

- East Cleveland formed an LSA in 1939, and by 1958 a column in the *Cleveland Press* referred to Bahá'í communities in Willowick, South Euclid, North Olmsted, and Euclid, as well as Cleveland.

By the 1950s, Bahá'í adults and youth around the state traveled to each other's towns and surrounding states for public meetings; to Bahá'í schools in Michigan and Maine; to state conventions in Mansfield, Cleveland, and Bowling Green; to national conventions in Chicago; and to the faith's first World Congress in London, England, in 1963, strengthening their bond through the teachings of Bahá'u'lláh.

In their home communities, there were card parties, family picnics, youth campouts, dances, and other social events that helped to knit together people of diverse races, religious and ethnic backgrounds, and economic strata who might otherwise not have been friends. It was their abiding faith that God has spoken anew to mankind, providing directions about how to move civilization forward, that kept—and keeps—Bahá'ís bonded and focused on doing the work directed through Bahá'í scripture.

For all their selfless efforts, the Ohio Bahá'ís suffered setbacks and tests of faith along with the rest of the Bahá'í community worldwide, at the deaths of 'Abdu'l-Bahá (1921), Dorothy Baker, an esteemed Bahá'í teacher and leader from Lima (1954), and Shoghi Effendi, 'Abdu'l-Bahá's

Some of the five thousand youth who attended the Bahá'í International Youth Conference in Columbus in 1985. (Courtesy of Houshang Ma'ani)

appointed successor, known as the Guardian of the Faith (1957). The Lima community was particularly tested during the 1930s, when local Christian ministers mounted a cruel campaign to defame Dorothy Baker, destroy her husband's business, and discredit the faith. But she eventually faced it with her usual grace by asking, and receiving, permission to explain the true nature of the faith to one of the congregations. That marked the beginning of a turnaround in community attitudes, but not before many —including non-Bahá'ís who worked at Frank Baker's Plezol Bakery— suffered.

Until nearly 1980, though, Bahá'ís all over the world suffered their trials in relative seclusion. Then, as knowledge of executions of Bahá'ís by the fanatical regime of the Ayatollah Ruhollah Khomeini seeped slowly out of Iran to the world, the faith was whisked from obscurity to the headlines of America's newspapers. Resolutions passed in Congress, in statehouses in Ohio and elsewhere, and in many city councils condemning the persecution were supported in Ohio by editorials in the *Vindicator* (Youngstown), the *Beacon Journal* (Akron), the *Tribune Chronicle* (Warren), and other papers. Soon, Iranian Bahá'í refugees began to populate

Ohio communities, and not long after, the American community's national newspaper, the *American Bahá'í*, began including pages in Farsi (Persian).

As a result of the publicity surrounding the persecutions, many more people heard the names "Bahá'í" and "Bahá'u'lláh," and references to the faith as a "sect" or "movement" or "cult" dwindled. Still, as late as 1991, when Loveland Bahá'í Hilda Stauss died, her obituary in the *Cincinnati Enquirer* called the eighty-nine-year-old publisher "an active member of the Bahá'í faith, an Islamic sect based on brotherhood and racial justice." The article subsequently mentioned that she had, at age ten, met 'Abdu'l-Bahá, whom the paper erroneously identified as the "grandson of the founder" of the faith (April 6, 1991).

Knowledge of the faith also spread after 1985, when the international governing body of the worldwide Bahá'í community issued a statement titled "The Promise of World Peace to the Peoples of the World." It opened by saying the peace so long sought and hoped for by the world is now within reach—not only possible, but inevitable—and went on to explain exactly how to achieve it. Bahá'í communities across the state, including Columbus, Cleveland, and Youngstown, responded by presenting the statement to public officials and hosting conferences and discussions on peace and its prerequisites.

The statement was re-emphasized after the September 11, 2001, terrorist attacks on New York City and Washington, D.C., when the National Spiritual Assembly issued a full-page response in the *New York Times,* focusing on the necessity of the unity of humankind in establishing peace in the world. Ohio Bahá'ís longtime recognition of that need had spurred their participation in community interfaith activities such as the Mahoning Valley's annual Multifaith Day and the Columbus-based Interfaith Association of Central Ohio.

Those activities and others, such as the satellite broadcast of the official opening of the exquisite terraced gardens leading to the Shrine of the Báb on the slopes of Mount Carmel (Haifa, Israel) in May 2001, also have enhanced public awareness of the faith, but some insensitivity still exists.

Bahá'ís all over the state engage in regular community devotions and study, stay united through regional newsletters, online message groups, and local and national websites, and participate in social and economic development projects, such as the following:

The Columbus Bahá'í Center on Sunbury Road was acquired in 1992 and is the first center in the state owned by Bahá'ís. Prior to 1992, Bahá'ís in central Ohio met in homes or rented facilities. (Courtesy of Dianne Small)

- A Youngstown area physician and his family lead an Ohio chapter of the Chicago-based Health for Humanity and provide basic health services, such as eye surgeries, to people in poverty-stricken countries, as well as speakers and programs to assist Ohio residents in developing and maintaining healthy lifestyles.

- A young Shaker Heights Bahá'í organized Safehaven, a multiracial and multireligious experience offering youth and young adults a place to stay "safe" on Friday nights while learning about each other's diverse beliefs. A movie is followed by discussion, cards, and/or a game of pool. The weekly program has attracted up to fifty people.

- Three young Bahá'ís started One Human Family Workshops, a multifaith project now headquartered in Columbus that uses the arts and other means to assist communities internationally in developing models of unity for their diverse populations.

- Two young Bahá'í artists, brothers who escaped from Iran years earlier, created a sculpture of two white birds of peace, some twelve feet in height, that became the centerpiece of the Peace Garden for Ameriflora 1992, an enormous international floral exposition in Columbus. The garden, which also included benches and writings on peace, continues to be maintained in Franklin Park near the city's downtown.

- Columbus also is home to Soul Miners, which offers children in an eastside neighborhood near the Columbus Bahá'í Center a monthly exploration of a historical person of African descent and the virtues that person exemplified. The children examine how they could practice those virtues and how it would help the world, their nation, their community, their family, or another individual. "We want the children to discover that they have the same virtues inside them that famous people do, and that they don't have to wait until they're grown to do great things," the founder told the *American Bahá'í* in November 2001.
- Central Ohio Bahá'ís have served on the board of the Interfaith Refugee Services of Central Ohio and the child neglect and abuse board.

These and other efforts to introduce others to this renewed approach to life remain primary to Bahá'ís everywhere and will go on throughout their lifetimes. Just ask Lillian Horn: In fall 2001, the devoted ninety-one-year-old retired teacher, who taught art lessons in 1971 to finance her pilgrimage to the Bahá'í World Centre in Haifa, Israel, was appointed to the executive committee for Crimson Ark Bahá'í School in Cleveland. Again, her mind raced with thoughts of lesson plans, classroom topics, and teaching techniques. This time, though, the stakes were higher. It was likely her last chance to impart God's latest message to his sons and daughters before they leave this planet. This was the lesson that lured her from bed each day.

"I cannot not teach the Faith," she declared to a gathering at her dining room table in Euclid, explaining her drive to share Bahá'u'lláh's message with the world. Gazing out her window, her dark eyes blazed, reflecting a salmon sun setting over Lake Erie. "I awake every day to a new challenge."

BELIEFS

- *God:* There is only one God, who has promised never to leave us without guidance. God educates us continuously through messengers sent to show us how to live and to enable us to know God through them. Through the ages these messengers have included Abraham, Krishna, Moses, Zoroaster, Buddha, Christ, Muhammad, the Báb, and most recently, Bahá'u'lláh. Each messenger reflects the same spirit of God, so their successive appearances can be described as returns.

- *Bahá'í faith:* The Bahá'í revelation is the latest of God's teachings sent to humanity. The teachings were delivered by Bahá'u'lláh, a Persian nobleman who gave up a life of luxury to spread the word of God. National and worldwide figures, as of February 2001, were about 144,000 and 5 million, respectively.

- *Bahá'u'lláh* (Arabic for "glory of God"): Born Mirza Husayn-'Alí Nuri on November 12, 1817, in Tehran, Iran, Bahá'u'lláh declared his station in 1863. He endured decades of torment and imprisonment to spread the teachings of God until he died on May 29, 1892. Through a long period of exile and forced travel, he and his family ended up in Palestine (now Israel), where the world center of his faith has become established among verdant gardens on Mount Carmel in the Holy Land. Throughout his life, he penned more than one hundred volumes of scripture. The two most important volumes, considered comparable to the Bible or Quran, are the Kitab-i-Aqdas (the book of laws) and the Kitab-i-Iqan (the book of certitude).

- *The Báb* (Arabic for "the gate"): The forerunner of Bahá'u'lláh, the Báb was also an independent messenger of God himself, who founded the Babi religion. The Báb, born October 20, 1819, declared his mission in 1844 in Shiraz, Iran, as the herald of "the advent of the Faith of Him Whom God will make manifest." The Báb escaped volleys of gunfire at his execution, though the cords that suspended him were destroyed by the bullets. The marksmen found him unharmed, completing his interrupted conversation with a follower. When he finished, he said to the gunmen: "Now you may proceed to fulfill your intention." Shaken by what had happened, the gunmen were unable to complete their task, and the Báb was shot to death by a another regiment on July 9, 1850, at the age of thirty.

- *'Abdu'l-Bahá:* Bahá'u'lláh's eldest son and appointed successor, to whom all Bahá'ís were to turn for interpretation of Bahá'u'lláh's writings. 'Abdu'l-Bahá was known to Bahá'ís as the perfect example of how to live Bahá'u'lláh's teachings. He shared the exile and banishment of his father, who called him the Master, the Most Great Branch, and the Mystery of God. After Bahá'u'lláh's passing, 'Abdu'l-Bahá chose his name, which means "Servant of Baha." He was born May 23, 1844, and died November 28, 1921.

- *Shoghi Effendi:* 'Abdu'l-Bahá's eldest grandson and successor, appointed in his will and testament as Guardian of the Faith. Shoghi Effendi was born March 1, 1897, and died November 5, 1957, without naming a successor. But he began the organizational system, known as the Administrative Order, which is intended, in time, to facilitate the creation of a world commonwealth of nations.

- *Purpose of life:* To know and love God, through His messengers and their characters, to develop one's soul for the next world, and to "carry forward an ever-advancing civilization" on earth. Bahá'u'lláh prohibited slavery, asceticism, and proselytizing; condemned cruelty to animals; and urged generosity and assistance to the poor.

- *Racial equality:* Humanity is one race and we must work toward eliminating prejudice. "Ye are the fruits of one tree, and the leaves of one branch," Bahá'u'lláh wrote. In 1991, the National Spiritual Assembly of the United States issued a statement on race unity, calling it "America's most challenging issue."

- *Equality of women and men:* Bahá'í scriptures say both genders were created in the image of God, so are equal in the sight of God. Attainment of this spiritual and moral standard is considered essential for the unification of the planet and the unfoldment of world order. Equality of the genders is also conducive to the elimination of warfare, the writings say, because women will not be willing to give their son's lives in battle after having reared them since infancy. Women are, however, given preference in education if a family has only enough money to educate either a son or a daughter. Bahá'u'lláh said women are the first educators of children, so must be educated themselves and explained: "The world of humanity is possessed of two wings, the male and the female. So long as these two wings are not equivalent in strength the bird will not fly. Until womankind reaches the same degree as man, until she enjoys the same arena of activity, extraordinary attainment for humanity will not be realized." ('Abdu'l-Bahá, *Promulgation of Universal Peace* [Wilmette, Ill.: Bahá'í Publishing Trust, 1982], 375).

- *Life after death:* All souls progress toward God after death, continuing their journey of spiritual development and understanding. Cremation is forbidden, as the body should be allowed to decompose as gradually and naturally as it was formed. "The world beyond is as different from this world as this world is different from that of the child while still in the womb of its mother," Bahá'u'lláh wrote. "There will he be informed of the secrets of truth, how much more will he recognize or discover persons with whom he has been associated . . . a love that one may have entertained for anyone will not be forgotten in the world of the Kingdom, nor wilt thou forget there the life that thou hadst in the material world" (Bahá'u'lláh, *Gleanings from the Writings of Bahá'u'lláh* [Wilmette, Ill.: Bahá'í Publishing Trust, 1983], 157).

- *Independent investigation of truth:* Each individual must seek and determine religious truth for him- or herself, using his or her own faculties of reason, conscience, and perception. Blind acceptance of scriptures, as understood by clerics, is what led to rejection of successive messengers of God in the past.

- *Harmony of science and religion:* Religion that does not correspond with scientific principles and reason is superstition; science without religion is materialism. If religion opposes science, then faith and, consequently, spiritual attainment are impossible.

- *Heaven and hell:* These are believed to be conditions of the soul, which can be experienced on earth and in the afterlife. Heaven, or nearness to God, can be attained by development of spiritual qualities and acceptance of His messengers and their teachings. Hell is experienced by turning away from God and becoming immersed in worldly interests and pursuits.

- *Giving:* Only Bahá'ís may contribute to the faith, to prevent outside influences from diluting its teachings. Only general appeals for funds are made; individuals are not solicited. Bahá'ís also contribute a portion of their wealth for promotion of the faith and upkeep of its properties and charitable works, as a means of drawing closer to God and purifying their material possessions. Donations from non-Bahá'ís are accepted only for charitable and socioeconomic development projects that extend beyond the Bahá'í community.

- *Worship, prayer:* Bahá'ís are obligated to pray and meditate every day and to fast, for a specified period, from the age of adulthood. Worship services, called the Nineteen Day Feast, occur once every nineteen days, on the first of each Bahá'í month, and consist of devotions followed by discussion of community business and the sharing of refreshments. There is no clergy, so Bahá'ís are responsible for educating themselves about their faith and its teachings. Consequently, universal education and independent investigation of the truth are primary tenets of the religion. The use of pulpits, kissing of hands, penance, and confession of sins to a human being are prohibited, and Bahá'u'lláh warned his followers to guard against fanaticism, noting that the purpose of religion is to establish unity among the people of the world, and it should not be made a cause of dissension.

- *Work:* Bahá'ís are told to engage in some occupation that will benefit themselves and others, even if they can afford not to. Work performed in the spirit of service is considered worship and draws the individual closer to God. Idleness and begging are condemned.

- *Family life:* Bahá'ís are encouraged to marry and are told to abstain from sex outside marriage and to educate their children. To promote family unity, Bahá'ís must have the permission of all living parents to marry, even if their marriage partner is not a Bahá'í. Divorce is discouraged, but is permissible if animosity develops and the couple is unable to reconcile during a full year in which they try to resolve their differences while living apart.

- *Politics:* Bahá'ís are prohibited from participating in partisan politics, but are told to obey a just government and may vote, as long as they vote on the merits of the individual and do not have to identify with one party or another. Bahá'u'lláh prophesied a world commonwealth, and cautioned against strident nationalism, saying, "It is not for him to pride himself who loveth his own country, but rather for him who loveth the whole world. The earth is but one country, and mankind its citizens" (*Gleanings,* 250).

- *War and peace:* Bahá'u'lláh urged nations to reduce their armaments to the level needed for self-defense and said if any nation rises against another, all nations must join together to defend that one from encroachment. Currently, Bahá'ís may serve in the military but must apply for noncombatant status. Bahá'u'lláh also proposed a universal auxiliary language and a common script to facilitate understanding and tranquility among all peoples. He said that if peace is to be achieved, the extremes of wealth and poverty must be eliminated and the unity of humankind must be firmly established. In 1985 the Bahá'í Universal House of Justice issued a statement titled "To the Peoples of the World," in which it addressed all the prerequisites to peace.

ATTENDING BAHA'I DEVOTIONAL SERVICES AND MEETINGS

Visitors are welcome to attend Bahá'í devotional services, holy day observances, children's classes, and informational and study group meetings, all of which are open to the public. Regular monthly worship services are open only to registered Bahá'ís, in order to ensure the free and open discussion of community issues during the administrative portion of the service.

CURRENT DEMOGRAPHICS

There were about 144,000 Bahá'ís in the United States as of February 2001. The number of Bahá'ís in Ohio was about nineteen hundred as of April 2001.

CONTACT INFORMATION

Bahá'í faith international website: *www.bahai.org*
Bahá'í National Center, 1233 Central Street, Evanston, Illinois 60201, 847-869-9039, *www.us.bahai.org*

RESOURCES

'Abdu'l-Bahá. *Paris Talks*. London: Bahá'í Publishing Trust, 1971.

———. *The Secret of Divine Civilization*. Wilmette, Ill.: Bahá'í Publishing Trust, 1980.

———. *Some Answered Questions*. Wilmette, Ill.: Bahá'í Publishing Trust, 1982.

Bahá'u'lláh. *The Hidden Words*. Trans. Shoghi Effendi. Wilmette, Ill.: Bahá'í Publishing Trust, 1980.

Freeman, Dorothy. *From Copper to Gold: The Life of Dorothy Baker*. Wilmette, Ill.: Bahá'í Publishing Trust, 1999.

Hofman, David. *The Renewal of Civilization*. Wilmette, Ill.: Bahá'í Publishing Trust, 1970.

Momen, Wendi, ed. *A Basic Bahá'í Dictionary*. Oxford: George Ronald Press, 1989.

Sears, William. *Thief in the Night*. London: George Ronald Press, 1980.

Smith, Peter. *A Concise Encyclopedia of the Baha'i Faith*. Oxford: Oneworld Publishers, 2000.

JAINISM

Tansukh Salgia and Bharati Salgia

HISTORY

THE HISTORY OF JAINISM IN THE UNITED STATES IS NOT DIFFICULT to trace. Jainism was introduced in the United States for the first time at the Parliament of the World's Religions, held in Chicago in September 1893. Virchand Raghav Gandhi of Bombay, India, an attorney and scholar of Jainism, traveled to Chicago and introduced Jainism to the West. Gandhi was the first Jain to visit Cleveland, Ohio, which he did on September 18, 1894, when he delivered a lecture on Jain science and philosophy at the Association Hall. His Cleveland lecture was profusely illustrated by means of a stereopticon and was warmly appreciated by the large number of persons in attendance. For two years following the parliament, Gandhi traveled to many cities east of Chicago and delivered speeches. During these speeches, he expounded on Jain philosophy about the universe and its uncreated nature and explained Jain principles and precepts. In America, Gandhi also established a society for the promotion of Jain religion and called it the Gandhi Philosophical Society.

Another Jain scholar, Barrister Champat Rai Jain, visited America to attend a World Fellowship of Faith conference in Chicago in August 1933. Furthermore, it is known that during the early years of Jainism in America, there were several individuals who were inclined toward the Jain way of life and learning. These included Wayne Steel of New York, Gary Benjamin of Buffalo, Leona Smith Kremser of Oregon, Mark J. Kayda of Lore City, Ohio, and Alice Avery of Oceana, California.

September 1971 marked the first North American visit by a Jain master. Gurudev Chitrabhanu from Bombay, India, came as a delegate to the third Spiritual Summit Conference at Harvard Divinity School, cosponsored by the Temple of Understanding and the Princeton Theological Seminary. Since then he has made the United States his second home, spreading the messages of nonviolence, reverence for life, and compassion for all. In September 1973 he established Jain Meditation International Center in New York City. He has inspired thousands of people in North America, including many from the entertainment industry, to follow the path of nonviolence and vegetarianism.

The migration of Asian Indians to the United States started gradually in the 1960s, when the immigration laws were relaxed and Asian Indians, including Jains, started settling in America. Most Jains who had newly immigrated to Ohio settled in Cleveland, Columbus, Cincinnati, Toledo, and the surrounding suburbs, where jobs were plentiful and facilities for higher education, research, and advanced training in medicine and engineering were readily available.

In the early 1960s there were five to ten families in each of the four major metropolitan areas of the state (Cleveland, Columbus, Toledo, and Cincinnati). These families got together once or twice a year in private homes to celebrate the birthday (Mahavira Jayanti) of Lord Mahavira and the festival of lights (Deepawali). Deepawali commemorates the day Lord Mahavira attained *nirvana* (liberation). In some cases they also assembled for the celebration of Paryushan, which literally means "abiding or coming together" with one's soul. It is an annual festival of eight to ten days when Jains study holy scriptures, reflect on past actions, and strive to purify body, mind, and soul through meditation, penance, fasting, and by forgiving and asking for forgiveness from others.

As word spread about these celebrations, Jains got together more often. People from distant suburbs, towns, and cities would gather, and the number of Jains began to grow. As the number of Jain families increased, it became difficult to accommodate members in private homes, so the communities rented nearby churches, schools, and community halls.

It was difficult for Jain families to practice their religion and raise their families in the Jain way while living and working in American society. Jainism is a religion that advocates the practice of nonviolence in thought, deed, and action. Thus one of the important parts of the religion is a vegetarian diet. In the 1960s, Americans often questioned their motives and beliefs because Jains could not associate, mingle, or share their food and customs with colleagues and neighbors. Jain children were embarrassed and disappointed when they could not share lunch with classmates. Questions were raised not only by their classmates but even by the teachers who would send notes home about students not getting enough protein from the vegetarian Jain diet. Many parents took time to meet with teachers and explain Jain beliefs. It took time and effort on everyone's part to get to know, understand, and respect one another's religious beliefs.

Naturally it was hard for Jain families to eat out. There were no vegetarian restaurants at the time. It was even harder for little children when their classmates visited nearby fast-food outlets and they could not join them. For college-bound students, food was a big problem. Food services at colleges were not geared to providing pure vegetarian food. Leaders in the Jain community intervened and, in some cases, concessions were made in the food plans. In spite of these efforts it was still difficult to get a balanced meal all the time.

Another area of difficulty that Jains faced was from the media. The news media rarely published news releases for Jain events in the local newspapers. Jains were told that Jainism is not a religion, but that it is a cult and/or an offshoot of Hinduism or a branch of Buddhism. In some world religion textbooks and encyclopedias, misinformation was printed, which was then used for public information and as school reference material. To a large extent the problems persist even today.

A positive breakthrough occurred in the summer of 1975, when a delegation of Jains, headed by a famous monk, Acharya Sushil Kumar, visited Cleveland as part of a worldwide goodwill tour to celebrate the twenty-five hundredth nirvana anniversary of Lord Mahavira. Large numbers of Jains welcomed the group. This was the first time Ohio-born children got a chance to glimpse and learn about the life of a Jain monk. (Traditionally, Jain monks are not allowed to travel by air or use any vehicle because complete renunciation of all worldly possessions is required.)

The Jain Society of Greater Cleveland and the Jain Center of Cincinnati/Dayton were formed, respectively, in 1978 and 1979; the International Mahavira Jain Mission in Parma was organized in 1980; and in 1991 the Jain Center of Central Ohio in Columbus was officially organized. Now things started changing at all levels. For Mahavira Jayanti and Deepawali programs, George V. Voinovich, then mayor of Cleveland, issued proclamations declaring April 8, 1979, as a day of *ahimsa* (nonviolence) in Cleveland. Congratulatory messages were also received from the governor and from Ohio's representatives in the U.S. Congress and Senate.

On February 8 and 17, 1979, the *Cleveland Press* newspaper (now defunct) printed positive articles about the visits of Acharya Sushil Kumar and Gurudev Chitrabhanu. On July 22, 1979, the local Catholic Radio station, broadcast at WMIH 1260 AM, WJW 104.1 FM, and WERE 1300 AM, hosted a live talk show with Sushil Kumar. He was also invited to speak about Hinduism and Jainism at Cleveland State University. Local people showed interest in learning more about Jainism. In August 1979 Jain Pontiff Bhattarak Charukeerty Swami of Shravanabelagola and Moodabidri of India were invited to participate in the Third Assembly of the World Conference on Religion and Peace at Princeton Theological Seminary. After the conference as a part of their peace mission, on September 14, 1979, they visited Cleveland. During the course of their one-week visit to Ohio they provided many discourses on the fundamentals of Jainism. Jains and non-Jains welcomed them with open arms. The local press provided positive coverage.

On April 24, 1981, Acharya Sushil Kumar was honored by the mayor of Cleveland at the city hall and also issued a proclamation to commemorate the anniversary of the birth of Lord Mahavira. In honoring Acharya Sushil Kumar, the mayor presented him with a key to the city. In return, the mayor gracefully received from the Jain community a set of four books on Jain art and architecture.

Jains of Ohio have played an important role at the national level. On May 22 through 25, 1981, the Jain Center of Southern California in Los Angeles invited Jain delegations from North America and founded the Federation of Jain Associations in North America (JAINA). Tansukh Salgia represented the Jain Society of Greater Cleveland, and he was elected vice-president of the new national organization. In 1985, at the third convention, held in Detroit, Salgia was elected president, a post he held through 1989. Salgia is the only director to have served on the federation's board continuously since the organization's inception. Sulekh Jain of Cincinnati was elected secretary in 1985 and later in Toronto at the fifth Jain convention in 1989 was elected president, a position he held until 1993. In May

The mayor of Cleveland, George Voinovich, honoring Acharya Sushil Kumar and a Jain delegation at Cleveland City Hall, 1981. (Courtesy of Tansukh Salgia)

1987 Surendra Singhvi of Dayton was elected treasurer. In 1991, during its organizational meeting in Cleveland, the JAINA Executive Committee formed the World Community Services Committee to focus and expand on the humanitarian role of Jainism. In 1993 Ramesh Shah of Cleveland was elected secretary of the federation. Ila Mehta of Toledo was elected to the national office to serve as a regional vice-president in 2001. In 2001 Soha D. Shah of Piqua, twenty-four at the time, became the youngest president of a North American Jain center when she was elected to that office at the Jain Center of Cincinnati/Dayton, where the first Jain temple in Ohio was built in 1995.

In 1987–88, under JAINA's leadership, Ohio Jains played a major role in the production and distribution of the first-ever documentary on Jainism, a PBS production entitled *Ahimsa-Nonviolence: A Story of the Jain Religion,* which was broadcast nationally in December 1988. This documentary has received many national and international awards. In 1983, with the help of Khusal Bhai of North Royalton, a program was established at Cleveland State University to bring Indian scholars to the university to teach eastern religions, including Jainism.

In July 1985 a national Jain magazine (*Jain Digest*) was founded in Cleveland. In the same year JAINA's national office was moved to Cleveland; from 1989 to 1993 it was located in Cincinnati. From these offices in Ohio, the messages of nonviolence, reverence for life, and compassion for all were taught through various seminars, workshops, documentary films, and weekend camps for Jains of all ages as well as the community at large.

In fall 1986 further progress was made. The Catholic Diocese of Cleveland recognized the importance of Jain religious beliefs; Jains were invited to participate in the planning committee of an interfaith dialogue which later became the Cleveland Conference of Religions, an independent organization which still sponsors conferences on religions. Also in fall 1986, the Jain Society of Greater Cleveland was invited for the first time to participate in a world peace forum organized by the Interchurch Council of Greater Cleveland. Through interaction with other faiths and to live up to the Jain principles of compassion and love, Jains across Ohio have been actively involved with soup kitchens and homeless shelters. They have also reached out to other parts of the world. As an example, Jaya Shah of Cleveland, as a part of a delegation of the Measles Initiative of the American Red Cross, traveled to Kenya to facilitate reduction of measles in fifteen African countries.

In August 1989 the Hindu Temple and Heritage Hall of Toledo was inaugurated; a Jain deity was installed along with Hindu deities. The temple is considered the first place of worship for Jains in Ohio. To commemorate its uniqueness, a historical marker approved by the Ohio Bicentennial Commission was placed at the site on April 27, 2003. In July 1998, Acharya Chandana, the only known female pontiff in the history of Jainism, visited Cleveland to offer the opening prayer at the fifth biennial convention of the National Federation of Asian Indians in North America. The mayor of Cleveland honored her for her efforts in spreading the message of nonviolence.

October 4, 1992, was a very auspicious day for the Jain community of Ohio, particularly for the Jain Center of Cincinnati/Dayton. On this day, under the spiritual guidance of the late Acharya Sushil Kumar, eleven acres were purchased for the future home of a Jain temple in Cincinnati. On May 28, 1995, temple facilities were opened to the public. On September 2, 3, and 4, 1995, with great festivity, idols of three Jinas (gods) were

The old Hindu Temple and Heritage Hall of Toledo was the first place of worship established for Jains in Ohio (1984). (Courtesy of Ila Mehta)

installed, and the temple and community center were ready for regular worship services.

In November 1995 the Jain Center of Cincinnati/Dayton honored the Reverend Maurice McCracken on his ninetieth birthday. Rev. McCracken was widely known as a Christian minister, a Gandhian, and a vegetarian and was very active in the nonviolent movement. This was a big event for the city of Cincinnati. Jains also participated in a vegetarian Thanksgiving Day and World Peace Bell celebration held in Newport, Kentucky, to observe the arrival of the new millennium. Since fall 1996 Jain leaders in Cincinnati have been teaching courses on Jainism at the University of Dayton and appearing on a National Public Radio talk show on Jainism broadcast from Xavier University in Cincinnati.

At the invitation of the Jain Center of Central Ohio, Gurudev Chitrabhanu graced the April 1997 celebration of Lord Mahavira's 2596th birth anniversary. He was later honored for his goodwill mission by State Senator Bruce Johnson and Columbus Mayor Greg Lashutka. In 1999 the Hindu Society of Greater Cincinnati also installed a deity of Lord Mahavira for Jains to worship.

On September 18, 2001, the Jain Center of Central Ohio made history when, in cooperation with Jain community members from across the

Jain deities installed at the first Jain Temple of Ohio, Cincinnati, September 1995.
(Courtesy of Tansukh Salgia)

state, it offered the Jain prayer for peace at the opening session of the
Ohio Senate. The prayer was lead by Sisters Samani Akshay and Sanmati
Pragya. Senator Bruce Johnson spoke eloquently about the Jain principle
of nonviolence and its importance in resolving the conflicts of the world.
At the conclusion of the prayer, Jain community leaders presented a set
of five books on Jain philosophy to Senate President Richard Finan and
Senator Johnson.

During the past thirty years, countless Jain monks, nuns, and scholars
have visited Ohio from India and presented discourses on Jain philosophy, meditation, and yoga at various colleges, universities, and churches
and to many interfaith groups. State and local political establishments
have honored these monks and scholars by presenting them with letters
of appreciation and proclamation and with keys to the cities.

In July 2003, for the first time since its founding in 1981, JAINA held its
biennial convention in Cincinnati. More than three thousand people
from the United States, Canada, Britain, Africa, and India attended. The
convention was hosted by the Jain Center of Cincinnati/Dayton.

Many more people understand and respect Jains and their religious
beliefs. The children are no longer teased and harassed. Many eateries
have special menus for vegetarians, and grocery stores also have labels on

food items listing ingredients so that Jains can choose what is edible for them. However, education of the general public about the fundamental principle of Jainism—ahimsa or nonviolence—needs more work.

BELIEFS

In Jain cosmology the universe is eternal, without beginning or end. Time rolls along in an eternal cycle of ascent and decline. A rising era is called an Utsarpini, in which human affairs and natural conditions improve and aggrandize over time. At the peak of the Utsarpini begins an Avasarpini, a "declining" era of the same length, in which the utopia which had evolved gradually corrupts and weakens, with life becoming more difficult to endure.

During each declining era are born twenty-four persons quite different from their contemporaries. Upon realizing the nature of worldly existence, the cycle of misery it entails, and the path to liberation from it, these twenty-four individuals renounce all physical, mental, and material ties to the world and blaze a path to perfection in their own lives. They are called Jinas ("victors" or "conquerors"). Jinas are also called Tirthankaras ("crossing makers"), those who show the path across the metaphorical "ocean" of worldly existence to final liberation and emancipation from a succession of births and deaths. A Jina has conquered the inner enemies of anger, ego, deceit, and greed and has uncovered the four inherent properties of the soul: infinite knowledge, perception, happiness, and will power. Those who follow the path of the Jinas are called Jains. Jains consider the Jain philosophy to be eternal. It has been revived and taught, again and again, by innumerable Crossing Makers for the benefit of humankind and all other living beings.

The ultimate goal of a Jain is to follow in the footsteps of these Crossing Makers and to likewise realize the inherent attributes of the soul. The first Tirthankar of the present declining era was the prehistoric Lord Rishabha. The twenty-third was Lord Parshva (877–777 B.C.E.), and the last was Lord Mahavira (599–527 B.C.E). Jain beliefs are based on the teachings of the Tirthankaras, which have been preserved in sacred texts called the Agamas.

The fundamental belief in Jain philosophy is that every single living being has a soul, or *jiva,* and that all souls are eternal (uncreated and indestructible), independent, spiritually equal to each other, and responsible for their own actions, whether mental, verbal, or physical.

Jainism is about living our lives in a way that respects and honors the spiritual nature of every living being, as well as our own, to the very best of our ability. The chief means of doing so is to strive to be as nonviolent as possible in thought, word, and deed at all levels, individual and social. In its philosophy, ethics, and rituals, the Jain religion invokes an intense and constant understanding not only of all living beings but also of all that exists. The directive principle of living is to live not "at the expense of others" or "by killing" but "with others."

The Jain religion presents an enlightened perspective of the equality of souls, irrespective of differing physical forms, ranging from human beings to animals and microscopic organisms. All life is sacred, irrespective of caste, color, creed, or nationality, and sanctity also covers species at all levels down to the tiny ant or the humble worm. Humans alone among all beings are endowed with all the six faculties of seeing, hearing, tasting, smelling, touching, and thinking. Therefore humans are instructed to act responsibly toward all life by being compassionate, egoless, fearless, forgiving, rational, and full of equanimity. All human beings have the potential to become Jina and realize the soul's true nature. Therefore, Jainism is sometimes called a "do-it-yourself" religion.

Jain religion has a clearly articulated scientific basis, which elucidates the properties and qualities of the animate and inanimate substances that make up the cosmos. Their interrelationship is described in terms of evolution and growth of "monads"—atoms, molecules, nonmaterial continuums, and souls. Jainism sets forth the existence of two fundamental categories of entities: *jiva* and *ajiva,* soul and nonsoul. The nonsoul "substances" are time, space, *pudgal* (all forms of matter and energy), and the media of motion and rest. Genius lies in this cosmology, which is comparable in many ways to the views of modern science. Elements of the Jain worldview include the subatomic makeup of matter, the charged nature of elementary particles, the interconvertibility of energy and matter, the conditions under which particles combine and dissociate, and a spacetime universe in which time is the fourth dimension. Jiva and ajiva are characterized as having distinct, immutable properties, which undergo modifications due to certain conditions. For the soul, those conditions are brought about as conscious and subconscious thought activity.

Through the inner workings of passions and attachments, the soul remains associated with nonsoul and persists in its cycle of material rise and decline, suffering and distress, delusion and wandering. Religious impulse is equated with the search for Truth, which begins with thought activity along the lines of "By soul alone I am governed" (*Appanan anusasay*). Dissociation from nonsoul is brought about solely through enlightened perception, knowledge, and conduct, which allow the soul to experience its natural attributes of infinite knowledge, perception, happiness, and will power.

The Jain code of conduct is made up of the following five vows: *ahimsa* (nonviolence), *satya* (truthfulness), *asteya* (nonstealing), *aparigraha* (nonpossessiveness), and *brahmacharya* (purity of conduct or chastity). Jain religion focuses much attention on aparigraha (nonpossessiveness) toward material things through self-control, self-imposed penance, abstinence from overindulgence, voluntary curtailment of one's needs, and the consequent subsiding of aggressive human urges. The code of conduct for the Jain monastic order, made up of monks and nuns, is more rigorous than that prescribed for the laity.

Vegetarianism, the way of life for a Jain, has its origin in the concept of compassion and mercy for living beings, or *jiva daya*. A Jain believes in doing his or her best to think, speak, and act with compassion and nonviolence toward the souls of other beings. This means the total elimination of animals from the diet. Animals typically have five physical senses and therefore experience greater pain and anguish than do plants, which are one-sensed (touch). While the vegetarian Jain diet does, of course, involve harm to plants and micro-organisms, it is regarded as the means of human survival involving the least violence toward other living beings.

Anekantavada (lit., "non-one-endedness"), another central doctrine, deals with the multifaceted nature of truth. It offers systematic, logical, and nondogmatic algorithms for understanding the multifarious aspects of truth behind different and even opposite statements, human perceptions, knowledge, and ideas about the nature of the true self. "Absolute truth" cannot be grasped from any one point of view alone, because any viewpoint is dependent on the time, place, nature, and state of both the viewer and whatever is being viewed. Hence, we can point to an infinity of partially valid perspectives. What appears true from one point of view is open to question from another. Naturally, we need to benefit from seeing things from different perspectives—including ones we might not prefer initially—in order to gain any kind of realistic impression. Anekantavada is a doctrine rooted in ahimsa and humility.

An important part of Jain teaching is the path of liberation, or the "The Three Jewels": Right Faith (Samyag Darshan), Right Knowledge (Samyag Jnana), and Right Conduct (Samyag Charitra). These three together lead to the development of higher consciousness. According to Jain metaphysics, the universe is without a beginning or end. It undergoes countless changes that are produced by the inherent natures of different substances.

Literally, *karma* means action. For every action, good or bad, there is an equally good or bad reaction or result, which the soul has to bear in this and any future life. However, by rigorous discipline, good deeds, and awareness one may be able to mitigate the density of karmas and shed them gradually. A theory of karma is essential to the Jain worldview and to the understanding of how one's own conduct—mental, verbal, and physical—affects one's present state and future destiny. For Jains, karma is not fate, luck, or predestination, but rather a very complex physical mechanism inherent to the physics that underlies the soul's eternal relationship with the universe it inhabits. Understanding how our thoughts, behaviors, and actions affect and are affected by this mechanism is key to understanding ourselves and the path of liberation in a very unique way. Jainism provides a logical explanation of our suffering and illustrates a rational way to eliminate suffering. It further states that the knowledge of reality and the realization of the true self lead the worldly soul to liberation (*moksha* or *nirvana*). The ultimate goal of Jainism is for the soul to achieve liberation through proper understanding and realization.

This is accomplished through the ideals of ahimsa, nonviolence, universal kindness, reverence for all forms of life, and nonpossessiveness and through the philosophy of Anekantavada. Jainism further states that the universe is not for humans alone. It is a field of evolution for all living beings. Hence compassion towards all is the most important code of conduct for all humanity.

ORIGINS AND RELATIONSHIP
TO OTHER FAITHS

According to Jain beliefs, Jainism originated in South Asia hundreds of thousands of years ago and is one of the world's oldest religions. It is not an offshoot or subsect of another religion. Jainism is sometimes known as Ahimsa Dharma, the religion of nonviolence. It is not an overstatement to observe that the Jain tradition has deeply influenced the fabric of Indian civilization in every field of human endeavor. Beyond South Asia, the Jain community has increasingly developed a presence in other parts of the world. There are Jain entrepreneurs, engineers, teachers, social workers, doctors, and professors in Ohio and all over the world. The presence of Jains in North America is growing rapidly and is being increasingly recognized. Today Jainism is an American religion of nonviolence and compassion.

Jainism tends to be less known compared to certain other religions, partly because Jains are not on a membership drive to convert others to their faith. However, Jain values have influenced many philosophers, writers, and humanitarians. Mahatma Gandhi, for example, was deeply influenced by Jain teachings. His principle of nonviolence gained independence for South Asia from the British Empire. Gandhi's insistence on the worth of every human being and his spiritual advocacy for vegetarianism have always been intrinsic to Jainism. Martin Luther King, Jr., was inspired by Gandhi's example and adopted nonviolent resistance as the core value of the American civil rights movement.

Jainism is an eternal philosophy whose benefits can be taken up by anyone wanting to improve his or her life and face stress with tranquility. Today, when suspicion and distrust are vitiating the atmosphere of international peace and the world is filled with fear and hate, we require a living philosophy that will help us recover ourselves. Love and goodwill, Ahimsa and peace, personally as well as universally, is the Jain philosophy of life. This system of thought and living stands for the highest and noblest human values and offers a path guaranteeing eternal peace and happiness. Wherever they are, Jains continue to be faithful to Lord Mahavira's teaching that "all life is bound together by mutual support and interdependence" (Tattvartha Sutra, J.21). Hence the principle of "Live, let live, and help others to live."

VISITING A JAIN TEMPLE

Jain worship services are open to the general public. However, guests attending such services are expected to observe certain basic requirements, such as wearing clean clothes; leaving shoes at the temple entrance; not eating, drinking, or bringing meat or liquor into or around the temple area; and having respect for all lives while in the temple area. A visit will reveal the inherent democracy of a Jain temple—different individual Jains might be found silently meditating, performing rituals, singing prayers, or studying scriptures all in the same space and without the intervention of priests or clergy. Jainism is an eternal philosophy whose benefits can be taken up by anyone wanting to improve his or her life.

CURRENT DEMOGRAPHICS

There are about 650 families in Ohio that belong to the Jain faith. The largest concentrations are in northeast Ohio (Cleveland, Akron, Canton, and Youngstown), Columbus, Cincinnati, Dayton, and Toledo.

CONTACT INFORMATION

There is no Jain administrative office in Ohio. Jain centers/societies are independent of each other. Each center has its own administrative office. The various Jain groups support each other based on their common roots, beliefs, and religious behavior. The following are the known public places of Jain worship in Ohio:

Jain Center of Central Ohio, 2770 Sawbury Boulevard, Columbus, Ohio 43235, *www.jcoco.net*

Jain Center of Cincinnati/Dayton, 6798 Cincinnati-Dayton Road, Cincinnati, Ohio 45044, 513-755-1400.

Hindu Temple of Greater Cincinnati, 4920 Klatte Road, Cincinnati, Ohio 45244, 513-528-3714, *www.cintitemple.org*

Jain Center of Toledo, 4336 King Road, Sylvania, Ohio 43560, 419-841-3662.

JAINA: *www.jaina.org*

Jainworld: *www.jainworld.com*
www.atmadharma.com

RESOURCES

Brown, Kerry, and Sima Sharma, eds. *That Which Is (Tattvartha Sutra), A Classic Jain Manual for Understanding the True Nature of Reality*. Translated by Nathmal Tatia. San Francisco: HarperCollins, 1994.

Eck, Diana. *On Common Ground: World Religions in America* (CD-ROM). New York: Columbia University Press, 2002.

JAINA Education Committee. *Jain Education in the New Millennium*. Raleigh, N.C.: JAINA, 2002.

Jaini, Padmanabh S. *The Jain Path of Purification*. Berkeley: University of California Press, 1979.

Salgia, Amar, ed. *Pure Freedom: The Jain Way of Self Reliance*. Torrance, Calif.: By editor, 2001.

Von Glasenapp, Helmuth. *Jainism: An Indian Religion of Salvation*. Translated by Shridhar B. Shrotri. New Delhi: Motilal Banarsidass, 1999.

ZOROASTRIANISM

Gulnar Surveyor

HISTORY

ZOROASTRIANISM IS ONE OF THE MOST ANCIENT RELIGIONS OF THE world still practiced today. It was the state religion of three great Persian empires that flourished almost continually from the sixth century B.C.E. to the seventh century C.E. Once the dominant religion in the civilized world, Zoroastrianism significantly influenced other religions that originated in the Middle East, including Judaism, Christianity, and Islam. Today its adherents, known as Zoroastrians, are a minority throughout the world. Most live in India, Iran, the United Kingdom, the United States, Canada, and Pakistan; others are scattered in many countries throughout the world.

The name "Zoroaster" is the Greek form of the name of Zarathushtra, the Prophet. Zoroaster was born, most likely, in the steppes of Asia near the Aral Sea, where he may have spent the early years of his life. There was little consensus among scholars in the first half of the twentieth century as to when he lived, and their estimates ranged from 6000 B.C.E. to as recently as 600 B.C.E. Today, on the basis of more recent research, many linguists, scholars of religion, historians, and archaeologists date his life around 1500 B.C.E.

From about 1500 B.C.E. to about 400 B.C.E., the Zoroastrian faith spread slowly across ancient Persia to become the state religion of the Medes and the Persians. During this period most elements of classical Persian art and architecture flourished.

The near extinction of the Zoroastrian religion commenced in the early seventh century C.E., as the Persian Empire was invaded and over time converted to Islam by the conquering Arabs. Those who did not adopt Islam were deprived of civil rights and civil liberties and heavily taxed to keep them subjugated politically and economically. Gradually, pressure to convert became extreme, and by the ninth century C.E., practicing Zoroastrians in Persia were a minority in their own country. The Mongol invasions of the thirteenth century further decimated the community.

In the tenth century C.E., some Zoroastrians fled Persia in order to preserve their faith. They settled on the western shores of India, where they were given asylum by Hindus, the followers of the predominant religion practiced there. In India, the newly arrived Zoroastrians came to be known as Parsis (from Fars or Pars, the southern region of Persia they were from). Despite subsequent centuries of suffering and hardship in India, the Zoroastrians, primarily agriculturists, eventually succeeded. While under British rule in India in the nineteenth and first half of the twentieth centuries, the Parsi Zoroastrians eagerly sought western education. They also took up general commerce, and some Parsi scientists were great innovators and were leaders in western-style industrial modernization and development in India.

Today the Zoroastrians are a small community numbering about two hundred thousand worldwide. About ninety thousand live in India, mostly in Bombay and the state of Gujarat. Approximately thirty thousand live in Iran, the ancient cradle of the Zoroastrian faith. The rest are scattered throughout the world, but mostly concentrated in the United States, Canada, Australia, the United Kingdom, Pakistan, and Africa. It is estimated that about fifteen thousand live in the United States and Canada (FEZANA).

In the United States and Canada, Zoroastrians have organized into associations, especially in big cities with large numbers of adherents. The different associations united to form one umbrella association called the Federation of Zoroastrian Associations of North America (FEZANA). FEZANA was registered in Illinois on June 2, 1987, as a nonprofit religious and charitable organization. Over the years, the FEZANA constitution has proved to be a viable document that has helped to resolve many questions and issues related to the orderly progress of a diverse and growing Zoroastrian community in North America.

There is no reliable data available on the history and demographics of Zoroastrians in Ohio. The earliest arrivals probably date back to the 1950s and 1960s, when the first wave of immigrants from India and Pakistan came to the United States. Beginning in 1979 many of the remaining Zoroastrians fled Iran to escape the regime of Ayatolla Khomeni. Some might have come to Ohio. Attempts have been made recently by FEZANA to obtain demographic data on Zoroastrians in North America. The existing data on Ohio indicate that most are concentrated in large cities, Cleveland and Cincinnati having the largest concentrations, followed by Columbus, Akron, Toledo, and Dayton. Ohio does not have an established Zoroastrian association. However, FEZANA recognizes two small groups that have organized in the last few years. One is the Cleveland Zoroastrian Community, whose members live mainly in the northeastern part of the state, and the other is the Zoroastrian Association of Kentucky-Ohio-Indiana, whose members live in the tri-state area.

BELIEFS

One Divinity—Ahura Mazda: Zoroaster was the first prophet to teach that there is only one universal divinity—that is, Ahura Mazda. This term consists of two Avesta words (a language used in the time of Zoroaster), *ahura* and *mazda.* The first word, *ahura,* was already used by the pre-Zoroastrians for any deity in their polytheistic pantheon. Zoroaster proclaimed a completely new concept—monotheism. He introduced Ahura Mazda as the sole creator of the universe who infused life into the physical world. This is probably why many scholars have derived the word *ahura* from the root *ahu,* meaning "life-giving force" and translate it as "the being, the essence," with a secondary meaning, "lord." The new word, *mazda,* which Zoroaster introduced, meant "super-intellect" or "supreme wisdom." Hence the term Ahura Mazda means "Lord of Wisdom" or "The Wise Lord." Zoroaster set down Ahura Mazda's eternal law in the Gathas (the divinely inspired songs), established the Law of Consequences, and prescribed the way to true happiness for the righteous.

Gatha—The Religion of Zoroaster: The five Gathas, which comprise seventeen songs that convey the precise and concise message of Zoroaster and are incorporated into the Avesta scripture, were essential to the survival of the religion. Much of the greater Avestan corpus was destroyed by conquerors such as Alexander the Great and others. The Gathas are the exact divinely inspired words of Zoroaster. They are the only authentic words preached by Zoroaster himself in the unique Gathic language of his time. The Gathas are mantras, or thought-provoking monologues, as well as preachings of Zoroaster. They stimulate the mind first, and so guide humanity to perfection and eternity. Thus, just three abstracted Gathic principles or tenets—*humata* (good thoughts), *hukhta* (good words), and *hvarshta* (good deeds), that is, being of critical mind, articulate speech, and purposeful action—have allowed Zoroastrians to live religious and ethical lives for millennia. The Gathas are chanted, providing direct communion with Ahura Mazda. These sacred songs survived the ravages of history due to the efforts of priests who had thoroughly memorized them for the performance of their liturgical ceremonies. The salient points of the Gathas are:

1. There is only one divinity recognized as being Great Wisdom—Ahura Mazda, who is a creator, sustainer, and continuous promoter of the cosmos.

2. The religion of good conscience (*daena vanguhi*) is universal and open to all who choose to be involved in it. There is divine enlightenment, *seraosha,* that reveals many divine faculties, which lead to the understanding of the principles that form the cosmos, an orderly universe.

3. The Zoroastrian universe has been created good and will always be progressing in an orderly manner towards completion, as intended by its creator, Ahura Mazda.

4. Humankind has been endowed with freedom of thought, word, and deed, and has a bright mind to discern between what is good and what is bad for all of society.

5. Humans are capable of expressing two forms of mentalities—*spenta mainyu,* progressive mentality, and *angra mainyu,* retarding mentality. Progressive mentality helps one to improve oneself and the world. Retarding mentality harms one and the world.

6. Humans are divided into two camps—the righteous and the wrong-

ful. The objective of the righteous should be to win over the wrongful into the righteous camp.

7. What is good can best be understood by studying nature, advancing knowledge, harmonizing with all that is good and beneficial, and preserving the environment.

8. Humanity may, if it chooses, develop all of the above divine faculties and become creative.

9. If human beings do not choose judiciously, this world continues to be chaotic and they suffer the consequences until they live by these divine principles.

10. Sooner or later humanity will correct itself and attain perfection and eternal life.

11. Caste, color, race, and nationality do not play a part in the universal message of Zoroaster.

12. Men and women are equal and enjoy the same rights in a free and responsible society.

13. Free human society should select only fully qualified persons of righteous records and merits for both temporal and spiritual offices in a true democratic environment.

14. The prime object of every human being should be to make a better world in spirit and body.

15. The good religion is a "self-renovating" religion. Its continuous progress makes it ever fresh, ever modern. Logical modernization of thoughts, words, and deeds, including traditional practices and rites, should be the order of the day.

16. Enlightenment and happiness come to the human being who gives happiness to others without discrimination.

17. Prayers help humanity to communicate with the Greater Wisdom. They help us to experience divine love. Prayers may be said in silent meditation, in a few words, in prose or poetry. They may be said plainly or with simple rituals (this is repeated throughout the Gathas). They may be said in the language that is understood best by the person, and not by rote.

To summarize, the Gathas are prayers to Ahura Mazda for spiritual guidance to humanity. "Good Thoughts, Good Words, and Good Deeds" is the quintessence of the Gathic message.

Life after Death: Zoroaster presented a belief in the resurrection of the body, a life in the hereafter, the coming of a savior, and rewards and punishments for the immortal soul. The divine law of justice prescribes that good will come to the good, and evil to the evil. Zoroaster says that every human being should be righteous for the sake of righteousness. He constantly reminds humanity that there is the spark of immortality in us, and life will continue after death. Some Zoroastrians believe in the concept of reincarnation, wherein the soul undergoes numerous cycles of birth and death to finally become one with God. This belief is likely the influence of Hinduism on the Parsis who have lived in India for several centuries.

SYMBOLS OF THE ZOROASTRIAN RELIGION

Fire: Fire is the outward symbol of the Zoroastrian faith and symbolizes the divine spark within. It is revered for its life-giving power in the sun. Fire was, however, a sacred symbol long before Zoroaster's time. Fire worship was an Indo-Iranian custom before the division of that civilization into Iranian and Indian peoples. Fire is also worshiped in the Vedas (Hindu scriptures) and is a sacred part of Hindu ceremonies. In his revelation, Zoroaster gave fire a new meaning. In the Gathas, he speaks of fire as a powerful creation of Ahura Mazda. When Zoroastrians stand in devotion before a fire they believe that they are standing in the presence of the sacred radiance of Ahura Mazda. To symbolize this, a fire is kept constantly burning in Zoroastrian places of worship.

Sudreh-Kusti: Every Zoroastrian after the initiation, or *navjote,* ceremony (described below) must wear a *sudreh* (sacred shirt) and tie a *kusti* (sacred girdle) around the waist. The sudreh is made of pure white muslin (a type of cotton) and the kusti is woven of seventy-two threads of lamb's wool. The kusti is tied thrice around the waist using square knots and is symbolic of the threefold path of good thoughts, good words, and good deeds. The sudreh-kusti is a symbolic suit of armor that Zoroastrians wear in the fight against evil.

The Fravashi: The Fravashi (or Farohar) is the symbol of the holy light or glory and is a holy guardian spirit. They are angels who accompany and guide every person, living organism, and inanimate object. They willingly come to earth to help all but the evil, and they are invoked in times of need. Their wings signify the ascent of the soul. The ring in the center symbolizes the eternity of the universe. The ancient man in the center represents the wisdom of age. This symbol is found inscribed on rock tombs of the Achaemenid kings, as well as in ancient ruins of Zoroastrians in Persepolis, in present-day Iran.

RITUALS

The Navjote (initiation ceremony): Navjote is the formal initiation of a person into the Zoroastrian faith. The word is derived from the words *nav,* meaning new, and *jote,* meaning one who offers prayers. Hence, *navjote* means a new initiate who offers prayers. Originally performed when a person was fifteen or older, it is now performed when a person is still in his or her childhood. The event is meant to bring the child into the faith and make the child directly answerable to Ahura Mazda for all thoughts, words, and deeds. It is usually performed between the ages of six and eleven. Both boys and girls are initiated with the same ritual. The sacred fire is kept burning throughout the navjote ceremony. Festivities with good food often follow the ceremony. After the ceremony, a Zoroastrian is expected to always wear the sudreh-kusti and recite the kusti prayers daily.

Funeral practices: Zoroastrians prefer not to bury their dead, because they believe that the decomposition associated with death pollutes the earth. For the same reason, the corpse cannot be disposed of at sea. Since fire is the symbol of righteousness, cremation would "defile" the pure fire. Zoroastrians believe that vultures and other natural scavengers were created by God to devour corpses. Feeding the corpse to vultures would be the natural way to dispose of the dead. In ancient Persia, the custom was to leave the corpse in a forested area for scavengers to devour. In India today, corpses are placed in a *dakhma,* also known as a "tower of silence," which is a circular stone tower with high walls that is open to the sky. Wherever there is no such facility, corpses are buried, with or without a coffin, or even cremated.

INSTITUTIONAL ZOROASTRIANISM

Institutional Zoroastrianism is the shape that the Zoroastrian religion that has taken in the last two millennia. This form is also commonly referred to as "Traditional Zoroastrianism." As a result of fourteen hundred years of cultural influence by Islam in Persia and by the caste system in India, Traditional Zoroastrianism has become a closed club of "born Zoroastrians" that does not accept converts. It believes that every human being is born into a religion by God's will and that conversion to a different religion goes against God's will. Traditional Zoroastrians strongly believe that marrying someone outside one's faith brings great harm to that individual and to the children of such a union. They also believe that only born Zoroastrians should be admitted into the Fire Temples. Traditional Zoroastrianism has a firmly established hereditary priestly class.

THE FIRE TEMPLE

As mentioned before, fire is an important symbol in the Zoroastrian faith, and a fire is kept burning constantly inside the place of worship; hence the term "Fire Temple." There are three grades of sacred fires, each representing a different level of holiness and ritual sanctity. The lowest form is called the Atash Dadgah and can burn in any clean place such as a home or a community center. The next grade, called Atash Adaran, is kept constantly burning, or at least smoldering, in Fire Temples by priests. The highest grade is called the Atash Behram; its creation requires elaborate rituals that take almost a year to complete. The fire in an Atash Behram is composed of embers from several different fiery sources, including lightning, which can be obtained only when lightning happens to ignite a tree.

There are no Atash Adarans or Atash Behrams in the United States or Canada. There are a few community centers in large cities where Atash Dadgahs are lit during religious ceremonies. The closest ones to Ohio are located in Chicago, New York, and Toronto.

CURRENT DEMOGRAPHICS

Approximately fifty to one hundred Zoroastrians reside in Ohio today, mainly in the Cleveland, Cincinnati, and Columbus metropolitan areas.

CONTACT INFORMATION

Federation of Zoroastrian Associations of North America (FEZANA), 951 Jordan Crescent, Edmonton, Alberta T6L 7A5, Canada, *www.fezana.org*
Zarathushtrian Assembly: *www.zoroastrian.org*

RESOURCES

Dhalla, M. N. *History of Zoroastrianism.* New York: Oxford University Press, 1938.

Jafarey, Ali. *The Gathas, Our Guide: The Thought-Provoking Divine Songs of Zarathushtra.* Cypress, Calif.: Ushta, 1989.

Mehr, Farhang. *The Zoroastrian Tradition: An Introduction to the Ancient Wisdom of Zarathustra.* Rockport, Mass.: Element Books, 1991.

THE RELIGIOUS EXPERIENCE
ADVISORY COUNCIL OF THE OHIO
BICENTENNIAL COMMISSION

The Religious Experience Advisory Council is one among twenty-two advisory councils established by the Ohio Bicentennial Commission to commemorate and celebrate the bicentennial of the state of Ohio. The Religious Experience Advisory Council was formed in January 2000. For about four years, more than twenty volunteers representing eight faith traditions served on the Religious Experience Advisory Council to plan events and projects for acknowledging the broad range of religious experiences in Ohio and the impact faith communities have had on our state.

Ohio is more diverse in religion and faith traditions today than it has ever been. Buddhists, Muslims, Christians, Hindus, Jews, Sikhs, Native Americans, Bahá'ís, Jains, and Zoroastrians are all now citizens of the Buckeye state. The religious pluralism of Ohio was evident in the composition of the advisory council and the multifaith activities implemented by the council to observe Ohio's two-hundredth birthday.

In addition to publishing this compilation on the history of religious experiences in Ohio, the advisory council sponsored the installation of more than ten faith-based historical markers. The historical markers, dedicated in collaboration with the Ohio Bicentennial Commission and the Ohio Historical Society, commemorate faith-based locations, events, and persons representing eight world religions.

BIOGRAPHICAL SKETCHES OF
ADVISORY COUNCIL MEMBERS

Rev. Ronald W. Botts is pastor at the First Congregational Church (United Church of Christ) in Columbus. He served as chair of the Religious Experience Advisory Council from 2000 to 2002.

Dr. Tarunjit Singh Butalia, a thirteen-year resident of Columbus, is secretary general of World Sikh Council–America Region and chairs its National Interfaith Committee. He is secretary of the Sikh Educational and Religious

The Religious Experience Advisory Council of the Ohio Bicentennial Commission, April 2003.
First row, L to R: Houshang Ma'ani, Molly Ryan, Ronald W. Botts, Rebecca Tollefson, Michael Morello. *Second row, L to R:* Paul F. H. Reichert II, J. S. Jindal, Winifred C. Wirth, Habib Khan. *Third row, L to R:* Tarunjit Singh Butalia, Dianne Small, Dilip Doshi, Meena Khan, Jack B. Davis. *Fourth row, L to R:* Alvin R. Hadley, Tansukh Salgia, Patrick Mooney, Bishun D. Pandey, Steven R. Dimler. *Not pictured:* Joyce Garver Keller, Ranbir Singh, Jayne M. Zborowsky
(Courtesy of West Ohio Conference, The United Methodist Church)

Foundation. He represents the Sikh faith at the national level on the North American Interfaith Network, and is a member of the Executive Council of Religions for Peace. He is an active member of the Interfaith Association of Central Ohio, the Ohio State University Interfaith Association, the Interfaith Center for Peace, Faith Communities Uniting for Peace, and the Religious Advisory Council of the mayor of Columbus. He lives in Dublin with his wife and two daughters.

Jack B. Davis is the president of Port Columbus Interfaith Services and served as the president of the Ohio Council of Churches from 2000 to 2002. He holds many leadership positions in his local church and his denomination (United Church of Christ).

Steven R. Dimler is past president of the Interfaith Association of Central Ohio (2000–2004). He is a longtime member of the Bahá'í Faith. Steve works as a food scientist at the Ross Products Division of Abbott Laboratories and lives in Pickerington, Ohio, with his wife and two children.

Dilip Doshi is president of Boson Technology Resources, an information technology company. He serves as Community Relations Commissioner for the City of Columbus, board member of the American Red Cross, and treasurer for the Interfaith Association of Central Ohio. He practices Jainism in central Ohio with wife Suresha, son Sagar, and daughter Sapana.

Alvin R. Hadley is the executive director of the Columbus Metropolitan Area Church Council. He has devoted much of his time to volunteer activities, serving on the General Board of Ohio Council of Churches and as a president of the American Baptist Churches of Ohio.

Dr. J. S. Jindal, a retired dentist and native of Meerut, India, is president of the Spiritual Sadhna Society and a trustee of the Asian and Pakistan Cultural Association. He lives in Columbus with wife Dr. Sneh Jindal, a retired psychologist and senior Vipassana meditation teacher, two sons Bipender and Lt. Col. Sudhir, daughter Sadhna, and eight grandchildren.

Joyce Garver Keller, a resident of Bexley, Ohio, is the executive director of Ohio Jewish Communities, Inc., an organization whose purpose is to enhance the Jewish community's ability to serve vital human needs. She is president of Ohio Women in Government and sits on the Capital Square Foundation's board of trustees.

Habib Khan is a businessman in the automobile industry. He has served in various capacities with the International Institute of Toledo, the Islamic Council of Ohio, and the Islamic Center of Greater Toledo. Mr. Khan participated in the opening of the first mosque in Ohio, in Toledo in 1954.

Meena Khan is a retired librarian from the University of Toledo. She is the founding librarian of the Islamic Center of Toledo Library. She is also treasurer of the Church and Synagogue Library Association (Maumee Valley chapter) and resides in Toledo, Ohio.

Dr. Houshang Ma'ani is a retired psychiatrist, and is chair of the Religious

Experience Advisory Council (2002–4). He worked as a physician in Indonesia for eleven years and in England for nine years, and came to Columbus in 1972. He is a member of the Bahá'í Faith and the Interfaith Association of Central Ohio.

Patrick Mooney, a native of Somerset, Perry County, and a fifth-generation Ohioan, is a retired elementary school teacher, historical researcher, longtime collector of historical and literary Ohioana, and chair of the Catholic Record Society, Diocese of Columbus. He has lived in Columbus for fifty years.

Michael Morello, a native of Ohio, is senior account manager for Motorola, Inc. He is a lifelong member of the Church of Jesus Christ of Latter-day Saints and has served in numerous lay clergy capacities for more than thirty years. He lives in central Ohio with his wife Pauline and their five children.

Dr. Bishun D. Pandey is professor of mathematics at the Ohio State University and has been serving the Bharatiya Hindu Temple in Powell, Ohio, for more than fourteen years. He is the president of the executive committee of the temple and resides in Lewis Center.

Rev. Paul F. H. Reichert II is a graduate of Trinity Lutheran Seminary and is the pastor of Calvary Lutheran Church (Evangelical Lutheran Church in America) in Northwood, Ohio, where he and his family live.

Molly Ryan is program coordinator with the Ohio Bicentennial Commission. She served as the liaison between the commission and the Religious Experience Advisory Council. She has a bachelor's degree in journalism from Ohio University. She is a Roman Catholic and volunteers for the Columbus AIDS Task Force.

Dr. Tansukh Salgia is the founding member and past president of the Federation of Jain Associations in North America and of many other Jain and Asian organizations, including the International Mahavira Jain Mission. He has authored many articles, edited several books on Jain subjects, and represented the Jain faith at national conferences.

Dr. Ranbir Singh is Professor Emeritus at the Ohio State University. He is past secretary of the World Sikh Council–America Region and is a founding trustee of the Sikh Educational and Religious Foundation of Dublin, Ohio. He is also a past president of the Interfaith Association of Central Ohio.

Dianne Small is an executive assistant with the Ohio State University Medical Center, and she has a bachelor's degree in history from the same institution. She is a member of the Bahá'í Faith and the Interfaith Association of Central

Ohio, and she belongs to the Ohio Arts and Crafts Guild and the Ohio Folk Art Association.

Rev. Rebecca Tollefson is the executive director of the Ohio Council of Churches. She is an ordained minister of the Presbyterian Church (U.S.A.), having receiving her M. Div. in 1981 from Louisville Presbyterian Theological Seminary. She has served churches in Iowa and Minnesota, as well on the Presbyterian Church's national staff.

Winifred C. Wirth has been active in the Buddhist Council of Ohio, the Interfaith Association of Central Ohio, and Amnesty International for over a decade. She lives in Columbus with her husband, a Protestant minister, and their son.

Jayne M. Zborowsky has been a member of the Old Stone Church in Cleveland for twenty years. She has been chair of the Board of Deacons, Member of the Session, chair of the Old Stone Church Mission Committee, and community liaison for many community projects.

CONTRIBUTORS

Jane A. Avner is Associate Curator of Jewish History at the Western Reserve Historical Society, where she manages the Cleveland Jewish Archives. She is the coauthor of "Historic Jewish Seattle: A Tour Guide," and has written articles about both the Seattle and Cleveland Jewish communities.

Rev. Marvin D. Bean is a retired member of the West Ohio Conference, United Methodist Church. He served as pastor of various churches and was Director of Intake at the United Methodist Children's Home. He is the conference historian and resides in Columbus.

Jonathan A. Binkley, a former educator, lives in Toledo, and is Chairman of the Historical Society and Editor of its News Magazine for the Churches of God, General Conference since 1997. He also held many positions in the former Ohio Conference.

Pamela Brown is Minister for Communication, Ohio Conference, United Church of Christ. She is editor of the Ohio edition of *United Church News*, conference webmaster, and publications designer. She is a member of Westerville Community Church UCC.

Juanita Bryant serves as the executive secretary of the Christian Methodist Episcopal Church, a position she has held since 1998. She is an attorney with a practice in probate and elder law and resides in Cleveland Heights.

Dr. Shive K. Chaturvedi teaches civil engineering and is also a member of the graduate faculty in the Department of Comparative Studies at the Ohio State University in Columbus. He serves as the educational coordinator at the Bharatiya Hindu Temple in Columbus.

Jacqueline D. Cherry is a graduate of the Ohio State University College of Nursing. She has compiled the history of *Vaud-Villities,* a musical production, and is currently writing the history of First Community Church (Marble Cliff), where she serves as archivist/historian.

Rev. Howard Collier is founder of the Church of Jesus, where he has been pastor for more than thirty-one years. He has been married to Alberta McNeal for forty-three years, and they are the parents of six. He has written more than seventy books, which have been distributed worldwide.

Rev. Roger L. Culbertson pastored two Assembly of God churches in Ohio (in Napoleon from 1955 to 1962 and in Defiance from 1962 to 2001, when he retired). He and his wife Geraldine have three daughters. He has written the column "Parson's Pen" for the *Defiance Crescent News* since 1972.

Charles J. Dawes, Ph.D., an administrator at Marietta College, holds a doctorate in Buddhist studies from the California Institute of Integral Studies, San Francisco. He has served on the boards of Karma Thegsum Choling Columbus, the Ohio Museums Association, and other nonprofit organizations.

Steven R. Dimler is the past president of the Interfaith Association of Central Ohio (2000–2004). He is also a longtime member of the Bahá'í Faith. Steve works as a food scientist at the Ross Products Division of Abbott Laboratories and lives in Pickerington with his wife and two children.

Rev. Wayne Evans is a superintendent (pastoring pastors) in the Evangelical Friends Church–Eastern Region, based in Canton. While forging ministries in the West Indies and studying for his doctorate, he and his wife Regina enjoy four children and one grandchild.

Rev. Arnold R. Fleagle, D. Min., is the director of church development for the central district of the Christian and Missionary Alliance. He serves as a consultant to the eighty churches of the district, primarily in the areas of church assessment, discipleship, master planning, and stewardship.

Rev. Dr. Albert H. Frank is a Moravian minister, the assistant director of the Moravian Music Foundation, and an adjunct professor at the Moravian Theological Seminary in Bethlehem, Pennsylvania. He has served as president of the Ohio Outdoor Historical Drama Association, which produces *Trumpet in the Land.*

Rev. Vincent T. Frosh is the senior pastor of the First African Methodist Episcopal Zion Church in Columbus and co-president of Building Responsibility, Equality, and Dignity (B.R.E.A.D.). He resides in Columbus with his wife and two children.

Rev. Clyde C. Fry is pastor emeritus, Northern Ohio District, having served First Church in Mansfield for thirty-one years. He has held posts in denominational and ecumenical organizations and is a consultant on church polity and pastoral education.

Rev. Jeff Gill, pastor of Hebron Christian Church (Disciples of Christ), writes for *Timeline,* the magazine of the Ohio Historical Society (OHS), works on a variety of archaeological and historical projects with OHS and Bethany College, and is a trustee of the Licking County Archaeology and Landmarks Society.

Jim Golding is a native of Athens, a graduate of the School of Journalism at Ohio University, a former information officer in the United States Air Force, a daily newspaper reporter and editor, and currently editor of the *Orthodox Observer*.

Alvin R. Hadley is the executive director of the Columbus Metropolitan Area Church Council. He has devoted much of his time to volunteer activities, serving on the Ohio Council of Churches General Board and as a president of American Baptist Churches of Ohio.

Dr. Richard H. Harms is a historian who serves as the archivist for Calvin College (Grand Rapids, Michigan), Calvin Theological Seminary (Grand Rapids, Michigan), and the Christian Reformed Church in North America. The author of numerous articles and several books, he is currently the editor of *Origins,* a publication of Heritage Hall at Calvin College.

Rev. Earl G. Harris is senior pastor of Greater Allen African Methodist Episcopal Church in Dayton. Pastor Harris holds a Master of Divinity degree from Payne Theological Seminary and is an ordained elder whose ministry has spanned more than thirty years.

Rev. Dr. Herbert R. Hicks is a retired pastor and a seventh-generation Ohioan with a three-hundred-twenty-year Quaker ancestry. Dr. Hicks was trained at Cincinnati Christian College, Lexington Theological Seminary, Mount Saint Mary's, and Princeton Theological Seminary. He is a member of the Wilmington Monthly Meeting of Friends.

Dr. Donald L. Huber is Fred W. Meuser Professor of Church History and academic dean at Trinity Lutheran Seminary in Columbus. A longtime student of Ohio history, he is a frequent contributor to *Timeline,* the magazine of the Ohio Historical Society.

Donley Johnson represents Christian Science in Ohio and works with the legislature and the media. He has been a Christian Science practitioner for more than thirty years. He and his wife, Nancy, live in Columbus. They have five grown children.

Linda D. Johnson is editor-in-chief for Salvation Army publications in the United States, Eastern Territory, based in West Nyack, New York. She is also a former editor of *Weekly Reader,* the national children's newspaper, and is the author of eight books for children.

Meena Khan is a retired librarian from the University of Toledo. Meena is founding librarian of the Islamic Center of Toledo Library. Currently, she is treasurer for the Church and Synagogue Library Association (Maumee Valley chapter). She resides in Toledo.

Rev. Joel L. King Jr., senior pastor of the Jerusalem Second Baptist Church of Urbana, was appointed executive secretary of the Ohio Baptist General Convention in October 2002. He lives in Gahanna and is married to Nancy Hayes; the couple has one son, Marcus Isaiah.

David Kline is an organic dairy farmer and writer who lives near Mt. Hope. He is the author of "Great Possessions" and "Scratching the Woodchuck," and is an editor for *Farming Magazine.*

Barry Landeros-Thomas is a native Ohioan of Cherokee and Lumbee descent. He was the director of education at the Native American Indian Center of Central Ohio. He and his wife and two daughters live in Columbus.

Lachlan Mackay lives in Kirtland and manages Community of Christ historic sites in Ohio, Illinois, Iowa, and Missouri.

Rev. Jeffrey Mansell is district superintendent of the Greater Ohio District of the Wesleyan Church.

Dr. John A. McFarland is a native of Ohio and a graduate of the Ohio State University, as well as Ashland Theological Seminary. He is a senior pastor and state ministerial credentials chairman for the Church of God in Ohio.

Patrick Mooney, a native of Somerset, Perry County, and a fifth-generation Ohioan, is a retired elementary school teacher, historical researcher, longtime collector of historical and literary Ohioana, and chair of the Catholic Record Society, Diocese of Columbus. He has lived in Columbus for fifty years.

Rev. Stephen M. Norden grew up in Japan as the child of missionary parents. He is a graduate of Hope College and Western Theological Seminary, both in Holland, Michigan, and is the founding pastor of New Hope Reformed Church in Powell.

Dr. Bishun D. Pandey is professor of mathematics at the Ohio State University and has been serving the Bharatiya Hindu Temple in Powell for more than fourteen years. Currently he is the president of the Executive Committee of the temple. He resides in Lewis Center.

James N. Pellechia is associate editor of Watch Tower Society publications, a lecturer on the modern history of Jehovah's Witnesses, and a member of the Society of Professional Journalists. His publications include *The Spirit and the Sword: Jehovah's Witnesses Expose the Third Reich.*

Willis C. Pollard is the editor of the *Ohio Baptist Messenger* and the historian for the State Convention of Baptists in Ohio. One of his responsibilities is to compile and publish the annual of the actions and activities of the convention. Mr. Pollard has lived in Ohio since 1967.

C. Robert Pryor is a native of Ohio and a founding trustee of Yellow Springs Dharma Center. He is associate professor in and director of the Antioch College Buddhist Studies Program.

Rev. Paul F. H. Reichert II is a graduate of Trinity Lutheran Seminary and is pastor of Calvary Lutheran Church (Evangelical Lutheran Church in America) in Northwood, Ohio, where he and his family live.

Rachel Reinhard is a lifelong resident of Ohio and a graduate of the Ohio State University. She has taught for most of her life in both the public schools and in the Church of Christ. At the time of her retirement in 1996, she was teaching British literature and humanities in Upper Arlington, where she resides.

Cynthia Rickard became a Bahá'í while studying journalism and politics at Kent State University and has served on the Kent and Youngstown Bahá'í Spiritual Assemblies. She has been a newspaper journalist for twenty-five years and is currently an editor for the *Vindicator* in Youngstown.

Rev. Dr. Susan Ritchie is a minister at the North Unitarian Universalist Congregation in Lewis Center. She teaches Unitarian Universalist history at the Methodist Theological School of Ohio and writes about her tradition's history and theology.

Mrs. Bharati Salgia received degrees in English literature and education from the University of Bombay, India, and is a teacher by profession. She is very active in the Jain community and has edited, compiled, and translated children stories and three books.

Dr. Tansukh Salgia is the founding member of the Federation of Jain Associations in North America and is the current president of Bramhi Jain Society. He has authored many articles and edited many books on Jain subjects. His passion is for interfaith and world peace.

Rev. James Schroeder is director of public relations and a member of the faculty at Circleville Bible College. He has been published in academic and religious periodicals and is a sought-after public speaker on various topics of historical interest.

Ernie J. Shannon has been a member of the Church of Jesus Christ of Latter-day Saints for more than twenty-seven years and has served in a variety of capacities. He is employed as a writer and communicator for Battelle Memorial Institute. He is married and has four children.

Dr. Ranbir Singh is Professor Emeritus at the Ohio State University. He is past secretary of the World Sikh Council–America Region and is a founding trustee of the Sikh Educational and Religious Foundation of Dublin. He was president of the Interfaith Association of Central Ohio from 1997 to 1998.

Rev. Dennis Sparks serves as executive director of the West Virginia Council of Churches. A Disciples of Christ pastor and native of Columbus, he has served the church as a pastor and ecumenical officer in Ohio and beyond.

Bruce Stambaugh is a retired elementary school principal. He is a newspaper columnist and a freelance writer. He works in marketing in a retirement community, attends Millersburg Mennonite Church, and lives near Berlin.

Kris Stevenson is the author of *So Much Summer* and *Delighting in God*. She lives in Mt. Vernon with her husband and two children and is currently teaching English and journalism at Mount Vernon Academy.

Rev. Dale R. Stoffer serves as the academic dean of Ashland Theological Seminary in Ashland. He also teaches in the areas of church history and theology, with special interests in Anabaptism and Pietism.

Gulnar Surveyor grew up in India and came to the United States to pursue graduate studies in biology. She worked in research and obtained a master's in business from the Ohio State University. She lives in Columbus with her husband and son.

Rev. L. Gordon Tait, a graduate of Harvard University, Pittsburgh Theological Seminary, and the University of Edinburgh (Scotland), is Mercer Professor of Religious Studies Emeritus at the College of Wooster. He is the author of *The Piety of John Witherspoon*.

Linda L. Thompson, Ph.D., is a retired educator who was with the Columbus Public Schools for seventeen years and the Ohio Department of Education for ten years. She is a choir member and church historian at the First Unitarian Universalist Church in Columbus.

Rev. Ken Turley has served in parish ministry since 1985 with terms on denominational boards and committees. He and his wife, Laurie, have produced five CDs of original music and continue to play and compose. They live with their two children in Fryeburg, Maine.

Dr. Peter W. Williams is Distinguished Professor of Comparative Religion and American Studies at Miami University. He is the author of several works on American religious history, including *America's Religions* and *Houses of God: Region, Religion, and Architecture in the United States*.

Rev. L. Cean Wilson is the United Methodist West Ohio Conference secretary and director of the Office of Ministry. She lives in Columbus. Previous appointments have included pastor and district superintendent.

Winifred C. Wirth has been active in the Buddhist Council of Ohio, the Interfaith Association of Central Ohio, and Amnesty International for over a decade. She lives in Columbus with her husband, a Protestant minister, and their son.

Anthony R. Zifer joined the Coptic Orthodox Church in 1997. He serves as deacon, bookstore manager, festival tour guide, and part-time preacher at St. Mary's in Columbus. He and his wife and two children live in Hilliard.

INDEX

Page numbers in italics refer to illustrations.

'Abdu'l-Bahá, 352, 354, 359
abolition movement, 7, 91, 134, 138–39, 168, 199, 203, 232, 268
Adams County, 2, 70, 167
Adena culture, 1, 31–32, 40
Afghani immigrants, 290
African Americans, 7–8; Baptists and, 59–62; Christian and Missionary Alliance and, 227; Church of God and, 210; community churches movement and, 113–15; Islam and, 286, 291–94, 296; Methodists and, 168, 172–84; Salvation Army and, 215–16. *See also* abolition movement
African Methodist Episcopal Church (AME), 7–8, 22, 172–76
African Methodist Episcopal Zion Church, 22, 177–80
Africa Wesleyan Methodist Church (Columbus), 204, *205*
Agamas (Jainism), 372
Ahimsa-Nonviolence (television documentary), 368
Akram, El Hajj Wali, 294
Akron, Ohio: Bahá'ís in, 352; Baptists in, 58; Buddhists in, 322, 328; Greek Orthodox in, 120; Hindus in, 312; interfaith movement in, 25; Jains in, 377; Jewish community in, 272, 278–79, 284; Methodists in, 178; Muslims in, 295–96, 302; Pentecostals in, 187, 189; Reformed in, 237, 239; Salvation Army in, 219; Unitarian Universalism in, 261–62; United Church of Christ in, 270; Zoroastrians in, 381
Al-Abdoney, Muhammad Yusuf, 288
Allen, Richard, 172–73
Allen County, 52, 71
Alliance, Ohio, 22, 186, 276
Alsbacher Document, 272, *273*
Amberley Village, Ohio, 279
American Bahá'í, 356
American Baptist, 54–58
American Indian Religious Freedom Act (1978), 29
American Muslim Society (Toledo), 289
Amish, 5–6, 11, 12, 44–48, 50
Amman, Jacob, 45, 50
amrit ceremony, 347
Anabaptists, 5–6, 45, 49, 71, 175
Andrews, J. N., 255
Anglican Church, 128–29
Anshe Emeth (Cleveland), 275
anti-Catholic riots, 13
Antioch College, 260, 266, 324
anti-Semitism, 12–13, 250, 275–76, 278–79
antislavery movement. *See* abolition movement
Apostle's Creed, 174–75, 179, 195, 238, 244

Appleseed, Johnny, 6, 89, 92–93
Arab immigrants, 286–87
Ariarajah, S. Wesley, 17–18
Asbury, Francis, 166, 206, 224
Ashland Brethren, 74–78
Ashland College (later University), 75–76
Ashland County, 48
Ashland Theological Seminary, 76
Assemblies of God, 185–88
Association for Community Centered Churches, 114
Athanasian Creed, 238
Athenaeum of Ohio, 248
Athens, Ohio, 65, 207, 325
Augsburg Confession, 164
Austinburg, Ohio, 266
Avondale, Ohio, 277
Awadalla, Shenouda, 125
Awrey, Daniel, 186

Báb, the, 359
Bahá'í Bulletin, 352
Bahá'í faith, 10, 28, 351–64
Bahá'í News, 353
Bahá'í World Centre (Israel), 16, 356
Bahá'u'lláh, 351, 359–62
Bailey, Francis, 90
Baker, Dorothy, 354–55
Balkans immigrants, 290
Ballard, David, 138
baptism: Adventists and, 257; Amish/Mennonite, 45, 49; Baptists and, 57, 61; Brethren and, 68; Christian Churches and, 82, 85, 87; Coptic Church and, 126; Episcopalians and, 131; Jehovah's Witnesses and, 147; Lutherans and, 164; Methodists and, 169, 179, 184; Mormons and, 152, 156–57; Pietist/Holiness and, 201, 213; Presbyterian/Reformed and, 233; Quakers and, 135
Baptists, 5, 9, 12, 54–67
Barnesville, Ohio, 141
Bates, Issachar, 102
Bates, Joseph, 255
Battle, Kathleen, 174
Beals, Thomas, 138–39
Beatty, Charles, 230
Beebe, Joseph A., 182
Beebe Chapel CME Church (Ripley), 182
Beecher, Lyman, 5, 7
Beedle, William, 102
Beidler, John, 198, *199*
Beissel, Conrad, 100
Bell, E. D. W., 178
Bellaire, Ohio, 276

403

Denison, Ohio, 121
Dennison University, 56
De Rooy, Jacobus, 235
Deshmukh, Suresh, 309
Dharmapala, Anagarika, 319
dietary practices, 282–83, 366, 371–72, 374
disaster relief, 65–66, 71, 217–18
Disciples of Christ. *See* Christian Church (Disciples of Christ)
discrimination. *See* persecution/discrimination
displaced persons. *See* refugees/displaced persons
Dover, Ohio, 194
Dublin, Ohio, 194–95, 242
Dublin Baptist Church (Dublin), 65
Duffield, George, 230
Dunbar, Paul Laurence, 174
Dunkers. *See* Brethren Churches
Dutch immigrants, 50, 235–37, 241–42

Earley, Charity Adams, 174
Eastern European immigrants, 6, 248, 250, 273, 275–77, 287, 290
East Liverpool, Ohio, 216, *217*, 276, 295
Eastman, Ephraim, 204
Eck, Diana, 17
Eckstein, Frederick, 90
ecumenism, 20–22, 86
Eddy, Mary Baker, 95, 97
education: Adventists and, 255, 257, 258; Amish/
Mennonites and, 47, 51–52; Bahá'ís and, 354;
Baptists and, 56; Brethren and, 75–76; Buddhists
and, 324–25; Christian Churches and, 81–82, 266;
Hindu Dharma and, 308, 316; Jehovah's Witnesses
and, 146; Judaism and, 279; Methodists and, 169,
173, 181–82; Muslims and, 287, 291–92, 295–96,
301; Pietist/Holiness and, 223; Presbyterians/Re-
formed and, 233, 266–67; Quakers and, 134,
140–41; Roman Catholic Church and, 250, 252;
Sikhs and, 341; Swedenborgians and, 90–91; Uni-
tarian Universalists and, 261; Zoarites and, 110
Eldorado, Ohio, 261, 262
Elyria, Ohio, 143, 187
Episcopal Church, 5, 21–22, 128–32
Eucharist. *See* Communion
Euclid, Ohio, 320, 354
Evangelical and Reformed Church, 265
Evangelical Friends Church–Eastern Region, 133–37,
142
Evangelical Friends International, 135
Evangelical Lutheran Church in America (ELCA),
21–22, 162–63, 165
Evangelical Synod of North America, 265–66
Evangelical United Brethren Church, 168
evangelism. *See* missions/evangelism

Fairborn, 64
Fairfield, Ohio, 261
Fairview Park, Ohio, 49, 244
Fakih, Abdul Jalil Abdo (Eddie Simon), 288
Fakler, James, 215
Fargo Wesleyan Methodist Church (Columbus), 204
fasting, 126, 298, 331, 362
Fayette County, 222
Fenwick, Edward D., *247*, 248–49
Ferguson, O. L., 222

festivals. *See* holidays and festivals
Findlay, Ohio, 186, *187*, 200–20
Finney, Charles, 267
First Baptist Church (Athens), 65
First Baptist Church (Fairborn), 64
First Church of Christ, Scientist (Lancaster), *96*
First Church of God (Wauseon), *211*
First Community Church (Columbus), 113–14, 116, 267
First Congregational Church (Cincinnati), 259–60
First Congregational Church (Marietta), 266
First Holland Christian Reformed Church (Cincin-
nati), *238*
First (Holland) Reformed Church (Cleveland), 242
First Unitarian Society (Marietta), 260
First Universalist Society (Belpre), *260*
Flake, Floyd, 174
Flower, J. Roswell, 186
foot-washing, 47, 201, 213, 257
Forster, William, 160
Fort Ancient people, 1, 32
Fox, George, 133, 136, 138
Frankel, Marcus, 273
Frankfort, Ohio, 328
Fremont, Ohio, 352
Friends (Quakers), 5, 100, 107, 133–42
Frost, Ohio, 261
Fulton County, 52, 196
Fye, Neil E., 227

Gahanna, Ohio, 242, 244
Galena, Ohio, 352
Galloway, Ohio, 207
Gambier, Ohio, 130
Gandhi, Virchand Raghav, 364
Gano family, 54
Gans, John, 70
Garfield, James A., 85
Gathas (Zoroastrianism), 381–83
Gaysport, Ohio, 352
Geauga County, 5
Geneva, Ohio, 277
Genthner, Robert, 326
German Baptist Brethren, 68, 74–75
German Evangelical Synod. *See* United Church of
Christ
German immigrants, 6, 11–12, 50, 100, 107, 160, 168,
216, 247, 272
German Reformed Church, 5, 6, 9, 11, 198. *See also*
United Church of Christ
Gilead, Ohio, 146
Gladden, Washington, 9, 267–68
Glenn, John, 233
Glenville, Ohio, 277
Gnadenhutten, massacre at, 3, 36, 194
God's Bible School, 222
"Golden Rule," 27–28
Golf Manor, Ohio, 279
Goshen, Ohio, 194
Gospel School Publishing House, *187*
Gospel Trumpet, 210
Gospel Visitor, 71
Grace Theological Seminary, 76
Grandview Heights Congregational Church (Colum-
bus), 113
Granville, Ohio, 56, 328